Lodi Memorial Library
Lodi, New Jersey

RULES

1. Books are due on date indicated under "Date Due" and may not be renewed.

2. A fine of two cents a day will be charged on each book which is not returned according to the above rule. No book will be issued to any person or his immediate family until fines in excess of 25¢ are paid.

3. All injuries to books beyond reasonable wear and all losses shall be made good to the satisfaction of the Librarian.

4. Each borrower is held responsible for all books drawn on his card and for all fines accruing on the same.

consumerism. Opportunity and self-fulfillment might replace enforced unemployment, repression and competition. It would be the beginning of an entirely different view of social relations. It would be very much like the vision Crystal Eastman affirmed in her many published writings.

March 1978
New York, N.Y.   B.W.C.

renamed in 1922 the Women's International League for Peace and Freedom. Members of Women's Strike for Peace who went to Geneva and The Hague in 1962 and 1963 in an earnest effort to stop the war in Vietnam told me seriously that they had just never known that other women had been there before, had done what they attempted to do—mobilize international opinion against imperialism and war.

Throughout the McCarthy period of the 1950s and during the antiwar demonstrations of the 1960s, the existence and work of the American Civil Liberties Union was acknowledged in the popular media. But almost nobody knew that the ACLU had been founded in 1917 to defend wartime dissenters and conscientious objectors by Crystal Eastman and Roger Baldwin, who had come to New York in 1916 to assist Crystal with her work as executive secretary of the American Union Against Militarism.

The reemergence of the women's movement in the 1960s revealed a feminist history that was so strong it has been surprisingly easy to repossess. From early urban feminist alliances, to abolition to suffrage to equal rights, from the 1800s to the 1920s, there had been women who supproted each other on behalf of political rights, peace, fulfilling and satisfying work for women. Frequently they were supported by men who shared their values. But more importantly, their ability throughout those long years of struggle to support and nurture themselves—to work with each other in the face of opposition both tedious and violent—communicated strength and unity to the contemporary women's movement.

And we have come to understand that the disappearance of politically active women from history was not an accident. Feminism has always meant independence of mind and spirit and body. Choices. It is revolutionary. To look deeply, fearlessly into how male society traditionally treats women is to see much more: the connections between repression, racism, poverty, sexism, imposed institutional ignorance and illiteracy. It is to recognize that many of the features of our discontent serve the same purpose: to divide people. Such divisions help to create and sustain violent, though false and contrived, antagonisms. Without those antagonisms people might unite on behalf of their own needs and wants. Security might replace women, or peace or movements for social change. Not until the civil rights and peace movements of the 1960s did historians begin to reclaim those aspects of our past. It is not surprising that errors have occurred during the reclamation process. Max Eastman, for example, apparently did not know that his sister's feminist writings had been published. Perhaps he had forgotten. Possibly he never knew. Yet Crystal and Max were very close. They lived together and they worked together for many years. Did she not tell him about her feminist articles? It seems unlikely. But the error was made; we do not know why. Possibly when Yvette Eastman publishes the book she plans to write using Crystal's letters to Max and their mother, some of these questions may be answered.

In 1966 when I visited Max Eastman I was writing about World War I, international diplomacy, foreign economic policy, civil liberties in wartime: "hard history." In 1966 I was not yet involved in the women's movement and although I was a "professional woman," I was not consciously a feminist. When Max Eastman suggested that I might want to write about his sister and offered to show me Crystal's letters to her mother and to him, an enormous collection, as well as the manuscripts of her feminist writings that Max believed largely unpublished, I politely refused his offer. My interest was limited to the war years. Reflecting my culture and socialization, I did not fully realize Crystal Eastman's importance until the women's movement altered my own consciousness and I began to think about all the women—activists and writers—who came before, and whom we have been, until recently, programmed to deny.

The effort to reclaim our past began during the early years of the peace movement in the 1960s when people rediscovered the contributions of earlier pacifists, so many of whom were women and feminists. Throughout World War II and the Cold War, popular interest in women like Crystal Eastman, who founded the Woman's Peace Party of New York and was, with Jane Addams, responsible for the emergence of the national organization, had been limited to a small group of political descendants who were members of that party,

PREFACE

For fifty years our entire culture militated so vigorously against our discovering Crystal Eastman's ideas and finding them usable that she practically disappeared from history. After her death in 1928 there were memorials and obituaries. But from that year to this not one essay, not one book has been entirely devoted to her work or to her life. The only historian who has written anything significant about her says mistakenly that Crystal Eastman "had no audience for her views; the unpublished nature of her writing attests the fact that the publishers did not consider her concerns worthy of print."*

But almost everything Crystal Eastman wrote was published. She had an enthusiastic and dedicated audience. She wrote for newspapers as well as magazines. She wrote boldly and well. And she was paid for what she wrote—and paid sufficiently to live for several years largely on that income. Part of the reason for such an historical error is the continued unavailability of her letters, which are in the possession of Yvette Eastman, Max Eastman's widow. There is, however, another and more pervasive part.

For many years professional history did not include the study of

---

* See June Sochen, *Movers and Shakers* (Quadrangle, 1973), pp. 48–49.

Crystal Eastman
on Women
and Revolution

EDITED BY
BLANCHE WIESEN COOK

New York
Oxford University Press
1978

Copyright © 1978 by Blanche Wiesen Cook

Library of Congress Cataloging in Publication Data

Eastman, Crystal, 1881–1928
    Crystal Eastman on women and revolution.

    Includes index.
    1. Feminism--United States. 2. Peace. 3. Women and socialism.
I.   Cook, Blanche Wiesen.   II.   Title.   III.   Title: On women and
revolution.
HQ1426.E26 1979   301.41'2'0973   78-59686
ISBN 0-19-502-445-1
ISBN 0-19-502-446-X pbk.

Printed in the United States of America

ACKNOWLEDGMENTS

I am grateful to the staffs of the Swarthmore College Peace Collection and the Schlesinger Library, Radcliffe College—particularly to Bernice Nichols, the dedicated curator at Swarthmore, and Barbara Haber at the Schlesinger for their considerate assistance. Jack Nordhorn of the microfilm department and the staff of the manuscript division of the Columbia University Libraries have been helpful and supportive. I am also grateful to Elizabeth Chittick, President of the National Woman's Party, for her assistance; to Judith Schwarz for the references to Crystal Eastman's F.B.I. files received too late for inclusion in this book; to Virginia Christenson of the Sophia Smith Collection; to David Klaassen, Assistant Curator of the Social Welfare History Archives Center, University of Minnesota; and to Virginia Gardener, William L. O'Neill and Barbara Sicherman for sharing material from their own research with me. I also want to thank my friend Marge Barton who made proofreading so pleasant.

Over many years, Crystal Eastman's family and several of her friends have generously provided information and encouragement. Until his death Crystal's son Jeffrey Fuller called me once a year to inquire about my continued interest in his mother. I am deeply grateful for his initial enthusiasm. Joyce Fuller and Crystal Eastman's grandchildren—Ann, Nick and Cordelia Fuller—spent an entire day with me in and out of the attic, going through trunks and boxes looking for letters, and finding several of the pictures reproduced in this book. I am also grateful to Crystal Eastman's grandchildren Chip, Deborah and especially Rebecca Young for their interest.

Annis Young spent many hours talking with me about her mother and made available Crystal Eastman's scrapbook, later letters and photographs. I am deeply appreciative of Annis Young's warm generosity and hospitality, and for Charles W. Young's shared enthusiasm.

Ruth Pickering Pinchot, Hazel Hunkins Hallinan, Roger Baldwin and Jeannette Lowe have given frequently of their time to talk about their friend Crystal Eastman. I am particularly grateful to Jeannette Lowe, who first referred me to the wide range of Crystal's published writings, and to Roger Baldwin, whose memories and analyses have informed my work over time. I also want to thank Penny Franklin and Philip Florence for their taped conversation about Crystal Eastman and Walter Fuller in London; and Yvette Eastman for her active interest in Crystal Eastman's writings.

Stephanie Golden, an outstanding editor, read this manuscript with rare sensibility. I am deeply grateful for Sheldon Meyer's enthusiasm, which made this book possible.

Finally, for their support I want to express my profound gratitude for my friends in the Friday evening and Sunday afternoon groups whose works have informed and influenced my own. In addition to benefiting from their work, and to our studies together, Clare Coss, Audre Lorde, Joan Kelly, Alice Kessler-Harris, Amy Swerdlow, Carroll Smith-Rosenberg, and Claudia Koonz read and improved early drafts of this manuscript. Clare Coss' valuable suggestions and sustaining companionship throughout the process of this project have been a continuing source of encouragement and deeper vision.

CONTENTS

Part Two   Crystal Eastman On Revolution

CRYSTAL EASTMAN
ON WOMEN AND REVOLUTION

INTRODUCTION

"Life is a big battle for the complete feminist." Crystal Eastman wrote those words in 1918, entirely convinced that the complete feminist would ultimately achieve total victory. Yet only now, fifty years after her early death in 1928, are women and progressives in large numbers turning to feminists and socialists like Crystal Eastman for theory and support.

Labor lawyer, social investigator, and pioneer in the field of industrial safety, Crystal Eastman's life involved compromise and contradiction, conviction and courage. She was in the vanguard of every major movement for social change. Committed equally to feminism and socialism, Crystal Eastman occupied a unique and, as the 1920s wore on, an increasingly isolated political position. She was generally the only socialist at feminist meetings, one of the very few feminists at socialist meetings.

During the 1920s equal rights feminists were generally attacked by representatives of organized labor and social reform humanitarians as enemies of working women. Because the debate over the Equal Rights Amendment focused on its potential for undermining the hard-won protective rights of working women, the controversy was cast as a class-based rather than a feminist issue. Furthermore, then, far more than now, the male-dominated socialist movement tended to dismiss the idea of equal rights for women as largely irrelevant to its programs for economic justice. Crystal Eastman's socialist-feminist position in support of equal rights was, under those circumstances, extremely difficult to communicate.

Her attempt to forge two radical visions that seemed unrelated to so many in both groups was the lonely task she undertook during the last years of her life. They were years marked by illness and an inability to find the steady and satisfying work for which she thirsted. Yet the writings of her later years relate to issues and visions of immediate concern to feminists, and to all women and men who seek a better, more humane environment—whether socialist, anarchist or liberal: visions of socialism that would end poverty, racism and privilege; the struggle for and dilemmas of civil liberties under capitalism and socialism, during war and in revolution; visions of feminism that would end dependence and subservience; visions of internationalism that would end imperialism and devastating warfare.

To lean on and be protected by a man, Crystal Eastman wrote over fifty years ago, is not the same as standing on your own two feet. Patriarchal protection of workers, men or women, is not the same as workers' control. Equal rights for all; work for all; peace and justice and equal opportunity; the end to privilege as well as poverty—those are very radical demands. They were Crystal Eastman's demands, and they are still unfulfilled. It is no accident that her work has for so long remained unknown—along with her joy in life and exuberance for people. The neglect and disappearance of Crystal Eastman's work is partly explained by the fact that history tends to bury what it seeks to reject. There was little room for the writings of a militant feminist who was also a socialist in the annals of America as it went from Red Scare to Depression to Cold War and back again.

Perhaps Crystal Eastman would not have been so lost to history if she had been more conventional. It is perhaps more comfortable to picture a woman of her views tragic in exile, rather than undaunted at the speaker's platform in Rome, Budapest, Paris, London. Surely it would have been simpler if she had not also socialized with Charlie Chaplin, titled nobility, black intellectuals and government officials; and when she partied with women she dressed entirely for herself and their company with a flamboyance for which she became noted. For women to dress for themselves and each other was really unfathomable. How was history to appraise the militant feminist wing of the international "smart set"? How could history appraise the life of a tough lady labor lawyer who was not only a feminist, but a mother and socialist?

There was nothing simple about her work, her political vision, or the nature of her personal relationships. And her vision demanded radical, profound, and absolute changes. Crystal Eastman's ideas were heretical and dangerous. Her life by its very example embodied a threat to customary order. "Freedom is a large word," she wrote in 1920. It demanded a large struggle, a long battle. She was committed to that struggle, and the range and intensity of her energy and spirit served her well.

Crystal Eastman loved life and was generally surrounded by friends. Protected and fortified by the support of women and men who shared her ideals and battled beside her, she was free and bold. Her close friend Jeannette Lowe said that "you wouldn't believe her freedom—she was entirely free, open, full of joy in life." Her brother Max wrote that "she poured magnetic streams of generous love around her all the time" and boldly plunged into new experiences. Roger Baldwin, who worked closely with her during World War I in the American Union Against Militarism and the Civil Liberties Bureau which they jointly created, remembered Crystal as "a natural leader: outspoken (often tactless), determined, charming, beautiful, courageous. . . ." She spoke in a deep and musical voice and could be entirely captivating as she dashed about the country on behalf of suffrage or peace or to organize against an injustice. Her sincerity was absolute and she frequently grew red with anger. She was impulsive and passionate and, her brother tells us, she once consulted Dr. A. A. Brill, the first Freudian psychoanalyst to practice in America, to bring her intense "libido down."

Crystal Eastman was a woman-identified woman. She neither sought male approval for her activities nor courted male protection. While she delighted in the company of women, she enjoyed male alliances wherever she found them genuine. She worked with and loved easily many women and men who were her friends and comrades. She was also firm and aggressive. Hazel Hunkins Hallinan, the suffragist organizer who knew Crystal best when she lived in England, recalled that she was "very realistic but not very docile. We used to call her a 'tigress' because she was so vital and aggressive. Whatever she felt she felt very strongly."

Born on 25 June 1881, Crystal Eastman spent most of her childhood in Glenora, a small town on the shore of Seneca Lake in New York. The daughter of suffragist parents, both of whom were ordained Congregational ministers, she claimed feminism as her birthright. Toward the end of her life Crystal wrote that "the story of my background is the story of my mother." Her mother, Annis Ford Eastman, was "the most noted minister of her time," an inspiring orator who found new ideas from Santayana to Freud "dangerously fascinating." And she encouraged Crystal and her two brothers, Max and Anstice, to be independent in thought and vigorous in action. A third brother, the oldest son, Morgan, died of scarlet fever in 1884. Crystal had scarlet fever at the same time and it marked her health throughout her life.

When Crystal was fifteen, her mother organized a summer symposium at which Crystal read a paper called "Woman." She dedicated the rest of her life to the fulfillment of the theme of that paper: women, she had written, "must have work of their own . . . because the only way to be happy is to have an absorbing interest in life which is not bound up with any particular person. No woman who allows husband and children to absorb her whole time and interest is safe against disaster."

Although Crystal Eastman hated the traditional institutionalization of marriage and "homemaking," she believed that most women shared "the normal desire to be mothers." An early advocate of birth control, she wrote in 1918: "Feminists are not nuns. That should be established." While she deeply desired children of her own and ultimately married twice, she did not marry until she was almost thirty and had occasionally doubted she would marry at all. Both she and her brother Max remained single until after their mother's death. And all their friends apparently believed that Crystal and Max really loved each other above all. In his autobiography, *Love and Revolution,* Max wrote very specifically about that: "As a boy . . . I used to announce that I would never marry any girl but my sister, and I suppose a passionate attachment underlay this firm resolution. Of all Freud's plain and fancy inventions, the concept of an 'incest barrier' is one of the most easily verifiable in my experience."

During her junior year at Vassar in 1902 Crystal wrote in her journal that men were typically "clever, powerful, selfish and animal"—except for her brother Max. And, she wrote, should she ever marry a man he would have to have Max's qualities: "I don't believe there is a feeling in the world too refined and imagined for him to appreciate." Crystal thought her brother might not like it, but she thought it was "the highest compliment you can pay a man to say that he has the fineness of feeling and sympathy of a woman. . . . All mothers ought to cultivate it in their boys."*

Many of Crystal's later writings reflect her high sense of gender injustice—bolstered not only by public law but everywhere propped up by cultural attitudes. She believed that for equality to be meaningful, an equality of emotional sensibility would have to accompany women's right to work and to vote. Throughout her life, homemaking—the notion that women's mission was to provide a comfortable home for men who shared no similar responsibility—symbolized women's servility, women's bondage. To end that bondage, women as well as men needed to be educated and involved with their own life's work; and both women and men needed to function efficiently in the home.

Personally, Crystal Eastman hated housework. Just as men traditionally declared themselves incapable of "woman's work," domestic chores literally made Crystal ill. Whatever political conflicts the contradiction of hiring servants may have caused, she required them. Her daughter Annis Young once told me, for example, that while she was certain of Crystal's love, she was equally certain that Crystal rarely, if ever, changed a diaper. On the other hand, Crystal insisted, women who wanted to work at home—or needed to work at home—should be paid for their labor. What is today referred to as "wages for housework" was featured in Crystal

---

* William O'Neill graciously sent me this excerpt from Crystal's journal, 9 June 1902. I am grateful to Annis Young for permission to use it.

Eastman's feminist program as a "Motherhood Endowment." In "Now We Can Begin," she wrote that the only way for women "at least in a capitalist society" to achieve "real economic independence" was for the political government to recognize and subsidize housework as skilled labor.

From 1903 to 1911 Crystal Eastman lived among people who shared her views. A settlement house worker while studying for her M.A. in sociology at Columbia (1904) and for a law degree at New York University (1907), she lived in and became a leading member of the new feminist and radical community just then emerging in Greenwich Village. She lived with suffragists who were her close friends from Vassar or law school. Madeleine Doty, Inez Milholland and Ida Rauh all became attorneys, and for some time Madeleine Doty and Crystal Eastman shared a Village apartment. Eventually Ida Rauh, who was later to marry Max, joined them; Milholland, who lived nearby, was there as often as not. Their apartment was one of the major communication centers for labor reform and suffrage activities.

Comfortable in many worlds, Crystal moved with ease among artists, social workers, poets, anarchists, socialists and progressive reformers. It was a time of experiment and change. And Crystal Eastman was committed to both. Appalled by poverty and its senseless waste, she was a socialist by nature and conviction. Her concern for the poor, nurtured by her mother from childhood, and her anguish over brutal economic conditions intensified during this period.

In 1907 Crystal graduated from law school second in her class with a particular interest in labor law. At the same time her good friend Paul U. Kellogg, then editor of the social work magazine *Charities and the Commons,* was organizing the celebrated Pittsburgh Survey for the Russell Sage Foundation and invited Crystal to join the staff. Crystal remained in Pittsburgh for over a year to complete the first in-depth sociological investigation of industrial accidents ever undertaken. Her work catapulted her to prominence, and in June 1909 Governor Charles Evans Hughes appointed her New York's first woman commissioner, the only woman among fourteen members of the Employer's Liability Commission. As secretary of that prestigious commission,* she drafted New York State's first worker's compensation law, which was soon used as a model by many other states.

She believed that industrial accidents happen almost inevitably because of organized neglect of workers' safety. Her goal was to shift the burden of guilt or blame from victim to industry and its management and to adopt, as almost every "civilized country except the United States" already had, the principle of worker's compensation. Industry's refusal to secure the safety and health of its workers remains today a primary labor issue. Unfortunately, corporations now prefer to pay insurance fees rather than make the necessary capital investments to secure safe working conditions. But in 1910 when the loss of a leg or an eye or a life generally resulted in no compensation to the worker or the worker's family, Crystal Eastman's book *Work Accidents and the Law*† resulted in a major progressive reform.

New York's worker's compensation law was a compromise. Initially, only a specific category of accidents in a few dangerous trades was covered. It was, Crystal argued, the best compromise possible considering that New York was one of the first states to insure any of its workers and industry was free to move to states without any such law. She hoped that with increased pressure to insure workers throughout the United States, the categories insured would be expanded.

The contribution Crystal Eastman made to labor law and industrial safety was internationally acclaimed. Moreover, her work in Pittsburgh and New York confirmed her radical vision and clarified her understanding of economics. She began to identify herself as a socialist in this period. In 1911 she wrote "Three Essentials for Accident Prevention," in which she referred to the Triangle Waist Company fire, in which 140 women locked into the room that was their "sweatshop" perished. When healthy women and men die because of preventable disasters, she wrote, we do not want to hear

---

* Officially called the New York Commission on Employers' Liability and Causes of Industrial Accidents, Unemployment and Lack of Farm Labor.
† *Work Accidents and the Law* (1910, 2d edition 1916) was reprinted in 1970 by Arno Press.

about "relief funds." "What we want is to start a revolution." Nothing short of revolution would finally end "this unnecessary killing and injuring of workers in the course of industry." At that time revolution meant, for Crystal Eastman, collecting the information necessary to prevent economic disaster and human suffering. It was a first step. Very early on Crystal believed that revolution was a process and not an event.

On 24 April 1910 a long interview with Crystal Eastman, New York's first woman commissioner, appeared in the magazine section of the Sunday *New York Herald*. "Portia Appointed by the Governor" represents the kind of vulgar sexism and classism Crystal Eastman spent her life battling. Written by a woman who seems slightly undone by Crystal's candor, it nevertheless provides a rare glimpse into her public personality. The interviewer suggested that the shirtwaist strikers of 1909 who had been picketing for decent wages, shorter hours and the kind of safe working conditions, including unlocked doors, which might have prevented the tragedy of the Triangle fire, were motivated by "vanity, a love of pretty things beyond . . . their pursestrings." Crystal Eastman's response to that was "vehement." According to the interviewer, when Crystal Eastman argued she became entirely the lawyer: "the adversary in every word and gesture. No, there's nothing particularly friendly in her method of argument. . . . It seems almost superfluous to add that Miss Eastman is a suffragette."

Suffrage was for Crystal a primary enthusiasm, and she expected the men in her life to be suffragists. According to Max, Crystal introduced him to political and social issues and, in 1909, encouraged him to organize the Men's League for Woman Suffrage. But the vote represented only a part of the power denied to women that Crystal Eastman believed women needed to reclaim. Tall, almost six feet tall, athletic and robust herself, she sought to extend the contours of women's strength and women's sphere far beyond suffrage. Max recalled that at some point during the year he lived with Crystal she met Annette Kellerman, a champion swimmer and diver from Australia who was then in New York to entertain Broadway audiences with her aquatic skills. Together she and Crystal attempted to work out a program for the physical "regeneration of the female sex."

To promote her vision of women's power, Crystal Eastman spoke before large audiences on "women's right to physical equality with men." Freda Kirchwey recalled that she pictured a Utopia of athletes, with women "unhampered by preconceived ideas of what was fit or proper or possible for their sex to achieve." Crystal believed that "when women were expected to be agile, they became agile; when they were expected to be brave, they developed courage; when they had to endure, their endurance broke all records." According to Kirchwey, who was at this time still a student at Barnard, as Crystal Eastman "stood there, herself an embodiment of tall, easy strength and valor, her words took on amazing life. . . ."

From adolescence onward Crystal was aware that fashion served to confine and limit women's ability to move freely. In matters of style, from short hair and short skirts to her insistence on wearing bathing suits without the customary stockings and skirts, her guiding principle was the achievement of greater and easier activity. Freedom involved discarding antique and unnecessary encumbrances. She never rode sidesaddle, and careened about her hometown "on a man's saddle in fluttering vast brown bloomers" that shocked polite Glenora society. When her neighbors complained to her father about her swimming clothes, she received her family's support. Although her father never said a word to her, Crystal believed that he was "startled and embarrassed to see his only daughter in a man's bathing suit with bare brown legs for all the world to see. I think it shocked him to his dying day." But Crystal was adamant. She was certain that "he would not want to swim in a skirt and stockings. Why then should I?"

In 1911, shortly after her mother died, Crystal Eastman decided to marry a ruggedly handsome insurance salesman named Wallace Benedict. Although she made it clear to her friends and family, including Max, that she was physically and romantically excited by Bennie, they remained puzzled by her decision actually to marry him. Because the letters for this period remain unavailable, the reasons for both her decision and their apparent disapproval remain unclear. We do know, however, that Bennie believed in and supported her work. According to Max, he was also full of "admiring passion." We also know that the decision was not easy for Crystal, partly because it involved moving to Bennie's home in Milwaukee.

After agreeing to the marriage she became sick and went to her parental home to rest. Max wrote: "perhaps the decision made her sick." Crystal apparently shared his conclusion. She wrote Max: "I've been feeling very scared about getting married all through this sickness. Getting back to New York and living with you was the hope I fed my drooping spirits on—not Milwaukee and the married state. Your suggestion that if I cant stand it, you'll know it's not for you, gives me a humorous courage. Perhaps after we've both experimented around a few years, we may end up living together again." In the spring of that year Crystal married Bennie and Max married Ida Rauh.

Crystal's marriage resulted in periods of deep melancholy. Within two years she returned to New York. The marriage ended officially only after she decided to marry Walter Fuller in 1916. The time Crystal spent in Milwaukee was devoted largely to the suffrage campaign.

In 1911 Wisconsin was the only large industrial state east of the Mississippi where a suffrage referendum was pending. The entire suffrage movement focused on Wisconsin, and Crystal served as the campaign manager and chaired the Political Equality League, which directed all activities in and out of the state. When it was over, Crystal attributed the suffrage defeat in Wisconsin to the dominating power of the brewery industry and its ability to pressure a variety of dependent industries: "There are whole cities of 20,000 . . . where not a single businessman dares to let his wife come out for suffrage . . . because practically every man's business is dependent . . . on the good will of the big breweries. . . ." The big corporations, she explained, generally "put their business . . . ahead of democracy, justice, simple human right."

In 1913, as a delegate to the Seventh Congress of the International Woman Suffrage Alliance at Budapest, Crystal met with the women who were soon to focus their efforts on the movement for international peace: Hungary's Rosika Schwimmer, Holland's first woman physician, Dr. Aletta Jacobs, and English suffragist Emmeline Pethick-Lawrence. As soon as the European War was declared she limited or suspended all other concerns to organize American sentiment against the war, against America's participation in the war and against militarism generally. She feared that if the United States entered the European War all recently achieved reforms such as her own efforts to improve and enforce industrial health and safety standards would be ended. She regarded the European War as a war of colonial ambition and believed that because all wars were organized for efficient international murder, they inevitably threatened to destroy those interests that most concerned people: labor legislation, public health care, decent housing, the movement for new parks and playgrounds, and all democratic institutions or, as Crystal wrote, "such beginnings of democracy as we have in America."

The international woman's movement, already organized on behalf of suffrage and clearly allied with the major movements for economic and social change, seemed to Crystal Eastman to be ideally suited to become the major force behind a new, bold and vigorous international peace movement. In November 1914, she called together the first meeting of the Woman's Peace Party of New York City and invited Emmeline Pethick-Lawrence to speak. A militant suffragist who had been imprisoned in Holloway gaol and brutally force-fed, Pethick-Lawrence maintained that there was "no life worth living, but a fighting life." It was time, she said, for the peace movement to learn from the women's movement. The established peace societies were "passive and negative," and it was time for women to be angry, "active and militant." Active and militant throughout the war, the Woman's Peace Party of New York, over which Crystal Eastman presided until 1919, differed dramatically in method and style from two other organizations she helped to create: the national Woman's Peace Party and the American Union Against Militarism.

To mobilize women for peace throughout the United States, Crystal persuaded Emmeline Pethick-Lawrence to go to Chicago and meet with Jane Addams. As a result, Jane Addams called a national conference of women's organizations in Chicago in January 1915 to found the national Woman's Peace Party, today called the Women's International League for Peace and Freedom. Also in 1914 Crystal met with Lillian Wald, the director of the Nurse's Settlement and the

Visiting Home Nurse Service, Paul Kellogg, Rabbi Stephen Wise, Oswald Garrison Villard, the publisher of *The Nation,* Jane Addams and others at Wald's Henry Street Settlement to organize what was originally called the Anti-Preparedness Committee. Lillian Wald became the president of this organization, soon to be renamed the American Union Against Militarism, and Crystal Eastman its executive director. The AUAM published antimilitarist analyses, lobbied in Washington against preparedness and conscription, and campaigned against American imperialism in Latin America and the Caribbean.

The social reformers within the Union believed that their testimony before congressional committees and their private meetings with President Wilson and his advisers (many of whom were personal friends or at least professional associates) were sufficient to make a difference in the forming of public policy. Their Washington lobbyist, Charles T. Hallinan, was well known and highly regarded. In the beginning their activities were analytic, educational, discreet, supportive of what they believed was the president's real desire: to keep the United States neutral. Crystal Eastman's ability as an administrator, the clarity of purpose she maintained during moments of high tension, enabled her not only to function effectively as the executive officer of the AUAM, but to persuade Lillian Wald and Paul Kellogg of the need to broaden the committee's vision and purpose, to expand and intensify its range of activities.

In November 1915 she launched a dramatic "Truth About Preparedness Campaign." Supported by both the AUAM and the Woman's Peace Party of New York, the campaign emphasized that economic profiteering was behind the industrialists' propaganda for military increases. Crystal Eastman identified the economic interests of the members of such prowar organizations as the Army League and the Navy League and called for a public investigation of America's defenses "to root out the graft and inefficiency" and to insist on the nationalization of the defense industries, in order to "clear the air of suspicion," to insure that the clamor for more and more capital for defense was "a disinterested clamor."

Both the AUAM and the national Woman's Peace Party accepted Crystal's suggestion and lobbied vigorously for congressional hearings on arms limitation and profiteering. To counter Theodore Roosevelt's claim that the United States had "a puny little egg-shell of a navy," their literature revealed the size and scope of the world's third largest fleet. When the AUAM's lobby failed and Wilson adopted a preparedness package that included a force of 400,000 trained "citizen soldiers," the antipreparedness activities intensified. The "Truth About Preparedness Campaign" held mass meetings in the largest halls of numerous cities throughout the United States. AUAM speakers addressed thousands of people and "won hundreds of columns of publicity from an unwilling press." The AUAM grew from "a small emergency committee of fifteen members to an organization of 6000 members with local committees in 22 cities. It conducted a national press bureau which served 1,601 papers— including labor and farm weeklies and regular dailies."

Under the auspices of the less restrained Woman's Peace Party of New York, Crystal organized public debates and forums between businessmen associated with the Navy League and antimilitarists. The leadership of New York's WPP was comprised largely of Crystal's closest friends—suffragists, socialists, militant feminists. Although there were many differences among them in age, affluence and position, to the press and the general public they seemed all to wear bobbed hair, believe in "free love," and belong to New York's "Bohemia." the WPP of New York was dominated by women like Margaret Lane, Anne Herendeen, Freda Kirchwey, Katherine Anthony, Madeleine Doty, Marie Jennie Howe, Agnes Brown Leach. They were members of Heterodoxy, an extraordinary luncheon club that met on Saturday afternoons for over twenty years to discuss women, literature and politics. They stood on street corners and handed out birth control literature. They helped organize strike committees and were occasionally arrested. They were rude to authority and careless about adverse publicity. Booing and hissing the business advocates of preparedness became a regular feature of their public meetings. When their meetings were broken up by violent patriots, frequently in uniform, the WPP was criticized in the press despite the fact that the women were the victims of the violence. Such publicity created additional difficulties for Crystal in her work with the AUAM leadership.

But Crystal Eastman believed that the activities of both organizations were necessary for success. She was convinced that lobbying by respectable and influential progressive Americans such as Lillian Wald, Paul Kellogg, Amos Pinchot and Jane Addams had not yet been rendered meaningless. She remained optimistic that democratic control of foreign policy might still play a role in presidential policies. Aware that the private lobbying of the AUAM without sustained public protest and as much publicity as possible would be futile, she supported entirely the more radical efforts of the WPP of New York. In addition, she believed that the international nature of the woman's peace movement was "unique and priceless" and urged women to "stand by it and strengthen it no matter what other peace organizations we may identify ourselves with."

Lillian Wald and Jane Addams shared Crystal Eastman's convictions and agreed with many of her poltical analyses. Their disagreements involved issues of emphasis, style. While Lillian Wald remained on the executive board of the New York party and Jane Addams maintained cordial relations with Crystal Eastman, the social reformers were unwilling to engage in certain kinds of public protest and opposed Crystal's more confrontational tactics.

Tensions over Crystal Eastman's flamboyant political methods and unconventional life-style persisted throughout the war. One example was a popular "War Against War" exhibit which drew crowds of five to ten thousand New Yorkers a day for several months. British pacifist Walter Fuller helped the WPP of New York erect this graphic exhibit, which featured a huge metallic dragon representing the war machine of Wall Street, vivid cartoons, colorful posters, and a series of militant speakers. The exhibit was costly and well publicized, and its spirited sense of protest became a major focus of contention.

Also, at this time Crystal divorced Bennie and married Walter Fuller, with whom she had been living. While such living arrangements would rarely be considered objectionable today, Crystal's private activities gave rise to additional criticism from some of her associates. Her good friends, however, delighted in her new happiness. Roger Baldwin recalled that Walter Fuller was "extremely

witty and totally pacifist and worked hard to make Crystal laugh—
and, you know, Crystal loved to laugh."

Others were not at all amused by his display of wit, especially as
represented in the "War Against War" exhibit. Mabel Hyde Kit-
tredge, a patron of causes associated with the Henry Street Settlement
and later president of the national Woman's Peace Party, resigned in
protest over the tone of the exhibit. She complained that the New
York branch "made fun" of the munitions-makers and "ridiculed"
certain American interests. Other New York residents bypassed the
branch over which Crystal presided to join the national WPP because
"the sentiments expressed" at the New York meetings were "very
extreme and dangerous"—not only impolite and daring, but socialist
and revolutionary.

Crystal Eastman's conviction that public activity and private
lobbying could have a real impact on presidential policy was bolstered
by the Union's success regarding Mexico in the summer of 1916. A
massive publicity campaign to avert war in Mexico resulted in an
"unofficial commission" of three Mexican and three United States
antimilitarists that met through June and July at El Paso. Organized
by Crystal, this effort at private mediation was supported by the
American Federation of Labor, whose officials met with officials of
sixty Mexican labor unions in "the most effective effort ever made by
the workers of two countries to avoid war." On 6 July 1916, Crystal
Eastman and her associates held a press conference in Washington
with three Mexican delegates and issued a press release which
compared the Mexican Revolution to the French Revolution and
analyzed the issues which jeopardized Mexican-American relations,
notably the fact that 75 per cent of Mexico's national wealth was
controlled by foreign capital, mostly North American. The AUAM
feared that United States policy in Mexico would impose a "suzerainty
from the Rio Grande to Panama," creating "a suspicious and embittered South America."

Crystal Eastman criticized the United States' entire Latin American policy, beginning with the Monroe Doctrine which, she wrote,
"contains the germs of future trouble." Why not, she asked, substi-

tute a truly "democratic union of American republics" to replace the "uncomfortable" and "possibly indefensible" Monroe Doctrine? Only in that way, she concluded, would the United States "rid itself of the temptation to establish profitable protectorates" where anti-American attitudes were "growing and perhaps warranted."

Wilson's response to the Union's activity was to appoint a Joint High Commission on Mexico to mediate differences. The commission sat from September 1916 to January 1917 and war was averted, intensifying the antimilitarists' expectations regarding the possibilities of mediation in Europe. In "Suggestions to the AUAM for 1916–1917," Crystal wrote that "we must make the most of our Mexican experience. We must make it known to everybody that *people* acting directly—not through their governments or diplomats or armies—stopped that war, and can stop all wars if enough of them will act together and act quickly."

But 1916 was an election year, and the victory for peace in Mexico was the final victory for the antimilitarists. The AUAM campaigned for Wilson despite the fact that Justice Charles Evans Hughes had been a progressive governor and had worked closely with Crystal Eastman, whom he had appointed to her post as commissioner, and with Lillian Wald—who had faith in his profound interest in protecting the "ordinary people." But most of the big preparedness spokesmen were Republicans, and Hughes did not promise peace. He promised suffrage. Therefore, most of Crystal Eastman's closest friends in the radical suffrage movement supported Hughes. They campaigned vigorously against Wilson, who refused to endorse the suffrage amendment.

That year was a tense and bitter time for the suffragist women who led the United States peace forces. It reflected the cruel dilemma of two historical movements that seemed temporarily antagonistic. It foreshadowed the dilemma feminists faced over the Equal Rights Amendment during the 1920s. While there was no correct position, there were priorities. In 1916 suffragists against the war had to vote for one or the other: Hughes, who seemed to promise suffrage with war, or Wilson, who promised peace without suffrage.

Several months before the election, in June 1916, Crystal Eastman gave a rousing and enthusiastic speech at the "Suffrage First" luncheon of Alice Paul's National Woman's Party convention. Nevertheless, all the AUAM's election efforts endorsed Wilson. From the beginning one of the members of the executive committee of the Congressional Union (reorganized in 1916 as the National Woman's Party), Crystal Eastman on behalf of peace now seemed to support the candidate some of her closest comrades—Doris Stevens, Alice Paul, Lavinia Dock, Inez Milholland—were picketing and jeering. It seemed incomprehensible.

One of Inez Milholland's last speeches before her sudden death during a lecture tour through the western states seemed specifically aimed at her friend Crystal Eastman: "Do not let anyone convince you that there is any more important issue in the country today than votes for women. . . . There are people who honestly believe— HONESTLY BELIEVE! . . . that there are more important issues before the country than suffrage, and that it would be very becoming on our part . . . to retire at this time. . . . Now I do not know what you feel about such a point of view . . . but it makes me mad. . . . We must say, 'Women First.' "

Milholland's criticism was not entirely justified. Crystal Eastman did not believe that suffragists should be silent in the interests of peace. In April 1915, with Milholland and Doris Stevens, she had participated in a well-publicized Congressional Union deputation to Senator James O'Gorman's New York office. The senator was one of the leading opponents of the federal amendment. On 8 May *The Suffragist* described the following exchange over the Susan B. Anthony amendment first introduced in 1878, not voted out of committee until 1887, and without a favorable congressional majority until 1918:

> Nothing, perhaps, was more indicative of the gulf which yawns between Senator O'Gorman and the suffragists of the country than his comment . . . : "Aren't you women going too hastily?" There was a long drawn breath of resentment. . . .
>
> "Too quickly! After forty years!"
>
> "Can freedom come too quickly?" asked Mrs. Inez Milholland Boissevain.
>
> "But, you know," said Senator O'Gorman, "the women do not have to depend upon amendments. They are very powerful. . . ."

"Yes," agreed Mrs. Crystal Eastman Benedict. "The women voters are a power in the country. They have tools with which to work. It is only a question of time when we will unite the voters to force some of our issues."

Nevertheless Crystal's support for Wilson while her closest friends were, as Doris Stevens later wrote, being "jailed for freedom" clearly established her 1916 priorities.

Personal divisions and anguish among the suffragists aroused by the election evaporated quickly, however. In December 1916 Crystal Eastman and Jane Addams testified on behalf of the national Woman's Peace Party before the House Judiciary Committee to endorse the federal amendment. Moreover, Paul's National Woman's Party opposed the war with consistent vigor; and when it became clear that Wilson had betrayed the antimilitarists, the pages of *The Suffragist* rallied to their support.

Contradictions in political life are commonplace. In this case the intensity of profound friendships transcended them. And Inez Milholland's sudden death transcended the election of 1916. Crystal Eastman arranged the largest and last memorial service for the beloved Amazon who had given her life to the suffrage movement. Representatives of all the major movements for change, as well as suffragists and pacifists, spoke. *The Suffragist* reported that Crystal Eastman "expressed the feeling of all these personal friends when she said, 'Here we are today, the representatives of so many great movements—and we all claim Inez Milholland. This is very wonderful to me; it simply means that her whole aspiration was for fuller liberty.'"

On behalf of her own aspiration for liberty, Crystal Eastman worked sixteen to twenty hours a day in the months prior to the declaration of war in April 1917. With only a few weeks off following the birth of her first baby, Jeffrey Fuller, Crystal campaigned tirelessly. In "War and Peace" she wrote that the radical peace movement had three major emphases: to stop the war in Europe, to organize the world for peace at the close of the war, and to defend democracy against the subtle dangers of militarism. More immediately, the demand for conscription and compulsory military training needed to be stopped. Stimulated "by the self-interest of capitalists, imperialists, and war traders, but supported by . . . thousands who call themselves democrats," the people needed to be de-mystified about alleged benefits of military training and service. "We must make this great democracy know," she wrote, "that military training is bad for the bodies and minds and souls of boys; that free minds, and souls undrilled to obedience are vital to the life of democracy."

As the United States hurtled toward war, Crystal Eastman's continued commitment to civil liberties in wartime and her support for *Four Lights,* the new newsletter of New York's WPP, created additional tensions within the AUAM leadership. First issued on 27 January 1917, *Four Lights* became the subject of the first serious antagonism between Crystal and Jane Addams, in her capacity as president of the national WPP, and Lillian Wald. Modeled on *The Masses* in format and style, *Four Lights* was gay, impulsive, sardonic and entirely disrespectful of authority. Although each issue was independently edited and Crystal Eastman had nothing specifically to do with its contents, she was directly responsible for its tone, and it was the official paper of the organization over which she presided. There was little doubt in the minds of such WPP conservatives as, for example, Lucia Ames Mead, that Crystal Eastman was no longer a sound ally.

Four Lights gave these women little choice. It devoted an entire issue, "The Sister Susie Number," to criticizing such women as Lucia Ames Mead, whose Boston branch abandoned its former position to assist the war relief work of more conservative groups. Some WPP branches complained the editors of *Four Lights,* spent the entire war knitting socks. Even Jane Addams and Lillian Wald, opposed to conscription in principle, administered registration programs in their settlement houses. In addition, Lillian Wald chaired the Council of National Defense's Committee on Public Health and Child Welfare, while Jane Addams volunteered to work for Herbert Hoover's Food Administration. As far as *Four Lights* was concerned Hoover had revealed "the cloven hoof of the military dictator," and without mentioning Addams by name, it editorialized that "Hoover Helpers" were those women "who accept their position beside the garbage cans

as they have always accepted what God and man has put upon them
to endure. . . ."

In its first editorial *Four Lights* promised to be "the voice of the
young, uncompromising peace movement in America, whose aims
are daring and immediate." Above all, *Four Lights* opposed the
mounting tyranny and wartime violence that quickly followed the
United States' declaration of war. Within three months after the
United States entered the war it editorialized against one of the
greatest wartime outrages, the race riot in East St. Louis in which
scores of black people were beaten, lynched, burned and drowned:

> Six weeks have passed since the East St. Louis riots and no public
> word of rebuke, no demand for the punishment of the offenders, has
> come from our Chief Executive. These American Negroes have died
> under more horrible conditions than any noncombatants who were
> sunk by German submarines. But to our President their death does
> not merit consideration.
>
> Our young men who don their khaki are thus taught that, as
> they go out to battle under the flag of the United States, they may
> outdo Belgian atrocities without rebuke if their enemy be of a darker
> race. And those who guard our land at home have learned that black
> men and women and little children may safely be mutilated and shot
> and burned while they stand idly by.

Uncompromising and bold, *Four Lights* announced on 24 March
1917 in dramatic banner headline that it hailed "the Russian Revolution with mad glad joy." It pledged itself to the cause of international democracy and claimed that all nations "must be democratized
before a federated world can be achieved." Moreover, it accused the
United States of "busily forging weapons to menace the spirit of
freedom struggling to life in an exhausted Europe."

Lillian Wald, Paul Kellogg, Oswald Garrison Villard, Jane
Addams and the other social reformers on the board of the AUAM
did not disagree theoretically with Crystal Eastman's position. They
endorsed her 15 June 1917 press release, for example, which announced that once the United States entered the war the AUAM
sought victory "in harmony with the principles outlined by the
Revolutionary government of Russia, namely, No forcible annexations, No punitive indemnities, Free development of Nationalities."

They disapproved, however, of her forthright public style and the order of her priorities. They particularly disapproved of the AUAM's new committee, the Civil Liberties Bureau founded by Crystal Eastman, Roger Baldwin and Norman Thomas.

Wald and Kellogg, for example, did not want to be identified with an "anti-war agitation." Rather than focus their energy on conscientious objectors and "an aggressive policy against prosecution of the war," they sought to influence the future peace negotiations in the interests of international democracy and federation after the war. Crystal Eastman insisted that the Civil Liberties Bureau represented a "democracy first" movement. "Our attempt to have the conscription act administered with due regard to liberty of conscience," she wrote, was only an attempt to save the United States from "the wholesale autocratic sweep which war-efficiency dictates."

Lillian Wald wrote Crystal Eastman on 28 August 1917 that the AUAM had been accepted by the public as "a group of reflective liberals." It was dignified and respectable. Its activities in the past had been legal. Crystal's enthusiasm for organizations like the Civil Liberties Bureau and the newly organized People's Council represented "impulsive radicalism." Wald wrote that Crystal Eastman's new activities demanded either her resignation or Wald's, and that "it would be lacking in sincerity for us not to be perfectly frank with each other."

For Eastman, Baldwin and Thomas the Civil Liberties Bureau was the inevitable development of all their convictions. On 2 July 1917 Crystal Eastman issued a press release to introduce the new bureau: "It is the tendency even of the most 'democratic' of governments embarked upon the most 'idealistic of wars' to sacrifice everything for complete military efficiency. To combat this tendency where it threatens free speech, free press, freedom of assembly and freedom of conscience—the essentials of liberty and the heritage of all past wars worth fighting—that is the first function of the AUAM today. . . . To maintain something over here that will be worth coming back to when the weary war is over. . . ."

By November 1917 the socialist activism of Crystal Eastman and her associates in the Woman's Peace Party of New York, combined with the activities of the Civil Liberties Bureau, ended the once-powerful alliance the AUAM had represented. Of her own resignation and the AUAM's disintegration Lillian Wald wrote in her 1934 autobiography, *Windows on Henry Street,* simply: "The fire and imagination of the Secretary, Crystal Eastman, were often impatient of more sober councils." The conservative wing of the national WPP felt more strongly.

An extensive correspondence between Lucia Ames Mead, Jane Addams and Emily Greene Balch—who consistently supported Crystal's activities—reveals that despite Crystal's formidable efforts throughout the war, the national WPP hierarchy attempted to prevent her from attending the Second International Congress of Women in 1919. They argued that her "extreme" radicalism and her "casual sex life" would confuse their mission and increase their difficulties. Although many of Crystal's associates shared her enthusiasm for the Russian Revolution at this time, they were more discreet about their views.

To continue their public works on behalf of the poor the social workers depended on the contributions of private financiers and government largesse. They placed a high value on cautious and respectable behavior, and feared to lose the kind of public approval Crystal Eastman never sought. She was bold and fearless about her political views and entirely open about her life. Her very openness threatened the closeted self-protectiveness of her critics.

During the postwar Red Scare when all social progress was suspended the attitude of the social reformers seemed justified. But it did not protect them. Their respectability in that period was illusory. When Jane Addams, for example, denounced the food blockade and insisted that the "United States should not allow women and children of any nation to starve," she was vilified as a traitor. Like Crystal Eastman, she was followed by secret agents and during the 1920s both their names appeared on all the lists of "dangerous Reds," enemies of America. The states' rejection of the child labor amendment, portrayed as part of a massive communist plot, symbolizes the collapse of progressive reform. While the nominal respectability of social reformers availed them very little, the inability of progressives to work together during the postwar period strengthened the militarist and antidemocratic forces they had so vigorously opposed.

Crystal Eastman's last activity as president of New York's WPP was to organize the First Feminist Congress in the United States, held on 1 March 1919. In her opening statement she examined the status of women in this self-congratulatory center of "freedom and democracy." Citing dismal statistics, including the fact that four-fifths of the women in America were "still denied the elementary political right of voting," she enumerated the essential changes required before women could be independent. She said that she did not intend to catalog the restrictive laws and repressive social customs that burdened women in a spirit of "bitterness," and she fully recognized "the fact that women by their passivity have made these things possible." Her one goal, her aim for this first feminist congress, was to "see the birth of a new spirit of humane and intelligent self-interest . . . which will lead women to declare: 'WE WILL NOT WAIT FOR THE SOCIAL REVOLUTION TO BRING US THE FREEDOM WE SHOULD HAVE WON IN THE 19TH CENTURY.' "

Throughout the postwar years, Crystal Eastman's entire effort involved feminism and the "social revolution," by which she meant socialism. As a feminist she had no illusions about the existence, or marginality, of feminist principles among the male-dominated socialist parties in the United States and Europe. Her own position, expressed vigorously in "Now We Can Begin," was entirely clear: "Many feminists are socialists, many are communists. . . . But the true feminist, no matter how far to the left she may be in the revolutionary movement, sees the woman's battle as distinct in its objects and different in its methods from the workers' battle for industrial freedom. She knows, of course, that the vast majority of women as well as men are without property, and are of necessity bread and butter slaves under a system of society which allows the very sources of life to be privately owned by a few, and she counts herself a loyal soldier in the working-class army that is marching to over-throw that system. But as a feminist she also knows that the whole of woman's slavery is not summed up in the profit system, nor her complete emancipation assured by the downfall of capitalism. . . . If we should graduate into communism to-morrow . . . man's attitude to his wife would not be changed."

Her socialist position, as expressed in *The Liberator,* which she co-owned and co-edited with Max from March 1918 until they both resigned in 1922, was equally clear. Crystal Eastman had been radicalized by her wartime experiences. While she had lobbied and campaigned through what were, before the war, legal and generally acceptable political channels against preparedness and conscription and America's entrance into the European War, many of her closest friends had been imprisoned and abused because they sought the most rudimentary political power—the vote—by exercising the most basic rights of free speech and assembly. The abolition of civil liberties in wartime revealed the fragile nature of bourgeois rights even in a country that boasted fiercely of its democratic heritage. The Espionage Act and the Sedition Act of May 1918 altered forever the nature of American freedom. Those laws rendered all Crystal Eastman's wartime activity illegal and resulted in the removal of all radical publications from the mails, including *Four Lights* and *The Masses,* as well as the imprisonment of countless dissenters, including her brother and Roger Baldwin. During the postwar Red Scare thousands of Americans were imprisoned or deported—anarchists, socialists, labor leaders, conscientious objectors.

A socialist before the war, she had maintained faith in the democratic principles generally associated with America. War, the counter-revolutionary mobilization and the secret Allied intervention in the Soviet Union (which was reported only in *The Liberator*) served to convince her that the only way to "restore liberty" was "to destroy the capitalist system." In July 1920 she wrote with scorn and wonder that there were duly elected socialists denied their seats in Congress and the state assemblies who preferred to sit on the legislative steps of this capitalist democracy with the doors closed in their faces rather than to "take a chance" and organize a real working-class movement "and [they] say so." Crystal was certain, however, that they did not represent the future. "The world's future," *The Liberator* editorialized in February 1919, "shall not be the League of Business Politicians at Versailles, but the New International, the League of the Working Classes of the World."

In March 1919 Crystal Eastman became the first American journalist to visit communist Hungary. Her report from Hungary is as valuable for its information as it is for her feelings regarding the inevitable conflicts and contradictions such situations present to "pacifist revolutionaries." There was, she concluded, nothing simple about the dilemma of force. On the other hand, the activities of the invading British, American and Japanese armies and Admiral Kolchak's "monarchist forces" helped resolve the conflict. The military invasion, intent on destroying all revolutionary movements, suspended Crystal Eastman's pacifism.

The Liberator was the only United States monthly to publish information about socialist movements throughout the world as well as news about the Allied intervention in Russia. In May 1919, for example, *The Liberator* published the startling news that "Japan has made an offer to England" to send troops to join the Allied intervention in Russia "and bear the expenses of the expedition alone—if she receives a mandate for Indo-China."

Filled with some of the most significant poetry and literature of the postwar period, this "journal of Revolutionary Progress" had an impact that reached far beyond the United States. Italian communist theorist Antonio Gramsci depended on it for international information, "so tight and bristling was the blockade around the Bolsheviks." *The Liberator* published John Reed and Louise Bryant from Russia, a regular column of international news by Alexander Trachtenberg (the founder of International Publishers), Bertrand Russell's "Democracy and Freedom," the works of associate editor Floyd Dell, contributions by Helen Keller, Norman Thomas, Roger Baldwin, Lenin and Dorothy Day, and the poetry of Claude McKay.

McKay's poetry had never been accepted by *The Masses,* which had sent him "so sorry" rejections. But when Crystal Eastman read his work in *Pearson's* she invited him to call at the *Liberator* office. One of the leading black poets of the Harlem Renaissance, McKay was still working on the railroads, writing poems on the trains whenever he had spare time. Impressed that Crystal suspended her conference with Margaret Lane, formerly the executive secretary of New York's WPP and now *The Liberator*'s business manager, as soon as he arrived, he wrote: "The moment I saw her and heard her voice I liked Crystal Eastman. I think she was the most beautiful white woman I ever knew. She was of the heavy or solid type of female, and her beauty was not so much of her features . . . but in her magnificent presence. Her form was something after the pattern of a splendid draft horse and she had a way of holding her head like a large bird poised in a listening attitude." Their life-long friendship began during that first meeting.

After the war, Crystal Eastman with her husband and son lived communally with her brother Max, their childhood friend Ruth Pickering—who had also graduated from Vassar and was soon to marry Amos Pinchot—the actress Florence Deshon, and Eugen Boissevain—who commanded "a whole fleet of merchant ships" and had married first Inez Milholland and then Edna Millay. According to Max, Crystal had engineered this "delightful half-way family," which included at least two servants, in 1918 to promote companionship and economy. With two houses and a collective courtyard and kitchen, they shared a comfortable communal space in Greenwich Village and also spent weekends and summers together in Croton-on-the-Hudson with, among others, Boardman Robinson, Margaret and Winthrop D. Lane, Floyd Dell, and—until they left for Russia—John Reed and Louise Bryant. Claude McKay, soon to become associate editor of *The Liberator,* was a frequent guest in both communities; his description of their parties and activities provides one of the few sources of information available about Crystal's life and society during these years.

Another fully detailed description of life at Croton and Crystal in particular is provided by Clare Sheridan's journal, published as *My American Diary.* Clare Sheridan was a British aristocrat and artist who scandalized polite London society, and especially her cousin Winston Churchill, when she became the first British woman to visit Russia and do portraits of the Soviet leaders. Ken Durant introduced the two women in March 1921 and Sheridan wrote: "I liked her. . . . She is good looking, and extremely decorative. She sails into a room with her head high and the face of a triumphant Victory." And the atmosphere in her home "was such as I recall in Moscow—hospitality that was simple and friendly, and discussions that were interesting and humorous."

In May, Sheridan visited Crystal and Walter Fuller in Croton on Mt. Airy Road, "in a roadside cottage surrounded by roses. It was

real country and luxuriantly green. . . . In the orchard on the steep
grassy hill behind the house the children climbed a cherry tree. . . .
There is a sort of colony at Croton, and every other house is inhabited
by someone one knows. . . . All work-worn journalists, artists and
Bohemians generally, who come there with their children for a rest.
The houses have no gardens, the grass grows long and the rose bushes
are weed tangled. Now and then a bunch of peonies survives. The
cottages have almost an abandoned look, for the town toilers are too
weary to work in their gardens. . . .

   "After a time, we sauntered into the garden of Mr. and Mrs.
Boardman Robinson . . . [where] a large party foregathered. . . . It
was as though Greenwich Village in summer array had been dumped
down with almost deliberate pageantry upon the grass. . . . And all
the children were good . . . and all the people were happy. One or
two of the mothers asked me (and I looked at them twice to see if they
were serious) when in my opinion conditions in Russia would be
sufficiently adjusted to enable them to take their children there for
education."

   The communal harmony and pastoral happiness of those years
were short-lived. From 1907 to 1921 Crystal Eastman's capacity for
work was intense and varied. Before the war her paying jobs, whether
as a social investigator or government appointee, occupied only part
of her working day. A variety of political activities and organizations
occupied the other time, in what amounted throughout those years
to a very long day. During the war sixteen-to-twenty-hour schedules
prevailed. Today we might call Crystal Eastman a "workaholic." She
thrived on work—it energized her and increased her strength. Only
when she was not working did she become morose or melancholic.
After the war the feminist movement and her travels for *The Liberator,*
both as fund-raiser and investigative reporter, enabled her to continue
this intense work pattern. Emotionally and fundamentally, hard
work was essential to her. Yet between 1911 and 1921 Crystal
Eastman's physical constitution had broken down several times. Her
blood pressure was frequently and dangerously high, and she had a
bad heart. Above all, there was nephritis. Diagnosed late and little
understood then, it is now known to be a slowly consuming and
painful kidney condition.

With complete disregard for her physical well-being, Crystal did not slow down until the birth of her second child two months prematurely. At the insistence of doctors, she removed herself from the management of *The Liberator,* became a contributing editor and agreed to rest while writing a book on feminism and taking more personal care of herself and her daughter Annis.

Hospital and medical expenses and the loss of her full-time *Liberator* salary devastated the Eastman-Fuller household. According to Max, Crystal "as joint editor really ran the magazine," and had received her "customary salary," $90 a week. Floyd Dell received $75 and Max, "to justify" his "truancy," received $60. Walter Fuller, who edited *The Freeman* at what we would today call a "movement" salary, was paid close to $50 a week. In the spring of 1922, when Annis was three months old, Walter Fuller left for England to look for a better job.

Although the full range of their difficulties, economic and emotional, is unclear, we know they were financially crushed by debts. On 14 April Crystal wrote that she was "so lonely it makes a sick feeling in my solar plexus. . . . I hope you will come back." To encourage Walter to return she arranged with Paul Kellogg to offer Walter a job on the *Survey Graphic.* It entailed more money, and Crystal believed that her husband "could work with Paul—he is sensitive and whimsical and humorous. And they have money in sight to run the *Survey Graphic* for three years—just about as long as you like a job to last. . . ." But Walter refused the offer.

In a subsequent letter dated 27 June Crystal discussed the possibilities of joining Walter in England as soon as she could raise sufficient funds and he could afford the company of his family. Crystal wrote: "Don't worry about harsh words. Have I said any? If I have they certainly can be forgotten now. I knew you had to run away. That you couldn't even send me a line to say so and say you were sorry will forever be incomprehensible to me. But then four-fifths of you is a closed book to me and four-fifths of me is a closed book to you,— and yet we love each other a great deal. Don't we?" At this time Walter Fuller, in partnership with Charles Hallinan, who had been the AUAM's lobbyist, began a literary agency in England. But Crystal's 27 June letter was full of doubts about his economic condition and apparent mistrust about his ability to alter the situation.

"Marriage Under Two Roofs," written for *Cosmopolitan* magazine largely for money, was not written largely as spoof. Crystal and her husband lived for years not only under two separate roofs, but in two separate countries. From 1922 to 1927 she and her children traveled back and forth between England and the United States with commuter regularity. Some years, such as 1924 when she organized the Women for Congress Campaign, were apparently spent largely in the United States. Then she would spend the summer in England with Walter. Other years were spent in England, with summer vacations in the south of France with such friends as Jeannette Lowe and their children. Walter might visit occasionally. Very much like "Marriage Under Two Roofs."

Wherever Crystal Eastman spent her time during these years, her life consisted of a continual battle to find meaningful work, to help organize the Anglo-American women's movement on behalf of equal rights, and to ignore the physicians, and several medical quacks, who all agreed on only one thing: Crystal Eastman needed rest. Crystal hated to rest, she hated inactivity and she hated to be without a steady job. Her inability to find work, the fact that she was actually barred from the kind of work she sought, was the hardest for her to comprehend. Today we are more familiar with the facts and effects of political blacklists. But Crystal Eastman, attorney, social investigator, noted orator and author, could not understand why a militant feminist, antimilitarist and socialist could not between 1922 and 1928 find regular employment. She could not understand it even when old friends like Paul Kellogg told her specifically that there were "practical difficulties in making a fresh start which it does no good to minimize." The United States, wrote Kellogg in a letter, "is not as tolerant as England; we still have a lot of beating up of bugaboos, and you will get a touch of that in any public work . . . and your various espousals—such as the Woman's Party—would not help in some of the few quarters where industrial research is still carried on, etc." Throughout the last years of her life, Crystal's only income was derived from her two houses, in Croton and Greenwich

Village, when she rented them, and from feminist articles contracted by the militant wing of the Anglo-American women's movement.

During the 1920s the contradictions between radicalism and reform, within the context of both socialism and feminism, were vividly apparent in the divisions of the women's movement. For twenty years social reformers like Jane Addams and Florence Kelley had championed protective legislation for women and children. To the extent that Crystal worked for protective legislation for workers, she too had been identified with that reform movement. But Crystal was a radical feminist who believed above all in equality. She regarded protective laws as cruelly discriminatory when they regulated working conditions for women only.

In 1908 social reformers such as Jane Addams and Florence Kelley had rejoiced in a Supreme Court decision that established the principle of protective legislation for women. *Muller* v. *Oregon* introduced "sociological jurisprudence" into constitutional law. Florence Kelley and Josephine Goldmark had hired Louis D. Brandeis to defend a protective law that established a ten-hour day for women laundry workers. The first of the famous "Brandeis briefs," two pages of legal argument and over 100 pages of sociological facts and statistics, demonstrated the physical inferiority of women, their need for protection—and the benefits for the human race should women's toil be specifically restricted by the state. Brandeis' brief was reprinted in the margins of the Supreme Court's unanimous opinion: Yes, declared the Court, "Woman's physical structure, and the performance of maternal functions. . . . justify special legislation restricting or qualifying the conditions under which she should be permitted to toil. . . ." These restrictions, the Court added, were "not imposed solely for her benefit, but also largely for the benefit of all. . . ."

This was the principle that the reformers, Addams and Kelley and all the others, sought to defend against erosion by the Equal Rights Amendment. When the National Woman's Party introduced this amendment in July 1923, at the seventy-fifth anniversary convention of the Seneca Falls Equal Rights meeting of 1848, the feminists and the women reformers became irreconcilably divided. *Muller* v. *Oregon* may have satisfied the humanitarians but it was repugnant to feminists. It classed women with minors, rested its decision on women's biological "inferiority," their potential maternity and "natural dependence" on man. It represented everything Crystal Eastman had opposed since her first speech called "Woman."

Since she was fifteen Crystal had considered arguments of women's physical inferiority male myths created to keep women untutored, unpaid and at home. The 1920s was a period when a great variety of social and economic forces were operating to achieve just that situation. Every victory for women's freedom was met by a counter-assault on behalf of the sanctity of the home. It was an era of new markets, experimental advertising methods and hysterical consumerism. With all Europe moving toward socialism, consumerism alone did not seem sufficient to keep workers invested in the capitalist system. Working women were urged to return home. It was believed that without patriarchal order there would be anarchy. The working class required stability. Women needed protection. Protection would preserve the home, and the entire human race. All the men in unions seemed to agree.

During World War I women in large numbers had moved into numerous industries and professions from which they had previously been barred. With war's end a great effort to dismiss them emerged. In Cleveland, for example, 150 women street-car conductors were dismissed after the men struck to eliminate women from the job because there was no longer a "manpower shortage." Also in Detroit white male conductors petitioned for the dismissal of women and black workers because their contract promised "women and Negroes could be employed only in an emergency, and the emergency was over." The courts and the National War Labor Board occasionally decided in favor of the recently employed. But by 1919 protective laws forbidding night work were used as a pretext for dismissing women workers from lucrative, interesting and sought-after jobs.

Nevertheless, Florence Kelley, Jane Addams, Dr. Alice Hamilton—all the friends of labor—opposed the equal rights movement because they did not want to lose hard-won protective laws. Organized labor women may have favored equality—but equality with protection; and they opted for protection first. Given the cruel hours and life-threatening conditions, most working women and their allies believed that it was absurd to abandon specific protective laws for the principle of equality that seemed then both abstract and far-fetched. Crystal Eastman's support for equal rights represented a socialist feminist tradition that has only recently begun to reemerge. In the 1920s she was almost isolated even among her allies in the National Woman's Party and its British counterpart, Lady Rhondda's Six Point Group.

The debate over equal rights divided and demoralized the women's movement. It did not reunite until the 1960s. Although the vision of the contemporary women's movement goes far beyond the ERA, it begins with the analysis that Crystal Eastman made during the 1920s. For Crystal Eastman protection was humanitarianism in the interests of "family welfare." It had nothing to do with the needs or rights or aspirations of women. It represented reformism at its worst. It served everywhere to bar women from well-paid jobs that men were eager to keep for themselves. Protective legislation, she maintained, protected male unionists who feared female competition and capitalist power which used intra-class competition between women and men just as it used ethnic and racial differences: to block real workers' unity, the necessary sense of connectedness that might stimulate a real workers' movement.

Crystal Eastman's commitment to equal rights was not an abstract enthusiasm. Case after case of individual privation moved her personally. With a rare empathy for all women, and an ability to imagine herself in each humiliating or repressive situation, her outrage was as specific as it was theoretical. In "Women, Rights and Privileges," for example, she wrote that "this sudden concern for the health of women when they set out to earn their living in competition with men seems a little suspicious. . . . What working-class mother of small children ever had nine hours consecutive rest? . . . What traditional union husband ever felt that it was his concern to see that she should have?" The example of women telephone operators in France, removed from their night jobs to protect their health and safety, illustrated well her point. The women were now protesting because they were limited to the busiest daytime hours "while the men, coming in at nine in the evening take the seven easiest hours . . . have two hours off for rest and are paid 3000 francs more per year than the women."

As a militant feminist who was also a socialist, Crystal Eastman was politically isolated in English society of the 1920s. In addition to her United States friends also in "exile", such as Hazel Hunkins Hallinan, Crystal's closest associates were the militant feminists Lady Rhondda, Lady Astor and Rebecca West. Margaret Thomas, Lady Rhondda, wrote Crystal Eastman, was "a wealthy woman, owner of vast coal properties, with no Socialistic tendencies whatsoever." Yet whenever Crystal lived in England she worked with the two equal rights groups associated with Lady Rhondda, the Six Point Group and the Open Door Council; and she was gainfully employed by Lady Rhondda's feminist weekly *Time and Tide*. When Lady Rhondda's father died he left her to administer the family coal properties in the Rhondda Valley in Wales, along with his peerage, "exactly as though she had been a son." But all of Lady Rhondda's energies went into the women's movement. And Crystal admired in her precisely those qualities she herself possessed in abundance:

"All her gifts, all her dreams, all her ambitions have . . . been concerned with the cause of making women free. . . . Lady Rhondda learned her Feminism at the militants' school and has never lost their fire. She loves to laugh. She loves to fight. When she calls upon the real Feminists of the world to find each other it is the call of a comrade. Perhaps it is the call of a leader, too."

By 1927, despite her activities in England, Crystal Eastman became desperate for more challenging work. Besides she never actually liked England very well. She loathed the climate and longed for the American seasons—the heat of the sun, the snow. She was neither well nor happy. In January she wrote to Paul Kellogg that she had decided, with finality, to return home. She asked him to help her as he had twenty-three years before: "I am rich in health and strength now. . . . Three lazy months at Antibes . . . have given me back myself." And, she wrote, she "was simply crazy to work. England holds nothing for me. . . . I have tried for two years to get a job—research, organizing, editorial, speaking, *anything*. . . . If you just say you *think* I can get work and begin to build my life again. . . ."

Kellogg's encouragement, his willingness to help her find work in her early field of health insurance, encouraged her enormously; she wrote that "nobody but Max ever helped me so much." Crystal left for the United States in August, having secured a temporary position organizing *The Nation*'s tenth anniversary celebration. Walter was to join her when she secured more permanent work. But in September 1927 Walter Fuller died of a stroke, and within ten months Crystal too was dead.

The last months of Crystal Eastman's life were given over to hard work and her final battle, to heal "this good for nothing body of mine." Ravaged by nephritis which was never properly diagnosed or treated, she blamed herself for her headaches, her loss of energy. On 11 October 1927 she wrote to Cynthia, Walter's sister: "I am fighting so hard not to drown and to get my health and hold on to it, so that I'll be equal to supporting the children and making a happy home for them." Writing in the hospital, after an operation and "still half doped with morphine and verinol," Crystal wrote that "the days and days of brilliant bracing sunny air have made it impossible to get permanently depressed. . . . I go from acute sorrow to my usual joy in activity, and there IS SO MUCH for me to do. . . ."

Even to the last weeks of her life Crystal's optimism prevailed over her pain. One of her last letters was to one of her closest friends, Ruth Pickering Pinchot. On 8 June she wrote: "Yesterday and today have been so wonderful that I am happy even with this nasty taste in my mouth and every mouthful more than doubtful—my eyes almost useless—and a roaring in my head at night like a train puffing up hill. And it is great to be here with the children. My heart is warm and life is sweet. . . ."

Crystal Eastman was forty-six years old when she died. Her last thoughts were of her children and all the work she had left undone. Many friends offered to adopt the children; Agnes Brown Leach and Henry Goddard Leach did so. Agnes Brown Leach had been among the most consistent supporters of the American Union Against Militarism, and she had been treasurer of the New York branch of the Woman's Peace Party and a member of the executive committee of the National Woman's Party.

Crystal Eastman was mourned by many, and all the articles written about her emphasized her unusual gift for inspiring friendship. Claude McKay, who believed that Crystal joined "in her personality that daring freedom of thought and action—all that was fundamentally fine, noble and genuine in American democracy," wrote of her many years later. He recalled that when in 1922 they were both scheduled to leave for England but on separate ships, they had arranged to have a final meal together. "But I waited until near midnight and she didn't appear. So I went out alone in Harlem, visiting the speakeasies and cabarets and drinking a farewell to the illegal bars. . . . Late that night, . . . I found a tiny scrap of paper thrust into my keyhole:

> Claude dear:
> I just dashed in to give you a hug and say good-bye—
> Bon Voyage, dear child!
> Crystal

"I tucked the little note in a corner of my pocket book and have carried it with me all these years, through many countries, transferring it, when one pocket book was worn out, to another." When McKay read of Crystal's death in *The Nation,* he took her farewell note out of his "pocket book and read it and cried. Crystal Eastman was a great-hearted woman whose life was big with primitive and exceptional gestures. She never wrote that Book of Woman which was imprinted on her mind. She was poor, and fettered with a family. She had a grand idea for a group of us to go off to write in some quiet corner of the world, where living was cheap and easy. But it couldn't be realized. And so life was cheated of one contribution about women that no other woman could write."

That farewell note, having been pasted by somebody into Crystal's annotated copy of Claude McKay's book *Home to Harlem,* is now in the possession of her grandchildren.

Crystal Eastman's contemporaries considered her "a great leader." In Freda Kirchwey's memorial in *The Nation* she wrote that when Crystal Eastman "spoke to people—whether it was to a small committee or a swarming crowd—hearts beat faster and nerves tightened as she talked. She was simple, direct, dramatic. Force poured from her strong body and her rich voice, and people followed where she led. . . . In her personal as in her public life her enthusiasm and strength were spent without thought; she had no pride or sense of her own power. . . . Her strength, . . . her rich and compelling personality—these she threw with reckless vigor into every cause that promised a finer life to the world. She spent herself wholly, and died—too young."

Crystal Eastman left us the legacy of her life, her determination and her work. Her vision, lost for so long, enables us to build with more clarity.

Sources

For biographical information I have relied largely on conversations with Jeannette Lowe, Roger Baldwin, Annis Young, Ruth Pickering Pinchot, Max Eastman, and Hazel Hunkins Hallinan. Quotations from Max Eastman's published writings are from *Love and Revolution* (Harper and Row, 1964) and *Enjoyment of Living* (Harper, 1948). See also Max Eastman's essays in my anthology *Toward the Great Change* (Garland Publishing, 1976), and Roger Baldwin, "Recollections of A Life in Civil Liberties," *The Civil Liberties Review* (Spring, 1975). See also June Sochen, *Movers and Shakers* (Quadrangle, 1973) and *The New Woman: Feminism in Greenwich Village, 1910–1920* (Quadrangle, 1972). In addition to Freda Kirchwey's memorial to Crystal Eastman in *The Nation* (reprinted here), see Katharine Ward Fisher, "Crystal Eastman," *Equal Rights,* (18 August 1928, p. 219); and the *Manchester Guardian* (15 August 1928).

Crystal Eastman's letters and writings for the World War I era are in the papers of the Woman's Peace Party, the American Union Against Militarism, the People's Council, and the Jane Addams and Emily Greene Balch collections—all in the Swarthmore College Peace Collection. Additional correspondence with Lillian Wald is in Wald's Papers at the New York Public Library and at Columbia University. Crystal Eastman's correspondence in the Max Eastman collection at the University of Indiana is not available at this time.

Published works relating to Crystal Eastman's wartime activities include: Blanche Wiesen Cook, "Democracy in Wartime: Antimilitarism in England and the United States, 1914–1918," in Charles Chatfield, ed., *Peace Movements in America* (Schocken Books,

1973); Marie Louise Degen, *A History of the Womans Peace Party* (Garland Publishing, 1975 [1939]); Charles Chatfield, *For Peace and Justice* (Schocken, 1974); C. Roland Marchand, *The American Peace Movement and Social Reform, 1898–1918* (Princeton University Press, 1972); Blanche Wiesen Cook, "The Woman's Peace Party: Collaboration and Non-Cooperation," *Peace and Change* (Autumn 1972). The entire collection of *Four Lights* is in the Swarthmore College Peace Collection. "Hoover How Can You?" in the 14 July 1917 issue of *Four Lights* is reprinted in *Toward the Great Change*. The article on the East St. Louis riots appeared in the 25 August 1917 issue. See also Blanche Wiesen Cook, "Woodrow Wilson and the Antimilitarists, 1914–1918" (unpublished Ph.D. dissertation, The Johns Hopkins University, 1970).

For information regarding Heterodoxy see the Inez Haynes Irwin Papers in the Schlesinger Library, Radcliffe College. Scattered Crystal Eastman correspondence regarding the suffrage movement is in the National Woman's Party Papers, the Library of Congress. The 1916 conflict between the suffragists and the antimilitarists is documented in the National Woman's Party weekly, *The Suffragist*. See especially the issues for 17 June 1916, 23 September 1916, 16 December 1916. For information about Inez Milholland see 25 November 1916, 23 December and 30 December 1916. See also Doris Stevens, *Jailed for Freedom* (Schocken, 1976 [1920]).

For the wartime relationship between Crystal Eastman and the social reformers see Lillian Wald, *Windows on Henry Street* (Little Brown, 1934), p. 311 and *passim;* Allen Davis, *American Heroine: The Life and Legend of Jane Addams* (Oxford University Press, 1973); and Blanche Wiesen Cook, "Female Support Networks and Political Activism: Lillian Wald, Crystal Eastman, Emma Goldman," *Chrysalis* (Autumn 1977).

In addition to Crystal Eastman's essays, Max Eastman's books and *The Liberator,* sources of information regarding Crystal Eastman's activities during the postwar years are: Claude McKay, *A Long Way from Home* (Harcourt, Brace and World, 1970 [1935]) and Clare Sheridan, *My American Diary* (Boni and Liveright, 1922). J. Stanley Lemons, *The Woman Citizen: Social Feminism in the 1920s* (University of Illinois Press, 1973) does not deal with Crystal Eastman directly but has material relevant to the equal rights controversy, and is well researched. See also Crystal Eastman's correspondence with Paul Kellogg in *The Survey* Papers, Folder 499, Social Welfare History Archives, University of Minnesota. All other letters quoted in this essay are from Annis Young's private collection.

One

CRYSTAL EASTMAN ON WOMEN

FEMINIST THEORY
AND PROGRAM

Mother-Worship

The story of my background is the story of my mother. She was a Middle-Western girl, youngest, cleverest, and prettiest of six daughters—children of an Irish gunsmith and a "Pennsylvania Dutch" woman of good family and splendid character. The gunsmith was a master of his trade but a heavy drinker, always ugly and often dangerous. My mother got away from home as soon as she could. After a year in a nearby coeducational college she taught school for a while and then married. The man she chose (for she was the sort of girl who has many chances) was a penniless but handsome and idealistic Yankee divinity student whom she met during that one college year. When he had secured his first parish, they were married.

For about eight years, during which there were four different parishes and four children were born, my mother was a popular, active, and helpful minister's wife. Then my father, who had always

Anonymous contribution to *The Nation*'s series "These Modern Women," 16 March 1927.

struggled against ill-health, suffered a complete nervous breakdown. He was forced to give up his church and his chosen profession. My mother had to support the family.

She began by teaching English literature in a girls' school. Before long she was giving Sunday-evening talks at the school. Then she began to fill outside engagements and finally she became a sort of supply-preacher to nearby country churches. About the year 1890, though she had had no theological education, she was ordained as a Congregational minister and called to be the pastor of a fairly large church in a well-to-do farming community. After three or four successful years, she and my father (who by this time had lost a good bit of money trying to be a farmer and a grocer but had begun to regain his health) were called as associate pastors to a big liberal church in a city of 40,000. It was my mother's reputation as a preacher that brought them this opportunity and she proved equal to the larger field. In time my father's health improved so that he could carry his share of the work, but my mother was always the celebrated member of the family.

I have a vivid memory of my mother when I was six years old. We are standing, my brother and I, in front of a run-down farmhouse on the edge of the town which had become our home. We have just said goodby to our mother and now we are watching her trip off down the hill to the school where she goes every day to teach. She turns to smile at us—such a beaming smile, such a bright face, such a pretty young mother. When the charming, much-loved figure begins to grow small in the distance, my brother, who is younger and more temperamental than I, begins to cry. He screams as loud as he can, until he is red in the face. But he cannot make her come back. And I, knowing she will be worried if she hears him, try to drag him away. By the time I was ten my mother had become a preacher.

Life was never ordinary where my mother was. She was always trying something new. She had an eager, active mind, and tremendous energy. She was preeminently an initiator. From the time I was thirteen we spent our summers like most middle-class, small-town American families, in a cottage beside a lake. And our life there, I suppose, would have been much like the life in thousands of other such summer communities, except for the presence of my mother.

For one thing, she organized a system of cooperative housekeeping with three other families on the hillside, and it lasted for years. A cook was hired jointly, but the burden of keeping house, planning meals, buying meat and groceries from the carts that came along three times a week, getting vegetables and fruit from the garden, collecting the money, keeping track of guests, and paying the bills, shifted every week. At first it was only the mothers who took their turn at housekeeping. But as the children grew older they were included in the scheme, boys as well as girls. Toward the end we had all the fun of eating in a big jolly group and only one or two weeks of housekeeping responsibility during the whole summer.

We used to have Sunday night music and singing for the whole hillside at our cottage, with the grown-ups in the big room, and the children lying outside on the porch couches or off on the grass. We had "church" Sunday mornings, too, in our big room; after all we were the minister's family. But it was a very short informal "church" followed by a long swim, and any one who wanted to could preach. We took turns at preaching as well as at keeping house, and we could choose the subjects of our own sermons.

Then one summer my mother started "symposiums." Once a week the mothers and older children and any fathers who happened to be around would gather on somebody's porch, listen to a paper, and then discuss it. I read a paper on "Woman" when I was fifteen, and I believe I was as wise in feminism then as I am now, if a little more solemn.

"The trouble with women," I said, "is that they have no impersonal interests. They must have work of their own, first because no one who has to depend on another person for his living is really grown up; and, second, because the only way to be happy is to have an absorbing interest in life which is not bound up with any particular person. Children can die or grow up, husbands can leave you. No woman who allows husband and children to absorb her whole time and interest is safe against disaster."

The proudest and happiest moment of my college days was when I met my mother in New York, as I did once a year, and went with her to a big banquet in connection with some ministers' convention she had come down to attend. She always spoke at the banquet, and she was always the best speaker. She was gay, sparkling, humorous, intimate, adorable. I would sit and love her with all my heart, and I could feel all the ministers loving her and rejoicing in her.

Almost always it is painful to sit in the audience while a near relative preaches, prays, or makes a speech. Husbands, wives, brothers, sisters, and children of the performers ought to be exempt from attending such public functions. My brothers and I always suffered when father preached, although, as preachers go, he was pretty good. At any rate he was beautiful to look at and had a large following of enthusiastic admirers. But when my mother preached we hated to miss it. There was never a moment of anxiety or concern; she had that secret of perfect platform ease which takes all strain out of the audience. Her voice was music; she spoke simply, without effort, almost without gestures, standing very still. And what she said seemed to come straight from her heart to yours. Her sermons grew out of her own moral and spiritual struggles. For she had a stormy, troubled soul, capable of black cruelty and then again of the deepest generosities. She was humble, honest, striving, always beginning again to try to be good.

With all her other interests she was thoroughly domestic. We children loved her cooking as much as we loved her preaching. And she was all kinds of devoted mother, the kind that tucks you in at night and reads you a story, and the kind that drags you to the dentist to have your teeth straightened. But I must leave her now and try to fill out the picture. My father, too, played a large part in my life. He was a generous man, the kind of man that was a suffragist from the day he first heard of a woman who wanted to vote. One evening, after mother had been teaching for some time and had begun to know her power as a public speaker, she came to him as he lay on his invalid's couch.

"John," she said, "I believe I could preach!"

"Mary!" he cried, jumping up in his excitement, "I *know* you could!"

This was in those early days when he had given up his own career as a minister, when he had cheerfully turned small farmer and had begun, on days when he was well enough, to peddle eggs and butter at the back doors of his former parishioners. From the moment he knew that my mother wanted to preach, he helped and encouraged her. Without his coaching and without his local prestige, it is doubtful if she could have been ordained. And my father stood by me in the same way, from the time when I wanted to cut off my hair and go barefoot to the time when I began to study law. When I insisted that the boys must make their beds if I had to make mine, he stood by me. When I said that if there was dishwashing to be done they should take their turn, he stood by me. And when I declared that there was no such thing in our family as boys' work and girls' work, and that I must be allowed to do my share of wood-chopping and outdoor chores, he took me seriously and let me try.

Once when I was twelve and very tall, a deputation of ladies from her church called on my mother and gently suggested that my skirts ought to be longer. My mother, who was not without consciousness of the neighbors' opinions, thought she must do something. But my father said, "No, let her wear them short. She likes to run, and she can't run so well in long skirts."

A few years later it was a question of bathing suits. In our summer community I was a ringleader in the rebellion against skirts and stockings for swimming. On one hot Sunday morning the other fathers waited on my father and asked him to use his influence with me. I don't know what he said to them but he never said a word to me. He was, I know, startled and embarrassed to see his only daughter in a man's bathing suit with bare brown legs for all the world to see. I think it shocked him to his dying day. But he himself had been a swimmer; he knew he would not want to swim in a skirt and stockings. Why then should I?

Beyond the immediate circle of my family there were other influences at work. My mother, among her other charms, had a genius for friendship. There were always clever, interesting, amusing women coming in and out of our house. I never thought of women as dull folk who sat and listened while the men talked. The little city where we lived was perhaps unusual. It was the home of six or seven distinguished persons, and not all of them were men.

In this environment I grew up confidently expecting to have a profession and earn my own living, and also confidently expecting to be married and have children. It was fifty-fifty with me. I was just as passionately determined to have children as I was to have a career. And my mother was the triumphant answer to all doubts as to the success of this double role. From my earliest memory she had more than half supported the family and yet she was supremely a mother. . . .*

* I have removed the last paragraph of this essay as originally printed. Crystal Eastman did not write it and crossed it out on all the copies she distributed, noting: "I am sorry the editor changed my ending. It was much better as I wrote it, more honest and sure. Far more interesting."

  Freda Kirchwey, who had changed Crystal's sentiments and style, wrote to Oswald Garrison Villard, publisher of *The Nation*, that she had had dinner in London with Katherine Anthony, Crystal Eastman, and Margaret Goldsmith, "the two latter boiling with deep rage" because Crystal's personality had been altered to suit the whim of *The Nation*. Kirchwey permitted Crystal to believe that Villard made the changes and wrote him, "you saved me from an awful fate."

  Copies of Crystal's annotations are in her scrapbook, now in the possession of Annis Young. See Kirchwey to Villard, 26 July 1927, Oswald Garrison Villard Papers, Houghton Library, Harvard University [B.W.C].

Birth Control in the Feminist Program

Feminism means different things to different people, I suppose. To women with a taste for politics and reform it means the right to vote and hold office. To women physically strong and adventuresome it means freedom to enter all kinds of athletic contests and games, to compete with men in aviation, to drive racing cars, to get up Battalions of Death, to enter dangerous trades, etc. To many it means social and sex freedom, doing away with exclusively feminine virtues. To most of all it means economic freedom,—not the ideal economic

The Birth Control Review, January 1918.

freedom dreamed of by revolutionary socialism, but such economic freedom as it is possible for a human being to achieve under the existing system of competitive production and distribution,—in short such freedom to choose one's way of making a living as men now enjoy, and definite economic rewards for one's work when it happens to be "home-making." This is to me the central fact of feminism. Until women learn to want economic independence, i.e., the ability to earn their own living independently of husbands, fathers, brothers or lovers,—and until they work out a way to get this independence without denying themselves the joys of love and motherhood, it seems to me feminism has no roots. Its manifestations are often delightful and stimulating but they are sporadic, they effect no lasting change in the attitude of men to women, or of women to themselves.

Whether other feminists would agree with me that the economic is the fundamental aspect of feminism, I don't know. But on this we are surely agreed, that Birth Control is an elementary essential in all aspects of feminism. Whether we are the special followers of Alice Paul, or Ruth Law, or Ellen Key, or Olive Schreiner, we must all be followers of Margaret Sanger. Feminists are not nuns. That should be established. We want to love and to be loved, and most of us want children, one or two at least. But we want our love to be joyous and free—not clouded with ignorance and fear. And we want our children to be deliberately, eagerly called into being, when we are at our best, not crowded upon us in times of poverty and weakness. We want this precious sex knowledge not just for ourselves, the conscious feminists; we want it for all the millions of unconscious feminists that swarm the earth,—we want it for all women.

Life is a big battle for the complete feminist even when she can regulate the size of her family. Women who are creative, or who have administrative gifts, or business ability, and who are ambitious to achieve and fulfill themselves in these lines, if they also have the normal desire to be mothers, must make up their minds to be a sort of supermen, I think. They must develop greater powers of concentration, a stronger will to "keep at it," a more determined ambition than men of equal gifts, in order to make up for the time and energy and thought and devotion that child-bearing and rearing, even in the most "advanced" families, seems inexorably to demand of the mother. But if we add to this handicap complete uncertainty as to when children may come, how often they come or how many there shall be, the thing becomes impossible. I would almost say that the whole structure of the feminist's dream of society rests upon the rapid extension of scientific knowledge about birth control.

This seems so obvious to me that I was astonished the other day to come upon a group of distinguished feminists who discussed for an hour what could be done with the woman's vote in New York State and did not once mention birth control.

As the readers of this magazine well know, the laws of this state, instead of establishing free clinics as necessary centers of information for the facts about sex hygiene and birth control, actually make it a crime, even on the part of a doctor, to tell grown men and women how to limit the size of their families. What could be a more pressing demand on the released energies of all these valiant suffrage workers than to repeal that law?

This work should especially commend itself, now in wartime when so many kinds of reform are outlawed. There is nothing about Birth Control agitation to embarrass the President or obstruct the prosecution of the war. If limited to the New York State laws it need not even rouse the indignation of Mr. Burleson. It is a reform absolutely vital to the progress of woman and one which the war does not interfere with. While American men are fighting to rid the old world of autocracy let American women set to and rid the new world of this intolerable old burden of sex ignorance. It should not be a difficult task.

I don't believe there is one woman within the confines of this state who does not believe in birth control. I never met one. That is, I never met one who thought that *she* should be kept in ignorance of contraceptive methods. Many I have met who valued the knowledge they possessed, but thought there were certain other classes who would be better kept in ignorance. The old would protect the young. The rich would keep the poor in ignorance. The good would keep their knowledge from the bad, the strong from the weak, and so on. But never in all my travels have I come on one married woman who, possessed of this knowledge would willingly part with it, or who not yet informed, was not eager for knowledge. It is only hypocrisy, and here and there a little hard-faced puritanism we have to overcome. No genuine human interest will be against the repeal of this law. Of course capitalism thrives on an over-supplied labor market, but with our usual enormous immigration to be counted on as soon as the war is over, it is not likely that an organized economic opposition to birth control will develop.

In short, if feminism, conscious and bold and intelligent, leads the demand, it will be supported by the secret eagerness of all women to control the size of their families, and a suffrage state should make short work of repealing these old laws that stand in the way of birth control.

Feminism

A Statement Read at the First Feminist Congress in the United States, New York, March 1, 1919

For two years the whole western world has been talking about freedom and democracy. Now that the war is over and it is possible to think calmly once more, we must examine these popular abstractions, and consider (especially here in America where the boasting has been loudest)—how much freedom and democracy we actually have. Above all it behooves women to determine frankly what their status is in this republic.—

> Four-fifths of us are still denied the elementary political right of voting.
> Only one woman has held a seat in the United States Congress.
> Only twenty-one women are sitting in our 48 state legislatures.
> With rare exceptions all the higher executive offices in both state

The Liberator, May 1919.

and federal governments are, by law or rigid precedent, open only to
men.

In only six states do women sit on juries.

With half a dozen exceptions in the lower courts, there are no
women judges.

In all government work, federal, state, county and city,—(notoriously in public school teaching),—women are paid much less than
men for the same work.

In private industry, where it is estimated that twelve million
women are now employed, the wages of women both skilled and
unskilled (except in a few trades) are on a scale of their own, materially
lower than the wages of men, even at work where their productive
capacity is equal or greater.

Most of the strong labor unions, except in trades where women
are in the majority, still close their doors to women workers.

Marriage laws in many states (including the guardianship of
children) are designed to perpetuate the economic dependence of a
wife on her husband. And nothing has been done in this country by
way of maternity insurance or by giving to a wife a legal right to a
share of her husband's earnings in recognition of her services as
houseworker and nurse, to modify that dependence. And the vital
importance of potential economic independence has yet to become a
recognized principle of modern education for girls.

Voluntary motherhood is an ideal unrealized in this country.
Women are still denied by law the right to that scientific knowledge
necessary to control the size of their families, which means that among
the poor where the law is effective, marriage can become virtual slavery
for women.

Laws, judges, courts, police, and social custom still disgrace,
punish and "regulate" the woman prostitute and leave uncensured the
man who trades with her,—though in case of all other forbidden vices
the buyer as well as the seller suffers if caught.

From this brief statement of facts it is fairly clear that women in
America today not only share the wholesale denial of civil liberty
which came with the war and remains to bless our victory, but carry
a special burden of restrictive legislation and repressive social custom,—(not in any way relieved by the war for freedom nor affected
by the two years' crusade of democratic eloquence)—a burden which
halts them in almost every field of endeavor, and effectually marks

them as an inferior class. This is stated without any bitterness and with full recognition of the fact that women by their passivity have made these things possible. But it is stated for a purpose.

It is my hope that this first Woman's Freedom Conference, held in New York City, will see the birth of a new spirit in American women—a spirit of humane and intelligent self-interest—a spirit of determined pride—which will lead them to declare:

"We will not wait for the Social Revolution to bring us the freedom we should have won in the 19th century."

Practical Feminism

The most revolutionary thing about the recent Labor Party Convention at Chicago was its decision to appoint a National Executive Committee composed of two members from each state, *one man and one woman*. To force women to take an equal share in the actual business of building up the executive machine,—it's never been heard of before in the history of the world, not in trades-unions, not in co-operatives, not in Socialist parties, not in Utopias. It means more for feminism than a million resolutions. For after all these centuries of retirement women need more than an "equal opportunity" to show what's in them. They need a generous shove into positions of responsibility. And that is what the Labor Party has given them. It is proof that there is some very honest idealism among the thousand delegates who gathered at Chicago.

Whether this quixotic generosity can be turned to good political account depends on how soon women get the vote.

Woman suffrage is an almost forgotten issue today, and yet the battle is not won. Despite the capitulation of Congress last June,

The Liberator, January 1920.

nearly three-fourths of the women of these States will be denied the right to vote in the Presidential Campaign of 1920, unless a miracle is accomplished in the next two months. The miracle will not fall from Heaven. If it occurs, it will be the result of hard work on the part of those same good fighters who picketed the White House and went to jail and finally wrung the Federal Amendment out of a distressed and embarrassed government,—Alice Paul's gallant band of militants.

They are still at it,—seeing that the necessary 36 states ratify the Amendment in time for women to vote next fall. Twenty-one States have ratified. Their chief effort now is to force the Governors of States whose legislatures hold no regular session this year, to call a special session in order to ratify the Amendment. If you go into their headquarters thinking this is unimportant,—women can wait another four years,—voting doesn't amount to much anyhow—you are pretty sure to come out thinking it is important, no matter who you are or how far to the left of the Left you stand on political action.

They are working more inconspicuously than in the old days, but with the same amazing clarity and tenacity of purpose. You come out wanting them to win and hoping with all your heart that those Western Governors who, for private political reasons, don't want to call a special session this year, will see that they are outmatched and hurry up and give in, so that the women of the country can declare themselves politically free on February 15th, 1920,—one hundred years from the day Susan B. Anthony was born.

Now We Can Begin

Most women will agree that August 23, the day when the Tennessee legislature finally enacted the Federal suffrage amendment, is a day to begin with, not a day to end with. Men are saying perhaps "Thank

God, this everlasting woman's fight is over!" But women, if I know them, are saying, "Now at last we can begin." In fighting for the right to vote most women have tried to be either non-committal or thoroughly respectable on every other subject. Now they can say what they are really after; and what they are after, in common with all the rest of the struggling world, is *freedom*.

Freedom is a large word.

Many feminists are socialists, many are communists, not a few are active leaders in these movements. But the true feminist, no matter how far to the left she may be in the revolutionary movement, sees the woman's battle as distinct in its objects and different in its methods from the workers' battle for industrial freedom. She knows, of course, that the vast majority of women as well as men are without property, and are of necessity bread and butter slaves under a system of society which allows the very sources of life to be privately owned by a few, and she counts herself a loyal soldier in the working-class army that is marching to overthrow that system. But as a feminist she also knows that the whole of woman's slavery is not summed up in the profit system, nor her complete emancipation assured by the downfall of capitalism.

Woman's freedom, in the feminist sense, can be fought for and conceivably won before the gates open into industrial democracy. On the other hand, woman's freedom, in the feminist sense, is not inherent in the communist ideal. All feminists are familiar with the revolutionary leader who "can't see" the woman's movement. "What's the matter with the women? My wife's all right," he says. And his wife, one usually finds, is raising his children in a Bronx flat or a dreary suburb, to which he returns occasionally for food and sleep when all possible excitement and stimulus have been wrung from the fight. If we should graduate into communism tomorrow this man's attitude to his wife would not be changed. The proletarian dictatorship may or may not free women. We must begin now to enlighten the future dictators.

What, then, is "the matter with women"? What is the problem of women's freedom? It seems to me to be this: how to arrange the world so that women can be human beings, with a chance to exercise their infinitely varied gifts in infinitely varied ways, instead of being destined by the accident of their sex to one field of activity—housework and child-raising. And second, if and when they choose housework and child-raising to have that occupation recognized by the world as work, requiring a definite economic reward and not merely entitling the performer to be dependent on some man.

This is not the whole of feminism, of course, but it is enough to begin with. "Oh! don't begin with economics," my friends often protest, "Woman does not live by bread alone. What she needs first of all is a free soul." And I can agree that women will never be great until they achieve a certain emotional freedom, a strong healthy egotism, and some un-personal sources of joy—that in this inner sense we cannot make woman free by changing her economic status. What we can do, however, is to create conditions of outward freedom in which a free woman's soul can be born and grow. It is these outward conditions with which an organized feminist movement must concern itself.

Freedom of choice in occupation and individual economic independence for women: How shall we approach this next feminist objective? First, by breaking down all remaining barriers, actual as well as legal, which make it difficult for women to enter or succeed in the various professions, to go into and get on in business, to learn trades and practice them, to join trades unions. Chief among these remaining barriers is inequality in pay. Here the ground is already broken. This is the easiest part of our program.

Second, we must institute a revolution in the early training and education of both boys and girls. It must be womanly as well as manly to earn your own living, to stand on your own feet. And it must be manly as well as womanly to know how to cook and sew and clean and take care of yourself in the ordinary exigencies of life. I need not add that the second part of this revolution will be more passionately resisted than the first. Men will not give up their privilege of helplessness without a struggle. The average man has a carefully cultivated ignorance about household matters—from what to do with the crumbs to the grocer's telephone number—a sort of cheerful inefficiency which protects him better than the reputation for having a violent temper. It was his mother's fault in the beginning, but even as a boy he was quick to see how a general reputation for being "no good around the house" would serve him throughout life, and half-consciously he began to cultivate that helplessness until to-day it is the despair of feminist wives.

A growing number of men admire the woman who has a job, and, especially since the cost of living doubled, rather like the idea of their own wives contributing to the family income by outside work. And of course for generations there have been whole towns full of wives who are forced by the bitterest necessity to spend the same hours at the factory that their husbands spend. But these bread-winning wives have not yet developed home-making husbands. When the two come home from the factory the man sits down while his wife gets supper, and he does so with exactly the same sense of fore-ordained right as if he were "supporting her." Higher up in the economic scale the same thing is true. The business or professional woman who is married, perhaps engages a cook, but the responsibility is not shifted, it is still hers. She "hires and fires," she orders meals, she does the buying, she meets and resolves all domestic crises, she takes charge of moving, furnishing, settling. She may be, like her husband, a busy executive at her office all day, but unlike him, she is also an executive in a small way every night and morning at home. Her noon hour is spent in planning, and too often her Sundays and holidays are spent in "catching up."

Two business women can "make a home" together without either one being over-burdened or over-bored. It is because they both know how and both feel responsible. But it is a rare man who can marry one of them and continue the home-making partnership. Yet if there are no children, there is nothing essentially different in the combination. Two self-supporting adults decide to make a home together: if both are women it is a pleasant partnership, more fun than work; if one is a man, it is almost never a partnership—the woman simply adds running the home to her regular outside job. Unless she is very strong, it is too much for her, she gets tired and bitter over it, and finally perhaps gives up her outside work and condemns herself to the tiresome half-job of housekeeping for two.

Cooperative schemes and electrical devices will simplify the business of home-making, but they will not get rid of it entirely. As far as we can see ahead people will always want homes, and a happy home cannot be had without a certain amount of rather monotonous work and responsibility. How can we change the nature of man so that he will honorably share that work and responsibility and thus make the home-making enterprise a song instead of a burden? Most assuredly not by laws or revolutionary decrees. Perhaps we must cultivate or simulate a little of that highly prized helplessness ourselves. But fundamentally it is a problem of education, of early training—we must bring up feminist sons.

Sons? Daughters? They are born of women—how can women be free to choose their occupation, at all times cherishing their economic independence, unless they stop having children? This is a further question for feminism. If the feminist program goes to pieces on the arrival of the first baby, it is false and useless. For ninety-nine out of every hundred women want children, and seventy-five out of every hundred want to take care of their own children, or at any rate so closely superintend their care as to make any other full-time occupation impossible for at least ten or fifteen years. Is there any such thing then as freedom of choice in occupation for women? And is not the family the inevitable economic unit and woman's individual economic independence, at least during that period, out of the question?

The feminist must have an answer to these questions, and she has. The immediate feminist program must include voluntary motherhood. Freedom of any kind for women is hardly worth considering unless it is assumed that they will know how to control the size of their families. "Birth control" is just as elementary an essential in our propaganda as "equal pay." Women are to have children when they want them, that's the first thing. That ensures some freedom of occupational choice; those who do not wish to be mothers will not have an undesired occupation thrust upon them by accident, and those who do wish to be mothers may choose in a general way how many years of their lives they will devote to the occupation of child-raising.

But is there any way of insuring a woman's economic independence while child-raising is her chosen occupation? Or must she sink into the dependent state from which, as we all know, it is so hard to rise again? That brings us to the fourth feature of our program—

motherhood endowment. It seems that the only way we can keep mothers free, at least in a capitalist society, is by the establishment of a principle that the occupation of raising children is peculiarly and directly a service to society, and that the mother upon whom the necessity and privilege of performing this service naturally falls is entitled to an adequate economic reward from the political government. It is idle to talk of real economic independence for women unless this principle is accepted. But with a generous endowment of motherhood provided by legislation, with all laws against voluntary motherhood and education in its methods repealed, with the feminist ideal of education accepted in home and school, and with all special barriers removed in every field of human activity, there is no reason why woman should not become almost a human thing.

It will be time enough then to consider whether she has a soul.

Alice Paul's Convention

"Mr. Speaker," said Sara Bard Field, turning the full force of her childlike smile and beaming eyes upon the unhappy Congressman, "I give you—Revolution."

With these naive words, gently spoken in a dim, echoing vaulted room at the heart of the national capitol, the victorious Woman's Party presented to Congress the statue of the suffrage pioneers, Lucretia Mott, Susan B. Anthony, Elizabeth Cady Stanton. Let me quote a few more sentences:

"Mr. Speaker, we do not commit to your keeping merely a block of marble wrought into likenesses which in a chaste repose like death itself will henceforth remain in Statuary Hall, but we commit to your keeping blood-red memories, alive and pulsing. . . . It is universal freedom for which the movement represented by these women has ever stood. . . . The very first Suffrage Association aimed to enfran-

The Liberator, April 1921.

chise the Negro as well as the woman. Listen to these words written
by Susan B. Anthony and introduced as part of a resolution in the
convention which formed the first American Equal Rights Association: 'Hence our demand must now go beyond women. It must
extend to the farthest bounds of the principle of the consent of the
governed.' Do you think that women who thought in those terms
would sit idle today because political democracy has become an
accomplished fact in this nation? Do you think that women like these
who published a paper in the Sixties called 'Revolution' would not see
the need of that brooding angel's presence still? Needless to say I
don't speak in terms of bloody revolution any more than did they.
But men and women are not yet free. . . . The slavery of greed
endures. Little child workers, the hope of the future, are sacrificed to
industry. Young men are sent out by the billion to die for profits.
. . . We must destroy industrial slavery and build industrial democracy. . . . The people everywhere must come into possession of the
earth."

And finally, "Mr. Speaker, you will see that if you thought you
came here to receive on behalf of Congress merely the busts of three
women who have fought the good fight and gone to rest, you were
mistaken. You will see that through them it is the body and the
blood of a great sacrificial host which we present—the body and
blood of Revolution, the body and blood of Freedom herself."

"What does all this mean?" I asked myself as I heard the words
go echoing up to the dome. If Alice Paul is such a confirmed
reactionary as many of her former followers say she is, why did she
feature Sara Bard Field at that impressive ceremony? Why did she
deny the claims of the Negro women and of the Birth Control
advocates for a hearing at the Convention, in deference to certain
powerful groups among her supporters, and then as if in complete
defiance of these same conservative groups insist that the only words
uttered in the name of the Woman's Party on the opening night
should be the obviously uncensored words of a fairly celebrated rebel?

And now that the convention is over, I find myself wondering
all the more: Why did Alice Paul stage this dramatic bit of Quaker
defiance at the beginning and then treat us to three dull days of
commonplace speeches, often irrelevant, often illiberal, with only a

few hours reserved at the end for the essential purpose of the meeting—the discussion of the future of the Woman's Party, which to many meant the future of the feminist movement in America? Five hours for that discussion—hardly time enough to determine the future of a high school dramatic society!

Nothing is more fun than to speculate about the motives and intentions of a shrewd and able leader who keeps his own counsels. I give my speculation for what it is worth: Alice Paul was not really interested in the convention, she was interested in celebrating the victory. After all, despite reports to the contrary, she is a human being. An explorer who had been away on a long and dangerous journey, whose best friends had doubted, whose foes had been many, whose rivals had been bitter, when at last he returned crowned with success, would rejoice in the celebration of his achievement. And the colder and lonelier had been his journey the more appropriate would seem the warmth and luxurious friendliness of his welcome. So it seems to me Alice Paul felt about the victory of woman suffrage—her victory.

In one respect, however, my simile of the explorer breaks down; it was strictly the achievement and not herself that Alice Paul arranged to have celebrated. Throughout that elaborate ceremony at the Capitol Alice Paul was not so much as mentioned by name. I had one glimpse of her behind the scenes after the show was over; with complete unconsciousness of herself as a personality, and with very effective indignation she was preventing the chief usher from covering up the statues and taking them away before the crowd outside had had a chance to come in and see them.

From beginning to end Alice Paul was never in evidence. But Jane Addams was there to say the first words. The name of the President's daughter appeared on the program. The press announced that Mrs. Harding endowed the affair with her official blessing. The Speaker of the House, who had fought the Party for eight years, graciously consented to receive the statues. No, Alice Paul was not there,—even the Woman's Party figured with one silent banner among hundreds—but the General Federation of Women's Clubs was there, the Association of Collegiate Alumnae was there, the Eastern Star was there, the Maccabees were there, the Army Nurses and the Navy Nurses, the Republican Women and the Democratic Women, the Daughters of the Revolution, the Daughters of the Confederacy, the Congress of Mothers, all, all were there, and dozens and dozens of others,—those who had scorned and condemned when the pickets stood for months at the White House gates, when they insisted on going to jail and starved themselves when they got there,—all these came now with their wreaths and their flowers and their banners to celebrate the victory.

Supremely neglectful of respectability during the long fight, Alice Paul saw to it that the victory celebration should be supremely respectable. All doubtful subjects, like birth control and the rights of Negro women, were hushed up, ruled out or postponed until the affair at the Capitol was over.* Nothing was allowed to creep into the advance publicity that was calculated to alarm the mildest Maccabee or dismay the most delicately reared Daughter. And when her radical friends called her a reactionary for all this, Alice Paul was adamant to their pleas as she had been adamant to the attacks of her enemies when they called her a wildcat.

But having corralled all this eminent respectability into the Capitol for the celebration she must needs give them a shock. So she made sure that the militants, speaking through Sara Field, should speak with no tame voice, but as usual with a voice quietly promising rebellion.

After that first evening in the Capitol the convention became dull and regular, everybody was well-behaved, there were no brilliant speeches, no surprises, no stormy and uproarious hours. The only thing that makes a convention exciting or worth while is the debate over resolutions and program. But in Alice Paul's convention there were no resolutions and hardly any program! No resolution on disarmament was passed to give expression to the overwhelming pacifist sentiment of the Convention. No resolution of protest against the disfranchisement of Negro women was passed, although the Convention was almost unanimous in its indignation on that subject. Even "simon-pure" feminist resolutions were discouraged.

---

* The Negro women were finally allowed to "lay a wreath" and the Birth Control advocates were at the last moment given a hearing at the convention. But in each case the action was taken too late for the name of the organization to appear in the program.

To all such complaints graduates of the Alice Paul school had one dogmatic reply: "Never endorse anything that your organization isn't ready to fight for. Never protest about anything unless your organization is ready to make that protest good." The more sacred a dogma is the more dangerous it is, and this one has the sacredness of the torn battle flag and the battered sword; it is the legacy of a victorious movement. Vital as this doctrine of extreme consistency was in the heat of the militant campaign—and no one can question that—what bearing had it on the deliberations of this body of women met to consider for the first time the actual status of women and lay the foundations of the movement which is to liberate them?

Last summer I went to Alice Paul with a roughly sketched but fairly complete feminist program. After a little discussion, she said, "Yes, I believe in all these things, but I am not interested in writing a fine program, I am interested in getting something done." That is the way she takes the wind out of your sails. But is she always right?

It reminds me of a story they tell about Alice Paul's first meeting with Bill Haywood. Bill grasped her tiny hand with hearty sincerity and began,

"Well, Miss Paul, the movement you represent and the movement I represent are the only movements in the country that have stood out against——"

"Yes," interrupted Alice Paul, who had been looking up at him with an expression of deep earnestness as though she were considering the philosophic relation between the Militants and the I.W.W., "and will you tell me, Mr. Haywood, how you went about it to raise that $300,000?"

Alice Paul is a leader of action, not of thought. She is a general, a supreme tactician, not an abstract thinker. Her joy is in the fight itself, in each specific drawn battle, not in debating with five hundred delegates the fundamental nature of the fight. "The Executive Committee have provided a good enough phrase—'To remove all the remaining forms of the subjection of women.' Let the delegates with the least possible debate adopt this phrase to serve for purpose, program and constitution." Of course she said nothing, but that, I believe, was Alice Paul's notion of what the Convention's action should be. "I will let you know what the first step is to be, how to act and when. Go home now and don't worry." These words were not printed in the program, but they seemed to be written between the lines.

Perhaps there are times in all movements that call for a leader just like that and for followers just like the majority in that convention who did what they were told. But this was not one of those times, and the proof of it is that the five hundred delegates, whether they voted with or against the leader, went home disappointed, without a quickened understanding, without a new vision. If their discontent could have been articulate it would have expressed itself in some such words as these: "We didn't come here just to state that women are still in subjection and that we are going to free them. We came to discuss and define the nature of our subjection and to outline the terms of our freedom. We came not merely to throw down a challenge, but to bring in a bill of particulars. For we are starting a new movement. We need a program in order to understand each other, we need a program in order to hold our mind and purpose steady and sure in this new field, we need a program as a first step in the process of education with which all new movements must begin."

A minority resolution looking toward such a program was actually introduced as a substitute for the Executive Committee's proposal, but the time limit and a very efficient steam roller disposed of it before the discussion had fairly started. The resolution was as follows:

"Having achieved political liberty for women this organization pledges itself to make an end to the subjection of women in all its remaining forms. Among our tasks we emphasize these:

"1. To remove all barriers of law or custom or regulation which prevent women from holding public office—the highest as well as the lowest—from entering into and succeeding in any profession, from going into or getting on in any business, from practicing any trade or joining the union of her trade.

"2. So to remake the marriage laws and so to modify public opinion that the status of the woman whose chosen work is home-making shall no longer be that of the dependent entitled to her board and keep in return for her services, but that of a full partner.

"3. To rid the country of all laws which deny women access to scientific information concerning the limitation of families.

"4. To re-write the laws of divorce, of inheritance, of the guardianship of children, and the laws for the regulation of sexual morality and disease, on a basis of equality, equal rights, equal responsibilities, equal standards.

"5. To legitimatize all children.

"6. To establish a liberal endowment of motherhood."

If some such program could have been exhaustively discussed at that convention we might be congratulating ourselves that the feminist movement had begun in America. As it is all we can say is that the suffrage movement is ended.

Is Alice Paul a radical? Is she even a liberal? Is she really a reactionary? These vague reformist terms are inappropriate in describing Alice Paul. Let us use the definite terms of the revolution. She is not a communist, she is not a socialist; if she is class-conscious at all her instincts are probably with the class into which she was born. But I do not think she is class-conscious. I think she is sex-conscious; she has given herself, body and mind and soul, to the women's movement. The world war meant no moment's wavering in her purpose, in fact she *used* the war with serene audacity to further her purpose. I imagine she could even go through a proletarian revolution without taking sides and be found waiting on the doorstep of the Extraordinary Commission the next morning to see that the revolution's promises to women were not forgotten!

Alice Paul does not belong to the revolution, but her leadership has had a quality that only the revolution can understand.

Personalities and Powers:
Alice Paul

History has known dedicated souls from the beginning, men and women whose every waking moment is devoted to an impersonal end, leaders of a "cause" who are ready at any moment quite simply

Time and Tide, 20 July 1923.

to die for it. But is it rare to find in one human being this passion for service and sacrifice combined first with the shrewd calculating mind of a born political leader, and second with the ruthless driving force, sure judgment and phenomenal grasp of detail that characterize a great entrepreneur.

It is no exaggeration to say that these qualities are united in Alice Paul, the woman who inspired, organized and led to victory the militant suffrage movement in America and is now head of the Woman's Party, a strong group of conscious feminists who have set out to end the "subjection of women" in all its forms.

Alice Paul comes of Quaker stock and there is in her bearing that powerful serenity so characteristic of the successful Quaker. Like many another famous general she is well under five foot six, a slender, dark woman with a pale, often haggard face, and great earnest childlike eyes that seem to seize you and hold you to her purpose despite your own desires and intentions. During that seven year suffrage campaign she worked so continuously, ate so little and slept so little that she always seemed to be wasting away before our eyes. Once in the early years, when the Union was housed in a basement impossible to ventilate she seemed so near to collapse that she was taken, under protest, to a nearby hospital to rest. But she had a telephone put in by her bed, and went right on with the campaign, forgetting, as usual, to eat and sleep. After a few weeks of this she got up and packed her bag and came back to the foul air and artificial light of that crowded basement headquarters. And nothing more was said about a breakdown. The truth is, of course, that she looks frail, as anyone would who was subjected to constant overwork and under-nourishment, but actually she possesses a bodily constitution of extraordinary strength, and a power of physical endurance that quite matches her indomitable spirit.

In America there were two ways to win the vote—by amending each of the forty-eight State constitutions or by amending the Federal constitution. Ever since the death of Susan B. Anthony, the National American Woman Suffrage Association had confined itself to the former method. And the movement already more than sixty years old, was progressing slowly. Only seven or eight States had won the vote.

In the winter of 1912 the Executive Board of the N.A.W.S.A. was approached by three earnest young women with the request that they be appointed a Congressional Committee to further the Federal amendment. The smallest and youngest of these young women, the one that nobody had ever heard of before, was Alice Paul. The committee was appointed and she was made chairman. In less than three months, raising the money day by day, she organized a suffrage parade in the national capital of such size and beauty and distinction that the arrival of Woodrow Wilson, the newly-elected president who was to be inaugurated on the following day, passed almost unnoticed. "The people were all on the Avenue watching the suffrage parade!" One month later a procession of women representing each of the 435 congressional districts carried a petition to Congress. There followed two months' intensive organization and agitation in the local districts at the end of which Congress was presented with a monster petition signed by hundreds of thousands of citizens, and woman suffrage was debated in Congress for the first time in twenty-six years.

Before the year was out the Congressional Committee had outgrown its parent; it became inevitably an independent body, the Congressional Union for Woman Suffrage with Alice Paul as its leader. And the American woman suffrage movement was born again. Suffrage was no longer a dull and rather obvious reform which our mothers and grandmothers had worked for. It had been dramatized for us. It was a glorious fight worthy of our best mettle.

Rebecca West once said, "The American struggle for the vote was much more difficult than the English for the simple reason that it was much more easy." And that is profoundly true. Indifference is harder to fight than hostility, and there is nothing that kills an agitation like having everybody admit that it is fundamentally right. If you can so frame your issue or so choose your method of attack as to precipitate discussion and difference of opinion among honest men, so that all your followers become passionate explainers, you have put life into a movement. Alice Paul knows this and she is a master at framing a meaty issue. As I look back over that seven-year struggle I sometimes suspect that many bold strategies were employed more to revive the followers than to confound the enemy.

The very concentration on the federal amendment created a new issue. "States rights" is an important political concern in America, and the agitation in Washington had barely started before the milder suffragists began to declare, "I am in favour of women voting but I am against the federal amendment. I believe the States should decide." This gave the movement something to feed on, it gave suffrage orators something to talk about besides "liberty" and "equality."

It is almost never a mistake to create a situation which divides the polite and timid advocates of a measure of justice from those who are really determined to get it. And every move that Alice Paul made had this effect. Organizing the women voters of the suffrage States to defeat democratic candidates, picketing the White House, the hunger strike, burning the President's war speeches—each of these policies was begun under a storm of protest from within and without the movement. Yet each proved in the end good political strategy and at the same time had an enormous re-enlivening influence on the suffrage movement. Those who stood by suffered so from the almost universal criticism that they gained the power and faith of crusaders. And the more conservative suffragists who opposed these policies were stimulated to more and more effective action along their own lines from a sense of rivalry. And so the movement grew and grew from the mighty dissension in its ranks.

Alice Paul's active leadership in the American feminist movement was almost an accident. She was a student at an English university intending to pursue the career of a scholar when she was caught up in the English militant movement and served a brief apprenticeship in jail. It was during this experience that she began to plan what she would do for women suffrage in America. American women owe much to the English militants, but this above all.

Political Equality League
(Report on the Wisconsin Suffrage Campaign)

A year ago Wisconsin was the only State east of the Mississippi in which a suffrage referendum was pending, and in view of its great reputation as pioneer among progressive states, suffragists everywhere felt that the Wisconsin campaign presented a tremendous national opportunity. And we, in Wisconsin, felt our responsibility to the whole national movement. In answer to our appeals, the word went out and echoed back and forth throughout the country, "Help Wisconsin! If we can win one big industrial State east of the Mississippi, it will put us ahead ten years." In answer to this word came money in large sums—thousands of dollars—from the National, from New York, from Illinois, from Minnesota, Nebraska, Indiana, Missouri, California, Kentucky, and from countless individuals. To all who came so splendidly to our aid we are deeply, profoundly grateful. We asked it believing we had a chance to win— you gave it believing we had a chance to win. The vast bulk of this outside help for Wisconsin was given or pledged a long time before anybody knew that Michigan and Ohio were also to have 1912 campaigns, and it was asked and given in the thought that Wisconsin might be our only hope of winning an eastern suffrage state in 1912.

Well, friends and helpers, we lost, but your money wasn't wasted. It went directly into the salaries and traveling expenses of organizers, and the suffrage leagues carefully and laboriously built up by these organizers—often beginning in towns where there was not even one suffragist to entertain the organizer,—these are alive and flourishing today, 50 of them, active, solvent, dues paying locals— your money was invested in them and they stand ready to win our next campaign.

But do not think we let you give all the money. You should know that one Wisconsin woman put $3,000 into our campaign last year and gave $1,000 to the National besides, Mrs. Charles W. Norris of Milwaukee. Others—men and women—gave lesser sums, ranging from $300 to five one-cent stamps—in all many thousands.

Before passing on to tell why we lost, I want to mention some of those to whom we owe that degree of success we had. First the older suffragists in Wisconsin, without whose early labors we never could have had a referendum to put before the people—those self-sacrificing pioneers, who have kept the torch burning for fifty years, under the inspiration of their devoted leader, the Rev. Olympia Brown. Next I

Proceedings of the 44th Annual Convention of the National American Woman Suffrage Association, Philadelphia, 21–26 November 1912.

want to speak of Miss Harriet Crim of Illinois—our girl orator of the Middle West—whose continuous services to Wisconsin were made possible by the National Association. North, South, East and West, wherever Miss Crim went, they clamored for her to come back and they are clamoring still. Next the La Follette's, all three of them, but in this recent campaign we owe most to Mrs. La Follette, who, from the moment Congress adjourned in July until election day, was a leading spirit in the campaign—writing, persuading, speaking, almost continuously.

Last but not least I must mention Miss Ada James, president of the Political Equality League, daughter of Senator James, who introduced our bill. Miss James is a rare combination, almost unfailing good judgment, keen political insight and the character of a saint on earth. Throughout the long months of the campaign, though she grew thinner and paler through her unceasing labors for suffrage, her spirit never failed. It was our constant inspiration.

Then I wish I could give a personal word of greeting from Wisconsin to the splendid speakers, the experienced campaigners and the brave new recruits who came in from other states to help us. First the Illinois women, without whose help we never could have begun our campaign, last the Ohio women, without whom we never could have made as good a finish as we made, and in between many another splendid woman, who put in a week or two weeks or six weeks, to help Wisconsin. Bless their hearts, one and all. I wish we might have won for their sake.

The vote on woman suffrage in Wisconsin barring one county from which returns have not yet come in, stood 132,000 for, 224,000 against. The papers have published it as a two to one defeat, but you see it wasn't nearly so bad as that. The majority against us fell 40,000 short of being a two to one majority. Nevertheless it was a heavy defeat. Now the only question which can possibly interest this great audience is why we lost, when our hopes were so high a year ago. Wherein were our calculations wrong? I have time merely to outline the situation. For one thing, we over-estimated the friendliness of the large Scandinavian vote. We counted on the Norwegians and Swedes of western Wisconsin standing in favor of equal suffrage as a matter of course, because women vote in Norway and are on the verge of it in Sweden, but when we came to campaign among them we found many on our side but many just as conservative about woman as the majority of the Germans. In short we found we couldn't count on their votes—they had to be brought over man by man and we didn't have time to get around. Next we over-estimated the support to be counted on from the Progressive Republican voters; we had hoped they would follow their great leader, Robert M. La Follette in this, as they have for so many years, in other Progressive measures, but thousands of them did not. I sometimes think the last thing a man becomes progressive about is the activities of his own wife.

Again, we over-estimated what the Socialist vote would mean to us. I believe that most of the Socialist Party members stood by their platform and voted for us, but their sympathizers did not. Thus, many of the wards in Milwaukee which gave Victor Berger enormous majorities went more than two to one against woman suffrage.

Finally, we under-estimated the far-reaching power of the great organized brewing industry in Wisconsin, and we under-estimated the extent of its hostility to woman suffrage. The open opposition of the retail liquor dealers is common to all suffrage campaigns. Wisconsin was no exception, but that alone was not enough to defeat us. The determined and united opposition of a great organized manufacturing industry is another matter.

Wisconsin stands second among the states in its output of malt liquors. The brewing industry ranks fourth in Wisconsin; its capital stock amounts to $85,000,000. I need not remind you of what made Milwaukee famous and I may say it deserves its reputation, but it is not in Milwaukee alone that good beer is made. A dozen other cities in the State are big brewing centers. Indeed there is hardly a town of 3,000 in the eastern part of Wisconsin which has not two or three big breweries.

Now, of course, the brewers didn't fight us openly. They didn't need to. The important thing was that everybody who did business with them from the farmer who sold them barley to the big city newspapers who sold them advertising space, knew how they stood. Thus, their mere enormous corporate existence in the State was a constant effective protest against the suffrage referendum. Have you ever thought how many industries there would be in a brewing state dependent upon the brewing industry for their success? The bottle makers, cork makers, barrel makers, malsters, etc. Why there are whole cities of 20,000 in Wisconsin where not a single business man dares to let his wife come out for suffrage? Why? Because practically every man's business is dependent for success on the good will of the big breweries in that city.

Whether they are wrong or right in their fears, the brewers of Wisconsin have decided that giving women the vote will hurt their business. They put their business, as, alas, most big corporations do, ahead of democracy, justice and simple human right, and they are determined to do all in their power to delay the coming of votes for women.

But what does this mean to the suffragists of Wisconsin? It is merely a challenge. The brewers do not control the majority of the voters of Wisconsin and they cannot defeat us alone. Their power can defeat us only when it is allied with ignorance and prejudice, and it is our business to cut off these allies,—to do away with the ignorance and prejudice that still exist in Wisconsin in regard to woman suffrage. When we have done that the issue will be clear and we shall win.

We made a great beginning last year; it will take two years more, perhaps four. Meanwhile all hail to Michigan for getting in ahead of us, she has made our task easier, and above all, all success to the campaign states of 1913.

CRYSTAL EASTMAN BENEDICT,
Campaign Manager.

1848–1923

In a little town of western New York State called Seneca Falls, about three hundred miles from New York City, there was celebrated last week the seventy-fifth anniversary of the first Woman's Rights Convention held there in 1848 at the instigation of Lucretia Mott and Elizabeth Cady Stanton. These two suffrage pioneers met for the first time in 1840 under unusual circumstances. Mrs. Stanton, then only twenty-five, had come as a bride to London to attend the World's Anti-Slavery Convention to which both she and her husband were duly appointed delegates. Among the other women delegates the most distinguished was Lucretia Mott, a Quaker from Pennsylvania, a woman approaching middle age, the mother of five children, an "acknowledged minister" in the Society of Friends, and President of the "Female Anti-Slavery Society." A shock was in store for these women who had come three thousand miles across the sea in the cause of human freedom—their fellow-emancipators refused to recognise them as delegates and even denied them admission to the floor of the hall, confining them to a curtained recess where they were allowed to listen in silence.

This exclusion was not accomplished without a stormy protest. William Lloyd Garrison was so outraged that he refused to take part in the proceedings, declaring, "After battling so many long years for the liberties of African slaves, I can take no part in a convention that strikes down the most sacred rights of all women." An English journal of the day, commenting on the debate, said: "Some have thought that although the ladies were defeated by a large majority of votes, the weight of argument was much in their favour. We shall not discuss the question here, as to whether it is right for women to take an active and prominent part with their brethren in promoting philanthropic objects; but we shall take the liberty to express our wish that half the temper, fullness of mind, warmth of heart, distinctness of utterance, facility of elucidation, and vivacity of manners which distinguish Lucretia Mott, had been the gift of nine-tenths of the gentlemen who raised their voices in the convention."

It is no wonder that the eager, highly intelligent, already rebellious, young bride Elizabeth Cady Stanton found Lucretia Mott a "revelation," and they "walked home arm in arm" from the convention hall to their lodgings in Queen Street declaring "it was high time some demand was made for the liberties of women," and "discussing the propriety of calling a woman's rights convention."

Time and Tide, 27 July 1923.

That was the beginning. Eight years later Elizabeth Cady Stanton, now settled in Seneca Falls, New York—a busy, harassed mother of several children—was invited to spend the day with Lucretia Mott who was visiting in a nearby town while attending the Friends' Yearly Meeting. The two women seem to have begun where they left off in London, and this time their indignation led to immediate action. "We decided then and there," writes Mrs. Stanton in her autobiography, "to call a Woman's Rights Convention. We wrote the call that evening, and published it in the *Seneca County Courier* the next day, July 14, 1848, giving only five days' notice as the convention was to be held on the 19th and 20th."

This "convention to discuss the social, civil and religious condition of and rights of woman" was held in the Wesleyan Chapel at Seneca Falls. Every session was crowded. A "Declaration of Sentiments" and twelve resolutions were adopted which but for the high-flown language, the almost religious earnestness characteristic of reformers of that day, might stand as the feminist protest of modern times. Equal educational opportunities, the opening of professions, skilled trades and the civil service to women, the right to equal voice in the councils of the church, an equal moral standard, the right to vote, equal guardianship of children, equal divorce laws, property rights unaffected by marriage, &c.—all these demands were made on behalf of American women at Seneca Falls in 1848. And, with the exception of the suffrage which was won by federal amendment in 1920, there is not one of these demands which is to-day completely realised in all of our forty-eight States. It is fitting then that this early convention should be commemorated by the Woman's Party which has reorganized since the vote was won to complete the programme laid down by the pioneers.

By its own announcement the Woman's Party is a "National non-partisan organization of women dedicated to the freedom of women, and open to all women who will put that cause before the interests of any political party. It works to remove all forms of the subjection of women—in the law, in custom, in the moral world, in the professions, in industry, in education, in elective and appointive positions, in the church, in the home. Its first object is the removal of discriminations in the law." During the past year changes have been made in the laws of nine different States and the legal status of four million women improved. These measures range from the equal guardianship law secured in Mississippi, one of the backward southern States, to the "Woman's Bill of Rights" secured in Wisconsin, which declares that "Women shall have the same rights and privileges under the law as men in the exercise of suffrage, freedom of contract, choice of residence for voting purposes, jury service, holding office, holding and conveying property, care and custody of children, and *in all other respects.*"

The third and best-loved of the three great suffrage pioneers in America was Susan B. Anthony. She was an intimate friend and co-worker of Mrs. Stanton's for forty-five years, a Quaker school-teacher who "hid her ferule away" in 1850 and devoted all the remaining years of her life to the freedom of women. Miss Anthony was not present at the 1848 convention, but her home was in Rochester, New York, a great industrial city not twenty miles from Seneca Falls, and she was buried there in 1906. As part of the seventy-fifth anniversary ceremonies the Woman's Party organized a pilgrimage to the grave of Susan B. Anthony led by the Mayor and city officials of Rochester. Thousands of women joined this pilgrimage—teachers, students, lawyers, government workers, doctors, business women, musicians, nurses, artists, writers, factory-workers—women from almost every walk in life who could truly say that they owe their present status in society in some measure to the work of Susan B. Anthony.

Thus is she honoured at last, that slim gallant Quaker girl, who for most of the years of her life was hounded by the mob and scorned by those in high places.

CREATING FEMINIST LIFE-STYLES

Short Hair and Short Skirts

A clever gray-haired woman said to me the other day, "I haven't the courage to bob my hair at my age, but I know that in another generation the woman with long hair will be an exception, and in two generations from now she'll be a freak."

And last week, my hairdresser who waves my hair for me whenever I have the money and the time to spare for such vanity, started her weekly monologue with:

"Everybody's having their hair bobbed nowadays, it seems to me. I cut off fifteen heads last week, and eleven the week before, and nine the week before that!"

In the theatre, between the acts, have you noticed how many girls are wearing short hair—in both the pit and the stalls.

Undated, unpublished essay, courtesy of Annis Young.

What does this vogue of short hair mean? Is it just a passing craze, a style that women will soon tire of, another expression of the average woman's love for change?

Or is it something more than that? Has bobbed hair come to stay, and does its coming mark a new stage in the progress of women?

I am old enough to remember the time when women wore long skirts that touched the ground on all sides and trailed in the back. If you younger women don't believe it, look at some old photos of your mothers and aunts in the nineties. A disgusting costume you will say—yes, and you are right.

But we women don't have to worry any more about wearing long skirts. Not all the propaganda of the cleverest dressmakers in Paris could bring back into general use a street costume with a long trailing skirt. The very thought of it makes us laugh. It would be like trying to stop us from smoking cigarettes.

The truth of the matter is that whenever a style comes in that is comfortable, clean and not unbecoming, and that is a step in the direction of freedom, it comes to stay, because women are moving all the time in the direction of freedom. When the short skirt "came in" women—especially younger women—were quick to see that it was comfortable, hygienic and becoming and they saw too, some of them perhaps unconsciously, that it was a step in the direction of freedom; for it gave women a freer use of their legs than they had known for hundreds of years. Incidentally, it gave them back the use of the left hand which in the days of trailing skirts had always to be used for holding the ugly things up out of the dust and dirt.

How does this apply to the fashion of short hair? Does it fall into the category of styles that are bound to last? It is certainly comfortable and clean, but is it really beautiful? For beauty and freedom must go hand in hand if they are to live. Here I confess opinions differ.

For my part, I believe that a girl's hair, whether it is naturally curly or just thick and healthy, is more beautiful short, with the ends free and visible, than it is with the ends always tucked up out of sight in a wad on the head. And for the rest of us, those who have what may be described as just ordinary heads of hair, it seems to me that it is easier to achieve success with it short than long.

So much for cleanliness, comfort and beauty. But surely the best thing about bobbed hair is the new sense of freedom it brings to the wearer. What the short skirt has done for women's legs, short hair is doing for their heads. And outside of musical comedy, a woman's head is ever more important than her legs.

Have you ever sat behind a bobbed haired girl on top of a London bus and seen her suddenly pull off her hat with a gesture of joy and relief to let the wind blow through her hair? She isn't doing it to show off, she is doing it for the glad sense of freedom it gives her. And though, perhaps, she doesn't know it, that new sense of freedom will always prevent her from willingly going back to the old style of long hair with its paraphernalia of pins and nets and all the rest of it.

Marriage under Two Roofs

"You're breaking up our home," my husband said.

"No I'm not. I'm trying to hold it together. You know we've had nothing worthy the name of home for years, and the thing we have is going to pieces so fast that nothing but desperate measures will save it. Try my scheme, then. Only try it, that's all I ask."

We tried it. And it has given us the one serene and happy period of all our married life. We no longer even think of separation, much less talk of it or threaten it. For the first time the fact that we love each other and have two splendid children is making us happy instead of miserable. My husband, who fought the scheme so bitterly, admits this now and often expatiates upon it.

Here is the story as well as I can tell it. To begin with, we had to move. The building in which we had lived for five years was to be torn down. Well, it just seemed to happen without our saying any more about it that we moved into two places instead of one. I took a small flat for myself and the children toward the edge of town where there are playgrounds and green spaces. My husband took a room in a clean rooming house within easy walking distance of his office. The two cost just a bit less than we had had to pay for a place large enough to hold us in reasonable comfort, all together. John's clothes and strictly personal possessions went to the room. Mine and the children's and our furniture, pictures and joint accumulations went to the flat. Technically he lives at one place and I at the other. But of course he keeps a change of clothes and all the essentials for night and morning comfort at my house, as might a favorite and frequent guest.

Every morning, like lovers, we telephone to exchange the day's greetings and make plans for the evening. Two or three times a week we dine together at my house and John stays all night. If we are to dine at a friend's house we usually arrange to meet there and at the end of the evening my husband may come home with me and he may not, according to our mood. If we are going to a theater I meet him in town for dinner, and after the show there are again always two possibilities—going home together like married lovers or parting on the street corner and going off in the night alone to our separate beds. And because neither course is inexorably forced upon us, either one is a bit of a lark. It is wonderful sometimes to be alone in the night and just know that someone loves you. In other moods you must have that lover in your arms. Marriage under two roofs makes room for moods.

Now about the children; for, paradoxical though it may seem, it is having children that complicates marriage so. Many pairs of lovers can have a house in common, a car, a cook, a club and all their Christmas presents; they can eat the same food, see the same plays, go to the same parties, cherish the same friends for years on end and enjoy it. But just introduce one or two children into that home, strong modern personalities, strange ebullient creatures neither his nor hers but mysteriously and indissolubly *theirs*—theirs to love, theirs to teach and train, theirs to be proud of, theirs to be ashamed of—and you have the material for tragedy. Obscure jealousies so often arise, deep resentments may be so long unspoken, rivers of cold misunderstanding may flow forever between the two who were at one before.

Perhaps I exaggerate the difficulty of bringing up children together. If the two parents come from an almost identical background, or if one has had a miserable childhood which he is glad to forget, there may be no difficulty at all. It is when, as in our case, both parents can claim a happy childhood but under totally different auspices, that their joint efforts to raise a family come so often to grief. I think my husband and I have quarreled with more anguish and bitterness over our children than over all other matters put together. But we quarrel no longer. The two-roof plan has made an end of quarreling.

"No wonder!" protests the indignant male. "You've got your way. You have the children, they live with you and you can bring them up as you like. But is that fair?"

Surely, as society is organized today, it is the mother's job to bring up the children. The father's job is to earn the living, and if he belongs as the father in our family does to the intellectual proletariat—people of education with expensive tastes and no capital, who must live by their wits—he will be hard at it for the first fifteen or twenty years of his married life. How can he be more than a "consulting partner" in the twenty-four hour a day job of bringing up children? He can criticize and interfere, or praise and suggest, according to his nature, but he cannot really do the job. Circumstances compel him to leave it to the mother. In big decisions about the children, of course, the father's will counts often more than the mother's, but in the everyday matter of training and association the most he can do is to "use his influence."

And in the usual American middle-class family, when is father's influence most often brought to bear? At breakfast! At breakfast of all times when everyone is already a little on edge from violating his natural instincts—children forced to "hurry up" and "be quiet" and "keep at it" when they long to dawdle and "fool"; mother forced to begin being patient and kind at a time in the day when it is against nature to be patient and kind; father, already heavy with his day's work, forced to spend his last precious half-hour in this crude confusion when his whole being cries out for solitude.

This at least can be said for the two-roof scheme: it automatically relieves father of the family breakfast, and the family breakfast of father! And no hard feelings anywhere. In our family father is now a treat. He might turn up some morning during the week, but if he does it is a surprise and everybody is so good that breakfast is almost a social occasion. Saturday afternoon father usually appears and takes you off for a lark somewhere, and Sunday he is just like a member of the family.

Is there really anything unfair in this arrangement? Are not the father's comments, criticisms and suggestions on the upbringing of his children apt to be better given and better received in the comparative leisure and freedom of Sunday than in the nagging, inescapable contact of a daily breakfast? Must a consulting partner review the raw, unfinished work every day?

At this point, I foresee, the passionate upholder of family life will try to compromise with me. "Why two roofs?" he will argue. "Why not a room for father at the top of the house and his breakfast served there? Is it necessary to drive him right out of the house?"

But I stand my ground. To begin with, for the type of family I am thinking of there seldom is a house. It is a flat, an apartment, a floor or two floors, at most a very small house. If father is lucky enough to have a room of his own it will not be out of hearing. He will always be acutely aware of the children in their noisy process of growing up. And mother will be aware of his presence in the house. The strain will still be there.

Moreover, even though you live in a palace, two rooms will not give you what two roofs will give you. Let us forget breakfast now— imagine it is evening, the long day's work is over, the children are asleep. Speaking from the woman's standpoint, can there be anything more irritating than a husband who shuts himself up in a room and says or intimates, "I want to be alone"? He is there with you in your common home. It is evening. You have been apart all day, and yet he wants to be alone! Outrageous! To sit and read in separate rooms under the same roof! Unnatural! Not to be borne! *Why did he come home if he wanted to be alone?*

Why?

Obviously because he had no home of his own to go to. Now

put my scheme into operation. Give him a place of his own, completely outside of your jurisdiction, a place where he keeps his clothes, where he normally sleeps, to which he goes quite simply and naturally whenever he wants to, without explanations and without fear of reproach. At the morning telephone rendezvous you have agreed not to spend the evening together. You may be a little lonely the first few times this happens, but you soon get to like your "vacations" and to plan for them. You may have a friend in for dinner whom your husband takes no pleasure in. You may arrange for some kind of recreation, dancing, music, lecture or what-not for which he has no taste, or you may be tired enough to enjoy a few hours of solitude by your own hearth.

In any case his absence is a refreshment, a chance to be yourself for a while in a rich, free sense which nothing but a separate roof can give you.

Women, more than men, succumb to marriage. They sink so easily into that fatal habit of depending on one person to rescue them from themselves. And this is the death of love.

The two-roof plan encourages a wife to cultivate initiative in rescuing herself, to develop social courage, to look upon her life as an independent adventure and get interested in it. And every Victorian tradition to the contrary, it is thus only that she can retain her charm down the years.

I wish I could set forth as freely and frankly my husband's feeling about this new scheme of life as I can my own. But he is not the sort of man who talks easily about himself. He is what the psychoanalysts call an "introvert." I know from a hundred signs that he likes it, but I can only guess why.

Most women tend to own and manage their husbands too much, and I am not free from that vice. Much of John's depression and irritability which used to be so baffling to me in the old days was due, I am sure, to his having no escape from me, no place where I did not come, no retreat from my influence. Now he has one. Often when we lived under the same roof he must have said to himself, "I love her but I can't stand her. She is too much for me." Now I know he never feels that.

People with very simple natures probably do not suffer from this pressure of one personality on the other in marriage. But for the usual modern type, the complex, sensitive, highly organized city dweller, man or woman, marriage can become such a constant invasion of his very self that it amounts sometimes to torture.

I am the last one to deny that there are successful marriages. I know ideally mated couples who can say to this argument with sincerity:

"But we don't want to get away from each other. We are perfectly happy as we are."

And I can answer only, "Bless you my children; there is nothing in this gospel for you."

Nor is there anything in it for young lovers in the first months of ecstacy and anguish, nor for parents, during the first baby's first year, nor for couples of whom one is a natural door-mat, nor for the excessively domestic man who wants to know the price of everything to a penny, how often the baby falls down and what the cook does on her afternoon off. (Though in this case no doubt the wife needs a retreat.)

No, I am speaking only to those who are discouraged with marriage, who have given it a good trial and found it extremely difficult. But I am sure I shall have a large audience.

Ours is not an extreme case. My husband is a bit temperamental but he has great charm. I am a "strong-minded" woman, perhaps, but not over-strong. We have hosts of friends who find us both good-natured, generous, easy to get along with. We are both of us intelligent. We can both take a joke. And I think we had more genuine love and respect for each other than is common.

Yet marriage was destroying us. We just lived from storm to storm, with tears, an emotional reconciliation and a brief lull of happiness between.

Now that we live under two roofs there are no storms, no quarrels, no tears. Our differences of opinion are not passionate and unbearable. They have an almost rational quality. Criticisms and suggestions are made with the gentleness and reserve that is common between friends. They are received with the open-minded forbearance of one who can be sure of the critic's early departure.

And as for love, we seem to have found it again. The hours we spend together have actually caught back some of the surprising gaiety and warm glow of sweetheart days.

What is the meaning of this all but universal habit of quarreling among the married?

When a friend irritates you or, as we say, gets on your nerves, you do not have to quarrel with her. You know she is going home pretty soon, or you are going home—a natural and inevitable separation will take place.

But with a husband or a wife there is no hope, nothing to look forward to. You cannot good-naturedly walk away, because you have no place to go. *His home*—or her home—*is your home.* This fact increases your irritation five hundredfold, and some outlet must be had.

Stormy quarrels, no matter how tender and intimate the interval between, are wearing to soul and body. But they are not nearly so devastating, I believe, as that much more common type of married quarreling which resolves itself into being a little mean to each other all the time.

Just who is there who does not know at least one couple like that—their conversation with each other made up almost entirely of small slighting remarks, each constantly belittling the achievements and enthusiasms of the other; kindly people in their relations with outsiders but always somewhat bitter and belligerent toward each other? Is anything less enjoyable than visiting in such a home? Is it really good for children to grow up in such an atmosphere?

Perhaps divorce is the only remedy for difficult marriages. But if my theory is correct, if it is the too constant sharing of one home, with no easy and normal method of escape, which primarily makes them difficult, then some loosening of the time-and-space conventions so bound up with marriage is worth trying. Separate beds, separate rooms, have not done much to reconcile people to marriage. Why not take a bold romantic step and try separate roofs?

It will seem to many that in setting forth this new plan for achieving a happy marriage I have avoided the crucial test, that my argument can be challenged at its very heart.

Crudely put, the challenge is: "If my husband sleeps under a separate roof, how do I know that he is always alone?" or again: "If I don't go home every night, how do I know that some other man is not there in my place?" In a literal and exact sense you don't know. That is the answer.

But after all, marriage, like business, is founded on trust.

When a husband goes off to work in the morning, does he *know* that his wife is not going to neglect her children and make love to the plumber? He hopes she isn't, of course, but he cannot be absolutely sure. It would not be practical to ring her up every fifteen minutes to inquire; if he is to get on with his work, he must trust her.

And as for the poor wife, how can she know that her bread-winner is not spending the entire morning kissing the stenographer, unless she squanders what she has saved up for the children's winter coats on a dictograph?

In the most conventional marriage there must be a considerable area of confidence as to the technical faithfulness of the parties. In marriage under two roofs you deliberately extend that area of confidence, that is all.

If one is of a very jealous disposition this may take some courage, but it is courage soon rewarded, for in this matter of marital faithfulness, as all wise women know, increasing the confidence usually lessens the risk. The two-roof scheme demands confidence during those very hours of ease when temptation is greatest; this cannot be denied.

But if it brings happiness where there was misery before, even that risk is well taken, for happiness is the only security.

Bed-Makers and Bosses

Many, many years ago I remember announcing to my mother that I would not make my bed unless my two brothers had to make theirs. To this my mother, who was really a feminist, agreed. We made it a family rule applying to all forms of household labour, and we felt like pioneers. And yet only yesterday I held this conversation with my six-year-old son, who has chosen a sailor's career.

Time and Tide, 12 October 1923.

"You know, Mother," he began, quite quietly and without conscious arrogance, "when I'm grown up I'm going to have my wife go with me on the ship."

"Yes, and what will she do?"

"Oh, make the beds, I suppose."

"Why have her a bed-maker?" I protested. "Why not a sailor like you? Why not the captain? Or why not have her be the wireless operator and then she would have a little office at the top of the ship where you could come and visit her?"

This last won a sparkle of enthusiasm from the brown eyes, but I feel sure he will revert to his original plan. How can I expect to counteract the steady insistent suggestion of school, story, song and game that girls are weak and boys are strong, that a proper heroine looks forward to a life concerned with "keeping house," while a hero has the world to choose from?

In this connection let me urge all mothers, fathers, nurses, teachers and trainers of the young to read "The Dominant Sex"* by Mathilde and Mathias Vaerting; to read and study it, to mark it and put it on the nursery or schoolroom shelf for frequent reference. It may surprise the authors of this excellent "Study in the Sociology of Sex Differentiation" to hear me recommend it as a Mother's Guide and Sure Nursery Favourite, but so I do. Never before have I felt so well fortified against the fast-accumulating masculine assumptions of my son. As I turned to the Encyclopaedia to answer his ceaseless enquiries about the natural world, so I turn to the Dominant Sex to make clear with example and wealth of detail that the bed-making, skirt-wearing, food-preparing, stay-at-home-and-mind-the-baby characteristics of woman are not exclusive, foreordained and immutable.

The thesis of the Vaertings is this: Whenever a period of feminine dominance has existed in any race (and we now have record of such periods among numerous races in the most diverse phases of development) women have exhibited what to-day we call masculine characteristics, followed "masculine" occupations, enjoyed "masculine" privileges, whereas men have been correspondingly "feminine."

---

* *The Dominant Sex.* By Mathilde and Mathias Vaerting. Translated by Eden and Cedar Paul. (Allen & Unwin; 10s. 6d. net.)

"Where women rule, woman is the wooer. The man contributes the dowry; the woman has the sole right of disposal over the common possessions. From the husband chastity and conjugal fidelity are demanded; but the obligations of the wife in this respect are less exacting. The wife's occupations lead her away from the home, whilst the husband attends to domestic affairs. The man adorns himself, but the woman's clothing is comparatively sober. Unmarried men are regarded with contempt. Girl children are valued more highly than boys. . . ." and so on. In short, "Masculine peculiarities in the Men's State are fundamentally identical with feminine peculiarities in the Women's State." The book abounds in specific references and careful footnotes, and it includes seven pages of bibliography. Here and there a rather heavy inference seems to be drawn from a very slight fact but on the whole one is inclined to be convinced.

It is comforting to learn for example that "when women ruled in Kamchatka the men not only did the cooking but all the rest of the housework, the sewing and laundry work. These were regarded as men's work and beneath a woman's dignity." And it is easy to agree with the authors in their conclusion that the time-honoured division of labour between the sexes was not due to woman's physique or reproductive faculties, but was a natural division "between a dominant sex and a subordinate sex."

However, despite some centuries of "bed-making," the most militant of us has no desire to see the race revert to a period of feminine dominance. All we ask, as the authors of this book express it, is that "humanity should find ways and means for the permanent realisation of sex-equality."

Boys and Girls

I am sure I was not more than fifteen when I formulated for myself the two corollary educational reforms essential to the freedom of women: Girls, *as well as boys,* must be brought up as a matter of course to earn their own living. Boys, *as well as girls,* must be taught, as a matter of course, the rudiments of home-making.

As might have been expected, great progress has been made in the first of these reforms. Twenty-five years ago a girl not driven by poverty was always called upon to explain why she wanted to go to work. To-day it is the other, the girl content to live on father until she finds a husband, who must explain and defend herself to her contemporaries. But has much progress been made in the equally important corollary reform? Public opinion actually applauds the young woman venturing into the business world, but it still obstinately (and quite illogically) protects the young man in his sacred right to know nothing of housework.

Just a year ago, in an otherwise thoughtful and modern-minded educational report on the "Differentiation of the Curriculum for Boys and Girls in Secondary Schools," I came upon this astonishing paragraph:—

> "Under the same conditions of health, and granted the same freedom from other demands on their time, there is every reason to believe that girls can match the achievements of boys when they enjoy the same training. But the conditions of health are not the same and the freedom from other demands is much less for girls than it is for boys. Girls are liable to seasons of lower vitality, in which nervous fatigue is serious; *and they have a part to play in the home and its duties which can hardly be shirked, even if its effects on their studies may be deprecated.* If, under such conditions and amid such distractions, the pace of education in girls' schools were made to keep time with that set in schools for boys, it is obvious that girls would, in effect, be required to do still more than boys in order to remain on a level with them. We have only to state the requirement in order to show its injustice; and *in the cause of justice and equality between the sexes* (!) we may thus suggest that, for many girls, a later age for passing examinations, and, for all girls, a shorter period of school hours, are imperatively necessary.

The italics and exclamation point are mine.

There were four women on that Consultative Committee. Did it occur to none of them that the cause of justice and equality would be better served by teaching the mothers to allot household tasks equally among boys and girls? And the seventeen men who were members, was not one of them chivalrous enough to suggest that brothers might be taught to do more than their share of housework during a sister's seasons of lowered vitality;—even as the lowest form of husband will help with the washing the week after the baby is born?

The members of that committee would no doubt reply that the scope of their inquiry did not include the home, that their task was to fit the curriculum to the boys and girls in the condition in which they come up the school-house steps. But surely the school has raised the home standards in many respects. Why not urge it to use its influence on behalf of fair-play for girls as well as clean teeth and clean faces? Such an effort, no matter how barren of results, would be more intelligent than to make a fundamental and permanent change in the school curriculum on the theory that little girls of the working-class will forever spend their leisure hours "helping mother" while their brothers play football.

In this connection there is still a word to be said, I think, about the report of the Domestic Service Inquiry Commission. Among other things this Committee recommended that a course in Domestic Science be made compulsory for girls in the elementary schools. Here it is again, this essentially masculine assumption that women will sacrifice everything to become proficient housewives. One set of inquirers would permanently lower the educational standards for a girl in order to allow her to be a faithful drudge in her leisure hours at home. Another set would still further handicap her, interfere with her general education and put off the time of special training for her chosen trade, by requiring her to take a course in these same household arts at school. It is a barbarous suggestion and I heartily concur in the feminist outcry against it.

But, it seems to me, by simply refusing to submit to this special training, women are missing an opportunity. After all housework has to be done by somebody sometime. As things are now, very few women escape all contact with it, direct and indirect. Their one hope of shifting or sharing the burden is to see that men get some elementary training in it. Why not welcome the idea of a compulsory course in Domestic Science but insist that it be general,—for boys and girls alike? Those who like it, of either sex, can take it up as a trade. Those who do not like it (and this will be the vast majority of both boys and girls) will not be injured by having learned how to take care of themselves in the daily emergencies of life, how to provide simple food and get rid of dirt. And it is impossible to exaggerate the importance of such common training in freeing the women of the generations to come.

Bertrand Russell *on*
Bringing Up Children

An Interview with the Noted Author of
"Education and the Good Life"

"Why should I read this book? His children are only babies. What does he know? Let him wait until his children grow up a little."

That is what my husband said when I tried to get him to read Bertrand Russell's book, "Education and the Good Life." You see, the Russell children are only three and five respectively, whereas ours are four and nine! Apparently, my husband, standing on his dignity as the father of a boy almost ten years old, looked upon Bertrand Russell as an upstart in the parent world.

Not a bit more in accord with my own enthusiasm was the response of my little girl's Montessori teacher to my eager question, "Have you read Bertrand Russell's new book?"

"No," she said. "I have only glanced at it. It seems all right. Nothing especially new. But isn't it rather foolish for a man of his age to start writing about children? He had a good subject. Why didn't he stick to it?"

I have quoted these two, the parent and the teacher, because they reveal how old-fashioned very intelligent people can be about

Children: The Magazine for Parents, March 1927.

the business of bringing up small children. There seems to linger even in some fairly modern circles a notion that bringing up children is a practical matter for individual parents and school teachers, that scientists and wise men generally better keep their hands off.

Yet, surely this is the most fundamentally important branch of all human inquiry—how to help these mysterious new, helpless creatures to unfold, to realize themselves, to be as happy and as great and as good as it is in them to be. Here, surely, is a task above all others for the thinkers.

Bertrand Russell is one of the most important men writing in England today. He has his place in the scientific world as a mathematician and philosopher; to the general reader he is known and valued as a student of the problems of government and a writer on social reconstruction. But, at the moment, what engages the mind and heart of this mathematician-philosopher-reformer above all else is the growth and development of his two children, John, aged five, and Kate, aged three.

What more natural than that he should turn his active and brilliant mind to the problems of the parent and the teacher? What more valuable thing could he do than what he has done—produce a book "On Education, Especially in Early Childhood"—a book so tender in its understanding of childhood, so practical in its grasp of the difficulties of parents, so able in its exposition of the aim and practice of the so-called "nursery school," that it would be hard to equal it in all the literature of modern education.

When I called on Bertrand Russell my mind was full of this book of his which I had just finished reading. I could think of nothing in it that I wished to dispute except his statement that "almost all children learn to read and write (under the Montessori system) without pressure before they are five years old." So when we had settled down in Mr. Russell's book-lined little study in Chelsea, I began boldly with that.

"Many of us in America think that it is a mistake to encourage children to learn to read and write so early," I said. "We feel that self-expression in drawing and painting, in building and modeling, and so on, naturally come first, and that too early a facility in reading and writing tends to put a stop to the development of skill and imagination."

"Well," said Mr. Russell, "of course it does not matter when children learn to read and write, so long as it is not put off too long. John loves to draw, in fact he is drawing and painting all the time. And yet he can read and write. He likes that, too. I think perhaps you in America are too insistent on the practical side of education, put too much emphasis on the utilitarian and not enough on the purely intellectual side of education."

I protested that, while this might be true, our emphasis on the training of hand and eye and ear and the artistic sense generally, in the very early years was surely not an expression of the utilitarian tendency but of a contrary tendency, our aim being to avoid being too utilitarian in our education. But we did not pursue this. Mr. Russell confessed himself completely ignorant of the modern school in America.

Later, when I saw little John Russell, and saw his drawing and painting book, I had to admit that learning to read and write had apparently not done him any harm. He draws much more firmly and paints with a much more daring imagination than does my daughter of the same age, who has but a languid interest in the letters of the alphabet, and whose "reading," though rapid and highly entertaining, is wholly a matter of her own creative fancy.

The nursery school, that is, the all-day school for very small children, does not exist in England except here and there in very crowded slum districts. John Russell goes for two hours in the morning to a near-by Montessori class; the rest of the day (barring rain) he spends in Kensington Gardens with his little sister and a young Swiss governess.

"Would you send your children to an all-day school if there were one near-by?" I asked Mr. Russell.

"Yes, I think we would, if it were large enough to have the advantages of a real nursery school, and if we could guard against infection."

"You think, then, that there is some special virtue in having small children spend most of their waking hours in another environment than that of their own homes?"

"Yes, decidedly. Perhaps the most valuable thing about it is that in such a school there is nothing you have to forbid them. A home is really not designed as a place for children to live in, it is not adapted to their needs. In the usual house, even with wise parents, children have to be told continually that they must not do this and must not do that. This constant repression of their natural instincts is harmful. Only the very rich could achieve the right environment for children, and even then there would not be the companionship of other children of the same age."

"In these days of small families, especially, we need the nursery school. The old-fashioned family of seven or eight children was better in many ways. It had some of the features of the nursery school; the attitude of the parents was more casual, they were less concerned, less intense over their children. It was a good thing, that is, if the children survived; of course, most of them didn't!"

"Have you begun to think yet what sort of schools you will send John and Kate to when they are past the nursery school age?" I asked.

"No," said Mr. Russell, smiling. "We have decided what schools we won't send them to. But we are still looking for a school we want to send them to. I think perhaps we won't send them to school, at all."

"You mean, you will teach them yourself?"

"Oh, no. Have a tutor, I mean. I was educated at home myself. There is something to be said for it. We should like to get several friends who have children to join us, and have more than one tutor. Then we could live by the sea in Cornwall all the year round, instead of for a few months in the summer as we do now. I should consider that a great advantage."

Next we discussed the differences between boys and girls. Throughout his book Bertrand Russell shows himself a good feminist. There is no suggestion that he would reserve certain branches of learning for boys, or that he would force on girls, as distinct from boys, a special training in the household arts. I asked him whether he thought there should be any difference at all between the education of boys and girls.

"The thing is to establish equality first of all, to establish it firmly. Then, in later years, when they come to specialize, there will be differences. The majority of boys will not, I believe, be interested in the same things that will interest the majority of girls. For example, girls are extraordinarily interested in the science of the body, in physiological processes. I don't think boys are, as a rule. Boys, on the other hand, almost all boys, have an intense interest in things mechanical.

"And the difference in their interests manifests itself so early," laughed Mr. Russell. "Mrs. Russell and I were, of course, very careful that there should be no difference made between John and Kate. As far as we could we gave them the same environment, the same things to play with. And we certainly never suggested to them that they were different. But we were shocked to see how young they began to manifest masculine and feminine characteristics! Take dolls for instance. We made a point of giving John a doll, and he tied it to his engine and made an engine-driver of it!"

"Kate, on the other hand, would nurse her doll, talk to it, sing to it, take it to bed with her. Baby girls *are* maternal, you can't get away from it."

"And what about co-education?" I asked.

"That is something I have never quite made up my mind about. I think on the whole the advantages of boys and girls being together outweigh the disadvantages."

"And surely younger children you would not separate?"

"Oh, before puberty there should be no question. Undoubtedly boys and girls should be educated together."

At this point I brought forward my favorite educational reform, i.e., that both boys and girls should be taught the rudiments of the household arts as a matter of course, as part of the essential preparation for life. To this Mr. Russell had no masculine objection to offer. Rather he made a valuable suggestion. "The time to teach those things," he said, "is when they are very young. Children have a real interest in such things as cooking at, say, ten years. It would not be a hard task to them then, whereas later on it would be.

Growing up should not be a burden. Learning should be without tears. Bertrand Russell believes that children need joy. We were discussing a certain Quaker school near London, known for its excellent educational features. "I would never send a child there," he said. "It's too joyless. You know, children need joy. It is really important for them to have a great deal of fun and foolishness and laughter in their every-day life."

Just then John and Kate came in and stopped for a few minutes with their father before going on to lunch. John is a sunny, gray-eyed boy who looks straight at you and begins to talk, one of those rare children who greet a stranger with a smile. Kate is a round, rollicking youngster just past babyhood.

If ever children had a fair start in life, I thought, it is these two, with their young, vital, feminist mother, author of "Hypatia, or Woman and Knowledge," and their learned, wise and very human father.

Schoolgirl Fiction for To-day

Wayfarer. By Kathleen Millay. (Morrow: New York. $2.00.)
Strangers. By Dorothy Van Doren. (Doran: New York. $2.00.)
Tin Wedding. By Margaret Leech (Boni & Liveright: New York. $2.00)

Here are three bright new novels from America. *Wayfarer* and *Strangers* are first novels written by young women unheard of as writers when I left the States two years ago. Neither has much literary distinction but both will prove extremely valuable to the social historian of these changing times a hundred years hence.

Wayfarer is a school girl novel, immature, without subtlety, without restraint, but far from dull; a book to read the first day after an operation when nobody can catch you at it but the nurse. It is easy reading like the Robert W. Chambers novels which were so popular when I was in school. But in matter how vastly different! The Chambers heroine always had a dash of the devil in her, just enough to make her "piquant." She was not really "bad," but through some accident due to her careless fun-loving nature she had allowed a doubt to arise as to her purity. Perhaps she had once missed a train and stayed out all night with a man. In the course of three or four hundred pages of passionate conversation, Chambers would clear that episode of all immoral implication and give her masterful lover the satisfaction of taking her to the altar, a virgin.

But for Miss Millay's young heroine there is none of this suspense—lovers are an old story for her before the book begins. Martha is living a happy-go-lucky, hand-to-mouth existence in an attic of Greenwich Village, New York's Bohemia. Men come and go, as friends, as lovers, or merely for breakfast, one never quite knows which. The author is much more concerned to tell how they keep house than who stays all night. In Martha's group it is taken for granted that a girl has a lover if she wants one.

Out of all this Martha suddenly marries a farmer and goes to live in a remote country district. When, after a few years, farm life has long ceased to be a romantic adventure for her and has come to be a bleak round of fire-building, cooking, cleaning, washing and baby-tending, in isolation unbearable, she runs off with a young summer visitor, who has a sailboat and a fast car and a flat in New York. Of course she goes back to her husband and child, but she goes back without any sense of guilt; she goes back because she is Martha—she cannot escape her responsibilities. She explains this to her lover, in the course of a long and very real conversation, before she leaves him.

> "I thought that being away would get me away. It doesn't. It was worse wondering whether Nancy had the croup last winter than it was being with her when she had it the winter before. It doesn't do any good for a person like me to try to run away from things. I can't do it. They go wherever I go."
>
> "Then you haven't loved me all this time?"
>
> "I don't know. . . . I have thought I loved you . . . and what is love other than what you think at the time? But now I know there is a deeper, more lasting feeling in me somewhere, somehow, for my husband . . . and that seems to me now to be more real. . . . He said once that 'home' was a place to come back to when you didn't want to be anywhere else. I guess he is right . . . and he is 'home' for me—wherever he is."

Martha's reunion with her farmer-husband is no less real. She feels how terribly he has been hurt, she is aghast at the havoc her going away has wrought. But she does not wish she had not gone. There is no remorse. She only suffers for his suffering. And John is generous in his understanding of her.

> "You face everything," he says, "you try everything—you use yourself up trying. And that's brave as anything can be. And I love you because you're like that. So, you see, I really love you because you were brave enough to leave me."

The more I think about this story, its honesty, its emphasis on realities, its putting of sex in its place, the more I like it. School-girl novel, did I call it? Well, the school-girl of to-day has her eyes open.

Strangers is another refreshingly modern story. Rachel, the heroine, and Anne, her sister, are women with an affirmative attitude to life and love. They know what they want and are not afraid to take it. Moreover, they work for a living both before and after marriage.

According to the last census there are two million wives in the United States who are "gainfully employed outside the home." Yet how often does one of them get into a novel or play? The same thing is true on this side of the Atlantic. The middle-class woman of fiction and drama never has anything to do but consider her love problems. But Mrs. Van Doren has given her women jobs. Rachel designs copy for an advertising firm even after she is married. Anne, who has a successful husband and a boy of five, is an editorial writer on a big New York daily. Edith, their best friend, who is married to a celebrated journalist and has two children, nevertheless "edits a magazine with a million circulation."

Strangers is not concerned with the business and professional lives of these women; it is concerned, like most novels, with their love affairs. But the author makes it clear that business and professional life is their normal background.

Tin Wedding, is in an entirely different class. It is genuinely fine writing. Miss Leech describes how a rich and beautiful New York woman discovers in the course of one day, her tenth wedding anniversary, that her husband whom she thought wholly hers has been unfaithful to her. It is interesting as a literary exercise, but not as life itself is interesting. *Tin Wedding* is a novel quite worth the attention of a first-class literary critic but of no possible value to the social historian of 2027.

What Shall We Do with
the Woman's Page?

I suppose there is nothing more irritating to a feminist than the average "Woman's Page" of a newspaper, with its out-dated assumption that all women have a common trade interest in the household arts, and a common leisure interest in clothes and the doings of "high society." Women's interests to-day are as wide as the world. I doubt if there is anything from deep-sea fishing to high-altitude flying that is not of absorbing interest to some woman somewhere.

By the last census, there are five million "females" in England and Wales who are "gainfully occupied" outside their homes, and that is one-third of all the "females" there are who have passed their twelfth birthday. The occupations of these five million women are divided into nearly a thousand classifications. They are, for example, foremen in foundries, electrical engineers, mosaic workers, haulage contractors, veterinary surgeons, farm bailiffs, shepherds, advertising agents, jockeys, round-about proprietors, and so on for pages and pages.

In view of all this it is nearly as foolish to assume that all women are interested in recipes as to assume that all men are interested in what to plant after wheat or the latest formula for artificial manure. As prospective eaters, we are all after a manner of speaking, interested in farming and interested in cooking, but in this modern world of specialisation it is not in reason to expect us all—either all men or all women—to take a keen professional interest in those highly-skilled occupations.

In recent years newspapers have begun to be aware of woman's changed and changing world. They feel vaguely that running the Woman's Page is not the simple thing it used to be in the 'eighties. They have begun to make some concessions to the modern woman, publishing from time to time in and among the recipes, patterns and

Time and Tide, 20 May 1927.

society notes, a short article on some new occupation for women. But they cling to the idea of a special department for women, as a circulation-getter. There is, I am told, an established tradition in newspaper offices that it is men who read the Woman's Page! And editors are afraid to abandon the feature for fear of losing male readers.

Now I wish to make a proposal which will do no violence to that tradition, which will, indeed, make the Woman's Page even more interesting to men, and which will at the same time challenge the attention of the sex for whom it was originally designed. Modern women need a forum, a clearing-house for the exchange of ideas, a meeting-place where they can learn of each other's experiments and benefit by each others conclusions. Such a forum the Woman's Page of the daily newspaper, if edited with some imagination, could provide.

Letters, intimate, honest, revealing letters from ordinary people are, I believe, the best "copy" in the world. On the Woman's Page, then, give us letters on the great woman question of to-day, the question that is at this moment agitating hundreds of clubs and thousands of firesides, how to reconcile a woman's natural desire for love and home and children with her equally natural desire for work of her own for which she is paid, for some normal work-contact with the world at large. This is not an easy question to solve though it may seem so to the young and confident who have never tried it. But it is of the very essence of feminism. And nothing would help more toward its solution than a full and free exchange of experience.

I should admire an editor who would know how to get letters from two or three hundred of those 700,000 married "females" in England and Wales who, the Census tells us, have jobs outside the home. Why not start them writing to each other through the Woman's Page, or writing to some central person, clever enough to analyse and sift and make the best use of their letters? And would it not be possible to get letters from half a hundred brides who have given up a pretty good job to get married and do housework, and then to hear from them again after a few years?

A series of letters on marriage finance would be invaluable. A questionnaire might be sent to brides of a year, to women who have been married ten years, and to those who have been married twenty years: "Please make your letter cover these points: (1) how much are you paid for your work in the home? Are you paid regularly? Are you and your husband financial partners in your marriage? Do you have a joint bank account? Can you suggest improvements on the usual financial arrangements in families, based on your experience? etc., etc."

I have said that the regular appearance of some such feature as this on the Woman's Page would challenge the interest of men as well as women. And I wish to emphasise this. No one is so bewildered by this modern woman's revolution as the average husband. If he could turn once a week to the Woman's Page, and find there scores of women stirred by the same unnatural discontent that seemed to be threatening his own home comfort, he would certainly be intrigued. He might even begin to understand.

WOMAN'S PLACE—
BEYOND THE HOME

Is Woman's Place the Home?

As a public character Rebecca West is getting to be a good bit like
Bernard Shaw; if she consents to make a speech she can be counted on
to say something so fresh, so impudent and challenging that the press
carries it right round the world. No doubt a sentence or two from her
celebrated debate with Duff Cooper on "Is Woman's Place the Home"
has appeared in the American papers. Perhaps it was only the Oxford
trousers joke: "I have known women," said Miss West in support of
her thesis that men are becoming more like women in dress and
physical type every year,—"I have known women so feminine that
they could not wear breeches. 'I am too feminine,' they said, 'I must
wear a skirt.' But I have never known a woman so feminine that she
insisted on wearing two skirts, which is what the Oxford trousers
are."

These so-called "debates," so popular in London as a means of

Equal Rights, 13 June 1925.

money-raising are in no sense expected to be a serious setting forth of two points of view. No continuity of thought, no consistency, seems to be called for and no meeting of the minds, just a series of clever and if possible humorous or satirical comments. Their unique value as entertainments, in my opinion, lies in the fact that they commence at 5.30 and finish at 6.30 so that one does not have to eat a bad dinner or lose a good evening to hear one. This measuring of wits on the old theme of "Woman's Place" between Mr. Duff Cooper, member of Parliament and husband of Lady Diana Manners, and Miss Rebecca West, novelist and celebrated critic, was second in a series of "Debates" held at the London School of Economics in aid of the King Edward Hospital Fund.

In the twenty minutes of sparkling inconsequential chatter with which Rebecca West opened the debate, I remember two rich thoughts.

"There are some remarks," she began, "which though they are not meant to be offensive, are in fact somewhat offensive. One of them is the proposition that 'woman's place is in the home.' There is really nothing offensive in it at all, it is a self-evident truth. As the mass of women between the ages of sixteen and forty-five get married they naturally live in homes. But when people say woman's place is at home they really mean that the *home is a symbol of a state of resignation to the male will.*"

I was startled. "There is a thought almost too good for this debate," I said to myself, "too wise and sad and true. How will she get herself back to the light bantering note expected of her?" And then she went on, "Personally, I have no objection at all to a resignation to the male will, because I am distinctly lazy; I would rather resign my will to anybody than use it."

A few minutes later she struck a rich vein of satire in describing man's special faculty in guiding public destiny, *"the faculty of virile failure,"* she called it. "Of course, we always exalt what we should like to be ourselves. When we choose a god we choose one as much like ourselves as possible, or even more so! Now there is one man whom men do really admire, and that is Napoleon, and the cause of their admiration of Napoleon is that he was an enormous and very expensive failure, who at his death had not only lost everything, but had also shorn his country of power, and had greatly diminished the vitality of the French people by calling for so much of their best for his army.

"Who, for instance, is the most invincible and popular of our contemporary politicians—who keeps on being popular no matter what he does? Winston Churchill. He has an extraordinary genius for failure. I think his popularity is due to the fact that he is so richly a failure in everything he does; he has that great power, which counts for nothing, of being full of beans—a power man has chiefly admired in the past.

"The Great War was a supreme example of the failure of men. We ought therefore to be sympathetic to men when they realize their failure and want to throw up their hands in the sphere of politics and go back to the home. After all, men do lose a lot by doing too much. One of the first consequences of overwork is lack of charm, and I ask, what is man when he has lost his charm?"

Mr. Duff Cooper supported his side of the question with some humor, but his contention was essentially the bald one that since a well-run nursery, two well-cooked meals a day and a drawing-room in which he can be quietly and comfortably entertained are essential to a man's well-being, therefore woman's place is in the home.

A lively exchange occurred when Mr. Duff Cooper introduced the name of Jane Austen as a supremely great "stay-at-home."

"It may be thought by some that I have put the task of the woman too low," he said, "but I am prepared to admit that there are none of the higher functions of the human race which woman is not adequately equipped to perform. Perhaps the greatest thing· which men or women can do is the production of scientific or artistic work. In my opinion, however, that too can always be done better in the home. There is no greater exponent of the art of literature in England, or possibly in the world, than one who never left the home for a moment—Miss Austen—and who probably spent more long and weary hours in the home, and in a small home, than any novelist or artist has ever done. Yet she found in these humble surroundings sufficient material to produce five complete masterpieces. I do not believe that our more travelled novelists have gained anything from their explorations which has put them on a footing with the stay-at-home artist."

"Mr. Duff Cooper has mentioned Miss Austen," said Rebecca

West when her turn came again. "But there never was a spirit who stayed at home less than Jane Austen. She never accepted a state of resignation to the male will which, I repeat, is what they mean by 'home' in this connection."

And Mr. Duff Cooper's reply to this, while it was the obvious and inescapable reply, gives the whole case away. "If," said he, "when a man gets home from his work in the evening, his wife is actually there in the flesh waiting for him, *he doesn't care where her spirit is!*" This seems finally to dispose of any lingering notion that a man's desire to keep women in the home is a romantic or idealistic notion.

Lady Rhondda Contends That Women of Leisure Are "Menace"

G. K. Chesterton Opposes Her in Public Debate at Kingsway Hall on This Thorny Subject, With George Bernard Shaw in the Chair

LONDON—The question "Is the Leisured Woman a Menace to Civilization?" the topic of the recent debate at Kingsway Hall between Viscountess Rhondda and G. K. Chesterton, with Bernard Shaw in the chair, had almost a Bolshevist flavor. Yet Lady Rhondda, who maintained the affirmative is a wealthy woman, owner of vast coal properties, with no Socialistic tendencies whatever; she is a peeress in her own right, only daughter of David Alfred Thomas, later Viscount Rhondda, who was given a peerage in recognition of his services as food controller during the war.

Viscount Rhondda left to his daughter not only his title but full possession, direction and control of his extensive properties, exactly

Christian Science Monitor, 8 March 1927.

as though she had been a son. She inherited not only his money but his directorships, his active place in the financial world. And she made a gallant and distinguished fight to take his seat in the House of Lords. Twice, however, it has been decided, after a long legal battle with counsel of the very highest rank on both sides, that no woman may sit in that august body.

Lady Rhondda's Objective

"Lady Rhondda is the terror of the House of Lords," said Bernard Shaw, in introducing her on this occasion. "She is a peeress in her own right. She is also an extremely capable woman of business, and the House of Lords has risen up and said, 'If Lady Rhondda comes in here, we go away!' They feel there would be such a show-up of the general business ignorance and imbecility of the male sex as never was before."

No, it was not radicalism that led Lady Rhondda to attack the idle women of her own class, it was feminism. She is a feminist, heart and soul, consistent to the last degree. She owns and edits a weekly journal, *Time and Tide*, which in style and matter and in general interest holds its own with the other serious English weeklies. It is in no sense a propaganda organ, and yet it never misses a chance to set forth, explain and uphold the feminist position on every issue which arises.

Now *Time and Tide* had published during the fall a series of challenging articles, signed "Candida," to show up the English woman of leisure, to reveal that despite her new citizenship and all the modern liberating tendencies, she is still leading an empty, idle life, a burden to herself and a danger to society. "Being a wife and mother in these days of labor-saving devices and small families is no longer a full-time job," said Candida.

A Critic Shocked

Among Candida's critics, the most celebrated and the most shocked was the brilliant G. K. Chesterton. He could not bear that anyone should call the sacred privilege of motherhood a job, and then, accepting the terminology he declared, "If it is not a full-time job it is because it is not being done." Having drawn such distin-guished fire, Candida revealed her identity as Lady Rhondda herself, and challenged Chesterton to debate the question. Chesterton ac-cepted, Shaw was induced to take the chair, radiocasting rights were disposed of at a good figure, and the house sold out three weeks in advance.

Now this debate, of course, was not a debate in any real sense, since, as Bernard Shaw pointed out in his summing-up, "both of the controversialists stuck closely to Robert Owen's famous precept, 'Never argue; repeat your assertion.' "

It soon became, as most discussions concerning women do become, a statement for and against that time-honored proposition: "Woman's place is the home." And it was of unusual interest because of the totally new light in which G. K. Chesterton put that ancient saying.

Chesterton detests modern civilization. For him it is the lowest form of slavery. He looks upon the home as a little island of individuality in a vast sea of dullness. "Home," he said, "is the only place where there is any liberty left, any chance for creative imagina-tion, any room for the development of personality." It is the greatest fallacy to think, as Lady Rhondda seems to think, that you are serving the community if you go out of the home. She seems to think the leisured woman will step out of her suburban home into Utopia. But what is actually offered? She can go and serve a joint stock company and help swindle the community. Or she can go to work for a patent food concern and poison the public. Or she can sell her services to a newspaper and spend her time writing lies for some millionaire, thereby mystifying, betraying and deceiving the people.

A Man's Idea of Home

According to Chesterton the only place where a man can call his soul his own in modern capitalist society is in that "self-willed, self-chosen group of the home. A man can have some fun in his home. He can do as he likes, say what he likes, even think as he likes. Why should women want to get out of it into the slavery of the commercial world?"

Chesterton's idealized picture of the home is what most people want in their lives. "Home is a place to come back to when you don't want to be any where else," says one of the younger novelists. Home is an escape, a safe retreat, an oasis of comfort and ease always waiting for you, in which you rest and relax and restore your egotism for another struggle with the world. Has it ever occurred to Chesterton, or to any other man, I wonder, that for women there is no such thing as home in this sense?

For the person who stays in it, whose business it is to "keep it," who is responsible for every detail of its comfort, whose struggle with the world it represents, the home can be no "island of liberty," no oasis of comfort and relaxation. That is why home-keeping women want to go out in the evening and business men want to stay in. The feminist does not want to abolish the home. She wants to find a man who will share the burden and joy of home-making as she would like to share the burden and joy of earning the living. "Home for women too" might be the new feminist slogan.

Personalities and Powers: Anna Wickham

Anna Wickham is a poet born of conflict, as perhaps all poets are. In "The Singer" she writes:

"If I had peace to sit and sing,
Then I could make a lovely thing.
But I am stung with goads and whips,
So I build songs like iron ships.
Let it be something for my song,
If it is sometimes swift and strong."

Time and Tide, 15 February 1924.

And much of her verse is swift and strong; much of it is tender, too, with that honest, daring tenderness so characteristic of the unsentimental modern woman.

Born in England of an Irish-Italian mother and an English father who was a musician, Anna Wickham was brought up in Australia. Most women artists start with a heavy domestic handicap and win through to their art only by fighting family tradition and prejudice. With Anna Wickham the story begins at the other end. "I was brought up to be an artist," she says. "I began to write poetry when I was nine to amuse my father, the way you would sing to a child. But music was my father's ambition for me. I could sing, and I was a great, tall girl of powerful build—the opera seemed to be my destiny."

At twenty she came to Europe to study with Jean de Reszke, and in a few months had become a pupil of great promise. Then came love, marriage into a conventional English family, motherhood, to all of which she abandoned herself with a sort of reckless passion, completely forsaking her operatic career and trying to forget her father's hopes. "But," to quote her own telling, "all those years when I was trying so hard to be a good wife and mother and a perfect housekeeper, my father was worrying at me to be an artist. I loved my boys, but my father was not interested; in every letter he was nagging at me to get to work. I suppose he kept the spark alive, for I knew no artists in those days."

Back in 1913, in those post-Edwardian times before the war, Anna Wickham, sitting safe behind her suburban hedges, happened to read an article in the *Poetry Review* to the effect that men have expressed women emotionally better than they could possibly express themselves. This was a challenge. As a foreword to her first volume of verse, "The Contemplative Quarry," she wrote:—

"Here is no sacramental *I*.
Here are more I's than yet were in one human.
Here I reveal our common mystery—
I give you 'Woman.'
Let it be known for our old world's relief,
I give you woman—and my method's brief."

Charlotte Perkins Gilman has written some clever feminist verse, but it is too intellectual, too sure. She is a better economist than artist. Anna Wickham senses, as an artist would, that the revolt of woman is not against her economic handicap alone, but against herself. The modern woman, longing as much as ever to be mastered emotionally, physically, yet determined to keep her mind free, striving to lose herself and yet not lose herself—it is for her that Anna Wickham has spoken with such vigour and sincerity. Read "The Wife," "The Pioneer," "Retrospect," "The Mother-in-Law," "After Annunciation," "The Angry Woman," "Meditation at Kew." Read her love poems too—frank and passionate enough, yet delightfully humorous sometimes.

Fine as many of these "woman" poems are, they are not her best. Who would say whether a man or woman had written "Choice," which is probably the finest thing in her first volume?

"No sleepy poison is more strong to kill
Than jaded, weak, and vacillating will.
God send us power to make decision
With muscular, clean, fierce precision.
In life and song
Give us the right to dare to be wrong
Who feared we were not right.
Regenerating days begin when I who made no choice choose
      even sin."

A poet's life-story is revealed so clearly in his verse, one may be forgiven for reading it. In "The Fresh Start" we can see that, once Anna Wickham had begun to write, the "perfect home" was abandoned with the same intensity with which it had been embraced.

THE FRESH START

"O give me back my rigorous English Sunday
And my well-ordered house with stockings washed on Monday.
Let the House-Lord, that kindly decorous fellow,

Leave happily for his law at ten, with a well-furled umbrella.
Let my young sons observe my strict house-rules,
Imbibing Tory principles at Tory schools.

Two years now have I sat beneath a curse,
And in a fury poured out frenzied verse,
Such verse as held no beauty and no good,
And was at best new curious vermin food.

My dog is rabid and my cat is lean,
And not a pot in all this place is clean.
The locks have fallen from my hingeless doors,
And holes are in my credit and my floors.

There is no solace for me, but in sooth
To have said baldly certain ugly truth.
Such scavenger's work was never yet a woman's,
My wardrobe's more a scarecrow's than a human's.

I'm off to the House-Goddess for her gift.
'O give me Circumspection, Temperance, Thrift;
Take thou this lust of words, this fevered itching,
And give me faith in darning, joy of stitching!'

When this hot blood is cooled by kindly Time,
Controlled and schooled I'll come again to Rhyme.
Sure of my methods, morals, and my gloves,
I'll write chaste sonnets of imagined loves."

Sometimes I think that the reason why women have not distinguished themselves more in creative art is not because they bear
children, but because they keep house. Who ever heard of a male
poet who had to keep house for a family? It is almost unthinkable.
Born in him along with the creative instinct is an imperious helplessness with regard to the details of food, clothing and shelter, which
acts as a sort of protective colouring to his genius. With shrewd,

instinctive wisdom he cherishes and cultivates this helplessness, knowing that it is far better for him to perish than to assume perplexing responsibilities such as the simplest housekeeping entails. But he does not perish—all his life long some woman looks after him.

A poet without a wife, that's what Anna Wickham is and as such bound to be a somewhat tragic figure. With someone to create the right background she would be a very celebrated personality as well as a writer of excellent verse. For she has a brilliant, challenging mind. Words never fail her, exciting, unusual words. She is a lover of talk and very gifted and original at it. And she is beautiful in her strange way. If the Amazons had born sons, we could call Anna Wickham the "Amazon Mother." She is six feet tall, broad-shouldered and lumbering, with a massive, noble head, brown eyes that are wide apart and droop a little at the corners, and the wistful, heart-taking smile of a young boy just past the awkward age. Her conversation is witty, shrewd, surprising. She smokes incessantly, and will talk all night or as late as she can get anybody to sit up.

She is a rare creature, and if, as I say, there was a loving wife to smooth out the background and keep the poet at her best, Anna Wickham would be the centre of a great admiring circle of men and women (boys and girls too, for she has a great way with children) who would stimulate her genius and be stimulated in their turn. Who was it who said that the tragic thing about women was that they could not have wives?

Caroline Haslett and the Women Engineers

One late winter afternoon, fifteen or twenty years ago, I was coming down in the elevator of the United Charities Building at Twenty-third street after a dull, disappointing day's work. At the floor below mine a handsome, gorgeously dressed woman stepped in; she was wearing a huge bunch of violets, single violets and extraordinarily beautiful, the biggest bunch I had ever seen. I fastened my eyes on them and stood frankly "drinking them in" as one would look at a cathedral or a sunset trying to remember it forever. Suddenly, just before we reached the ground floor, the woman took them off and handed them to me with one swift eager gesture and a look of understanding, and then dashed off into the night.

It was a similar experience when Caroline Haslett smiled at me so unexpectedly from the platform.

I had gone to a small branch meeting of the Women's Freedom League because I saw that Miss Haslett, secretary of the Women's Engineering Society, was to speak, and I had always wanted to meet her. There was a row of speakers, six or seven perhaps, but I knew which was Miss Haslett at one glance. Yet she did not look in the least as I had expected a woman engineer to look. She is young, of course, not more than thirty, a big broad-built girl with a wide serene face, like a poet's dream of a peasant woman. Her hat was off (must I after all devote my remaining years to a campaign for "hats off indoors" in the name of beauty, sincerity and freedom?). Her hat was off and her long dark hair was parted in the middle and worn in flat rings over her ears. Big mouth, strong nose, shining eyes, a grave and lovely face. Maternal, too, I thought, in that rich universal way in which some women's faces are maternal—suggesting strength, security, happiness and saying "Take all you want—I am inexhaustible."

There it was again, rare unexpected beauty, and I sat feasting my eyes and trying to think of adequate adjectives as one might if suddenly faced with a wide happy view of hills and meadows. I was only half listening to the speeches and I must have showed my pleasure frankly in my face, for all of a sudden the girl smiled at me, an easy, friendly, humorous smile as though she said, "All right, here I am, if you like me so much!" And then I remembered that woman in the elevator so many years ago, whose smile had said, "Here, you love these violets, you're thirsty for them—they're yours."

I suppose that is a very sentimental way in which to open an article on British women and the engineering trades, but I am going to risk it. I can see no point in writing, certainly no *fun* in writing, unless you try to describe the things that really happen to you.

Next day, over a long lunch at her club, Caroline Haslett told me her story and the story of the society to which she has given the last seven years of her life. She is not difficult to interview as so many English women are—shy, reserved, fighting you off all the time. She seemed more like a radiant California girl, except for her deep, musical voice, and she pours herself out to you in a rich careless stream, eager, confident, trusting. She likes to talk and it is a good story she has to tell.

"Are you really an engineer?" was almost the only question I had to ask.

"No, I'm not an engineer and I never say I am. I'll tell you how I began, if you like. I began by being a failure. I was never bright at lessons. Sometimes they thought I was mentally deficient! And when I finished the ordinary school nobody knew what to do with me. We were not well off. My father was an engineer but not a man that cared about getting on in the world. He never could see any reason for making money; all he wanted was to live a quiet life in the country. There were four of us children. So I had to do something. First I thought I would be a teacher because the training school for teachers was in another village quite a distance from our house, and I knew I would have to take the train every day. That was what I wanted, to get away from home. So I got the local teacher to coach me and to everybody's surprise I passed the entrance examination. The first year I did brilliantly. The second year I did nothing, I dropped to the bottom of the form. You see, I was terribly in love but they didn't know it. I was only seventeen then. Anyhow they did not want me there any more. So I was at home again. Just about this time I became a suffragette and fell out with the young man over that. Then I was ill for a while, and after that I just seemed to be settling down to nothing. My mother, who was a very energetic, able woman and ran most of the committees in the village, was in despair over me. She gave me up and was thinking there was nothing for me to do but sit home and crochet. I was just a failure. Everybody thought so. So did I.

"Then one day a friend of my father's, an engineer, a man who made boilers for ships, came to visit us. He saw me and he must have liked me. He said to my mother, 'I don't think there is much wrong with that girl. She has a brain. She only wants waking up. She needs to find something she likes to do. I believe I'd like to take her into my office.' So that was how I began my engineering career."

"But, didn't you ever study engineering?"

"No, I never studied, not even in a night school. But I had some great training and I would have gone on and qualified if this job had not come along. You see, soon after I went to work for that man the war came. And before long all the responsible heads in the concern had to go. I understood things by that time, they knew I was intelligent and reliable, and they began to leave things to me. In the end I was left with all sorts of big contracts to handle. Afterwards I made them give me four months in the shops to get practical experience. It was all right while the war lasted but when the men came back and took up their old positions again, they gradually took my work away from me. I found myself only a sort of super-clerk or secretary. When I asked for a better job they would laugh and tell me I'd soon be getting married. But I was serious. I meant to leave and try to get into a firm where there was more opportunity.

"Just then I happened to hear that someone was advertising for a secretary to organize a Woman's Engineering Society. It was Lady Parsons, the wife of Sir Charles Parsons, a famous engineer. I was interested in the idea, of course, but I applied for the post without thinking or caring much about it. I was twenty-three then. There were sixty-odd applicants, all of them older and many with university degrees, but for some reason Lady Parsons chose me."

It was a wise choice. Caroline Haslett has turned out to be a true child of her energetic organizing mother. I think she is the sort of "secretary" we know so well in America, whose title should be "promoter-executive-editor-organizer-publicity-man" and who needs a committee only to hold her down. At any rate the Women's Engineering Society, which began in 1919 with twelve qualified members, has grown and flourished in her eager and capable hands. There are several hundred members now, they have held three successful conferences, the last one at Wembley with audiences of over a thousand; they publish a competent and dignified illustrated quarterly with highly technical and scientific articles by women engineers, and, most important of all, they have gained admission for women to all the engineering societies.

Miss Haslett explained the significance of this last achievement.

"It was not difficult for a woman to get her engineering education nor to get her degree. But the B. S. C. is not enough. Every branch of engineering has its own society, mechanical engineers, marine engineers, civil, electrical, automobile, etc. And professional standing requires membership in one of these societies and the right to print its initials after one's name. When we began none of the societies except the Electrical Engineers were open to women. Almost the first thing I did was to write to all these societies and ask them if they would be willing to admit women who duly qualified for membership. None of them was willing. My next move was to invite each society to send a representative to sit on our Council. This they all agreed to do, and they have done it every year. I've tried from the beginning to get the cooperation of men engineers because I thought by advising and helping us they would get interested in us and want us to succeed. This plan worked well; after about two years all the societies let down the bars and opened their doors to women. Of course the qualifications are high and the examination is stiff; they probably scrutinize the women applicants harder than the men. That would be natural. But women do get in.

"The hardest problem now is for women to get their shop experience. One of the qualifications for admission is always shop experience, and there are very few firms that will take on women students into their shops, only two or three in the entire country. But that will come. Everything would be easier if we were not in the midst of a trade depression. Given a boom in industry there would be a great chance for the woman engineer."

Another organization quite recently formed in England to which the Women's Engineering Society acts as a sort of parent and of which Miss Haslett is also secretary, is the Women's Electrical Association. It was established in order to teach women, especially home-makers, the possibilities of electricity in reducing drudgery, and not only this, but to teach them the elementary facts about electricity so that they can make their own ordinary repairs. This association is growing faster than even Miss Haslett expected. She is in constant demand to come and establish branches.

"Home making," she says, "is the oldest industry in the world, it is a skilled job if ever there was one, but it has never had good tools. During the war women got a chance to see how differently industry is organized, how the whole emphasis is on eliminating drudgery, eliminating fatigue, and always on perfecting tools. Women engineers, while I want them to go into all lines of work, will perhaps, make their first big contribution by bringing this emphasis into the work of the home."

Miss Haslett spoke most appreciatively of the women engineers in America. At all their conferences American representatives had spoken, and as early as 1924, three outstanding American women had joined the Women's Engineering Society: Mrs. McBerty, Dr. Lillian Gilbreth, and Kate Gleason representing respectively the electrical, industrial and mechanical aspects of engineering. Other American members are Ethel H. Bailey of New York, Society of Automotive Engineers; Florence M. Paley, civil engineer on the staff of the Nickel Plate Railroad; and Mary Dillon of the Brooklyn Gas Company.

"American women engineers," according to Miss Haslett, "have little opposition to meet. They are admitted to all engineering institutes and societies, but nevertheless, they feel the need of an organization to take care of those special questions which naturally present themselves to women entering a new profession." And so, since they have no society of their own, Miss Haslett invites them to join the British Women's Engineering Society. It is what one would expect of a secretary who asked all the men engineering societies, which had refused admission to women, to send representatives to sit on her council.

We need more Feminists like Caroline Haslett.

Who Is Dora Black?

"I admit I should not like to have become Mr. Dora Black," was Bertrand Russell's quick response to the Lucy Stone challenge with which I began the conversation. I had come to ask Mrs. Russell why, in publishing her little book, "Hypatia, or Women and Knowledge" (described by the Manchester *Guardian* as a "passionate vindication of the rights of women," and enthusiastically reviewed by Ruby Black in our own EQUAL RIGHTS), she had seen fit to adopt the manner of an early Victorian "authoress" and sign herself "Mrs. Bertrand Russell."

I had not expected to interview Mr. Russell too, but there we were in his study, and there did not seem to be any place for him to go. So he graciously stayed and helped us on with our interview. On the whole, I was glad. There is comfort in discussing new and startling ideas with a philosopher who is capable of honest thinking at a moment's notice, even though his personal life may be as much controlled by convention, tradition and prejudice as the lives of most of us are. And in England it is a new and startling idea that a woman might keep her own name after marriage.

"To tell the truth," Mr. Russell went on, "it never occurred to us that Dora might keep her own name when we were married. We made no decision about it because we never thought about it."

"No," broke in Dora, "I certainly never thought of it. I was thinking about the children. You see, their father's name is a very distinguished one with great traditions behind it. It would not seem right to deprive John of all that it might mean to him to be a Russell."

"It seems to me," said the philosopher, taking up this thought, "if you are going to make so much of this matter of names you must go to the bottom of it. It is the child's name that counts. That should concern us much more than the wife's name. For it is by the passing on of the name that the family tradition is carried on, and that is important to the race. Great names, great family traditions must not be lost."

"Very well, then," said I. "Agreed. But there are just as many girls born to distinguished families as boys. Why should the name be lost when the daughter of a distinguished family marries a man of an obscure family? Let the children bear whichever name means the most. But why force the undistinguished father or mother to become still further undistinguished by also assuming that name?"

There is no doubt that I am the world's worst interviewer. I go with the sincere intention of sitting quietly, pencil in hand, and speaking only to "draw out" the famous man or the celebrated lady, as the case may be. But the affair always ends in a free-for-all discussion, a search for essential truth and justice, during which I become quite as much interested in what I say to the victim as in what he or she says to me.

Bertrand Russell, as all reading America knows, has a right to be proud of his name in respect of his own achievements. He is, I believe, a very great mathematician. But he is also a profound thinker on human affairs, and unlike so many important thinkers, he can write. His thoughts do not have to be dug up for general consumption out of long, badly constructed books full of highly technical terms. They reach us in small, clearly constructed books, and in English that is not only beautifully simple but often poetic.

Perhaps it is not quite so well known in America that Bertrand Russell comes of a famous line. He is a grandson of Lord John Russell, who introduced the Reform Bill of 1832, and became a great Whig leader. He was prime minister several times and was a power in public life until well on in the 'sixties. In recognition of his distinguished services to the country Lord Russell was made an earl. When the present Earl Russell dies, Bertrand Russell (his brother) will succeed to the title, with all that that means in English society.

And who is Dora Black? When I came to England in 1919 I met her at Cambridge—a slender, vivacious, dark-eyed girl with the reputation for being brilliant and unusual. She was then considering, I remember, whether she should go on with the scholastic career, which seemed to be opening up for her, or abandon it and try to make her living as an actress. A short time after this she became Bertrand Russell's secretary, then his wife, and the mother of his two children. Mrs. Russell is 31 years old now, and seems to have given up all thoughts of the stage and of the scholar's life in which she had made so fine a beginning. However, she has by no means retired into obscurity. Although her children are but two and four she has found time to stand for Parliament; she is the secretary and active leader of the Workers' Birth Control Group which is doing such splendid work in forcing this issue on the attention of the Labour Party; and she has begun to write books.

So there you have it: a spirited young woman of great promise marries an older man of many achievements and considerable fame. Shall she struggle on as "Dora Black" until she has won a hearing for herself on her own merits and such distinction as her achievements entitle her to? Or shall she make the most of her husband's name?

What would Lucy Stone say?

Mrs. Russell's explanation about "Hypatia" was very frank. "I wanted to publish the book as 'Dora Russell,' " she said. "But the publisher persuaded me to allow him to put 'Mrs. Bertrand Russell' in parentheses under my name on the title page. He said it would add two thousand to the sales, and the thing I cared most about was to get the book read, to make my ideas known, and besides we needed the money. Our only income is from our writing. So I agreed. You see, I used to write a good deal, but I could not get any paper to print what I wrote when I was Dora Black."

As a matter of fact in the English edition "Mrs. Bertrand Russell" appears twice on the jacket and twice on the cover without any parentheses and with no hint of "Dora." But this Mrs. Russell did not intend.

I stand somewhere between Shakespeare and Ruth Hale on this matter of names. Symbols are vastly important, and certainly this taking your husband's name is one of the most devastating symbols of "subjection" that remain. And yet I don't think keeping your own name is the ultimate test of a Feminist. I don't feel like walking out of a woman's house because she has not done it. I wanted to know some more about Mrs. Russell.

She was one of four children, she told me, in a lower middle-class English family. There were three girls and one boy and very little money. The father, unlike many British fathers treated his boy and his girls alike in the matter of education. He said to Dora when the time came, "I'm not going to make a fine lady of you. I'll spend what money there is on schooling." She was sent to a good grammar school and did not really want to go to the university. She had wanted to be an actress from the time she was four years old. But she happened to win a scholarship and so she went to Cambridge almost by chance. The rest of the story we know.

"What phase of Feminism interests you most, Mrs. Russell?" I asked.

"Working-class Feminism," she answered promptly. "I am especially interested in the lives of married women in the working-class. And I think the freedom of women will be very unstable until the position of these working-class wives and mothers is improved. Today they are like slaves. They need, first of all, to know how to limit their families. That is why we founded the Workers' Birth Control Group. But that isn't all. They need, terribly, ante-natal and post-natal care. Bearing children for working-class mothers in England today is four times as dangerous as coal mining. I could show you the figures. Well, then, there is motherhood endowment. They must have that so that if they want to stay home and take care of their children they can."

"But isn't it also part of the married woman's battle to get rid of all these increasing restrictions against her holding various jobs outside the home?" I asked.

"Yes, yes, I am heart and soul against putting any restrictions on the right of married women to work. And I was so glad to see the generous way in which the single women at the last Labour Women's Conference stood up for this right. It was splendid to see single women get up on the floor and defend the married woman's right to hold her job. The old spinsterish attitude is dying out.

"But there is another thing I want to say. Feminists have emphasized for a long time the importance of each woman's individual entity and the necessity of economic independence. Perhaps it was necessary. But now I think we need some emphasis on the instinctive side of life, sex and motherhood. I am writing another book now called 'The Right to be Happy,' and trying to say what I mean. Life isn't all earning your living. Unfortunately we fall in love and Feminism must take that into consideration."

If I have seemed at times ungracious in this interview it is because I am ignorant of the art of interviewing. There is much that I admire in Mrs. Bertrand Russell: a little young, a little inconsistent, a little sure of herself perhaps, but very, very genuine, and so rich in energy, initiative, and confidence that she is bound to do great service for women. Incidentally, I think, if England had had a Lucy Stone League she might still be Dora Black.

Lindbergh's Mother

I saw with joy that my favourite morning paper had nine columns on Charles Lindbergh's one-man flight across the lonely wide Atlantic. Eagerly my eyes raced through those columns, eating up the words in a passion of admiration and excitement. As I read on my heart beat faster, my skin was tingling with delight, tears came into my eyes. I wanted to write a poem, I wanted to sing, I wanted to shout— "Glory! Glory!! Glory to the human race!!!"

Then I came to the wireless telephone conversation with Lindbergh's mother in Detroit. How enterprising these newspaper people are, I thought. Not content with recording the first non-stop flight from New York to Paris, they have to "jazz up" the story with a 4,000 mile telephone conversation! Alas, however, this reporter's enterprise was entirely exhausted in having the idea of talking to Mrs. Lindbergh; there was none left for the interview.

These copiously reported cross-Atlantic telephone conversations have, so far, been just about as interesting as communications with the spirit world. When, in the course of a spiritualistic seance, a group of yearning humans do at last get in touch with the spirit of some great man, the most he has to say to them is, "I left that rusty saw you are looking for under a box behind the wood-shed door," or something equally stimulating.

Mrs. Lindbergh did no better. But who can blame her? A dull reporter cannot get a good interview, whether the celebrity to be questioned is a spirit of another world or the mother of a hero 4,000 miles away. All this man could think of to ask Mrs. Lindbergh, when she answered his London call, was what she would give her son to eat when he came home.

"His favourite pudding?" he brilliantly suggested.

"No, not pudding—pie," Mrs. Lindbergh genially played up, being an American.

Time and Tide, 27 May 1927.

That was the high-point of the interview. One was left with the impression that Mrs. Lindbergh is a hearty good soul, sitting with hands folded until it is time to make that pie.

And what is the truth about Mrs. Lindbergh? I find it on an inside page of the same paper.

> "Charles Lindbergh's father, who was a former member of the United States Congress, died on May 24, 1924. The family was not well off, and Mrs. Evangeline Lindbergh, his mother, *was forced to take a position* as school teacher at Detroit, Michigan, where she now has a chemistry class in a high school" (*Italics mine.*)

Now, Detroit is one of those marvel cities of the middle west, with a population of a million or two. It is beautiful, clean, modern, aspiring. Its high schools would be, each one, a triumph of architectural design and practical construction, with science laboratories equipped to the last degree. Evangeline Lindbergh has specialised in chemistry, no doubt, and now, in one of the perfect laboratories of one of these beautiful schools, she has the privilege of revealing the simpler mysteries of chemistry to boys and girls of seventeen to twenty who are preparing for the universities. This is her work, for which she is no doubt paid an excellent salary.

But, in the opinion of the Press, the fact that Lindbergh's mother teaches chemistry for a living, is a family misfortune—almost a disgrace—a matter for low-voiced regret to be mentioned on an inside page along with the fact that his father is dead.

Just a hint of shadow in the hero's triumph—his mother works, she teaches school. But surely now with all his prizes and rewards he can lift her from that humiliating position and establish her permanently in a rocking-chair at home? Surely from now on Lindbergh's mother will have no work more arduous than to tell some other woman what kind of a pie to make for his dinner?

Mrs. Pankhurst Comes Back as Candidate for Parliament

Lady Rhondda, at Six-Point Dinner, Urged Militant Leader to Resume Political Life, While Lady Astor Offered to Resign

LONDON, April 13—The chief topic of conversation among feminists in London just now is the return of Mrs. Pankhurst and her probable candidacy for Parliament. It is seven years since the famous militant leader left England, and almost 12 years since she gave up the suffrage battle, and on the eve of victory offered her services and those of her organization, in so far as she could control it, to the British Government in the Great War.

In 1903, as some suffragists will remember, Mrs. Pankhurst, widow of a distinguished Manchester lawyer, with her daughter Christabel, organized the Women's Social and Political Union, dedicated to "deeds not words," and set out to make votes for women, which had been for 50 years a matter for discussion and polite agitation, a fact in Great Britain. The campaign of the "militants" which followed challenged the attention of the world. It has been called, with some reason, "the most remarkable fight in the fighting history of the world." And Emmeline Pankhurst, heroic and determined leader of that fight, has her place secure in the history of progress.

But can a leader, no matter how great, "come back" after so long and complete a break with her followers? Is Mrs. Pankhurst, who has endured 10 or 15 extreme hunger strikes in the course of her amazing contest with the British Government, still able to face a political campaign? These questions and others were in my mind when I decided to attend the dinner of welcome given by the Six-

Christian Science Monitor, 14 April 1926.

Point Group at the Hyde Park Hotel, at which I knew Mrs. Pankhurst's parliamentary candidacy was to be proposed.

The Six-Point Group

The Six-Point Group (so named for its six immediate demands) is a feminist society organized since the war, of which Viscountess Rhondda is the founder and active head. Lady Rhondda was herself a militant and served her time in prison. She has always been a stanch admirer of Mrs. Pankhurst and I have no doubt it was her idea to bring Mrs. Pankhurst back to London and persuade her to stand for Parliament. The women's program of freedom is by no means achieved in England. Even the suffrage is a halfway measure which denies the vote to all women under 30 and to thousands of single women over 30 who are not house-holders. To remove this and many other obstacles to women's equality which still stand in the British law, strong women are needed in Parliament, and, in Lady Rhondda's opinion, no woman could be so useful there as Mrs. Pankhurst.

And so the Six-Point dinner was arranged not only as a tribute to Mrs. Pankhurst's past great achievement but in order to claim her for the future. Lady Rhondda herself presided and proposed the toast of Mrs. Pankhurst.

"I wonder what Mrs. Pankhurst is going to do for us in the future," she said after some gracious and amusing references to the militant past, "I should like to ask her a straight question. I should like to ask her why she does not go into Parliament."

Lady Astor Offers to Resign

Mrs. Philip Snowden and Mrs. Drummon followed in the same vein. But it was Lady Astor, hurrying over from the House of Commons to speak, who made the occasion dramatic. "I have only come to pay my humble tribute to Mrs. Pankhurst," she began, looking very young and earnest in her severe black suit and effective close-fitting black hat in contrast to all the women in evening gowns. "Of course her place is in the House of Commons. There must be no rest for any of us until we get her there. I first saw Mrs. Pankhurst when she came to Plymouth to make a recruiting speech at the beginning of the war. I heard her put the case for war better than any man could put it. Now the war is over. Let her put the case for humanity. We need her in Parliament, and there is no sacrifice I am not prepared to make to see that she comes in. I would gladly resign my seat tomorrow if she saw her way to take it."

When Mrs. Pankhurst rose to respond to these tributes and answer Lady Rhondda's question, it seemed to me that she had not changed. She is the same slight, gentle, intensely quiet woman, with soft waving grey hair and a low singing voice, which some 15 years ago stirred vast audiences in America to sympathy for the militant's cause. That must have been in 1910 or 1911. She speaks with the greatest possible simplicity, almost with the naïve charm of a young girl making her first speech. That is one of her special gifts as an orator.

Mrs. Pankhurst Accepts

Mrs. Pankhurst referred to her long absence, and said how much she had learned, and what a privilege she felt it to be a citizen of the great British Empire. Replying to Lady Rhondda's question, she said she felt deeply moved that so many friends thought her worthy to take a place in the Mother of Parliaments. Her answer was—to quote her own words which might well have been the words of a missionary in accepting a distant and dangerous post: "If you want me there, if you think I can serve, if you think I can help, then, hard as the work is, I will go there if I am sent."

Then, turning to Lady Astor, she went on, "But, touched as I am by Lady Astor's offer to give me her seat, I must decline. Because if I go to Parliament I must fight for my own seat—with your help."

Mrs. Pankhurst herself and the proposal to put her in Parliament were received with great enthusiasm by the 200 or 300 women (ex-militants most of them) who had gathered to do her honor. But there are at least two large sections of British feminists who will not look upon any proposal concerning Mrs. Pankhurst with enthusiasm: first, those who belonged to the "constitutional" wing of the suffrage movement and still regard the Pankhursts and all their works with horror; and, second, the vast following of younger militants of radical and labor, or pacifist leanings who have not forgotten what happened in 1914.

Possible Opposition

According to these young women, Mrs. Pankhurst turned their beloved Women's Social and Political Union, for which they were ready to give their all, into a war organization, over night; she offered the services of this rebel society to the British Government, without so much as a notice to the members, and this while a score or two of those members were lying in jail!

However, the British are a sentimental race, much given to forgiving their leaders and forgetting past disputes and disappointments. These feminists, even though they are critical of her, recognize Mrs. Pankhurst's greatness. Most of them realize that they owe their present suffrage more to Mrs. Pankhurst than to any other one person. If she has come back to give herself once more to their battles, if she has come back to help them win the vote for women under 30, the right of married women to work, equal pay and equal opportunity in industry, the professions, and the civil service, etc., and if her singular power to inspire devotion is unimpaired, as I think it is, they will follow her.

Even without such a following, Mrs. Pankhurst can easily become a member of Parliament. The Conservatives, it is rumored, are by no means unwilling to give her a constituency at the first opportunity. And as we have seen, she has the whole-hearted backing of two feminist leaders of wealth and distinction. With Lady Astor and Lady Rhondda to campaign for her, and a hopeful constituency, there is little question but that Mrs. Pankhurst will be returned to Parliament.

A FEMINIST CONCEPTION OF CRIMINAL LAW

Protection of Children

Measured in terms of lost youth and forgotten happiness, there is perhaps no crime more devastating than the crime of child-assault. Yet in actual practice, as was brought out by Mr. Briant during the debate on the Home Office Vote in the House, "the penalties imposed would be ridiculous if they were not tragic in their leniency."

Mr. Briant cited case after case to prove his point.

"In a case of indecent assault on a child of nine the penalty was four months' imprisonment. About the same time a man received five months' imprisonment for hanging a Pekingese dog. In another case of assult on a child of six there was a sentence of one month's imprisonment, in another on a child of seven, in which the man who was convicted gave as a reason that the child had given him any amount of encouragement, the total penalty was a fine of £3 . . . There is a case of a child of seven in which the man was only bound

Time and Tide, 20 July 1923.

over. In another case, in which the child is or was about to become a mother, the sentence was one week's imprisonment."

In his moving plea for more adequate penalties Mr. Briant was ably supported by Lady Astor and Mrs. Wintringham. Lady Astor recalled a case of a magistrate personally known to her who on the same day sentenced one man to two years' imprisonment for some small theft and another to six weeks' imprisonment for assaulting a little girl of seven. Mrs. Wintringham called attention to the fact that the men who commit these offences usually commit them again and again, being repeatedly sent to prison, and released, only to assault some other child. She urged that such cases be looked upon as mental degenerates and treated as such.

> "I would ask the Home Secretary to appoint a Committee consisting of medical men and representative women and lawyers who have knowledge of crime that could inquire into this question with a view to setting up machinery, such as that which is working with such extraordinary success, although it is only in its early stages, in Birmingham and in Essex, which would bring about the examination from the psychological and scientific point of view of the men who commit these offences. Such machinery with proper medical inspection would give us more scientific knowledge than we have at present and would lead to the treating of these men as moral degenerates rather than as ordinary persons."

Certainly if committing an assault on a child of tender years is a crime at all it is a crime that demands a grave penalty. If on the other hand it is the act of a moral pervert, of a man who cannot be said to be responsible for his actions, then the State has a right to detain that man, to put him under scientific observation and keep him from roaming at large as a menace to childhood.

Yet it can be argued that in cases of this kind where the evidence is of a delicate nature and difficult to get at because of the youth of the victim, convictions must always be rare, however much we may improve our method of dealing with the criminals. The truth is that a case of child-assult once committed is no easy thing to handle, either from the point of view of the child or the accused. The only sure and immediate remedy is prevention. And here the importance of having an adequate force of well-trained women police can hardly be over estimated. This was not lost sight of in the debate. Lady Astor sketched the history of the women's police force from its small beginning in 1914 up to 1918–1919 when London had a properly organized women's Police Patrol of something like a hundred women. In 1920 their work was investigated by a Departmental Committee, of which Lady Astor was a member. Though they had no power of arrest it was learned that

> "nearly 2,000 persons were cautioned by these women police for acts of indecency in parks and public places. There were nearly 3,000 persons cautioned for unseemly behaviour in parks, and 2,700 young girls were cautioned for loitering in the streets, and advised as to the danger of doing so; 1,000 girls passed into homes and hospitals, and 6,400 respectable girls and women stranded at night were found shelter."

> "We had the evidence of Sir Nevil Macready, Sir Leonard Dunning, and chief constables and social workers, and the Committee unanimously reported that in thickly populated areas, where offences against the law relating to women and children are not infrequent, there was not only scope, but urgent need, for the employment of women police, and they also said that the women should be specially qualified, highly trained and well paid."

Yet on mere police evidence that their "utility was negligible" the Geddes Committee recommended that the Women Police be disbanded, and the force was reduced to twenty.

"The most alarming thing," Lady Astor went on, "is that there are practically no women patrolling at Hampstead Heath, Clapham, Wimbledon and Putney Commons, and yet it has been proved that this patrolling is the greatest preventative of criminal interference with children. It is almost better not to have parks unless you have them properly patrolled."

For £18,000 a year, Lady Astor declared, an efficient women police force for the whole of London could be maintained. £18,000 to save perhaps thousands of children from a blighting and never-to-be-forgotten horror, to relieve the mother's heart of its most constant fear—this seems little to ask of a Government which feels financially confident enough to remit £13,000,000 of the tax on beer.

Justice For the Prostitute—
Lady Astor's Bill

No more astounding relic of the subjection of women survives in western civilization than the status of the prostitute. In the United States for instance, where her trade is nominally illegal, it frequently happens that in case of detection, she alone is arrested and her "customer," the man who bought what she offered to sell, not only goes scot free and escapes all publicity, but has the money he paid to the prostitute refunded by the State. In connection with what other illegal vice is the seller alone penalized, and not the buyer?

In those countries of Europe, such as France for example, where the system of legalized prostitution still maintains, the prostitute "enjoys" a certain protection from the State, even encouragement in her trade, but at what a cost! She is registered, she must submit at frequent intervals to compulsory medical examination and treatment; she is marked, set apart by the State for one purpose only, caught in a net from which she can never escape. And under this system, too, the "buyer" comes and goes as he likes. Of all ugly, foolish, and cruelly unjust institutions designed by man for his own protection, the so-called system of "regulated vice" seems to a casual inquirer the worst.

For fifty years and more reformers have been active in the field of "morals" legislation, but today I believe,—certainly in England— there is a new note in this agitation, a feminist note. Women are beginning to demand as a first step *justice for the prostitute*. On July 9 last a bill was introduced in the House of Commons by Lady Astor for the "Repeal of the Solicitation Laws." A bill as simple and direct as Lady Astor herself, a bill as honest and daring as the feminist movement must always be.

In England, solicitation is not illegal nor is prostitution itself illegal. However, there are three provisions in the law under which prostitutes are arrested for solicitation, loitering, etc., and convicted on the evidence of the police officer alone. Thus in theory prostitution is not a criminal offense, but in practice here in England as everywhere else it is a *one-sided* crime; *i.e.,* it takes two to commit it but only one is penalized.

These solicitation laws which Lady Astor's bill would repeal provide as follows: (1) Every common prostitute wandering in the public streets or public highways or in any places of public resort and behaving in a riotous or indecent manner is liable to one month's imprisonment on police evidence only; (2) Every common prostitute or night-walker loitering or being in any thoroughfare or public place for the purpose of prostitution or solicitation to the annoyance of the inhabitants or passengers is liable to a penalty of 40 shillings or a term of one month; (3) Every common prostitute or night-walker loitering and importuning passengers for the purpose of prostitution is liable to be arrested by a constable without warrant and on summary conviction to be fined 40 shillings or to be imprisoned for 14 days.

The new bill, known as the Public Places (Order) Bill, would substitute for all the above these two clauses:

> "Every person who in any street or public place wilfully causes annoyance to any person by words or behaviour, shall be liable to a penalty not exceeding 40 shillings for each offense."
>
> "Any constable or other peace officer may arrest without warrant any person committing an offense against this act, provided that no person shall be taken into custody for such offense except upon complaint by or on behalf of the party aggrieved."

Lady Astor said in moving the bill, "Our present laws on street offenses go right in the teeth of British justice in two respects. First, they discriminate against one particular class of persons; and secondly they permit the conviction of a person for a grave offense on the evidence of one police officer alone, with no evidence as to whether annoyance has been caused, or how it has been caused." She made a plea that the prostitute should be given "what we want everyone to have, common justice in the eyes of the law."

Now everybody knows that a bill of such sweeping character is not brought to the stage of being introduced by a prominent member

without years of effort and study and organization. For the last two
years the drafting of this bill, the preliminary work connected with
it, and the creating of a body of public opinion behind it, has been
the chief work of the Association for Moral and Social Hygiene of
which Alison Neilans is secretary. She more than any one other person
is responsible for it.

Miss Neilans was a militant, who suffered three imprisonments,
and knew the hunger strike. Later she was an organizer for the
Woman's Freedom League, which she left to become secretary of the
A.M. and S.H., as it is called. This society was founded in 1870 by
Josephine Butler, a great woman of the last century who led the fight
against State regulation of prostitution throughout Europe. Unlike
some enthusiasts for social purity, Josephine Butler had a real feeling
for liberty and a passion for justice. Alison Neilans is her true
disciple.

I will quote a few paragraphs from a memorandum prepared by
Miss Neilans from which the reader may judge of the importance of
the new Street Bill, and get some conception of the strong intelligence
and clear purpose behind it:

"The object of our bill is to repeal the special laws against
'prostitutes,' and to substitute an equal law applicable to all persons
who annoy or molest others in the streets or public places, and to
provide that such persons shall be taken into custody only on
complaint by or on behalf of the person annoyed. * * * Most people
would agree that respectable men and women should not be convicted
on a charge of molesting or annoying persons of the opposite sex on
police evidence only, but they may think that known bad characters
should be convicted on police evidence. But 'annoyance' is annoyance,
whether the person who annoys us is of good or bad character. The
law is not concerned with people's moral character, but with what
they *do*.

"Moreover, the question of character and previous convictions is
not in order until the defendant is convicted of the offence of which
he is at the moment charged. This legal protection is, however, not
accorded to the prostitute; the very fact that she is charged as a
'known common prostitute' is in itself evidence as to character.

"We contend that there is no reason for special legislation

against alleged prostitutes. They should be subject to the same restrictions on their conduct in the streets as are applied to other people, but not to special restrictions. * * * The existing law against solicitation differentiates not only between men and women, but also between women and women, *e.g.,* three of the sections which our bill proposes to repeal do not refer to men nor even to all women, but only to 'common prostitutes.' And no statutory definition exists of the words 'common prostitute,' nor of the word 'prostitution.' (Yet if 'solicitation for immoral purposes' is to be made an offence, it is obvious that prostitution itself should be made an offence. It is totally illogical to make it a legal offence to solicit a person to an act when the act itself is not an offence.)

"Under the Vagrancy Act alleged 'common prostitutes' convicted of 'riotous or indecent behavior' are liable to one month's imprisonment on police evidence only. *'Riotous or indecent' behavior is, in practice, interpreted to mean mere solicitation.* The effect of repealing this clause is to put the common prostitute under the same laws as other people. There seems to be no reason why 'common prostitutes' should be especially forbidden to behave in a riotous or indecent manner. Such conduct should be an offence in all persons equally."

In another article, Alison Neilans has said: "The prostitute is the scapegoat for everyone's sins, and few people care whether she is justly treated or not. Good people have spent thousands of pounds in efforts to reform her, poets have written about her, essayists and orators have made her the subject of some of their most striking rhetoric; perhaps no class of people has been so much abused, and alternatively sentimentalized over as prostitutes have been *but one thing they have never yet had, and that is simple legal justice.*"

It would be hard to exaggerate the legal and social and feminist significance of Lady Astor's bill. *Time and Tide* says, in an editorial of July 17, "The Bill would if it were passed constitute on the legal side the biggest step forward which it is possible to take towards doing away with a recognized prostitute class." And I think this is no exaggeration.

ORGANIZING
AN INTERNATIONAL
SOCIALIST
FEMINIST FUTURE

Suffragists Ten Years After

Ten years ago I was a delegate to the Seventh Congress of the International Woman Suffrage Alliance at Budapest. The Ninth Congress of the same organization, held in Rome this May, resembled the one held in 1913 about as much as a gathering of town-planning experts would resemble a mass-meeting of Indians, Egyptians, East Galicians, or any other small and oppressed nationality which was demanding independent national existence. There is nothing to compare with the single-minded and absolutely unanimous enthusiasm of the oppressed. Ten years ago the women of the civilized world, with the exception of Finland, Norway, and a half dozen of the American states, had no right of franchise, a right which they had been demanding for more than half a century. Today, as Mrs. Carrie Chapman Catt, the retiring president, said in her reply to Premier Mussolini's address of welcome, "the delegates of twenty of the forty

The New Republic, 27 June 1923.

nations represented are voters and among them are members of parliaments and councillors of great cities."

Feminism, ten years ago, demanded of its leaders eloquence and passion, of its followers devotion and hard work. Today when there is no longer a single, simple aim and a solitary barrier to break down, there are a hundred difficult questions of civil law, problems of education, of moral and social custom to be solved, before women can come wholly into their inheritance of freedom. Feminism today demands patient research rather than eloquence, and brains even more than devotion. So if there were no thrilling moments in the recent Congress, there was nevertheless evidence of genuine intellectual effort and solid achievement.

For nearly two years four committees had been at work collecting material. By means of international questionnaires and personal research and with the aid of the various affiliated national associations, these committees made a practically world-wide inquiry into the status of women in regard to (1) the right to work and equal pay, (2) the maintenance of motherhood, (3) the nationality of married women, and (4) moral questions. The findings of these inquiries were published in *Jus Suffragii*, the official organ of the Alliance, a month before the Congress, and in Rome on the Saturday before the formal opening each committee held an all-day preliminary conference for the purpose of considering the findings and of drafting recommendations to be presented at the conference. With such preparation, it was no wonder that the debate on the floor of the Congress was like that of experts discussing complex points, rather than of enthusiasts championing a "cause."

I select two of the resolutions adopted by the Congress for mention in this article, because they seem to have especially important feminist significance. In regard to the nationality of married women the Congress declared not only that "a married woman should be given the same right to retain or to change her nationality as a man," but it recommended the calling of a conference of the governments of the world to adopt a resolution embodying this principle and drew up a provisional draft for such a convention. The Cable Act, passed by the United States last September, giving an American woman who marries a foreigner the right to retain her nationality and requiring a foreign woman who marries an American to go through naturalization proceedings if she desires to become an American citizen, has caused so much confusion in the passport offices of the different nations that the governments will doubtless welcome the proposal of the Congress. They will find much of their preliminary work done for them by the special committee of the Woman Suffrage Alliance, the chairman of which, Miss Chrystal Macmillan, is ably qualified to act in the capacity of adviser.

Another rock of the common law that as yet stands unmoved by present feminism is the legal conception of a wife as a dependent, entitled to "bed and board" in return for services, but to nothing more. A resolution introduced by Miss Eleanore Rathbone's committee on the maintenance of motherhood and adopted by the Congress, put a little charge of dynamite under the rock. It reads:

> This Congress believes that married women who are bringing up children . . . are doing work of as great importance to the community as those men and women who are producing material wealth. . . .
>
> This Congress therefore declares that such improvements in the laws of the various countries should be made, as will secure to married women a real economic security and independence.
>
> This Congress declares that a husband and wife should each have complete control of their earnings, income and property, except that, in view of her care of the home and the children, a wife should have a right to a certain proportion of the husband's income. . . . And that where the husband refuses to allow his wife the share of his income to which she is entitled the court may order a certain proportion of his wages or other income to be paid to her direct.

Not very happily worded perhaps, but nevertheless these clauses embody the germ of an important new conception of marriage, in which the home-keeping, child-rearing wife will have a working-partner's claim on the family income, not the claim of an unpaid dependent to her "keep." To establish in law and custom this conception of marriage may take a generation or two, but its establishment is essential to the greater freedom of women and should therefore become a major task in the program of the feminists.

So complex is the nature of the problems which women in all countries are destined to deal with as soon as they get the vote, that it may be wise to divide the Alliance into two groups, the enfranchised and the unenfranchised. Women who have the suffrage still to win, above all, women from countries where a wife is still a chattel without the right to hold property or keep her own earnings, grow impatient in listening to the prolonged discussion on advanced economic legislation contemplated for countries where the vote is an old story. A Junior Alliance of the non-voting women, from which each country would graduate and be received into the parent body upon winning the suffrage, might be a solution to the problem. I have suggested this plan to many delegates, but they seem to feel that the backward countries need the help and advice of the more experienced women. It is my feeling, however, that new movements need to be let alone in order to develop their own leaders and their own type of activities, and that the loss in wisdom and experience would be more than offset by the gain in power and enthusiasm that comes with concentration upon a single aim.

Keeping Abreast of the Times

"If it weren't for the Guild the Co-Operative movement would be nowhere." I had heard this so many times since I came to England that I decided to go to Cardiff, where the Women's Co-Operative Guild was holding its fortieth annual Congress, and see the representatives of these 52,000 working-class housewives in action.

If you were a professional woman and also a mother, and had been looking all your life for an ideal helper who would make your double life practicable, a sort of "substitute mother," you would have exclaimed as I did when I opened the door into that small crowded Congress Hall at Cardiff.

"Why, here they are, all of them!" Eight hundred, bright-eyed,

Equal Rights, 14 July 1923.

kindly competent faces, and nearly every one had the beaming, reliable look that a mother's face ought to have.

Of course, they *are* mothers, working-class mothers for whom there is no servant problem because there are no servants; and the bravest of these because they do it all—nursing, cooking, cleaning, washing, sewing—and yet keep their souls alive, their minds active, their hearts warm toward the world and its hard problems of progress.

In one day's session I heard these guildswomen discuss ably half a dozen problems of internal management in the vast Co-Operative movement of which they are so vital a part; I heard them advocate and adopt intelligent resolutions on birth control and on peace; I heard them attack the Government's housing policy from every point of view, human and economic, and make constructive suggestions of real importance. Never have I known so much business put through on the opening day of any other congress.

Is it the housewives' training that makes these women so able to dispense with heroics, to follow a plan and get through the day's work? Then I am tempted to conclude that it is the best possible training for active political life.

A Matter of Emphasis

In order to justify their separate existence within the parties the women's political organisations must serve a distinct purpose. This purpose would seem to be threefold; (a) to give scope and training to potential women leaders who might never be given an opportunity to show their gifts in the main party organisation; (b) to give organised expression to the women's demand for place and power in the party councils and genuine chances for political advancement in accordance

Time and Tide, 5 June 1925.

with their service and ability; (c) to make felt the women's viewpoint in politics,—or rather the women's emphasis. We were moved to these reflections as we journeyed to Birmingham last week to attend the National Conference of Labour Women held in the Town Hall, May 27 and 28. For surely if a women's party conference is to be merely an echo, no matter how enthusiastic, of the platform already adopted by the main party organisation to which the women are as individuals affiliated, it is hardly worth the paper and print and postage required to call it together.

The Conference at Birmingham, we hasten to say, was anything but an echo. Though some of its leaders would resent the imputation, it had in our opinion, great feminist weight and significance. The first Woman's Labour Conference, which was called eighteen years ago under the inspiration of Margaret MacDonald, Mary Middleton and Mary MacArthur, numbered 40 women. At Birmingham last week 860 accredited delegates assembled, nine-tenths of them representing Women's Sections of the Labour Party, the balance representing trades unions, the Women's Co-operative Guild, the I.L.P., Fabian Society, etc. It goes without saying that this increase in numbers has meant a corresponding increase in vigour and independence. One can be sure that the Woman's Labour Conference has fed on something stronger than "echoing and endorsing" to make such a lusty growth in 18 years.

We do not suggest for a moment that this was a feminist conference. It was emphatically a labour and socialist conference, outspoken in its denunciation of the capitalist system, confident in its hope of a co-operative commonwealth. "We are socialists first and foremost and all the time," said the Chairman, Ellen Wilkinson, M.P., and she might have added (so far at least as an outsider could judge the temper of the delegates), "socialists with a leaning to the left." But we are not here concerned with the economic philosophy underlying this gathering of women, nor with the political platform to which they as party women give their adherence. What concerns us is to point out to what a remarkable extent they spoke not as socialist women, not as party women, but as *women*.

Take first these sentences from the Chairman's opening address: "It can almost be said that women sidled into politics. We peeped around the door and said humbly: 'Please can we come in just to look after the babies while you are busy?' . . . But that period is now ended, and while women will naturally specialise on certain matters, we must as a Labour Women's Movement regard ourselves as whole human beings interested in all sides of human life. We need to emphasise this in our local sections and trade unions; we want women on the finance as well as on the social committees; and we want to see women taking their full share in the management of the great trade unions. . . . It is important that women in the Labour Party branches should realise their responsibility to their women comrades, and press for suitable women to have a chance of the good seats. I once heard a very responsible organiser of the Party say in all seriousness: 'There is a hundred to one chance in that division, but it might be won. It is just the sort of seat a woman ought to fight.' . . . ."

Here surely is the suggestion that in the Labour Party as in other parties women must fight for their "place in the sun." It was repeated during the debate on the franchise resolution, demanding "full adult suffrage for men and women at twenty-one without further delay." More than one speaker spoke with heat of the opportunity missed by the Labour Government in not pushing the full enfranchisement of women during its months of office. And, if we are not mistaken as to the procedure, the section of the Report dealing with enfranchise-ment was referred back for re-drafting so as to include some expression of this criticism. A more emphatic note of criticism appears in the resolution calling upon the Labour Party "to deal stringently with any representative of the Labour Party who does not support sex equality economically, educationally and politically. Finally and most significantly, a practical step was taken toward securing fuller political representation in the resolution calling "upon all members of the Women's Sections to immediately levy themselves a small sum weekly as a political fund for the express purpose of running Working Women Candidates for Parliament." The enthusiasm and unanimity with which this burden was undertaken was unmistakeable.

"We must work to create a new point of view toward women in the labour and socialist movement," said Mrs. Bruce Glazier during one debate and it was gratifying to find this great conference of Labour women recognising to some extent that necessity.

But it was not only by this recurring note of vigilance in the matter of recognition and equality that the conference demonstrated its importance as a separate organisation within the Labour Party. Again and again throughout its reports and debates and resolutions it revealed what we have called the "women's emphasis," an emphasis on the supreme importance of human well-being, especially the well-being of children. In the criticism of the pensions scheme, in the discussion on housing, on health and maternity insurance, in the demand for stronger regulations to ensure clean food and pure milk, above all in the discussion of the health environment in elementary and secondary schools, there was evidence of detailed knowledge and patient study, there was evidence of that homely wisdom which is based on personal experience and cannot be gainsaid, there was a wealth of concrete practical suggestion, which no ordinary Labour conference would have brought to light. Labour men might endorse the same propositions but they would not spend so much time and thought and fireworks on them.

It is not so much that women have a different point of view in politics as that they give a different emphasis. And this is vastly important, for politics is so largely a matter of emphasis.

Britain's Labor Women

Eighteen years ago Mary MacArthur, Margaret MacDonald, and Mary Middleton called the first Conference of Labor Women. There was no franchise for women in England then, and little prospect of any. This year a thousand delegates and visitors packed Birmingham Town Hall. Presiding over them was Ellen Wilkinson, M. P., witty and red-haired, ex-Communist, and now the only woman sitting for the British Labor Party at Westminster.

The Nation, 15 July 1925.

Forty of the delegates represented the Women's Co-Operative Guild, the Independent Labor Party, and the Fabian Society; seventy-five represented trade unions. Seven hundred and thirty-one represented women's sections of the Labor Party from all over England, Scotland, and Wales. Nearly all were working-class housewives whose absence from home meant that friendly neighbors had to volunteer care for husband and child. The husbands of these women were Welch miners, shipbuilders from Tyneside, shop assistants, railway conductors, cotton-mill workers, seamen, carpenters. Never have I seen a conference of American women where the same forces were gathered together. England is small. Third-class railway fares are cheaper than fares for the same distances in America. Even with the low wages and unemployment now prevalent, it had been possible to achieve a representative convention.

I walked to the platform and looked at the earnest tired faces of these women. Their plain, often shabby clothes, and their sallow complexions were evidences of the poverty that is the common lot of the English working class. Poor food and strain had done their best to remove the beauty from the faces before me; but the beauty of courage was still there.

As the meeting opened, messages of greeting were read from Sweden, Finland, and Russia. A small but significant feature to record. These women are opening their own channels of communication with the Continent, and they have begun to learn much from the determined and educated feminist groups in Scandinavia and Russia. Not only domestic problems, of food, housing, old age, and maternity, are now recognized on the agendas of women's conferences, but foreign affairs are boldly discussed. Not long ago foreign affairs were considered the preserve of highly placed men.

The uses of the convention are three. It is the occasion for direct representatives of working-class women to formulate their own program, so that with some sort of united front they can make themselves felt in the Labor Party Congress that follows later in the year. At the conference the women leaders from National Labor Party headquarters meet the delegates who must in turn educate the women in the villages and factory towns. Second, the conference is the debating ground extraordinary for the home women, workmen's wives whose money income is derived from their husbands' wages, and the working women in stores and factories. Considering how often in the past women workers have been used, if not as strike-breakers, at least as the undercutters of wages, this meeting of two groups of women has been needed to make clear to the wives of men trade unionists that for their own sakes and their husband's sakes the principle of equal pay for equal work must prevail, if the standards within an industry are not to be lowered. The cleavage between the home women and the women trade unionists is steadily growing less. Finally, the conference offers a forum for definite feminist propaganda, the furtherance of the women's franchise bill, the formulations of demands for more women candidates for Parliament, and the discussion of such subjects as birth control and other feminist issues.

Ellen Wilkinson opened the convention with a denunciation of the Churchill tax on artificial silk. "Every bit of color and gaiety is to be taken from the life of the working woman. Her hard-earned little fineries are to be taxed by nearly ten millions for the benefit of the richest people in the country." Ellen Wilkinson knows that to clerk and shopgirl neat appearance is a necessity if she is not to lose her job. She went from the Churchill tax to an analysis of the proposals for widows' pensions and compared the eighteen shillings a week proposed for a workman's widow with two children with the army private's widow's forty shillings. Dr. Marion Phillips, the energetic Australian who is chief woman officer of the Labor Party, reported 1,450 women's sections with a total membership of 200,000; and an increase in Labor women holding municipal, county, and district-council offices in the past year. This was salve to those delegates who feel keenly the loss of Dorothy Jewson, Margaret Bondfield, and Susan Lawrence in Parliament; and who have resented the ready alibi of certain of the men who lay the blame for the Baldwin victory on the women voters. Women voters, indeed. This conference chided Ramsay MacDonald for neglecting to make the women's franchise bill admitting the younger women a party issue.

The birth-control resolution which was carried read:

> This conference is of the opinion that it should be permissible for doctors employed in any medical service for which public funds are provided to give information on birth control to married people who desire it.

It is not illegal in England to distribute information in regard to contraceptives. The issue was whether the public health centers should do carefully and scientifically what so many women manage to do as best they can. Two years ago the subject was very timidly discussed. Last year Dora Russell and Freda Laski put through a resolution asking that the health centers give out such information, but the Roman Catholic Minister of Health in the Labor Government would not move. This year no two women "put through" the resolution. The whole floor was for it, with a few bitter exceptions who regard contraceptives as a frustration of God and the moral order. However, "I am a Catholic," said a stout motherly woman, climbing on her chair as is the custom for speakers from the floor, "and I want to say that the Catholics better be honest. They are practicing birth control if they've got the information." To two firm young socialists who rose to explain that birth control was an economic issue that would not survive the social revolution an earnest woman replied firmly: "Even in the cooperative commonwealth I think a woman will want to choose her time and say how many."

Another resolution which was passed unanimously called on the Labor Party "to deal stringently with any representative of the Labor Party who does not support sex equality, economically, educationally, and politically." The demand set forth in Ellen Wilkinson's opening speech that the Labor Party propose women candidates in a reasonable number of parliamentary seats was echoed in the resolution which demanded that "the women's sections immediately levy themselves a small weekly sum as a political fund for the express purpose of running working-women candidates for Parliament." There is a suspicion that certain of the men who direct Labor party affairs are willing to have women candidates but not in the sure districts, and that there is not the same zest in the men's efforts to raise campaign funds for the women that there is among the women to support the men.

Among the other resolutions passed were demands for a National Wheat Board to solve the problem of cheap bread, a demand for a trained nurse in every secondary and primary school, a demand for the passage of the women's franchise bill admitting the younger women to the polls. Various resolutions calling for an international conference of labor women; for enforcement of the Wheatley housing act, for family migration, and for study of the labor market in the colonies were all on the agenda.

These Englishwomen speak well, briefly, and with much caustic force. The various English dialects give a certain rich savor to the debate for an American observer. Noteworthy as contrasted with American meetings I have attended is the hard-mindedness and attentiveness of these women. The rank-and-file delegates, scrambling on their chairs to speak, match the platform in thoughtfulness and directness. The impression is of women who are going to fight to get their full share of power within the Labor Party. They intend that the men shall be helpmates in their feminist projects.

The New
British Commonwealth League

Is it a retrograde step to establish at this time a special organization "to secure equality of liberties, status and opportunities between men and women" within the British Empire? This point was raised by Ellen Wilkinson in an address before the Conference recently called in London by the British Commonwealth League. This League, of which Mrs. Corbett Ashby is president and M. Chave Collison of Australia, secretary, has been organized, as I understand it, to take the place of the British Overseas Committee of the International Woman's Suffrage Association, and also of the British Dominions Women Citizens' Union. It does not, therefore, represent in any sense duplication of effort, but rather a unifying of effort, a plan of action which will enable women who call themselves British subjects to pull together, wherever they find themselves on the five continents of the world.

Equal Rights, 22 August 1925.

Miss Wilkinson's point, of course, was that it was a mistake for a group of reformers to emphasize British imperialism in this day when the whole emphasis of liberal thought is upon internationalism. However, internationalist though I am, I think my favorite member of Parliament is wrong. She probably gave expression to a first thought, a very natural first reaction.

For good or ill, the British Empire, or the "British Commonwealth of Nations," as the Liberals prefer to call it, is becoming every day more distinctly and in more important ways a political entity. So long as this is true, and so long as women are living under unequal laws in any part of that vast "entity," it would seem to be perfectly logical, if not essential, to maintain a feminist organization corresponding to it in province and purpose. In securing to British women the right to retain their nationality after marriage, for example, such a league will almost immediately justify its existence.

I wonder if the American feminists who secured the passage of the Cable Act had any idea how disturbing it would be to the whole diplomatic world, and how delightfully stimulating it would prove to those pursuing Equal Rights in other lands? That act, which established the right of an American woman to retain her nationality on marriage, also established the corresponding obligation upon a foreign woman marrying an American, if she wished to adopt his nationality, to become "naturalized." Thus, for example, an Englishwoman marrying an American, by British law automatically loses her British nationality, but she does not now, as formerly, automatically acquire her American husband's nationality, and thus for a considerable period she has no nationality! This results in injustice and difficulty for the woman in question, and it also results in hopeless confusion in consular offices the world over. It is not at all surprising, then, that the "right of married women to retain their nationality," which has been a sort of latent demand of all feminist programs for years back, has become almost over night an immediate political issue.

In England, Chrystal MacMillan is the great protagonist of this nationality measure. On the second day of the Conference Miss MacMillan explained the status of the matter and urged the new League to act as a unit throughout the empire on it. On February 18, it appears, the House of Commons adopted the following resolution without a division: "That in the opinion of this House a British woman shall not lose or be deemed to lose her nationality by the mere act of marriage with an alien, but that it should be open to her to make a declaration of alienage." However, a similar resolution must be passed by all the Dominion parliaments before effective legislation can be secured. Therefore, as soon as the House of Commons acted, the officers of the International Woman Suffrage Association cabled to the affiliated societies in the various dominions and asked them to co-operate. But as yet the dominions have not acted. Miss MacMillan therefore warmly welcomed the formation of a league devoted to the Equal Rights campaign solely within the Empire, and recommended this measure for its immediate attention, "Women must bring pressure to bear on their own dominion parliaments and also on the next Imperial Conference," she said.

There was something very direct and spirited about this meeting of British women—a note of impatience, one might say. It struck me first in Mrs. Corbett Ashby's opening words.

"There was a time," she said, "when the only qualities admired in women were chastity and self-sacrifice, but that time has passed. Women are no longer in that mood. Patience with ills you can cure is the greatest evil, and the only justification for self-sacrifice is that it be for a wide and good end."

In the discussion of the franchise it was revealed that in many parts of the Empire women do not yet vote (notably South Africa and Bermuda), and appropriately indignant resolutions were adopted. It was pointed out again and again that fully enfranchised British women in going from one part of the Empire to another would lose their vote.

After an exceedingly able survey of "morals" legislation throughout the Empire by Alison Neilans, secretary of the British Association for Moral and Social Hygiene, a resolution was adopted calling upon the British governments, at home and in the overseas dominions, "to extend the principle of *moral equality* throughout all their legislation and particularly in regard to the laws governing marriage and divorce, illegitimacy, prostitution, street order and venereal disease." Women were especially warned to watch the *administration* of laws in this connection so as to guard against "measures of exception" being applied to women under pretext of morals.

It is a great day for feminism when women of all classes demand justice for the prostitute.

The final session of this two-day conference was devoted to the question of economic equality and how to secure it, with Lady Rhondda in the Chair and Mrs. Oliver Strachey giving the principal address. The resolutions adopted at the close of this session have such a modern note that it is a pleasure to quote them in full:

1. "Equal pay for equal work must be established.

2. "The existing division and subdivision of labor into men's and women's work must be replaced by a free field.

3. "No obstacle must be placed in the way of the employment of married women.

4. "Protective legislation in industry must be based on the nature of the work and not on the sex of the worker.

5. "The economic value of the work of women in the home must be recognized."

Socialist Women of Eighteen Countries Meet at Marseilles

"This day's work will lay the foundations for a Women's International," said Mrs. Dollon, City Councillor of Glasgow, as we drove up to the Chateau des Fleurs early in the morning of August 21st. And when we drove back to our hotel in Marseilles that night after eleven hours struggle in a dim green light, with three languages and the worst acoustics the human voice has ever tried to conquer, I remembered what she had said and I knew she was right. Despite everything the foundations had been laid, and solidly laid.

Equal Rights, 26 September 1925.

Every new effort at organized expression on the part of women acting by and for themselves must interest a feminist. And I would ask my readers, whether they belong so far to the right that they regard Labour and the Socialist International as a menace to the human race or so far to the left that they regard it as a pitiful counterfeit movement deserving only contempt—I would ask them in either case to consider this first independent step on the part of the women allied to that International with sympathy and enthusiasm.

There has always been a scattering of women delgates at the meetings of the Socialist International and in recent years there have been two women on the Executive, Adelheid Popp of Austria and Mrs. Harrison Bell of England. Two years ago when the International met at Hamburg, the women delegates who happened to be present met together in an effort to form some permanent association. The attempt was not successful however. The women present could not agree as to what the function of a woman's committee within the International would be; many of them were doubtful as to the wisdom of forming a distinct group. The only outcome was the election of a "Praesidium" of four, [Dr. Marion Phillips of England, Marie Jucharz of Germany, Alice Pels of Belgium, and Adelheid Popp of Austria], whose duty it should be to keep the project alive, to secure a permanent woman correspondent in every country, and to call a woman's conference in connection with the next meeting of the International. It is the conference which has just been held at Marseilles, the first official International Conference of Socialist women.

The Chateau des Fleurs is a long, low one-roomed building set in the midst of a shady park. The walls and low curved ceiling of the hall inside are completely covered with mural decorations representing flowers, fruits and hanging gardens, very much like those one sees in a cheap French or Italian restaurant in New York, except that they are dim and half-erased instead of new and shiny. The effect of these decorated walls is to darken still more the green light that filters through the shaded windows. A perfect setting for a gentle afternoon slumber, but hardly one I should choose for hammering out the foundations of a new movement. In the center of this very rectangular hall capable of seating perhaps two or three thousand people, was a small platform and a few rows of tables and chairs, and here, with echoing spaces on either side, the eighty odd delegates assembled and tried to confer.

I think all reformers should be required to take a course in lighting and acoustics. Not contented with the difficulty of understanding each other and the still greater difficulty of agreeing with each other, we seem so often to meet in places where we can neither see nor hear each other!

The conference opened with Frau Popp in the chair and five men surrounding her on the little platform. These turned out to be members of the Executive of the International who had come to extend greetings to the women's meeting. The greetings I thought a bit overdone, especially as the women had but one day, and each of the five men made a speech which had to be translated into two other languages. Perhaps I was impatient for the business of the day to begin and therefore unduly critical, but these men, with one exception, seemed to me to have no sense of the conference as having any feminist significance. They had the smiles and gracious complimentary manner of a deacon addressing the "Ladies' Auxiliary." It was only old Wiebaut, a Socialist leader of Holland, who seemed to take the conference seriously. He was genuinely indignant over the fact that most countries deny to a married woman the right to retain her own nationality, and he urged Socialist women to work for "equality of the personality" in every respect.

Half the morning session having been given over to greetings, the second half was devoted to a confused deafening wrangle over a sort of "side" resolution brought in by the British delegates, dealing with war and poverty. It was a feeble resolution and vague, declaring that "as the interest of the great mass of women are centered upon the welfare of their homes and their children, so their interest in socialism is mainly concerned in its power to secure them against war and poverty"; and going on to urge that "in order to arouse this interest to its fullest extent" the Socialist movement should advocate a strong peace policy and a policy of co-operation among the workers of all countries in the production of food supplies, etc.

Surely this is unsound from both a feminist and Socialist standpoint. Men are no less interested than women in something which will "secure them against war and poverty." And every Socialist knows it is impossible to achieve co-operation in production internationally so long as capitalist nationalism exists. So I think the opposition to this resolution, from whatever confusion of motives it arose, was a healthy one; and the result of the discussion by which the idea of the British resolution was confined to a brief addendum to the main resolution, was on the whole a victory for intelligence.

When we adjourned for lunch I found most of the British delegates believed that the opposition to their resolution came from timidity on the part of the Germans and Austrians, their unwillingness to take any action independently and separately from the men. Many were in despair over the outcome of the conference. But they were wrong, as the afternoon session proved. When the main resolution came up, with its straight feminist contentions it was the continental women who held out most strongly for the necessity of independent action on the part of women. And the amendments which were proposed to strengthen and broaden the demand for equality were proposed not by British women or American women but by continental women.

Coming now to the main resolution, in which there was an attempt to embody the principles as well as the form and machinery of the proposed organization, I will quote its main clauses in full, putting in italics the amendments added after discussion.

"I. For the accomplishment of Socialism it is necessary that the masses should be roused to assist in the active work of the re-organization of society, and the masses consist of women as well as men. It is therefore essential that the Socialist parties in all countries should do their utmost to assist in the organization of women within the labor and Socialist movement, and in order to accomplish this, every Socialist Party should regard the complete emancipation of women as the primary aim of their policy. It is their duty to work for the full political, *economic and social,* equality of men and women, especially in regard to electoral equality and equality in laws dealing with the family, citizenship and marriage, and equality of rights between legitimate and illegitimate children. They must also demand full freedom for women to enter administrative, professional and industrial life, *without regard to her family status (whether married or not*) *and without regard to her need,* and economic equality in regard to wages.

"II. As it is necessary that the policy of the Socialist movement should be based upon the needs of women as well as men, Socialist women in all countries should have the right to discuss and formulate for themselves their views of social problems of interest to women.

"III. The development of capitalist society has left women under many social and educational disadvantages, so that from a political and economic point of view their position is weaker than that of men, while the obligations and burden of motherhood require that they should have special care and protection in industrial life. It is therefore necessary that the Socialist movement should advocate all such measures of protection and care as the workers and especially the women workers think requisite, in order to secure the welfare of mothers and children.

"IV. In order to get full understanding between the Socialist women in the different countries, an International Advisory Committee of women should be formed consisting of representatives of the women; with the special duty of advising the Executive Council of the Labor and Socialist International; and to assist in organizing an international conference of Labor and Socialist women *in connection with each conference of the International.*"

Now that is not a good resolution, it is not brief and succinct, it is not eloquent, it is not even entirely clear or altogether consistent. My editorial pencil was itching to get at it all day. But considered as the output of women associated together in their own interests for the first time, considered as the first feminist utterance of women brought up in a movement whose primary attitude to women seeking equality has always been, "Help us get socialism first and all these equalities will follow"—it is a surprisingly strong and purposeful declaration. There is the admission that the present order, hard as it bears on the masses of men bears harder on the masses of women; and there is the demand that "complete emancipation of women" be put in the forefront of Socialist policy the world over. Surely this is all we ask of "la femme socialiste."

And these women seem to know what they mean by freedom and equality. They do not confuse it with humanitarianism or family welfare. This, I think, is suggested by the amendments which were accepted as a matter of course, and it was revealed still more clearly by the tenor and emphasis of most of the delegates' speeches on the resolution, which continued without a break from two o'clock until eight.

"The resolution is not clear enough on equality," said Mme. Budzynska, a Polish doctor; "we should demand equality not only in marriage laws, but in all civil laws."

"We must proclaim the right of women to work," declared Betty Karpisek, one of the two Czech delegates, "too often women are excluded from the public service or badly paid when they are allowed to remain."

Frau Wurm, a handsome, powerful looking delegate from Berlin (member of the Reichstag as nearly all the German delegates were), added a still more modern note to the discussion: "It is necessary to demand equality of opportunity to work, yes. Indeed, married women are in danger of being ousted altogether. This must not be. We must ask for protection of motherhood as proposed by the Washington convention, but otherwise opportunities must be equal. I do not agree to the idea of a family wage. We need a change of mentality on the part of women. They must cease to consider their work or profession as a temporary thing, dependent on marriage."

"In my country, Latvia," said Klara Kalnin, "women are still under the tutelage of men, though they vote. It is all right to demand protection of motherhood but that is not our only question. We must have full civil rights, men must be educated to a different attitude to us, we must have a complete transformation of family life."

"There is no atmosphere of equality between men and women in any country," said Mary Carlin, when it came her turn. Mary Carlin is a splendid big Irish woman who is the National Woman Organizer for the Transport and General Workers Union of Great Britain, and she ought to know. "Our International Advisory Committee will be a step forward, it will give us a chance to bring forward our special viewpoint. Men are very gracious but we do not enjoy equality even in the Socialist Party."

And Frau Popp: "Political equality does not correspond necessarily to real social equality. We have the vote in Germany and

Austria but women's labor has gone back since the war. Women are being driven out of all the better paid positions. We shall get ahead faster with our equality program if we have a central committee and can co-ordinate the reforms in different countries. It is not enough to have two women on the Executive—we must have our own international committee in contact with women in every country."

Toward the end of the afternoon a French woman spoke, Louise Saumoneau, editor of La Femme Socialiste, for many years on the Executive of the French Socialist Party. She is a small keen gray-haired woman, with deep burning eyes and a look both shrewd and earnest. The resolution, she said, was too theoretical. "We must go into details in our demands and in our criticisms. For example two socialist governments of Europe, when they had the opportunity to achieve political equality for women, failed. We should not be quiet about this." One of these was the Catholic Socialist government of Belgium, which, as a Belgian delegate admitted, voted against woman suffrage at a critical moment when the issue was precipitated by its enemies as a means of embarrassing the government and precipitating its downfall. The other must have been MacDonald's Labour government in England, which failed to extend the vote to women over twenty-one although with the help of the Liberals it had the power to do so.

Mrs. Dollon, who spoke soon after Louise Saumoneau, agreed that Socialist leaders could not always be trusted to stand up for equality: "For example, when the question came up in England of dismissing married women large numbers of Socialist members of Parliament were in favor of it."

In the point raised by the last two speakers I have quoted lies the answer to the question whether women should maintain separate committees or merge completely as individuals in the political parties with which they are in sympathy. Morris Hillquit, one of the five men who spoke in greeting at the opening of the conference, said among other things, "I hope you will soon grow to the point where you will abolish your separate existence, to the point where women will take their place in the general movement for the emancipation of the working-class."

The answer to Mr. Hillquit, as I am sure most of those Socialist women at Marseilles would agree, is this:

"When the Socialist parties of the world do genuinely decide to make equal rights for women a primary aim of their policy, never to be side-tracked for political expediency, then and not till then will we abolish our separate existence."

THERE IS NO PROTECTION WITHOUT EQUALITY

An Acid Test for Suffragists

Should there be special restrictions upon the hours and conditions of women workers?

In this article Miss Crystal Eastman tells how the issue is dividing the feminist movement in the countries where the vote has been won, and how evenly balanced were the two camps at the recent congress in Rome.

In all countries where women have won the vote Suffragists tend to separate into two distinct groups so far as their public activities go: there are the humanitarians who devote themselves to securing those measures of general human betterment for which enlightened women have always stood, and there are the feminists, who, as long as any inequality exists between men and women, regard it as the chief object of organised women to remove it.

Already in the United States the line is clearly drawn, and the

London *Daily Herald,* May 1925.

two groups are organised. There is the Woman's Party, which exists solely "to remove all forms of the subjection of women," and the League of Women Voters, which takes up child welfare, education, social hygiene, international co-operation to prevent war, etc., as well as uniform laws concerning women.

Elsewhere the same division will inevitably take place; women who have worked side by side to win the vote will divide according to whether their interests are mainly humanitarian or mainly feminist.

Sometimes the two groups find themselves directly antagonistic, as for instance in the matter of special labour restrictions for women. The feminists oppose such restrictions, when they apply to women and not to men, as an unwarranted interference with woman's freedom and as a serious handicap in competition with men. The humanitarians defend them as a necessary protection to motherhood and the race.

A lively debate on this subject took place at the recent International Congress of Women at Rome, in connection with the resolution that "no special regulations for women's work, different from regulations for men, should be imposed contrary to the wishes of the women concerned."

Miss Anna Polak, director of the National Bureau of Women's Work of Holland, led the anti-restrictionists, and was supported by the entire Dutch delegation. The Scandinavian delegates were on the same side. Dr. Dagny Bang, of Norway, speaking for them, said:—

"Norway, Denmark and Finland have no prohibition of night work for women in industry. Sweden has got the law, but it was much opposed by women, and they are working now to get rid of it. As soon as the law passed it had the effect of driving women out of several highly-paid trades, such as printing and bookbinding. And that is the effect it will always have."

Lady Dockrell, head of the Irish Free State delegation, declared that special restrictions on women's work did more harm than good. The English delegates, while they took no part in the debate, were, I believe, chiefly with the Dutch and Scandinavians on this matter.

On the other side were the American delegation representing the League of Women Voters, the Australian delegates, and the

Austrian and German delegations, all of whom took the humanitarian rather than the purely feminist position on this question.

After a full discussion a vote was taken, and the figures were extremely close, the resolution being carried by only a dozen votes.

Later in the day I had an opportunity to ask Miss Polak what she had meant in her speech when she demanded "no restrictions on women's work along general lines."

"What is dangerous for women," she replied, "is not always dangerous for men. We are not opposed to every kind of restriction. For instance, I have known a weak man who could carry a much heavier load than I can carry, and yet I am very strong. Women can be permanently injured by carrying loads too heavy for them.

"In certain kinds of dangerous work we in Holland allow a restriction on women's labour. But in the four main divisions of labour legislation, restriction of hours, prohibition of night work, prohibition of Sunday work and the Saturday half-holiday, we do not recognise any reason for making special laws for women, and we know those laws are unfair to women and do much harm to them in the economic struggle."

Equality or Protection

A good deal of tyranny goes by the name of protection. For example, there is a law in Connecticut, one of the eastern American states, which reads:

"No public restaurant, cafe, dining-room, barber shop, hair-dressing or manicuring establishment or photograph gallery shall employ any minor under sixteen years of age or any woman, between the hours of 10 o'clock in the evening and 6 o'clock in the morning."

Equal Rights, 15 March 1924.

Classification of Women

For a woman engaged in these pursuits there may be as much insult and injury in such a law as there was for all women in the pre-suffrage classification of minors, idiots, criminals and women as persons denied a voice in democratic government. And this law is not peculiar to the State of Connecticut nor to the United States of America. It is quite usual to prohibit night work for women in advanced industrial countries. It is one of the most commonly advocated industrial "reforms." Yet it is not maintained that women's lungs are more susceptible to the night air than the lungs of men, or that women's eyes are more injuriously affected by artificial light than the eyes of men. If this were true, we must begin by legislating against the full work-basket which the working-class mother takes up by lamp-light after her children are asleep and the dishes of the last meal are washed and put away.

Dangers of the Dark

No, the implication of such laws is really a moral one—women must not be allowed to work after dark lest they succumb to the dangers of the midnight streets. Although it must be obvious that in the agitation preceding the enactment of such laws the zeal of the reformers would be second to the zeal of the highly paid night-workers who are anxious to hold their trade against an invasion of skilled women.

To this sort of interference with her working life the modern woman can have but one attitude: *I am not a child.* I will have none of your protection.

But all the so-called protective legislation for women is not so indefensible. A great deal can be said for minimum wage laws and laws limiting the hours of labor for women on the ground that woman's labor is the least adapted to organization and therefore the most easily exploited and most in need of legislative protection. Less can be said for the type of law which prohibits certain trades to women on the ground of their physical inferiority. The danger that women will rush in large numbers into trades for which they are by constitution manifestly unfit is not so great as the danger that such a principle of sex prohibition once admitted in the law will be used by the influence of powerful unions to keep women out of trades for which they are manifestly fit.

Equality Versus Protection

Sooner or later in every industrial country where women have won the franchise this vexed question of equality versus protection is bound to arise. The good suffragist, after she has won her vote, takes one long night's rest, awakes refreshed and eager, and begins to look around for equal opportunities in every field of human endeavor. On the very first corner she meets the earnest reformer, who stops her, saying, "My dear you must not ask for Equal Rights in industry. If you do, what will become of this whole body of labor law which I have built up by years and years of patient effort to protect a weaker sex from the extreme rigors of industrial competition? Is all my work to be wasted?"

The Equal Rights Amendment

This is no idle rhetorical question. It is a very real question indeed. To meet it and answer it with courage and consistency and yet with sympathy and sound practical human judgment may well be the major concern of feminists for the next decade. In America, with the introduction in Congress last December of the Lucretia Mott amendment—(*Men and women shall have Equal Rights throughout the United States and every place subject to its jurisdiction*)—a battle royal has commenced. The amendment, sponsored, of course, by the younger and more militant element led by Alice Paul and the Woman's Party, was hardly 24 hours old before every member of Congress received a letter protesting in the strongest terms against it, signed by the official representatives of seven other national women's organizations, all of the more solid, more established, more distinctly humanitarian type.

The leading spirit in this opposition is Florence Kelley, founder and secretary of the National Consumers' League, known the world over as a passionate advocate of protective laws for women and

children in industry, an exceedingly forceful, almost violent personality, a born fighter, and a leader as devoted and able in her generation
as Alice Paul in hers. Thus at its beginning the battle is dramatized
in the figures of these two lionhearts.

The Claim of the Opposition

To the claim of these seven opposing societies that the amendment is not supported by any national organization except the one
that proposed it, the Woman's Party replies: "When Susan B.
Anthony introduced the National Suffrage amendment in 1878, few
women supported it." To the objection that the Equal Rights
Amendment "would endanger existing statutes providing a 48-hour
week, eight or nine or ten hour day and other industrial standards
governing the employment of women," the reply is:

The Answer to the Opposition

"The Equal Rights Amendment would not affect existing labor
legislation, except to establish the principle that industrial legislation
should apply to all workers, both men and women, in any given
occupation and not to women workers alone. Examples of states
where labor legislation already applies to both sexes are Oregon,
where there is a 10-hour law for both men and women employes in
mills, factories and manufacturing establishments, and Florida,
which requires seats for both men and women employes in stores."

Time on the Side of Equal Rights

"It may be," the official organ concludes, "that the Woman's
Party now stands alone for the Equal Rights Amendment—but time
is on our side and as the principle of Equal Rights in the suffrage field
has at last prevailed, just as surely will the principle of Equal Rights
for men and women be established in every field."

It behooves us to watch carefully the contest of these two ideals
in American legislation. For the issue will be raised before long on
this side. The time will come when British women will have to do
some hard thinking and declare their faith in this matter.

Feminists Must Fight

TO THE EDITOR OF THE NATION:

SIR: In a recent issue of *The Nation* there appeared, under the title A Women's Bloc? a thoughtful and yet I believe somewhat confused criticism of the election policy of the National Woman's Party. That policy had been announced as an effort "to elect all women nominees, irrespective of their political affiliations, who seem qualified to sit in Congress and who will support the Equal Rights Amendment and a general feminist program." Your writer held that this was good publicity but bad politics, that while it was possible to hold women as a disfranchised group together in a fight for the single issue of their enfranchisement, across party lines and irrespective of economic and class interests, such tactics were no longer possible. Now that women were voters economic and class interests would prove stronger than sex interests. "There are other revolutions going on in the world besides the women's revolution."

"For every party job," the writer concedes, "for every political office, for every legal change in the direction of equality, women will have to fight as women. But the lines will be drawn inside party lines, not across them. Inside the party organizations the women will have to wage their own battle for recognition and equal rights."

At this point some very careful thinking must be done. It is probably true that the battle for "recognition," political and official, will have to be fought inside party lines. If women want to be in politics they must be politicians, they must choose their party and play the political game from the ground up. But it seems to me most emphatically not true that the battle for "equal rights" must be fought within party lines. It can never be won there. It must be fought and it will be fought by a free-handed, nonpartisan minority of energetic feminists to whom politics in general, even "reform" politics, will continue to be a matter of indifference so long as women

Letter to the editor, *The Nation,* 12 November 1924.

are classed with children and minors in industrial legislation, so long as even in our most advanced States a woman can be penalized by the loss of her job when she marries.

If I am right about this distinction, then perhaps it is unfortunate that the National Woman's Party has undertaken for the moment a double role. But the principle of the Equal Rights Amendment is supremely important. The very passion with which it is opposed suggests that it is vital. To blot out of every law book in the land, to sweep out of every dusty court-room, to erase from every judge's mind that centuries-old precedent as to woman's inferiority and dependence and need for protection, to substitute for it at one blow the simple new precedent of equality, that is a fight worth making if it takes ten years.

And I expect to see the writer of your editorial, who is I am sure a feminist, backing the National Woman's Party in this fight long before the time is up.

CRYSTAL EASTMAN

New York, October 30

English Feminists and
Special Labor Laws for Women

I have just come from the annual council meeting of the National Union of Societies for Equal Citizenship. It may interest American women to know that this highly regular and conservative body, direct successor to the "Constitutional" and the non-militant suffrage group, whose retiring president, Mrs. Fawcett, has recently been

Equal Rights, 18 April 1925.

made a "Dame" of the British Empire, declared itself with only a few dissenting votes against protective legislation applying to women, but not to men. This is not a revolutionary departure on the part of the N.U.S.E.C. A similar resolution was passed in 1919 and reaffirmed in some form or other, I am told, at every annual meeting since.

This year the resolution read: "This council reaffirms its conviction that legislation for the protection of workers should be based not upon sex, but on the nature of the occupation . . . and it regrets that certain of the Washington conventions are not in accordance with these principles." It was introduced by Miss Helen Ward, who is on the executive board both of the National Union and of the National Council of Women, who is a vice-president of the Council for the Representation of Women on the League of Nations, and a member of the womens' advisory committee to the League of Nations Union.

The "Washington Conventions" adopted by the International Labor Office of the League of Nations include, of course, the famous "prohibition of night work for women," which has been incorporated in the industrial legislation of Great Britain and of so many other nations affiliated with the league. Miss Ward pointed out that the International Labor Office has recently extended the night work convention to cover agriculture and that there is nothing logically to prevent its being further extended to include brain-workers. She declares, moreover, that there is a very strong group in the International Labor Office that wishes to establish "differential sex legislation" as a fundamental principle of the league—as the "ultimate international ideal." This tendency, she believes, is most important for feminists to combat.

Miss Ward's own position is well covered by "View B" in the following paragraphs with which she concluded a recent article:

"To sum up, there is, among women, a large variety of opinion in regard to the best methods for the protection of workers, whether men, women, or children, in particular, there are two views which may be called View A, and View B, as follows:

"*View A.*—That women and children being, not only when the former are bearing children, but at all times, subject to such natural disabilities, that they cannot be adequately protected by means of the raising of standards of welfare and wages for all workers, regardless of sex, it is for their good to build up a permanent international system of protective or restrictive legislation for them, as a class apart.

"*View B.*—1. That in some backward countries, some temporary legislative restrictions upon women's work may be the lesser of two evils.

2. That an international system of restrictive legislation for non-adults is desirable, and that a very large measure of protection for young women will thus be secured without the evils of the differential system for adults.

3. But that, to segregate women permanently by an international system of restrictive legislation, based on sex, is, in spite of any apparent temporary advantage, to afford them no stable protection, but rather to add to the difficulties they already have to contend with; that the ideal therefore is, to base protective legislation, not on the sex of the workers, but on the nature of the work."

Miss Ward was ably supported in the debate by Mrs. Elisabeth Abbot, also on the board of the N.U.S.E.C. and a prominent leader of the women's movement in Great Britain.

The resolution did not pass without opposition. There was an effort to weaken it by amendment, and after this failed an effort to get it tabled, which also failed. It is significant that the National Union's position on protective legislation is now so well established that only a short time was reserved for debate on this resolution and only two delegates were found to speak against it.

The N.U.S.E.C. is made up of some 200 local affiliated societies throughout Great Britain. There were 300 delegates at this year's annual meeting and 14 new societies were admitted. It is a live, flourishing and highly representative society.

But the National Union is not the only woman's organization in Great Britain which is opposed to restrictive industrial legislation on sex lines. The Women's Freedom League, of which the distinguished Mrs. Despard was for so many years president, has taken even stronger action. In 1919, on motion of their national executive, the league declared "uncompromising opposition to any efforts, whether national or international, to limit the opportunities of women in industry under the name of protection."

"Again and again," said the secretary, Miss Florence A. Underwood, "this resolution has been reaffirmed by our committee and by our delegates to conferences convened by other societies. At the Congress of the International Woman Suffrage Alliance at Rome in 1923 our delegates maintained that no restrictions should be imposed on the work of women which are not also imposed on men's work. We ask for equal opportunities and equal pay for women with men in all branches of industry, in commerce, in the professions and in the civil service. We hold that any special protective restrictions can only undermine women's chance for equality. A fair field and no favor is the watchword of the Women's Freedom League."

This organization did not stop at resolutions. In 1920, when a bill was brought in (following the Washington Convention) to prohibit women, young persons and children from night work in factories, the Freedom League fought against the inclusion of women with all its force. Their view is, quite frankly, that all restrictive legislation in regard to women's work is engineered by men who do not wish to have women's full competition in their particular trades, and in the interests of women should be uncompromisingly opposed.

The third active feminist organization in Great Britain, the Six-Point Group, of which Lady Rhondda is the founder and chairman, has never taken formal action on the matter of industrial restrictions, but it is well known that its officers are opposed to such restrictions except when applied to men and women alike. An unsigned editorial in *Time and Tide* (Lady Rhondda's paper) for March 20, in commenting on the recent action of the N.U.S.E.C., says: "For our part we are glad that this important body of women should have taken the line they have . . . against protective legislation for women."

This would seem to make it unanimous so far as the distinctively feminist organizations go. The National Union of Societies for Equal Citizenship, the Women's Freedom League and the Six-Point Group, so far as I know the only societies of national scope in this country which are devoted to the object of securing equality for women, take the same stand on the matter of so-called "protective legislation" for women that the National Woman's Party takes in the United States.

International Co-operation

April 7, 1925—as I write the date I realize that it may become as famous in feminist history as July 20, 1848, the date of the Seneca Falls Conference. For today there met together for the first time, at the American Women's Club of London, eight distinguished women who have formed the first national group of what is bound to become a world-wide Equal Rights Committee. "An International Feminist Lobby," an American correspondent has called this proposed committee, and such in a sense it will be,—a vigilant group to guard the rights of women and watch over their real interests in all international agreements, treaties and "conventions," and to advocate and proceed with the full program of Equal Rights for men and women throughout civilization. This group in London has been formed as the British Section of an International Advisory Committee to the National Woman's Party.

The creation of this British Advisory group is in accordance with the program adopted at the last National Convention of the Woman's Party in 1921. At that convention, suffrage having been won, the Woman's Party resolved to work for Equal Rights and recognition for men and women not only in the United States but in any international association or gathering to which our country should become a party. In line with this program, at the conference of National, State and Local officers of the Woman's Party in Washington in November, 1923, Mrs. Oliver H. P. Belmont, president of the Woman's Party, proposed that the organization should get in touch with the women of other nations in order to establish "greater co-operation in dealing with problems of common interest to women, and in order to aid the movement to end the present world-wide subjection of women." The resolution to this effect, introduced by Mrs. Belmont, was adopted by the conference, and Mrs. Belmont was appointed chairman of a committee (with

Equal Rights, 9 May 1925.

power to appoint the other members) to carry out the resolution as soon as possible.

Mrs. Belmont is now in Paris working actively upon the plans for establishing a closer relationship among feminists the world over.

"The formation of our British Advisory group is our first step," said Mrs. Belmont, "toward carrying out the plan agreed upon at our last national conference. We have taken no action heretofore toward carrying out this resolution because no one has had the necessary time to devote to it, owing to the pressure of work involved in the campaign for the Equal Rights Amendment at home. But the opportunity seems opened to us now to lay the foundations for co-operation with the women who are in the vanguard in the feminist movement in all lands.

"While the United States has never joined the League of Nations, it is being inevitably drawn more and more every day into common action with other nations. President Coolidge announces that he will soon call a World Conference. Our nation will undoubtedly go further and further in international action. We must be ready."

The formation of the British Committee was effected by Alice Paul, of the National Council of the Woman's Party, who has spent the last few weeks in London after spending some time in France with Mrs. Belmont, laying the general plans for obtaining closer international co-operation among feminists.

The membership of the newly formed British Advisory group is as follows:

Lady Rhondda: Owner and co-editor of the brilliant feminist weekly, *Time and Tide;* founder and chairman of the Six-Point Group; active financier of extensive interests, known the world over as the first woman to claim a seat in the House of Lords as a peeress in her own right.

Elizabeth Robins: Well-known novelist, author of "Ancilla's Share," a profound satirical study of the position of women through the ages, which is rapidly becoming the feminist "Bible." (Miss Robins is the sister of Raymond Robins of Chicago.)

Dr. Louisa Martindale: Celebrated physician; justice of the peace; past-president of the British Women's Medical Association; a leader in International Woman's Medical Associations; head of the

Woman's Hospital at Brighton, one of the few hospitals in the world staffed and officered entirely by women.

Mrs. Emmeline Pethick-Lawrence: Treasurer of the Women's Social and Political Union throughout the Militant Campaign; one of the founders of the Women's International League for Peace and Freedom, and for many years on the Executive Board of the British Section; a speaker of international repute.

Dorothy Elizabeth Evans: Former secretary of the Women's International League for Peace and Freedom; now secretary of the Women Civil Servants' Association of Great Britain.

Alison Neilans: Secretary of the British Association for Social and Moral Hygiene and editor of its organ, *The Shield.*

Dr. Elizabeth Knight: Treasurer and one of the chief financial supporters of the Women's Freedom League of Great Britain (founded by Mrs. Despard).

Mrs. Virginia Crawford: President of St. Joan's Social and Political Alliance (the great Catholic Feminist organization of Great Britain); a poor law guardian and borough councillor; one of the founders and honorary secretary for six years of the Catholic Social Guild of Great Britain; for many years on the Executive Board of the Catholic Truth Society; well-known author and lecturer on social and political movements.

The first act of this new group was to send a courteous and well-considered cable to the American Association of University Women, meeting in convention at Indianapolis on April 8th, setting forth the position of British feminist leaders on the question of industrial equality for women. The cable was addressed jointly to an English woman, Mrs. Corbett-Ashby, president of the International Suffrage Alliance, who was a guest and speaker at the convention, and to Miss M. Carey Thomas, who had been appointed by the Association of University Women to gather information for the Association on this subject which is so controversial in the United States.

The cable read:

> "We understand that the Convention of the American Association of University Women will consider the question of Equal Rights legislation for men and women. May we ask you to bring before the convention the fact that there is wide-spread support among English feminists for Equal Rights legislation in all fields including the

industrial field, and strong opposition to all so-called protective laws applying to women and not to men.

(Signed),

ELIZABETH ROBINS,
EMMELINE PETHICK-LAWRENCE,
VISCOUNTESS RHONDDA,
DR. LOUISA MARTINDALE,
DOROTHY EVANS,
DR. ELIZABETH KNIGHT,
VIRGINIA CRAWFORD,
ALISON NEILANS."

The newly formed British Advisory group, in addition to cabling to the American University Women's Convention, arranged for the sending of another cable-message on the same day informing the convention that the leading British feminist organizations have endorsed Equal Rights in all fields, including the industrial field, and are opposed to special labor laws applying to women and not to men.

This cable read:

"We understand that American Association of University Women will consider question of Equal Rights legislation for men and women. Please convey to the convention the information that the undersigned British Women's organizations have endorsed Equal Rights legislation for men and women and are opposed to special labor laws applying to women and not to men.

(Signed),

Women's Freedom League,

FLORENCE UNDERWOOD,
Secretary.

National Union for Equal Citizenship,

ELEANOR RATHBONE,
President.

Women's International League for Peace and Freedom,

K. D. COURTNEY,
Chairman.

St. Joan's Social and Political Alliance,

VIRGINIA CRAWFORD,
President."

The British Advisory Committee is a practical bit of co-operation between British and American feminists, the creation of a very
informal alliance, which it is hoped, may be the nucleus of a genuine
international movement for Equal Rights for men and women
throughout the world.

"And you have been encouraged by the response of the British
women?" I asked Miss Paul.

"Yes, indeed. The response was extraordinary. To begin with,
Mrs. Corbett-Ashby, president of the International Suffrage Alliance,
whom I saw first in London, was most helpful. From her wide
international experience she was able to give me the names of
distinguished feminists in a dozen countries who would be likely to
welcome our effort and gladly ally themselves with it. Mrs. Corbett-
Ashby also expressed her desire to have the Woman's Party affiliate
with the International Alliance and we made the preliminary arrangements for this affiliation. Every one else whom I have met has been
equally enthusiastic."

To me as an observer, Miss Paul's brief weeks in London seemed
a sort of triumphal progress. She has found practically no opposition,
but everywhere people eager to meet her because of her magnificent
record of service, and most ready to listen and believe in her plans for
future battles. For what it may signify let me say that she has dined at
the House of Commons with Mr. Pethick-Lawrence, M.P., who gave
a dinner to enable Lady Astor, M.P., and Ellen Wilkinson, M.P., to
meet her; that she has been informally entertained by Mrs. Pethick-
Lawrence; by Lady Rhondda; by Rebecca West; by Mrs. Curtis
Brown, president of the American Women's Club in London; by
Elizabeth Robins; by Mrs. Sydney Webb; by Dr. Louisa Martindale;
by Mrs. Corbett-Ashby; by Chrystal Macmillan; the distinguished
barrister who argued the case for woman suffrage before the House of
Commons; by Mary Borden, the novelist; by Nina Boyle, one of the
leaders in securing recognition for women in the League of Nations;
by Ellen La Motte; by Helen Ward, the well-known pioneer feminist
leader, etc.

I may add that Alice Paul's visit to London has brightened the
lives of such Woman's Party exiles as Hazel Hunkins, Betty Gram
and myself. To see this wonder-worker—so quiet, so indefatigable,

so sure,—once more beginning to move mountains, revives one's faith in the future.

Protective Legislation in England

There is in England a marked cleavage in opinion among women on the matter of special "protective" laws for women, just as there is in America, but the line seems to be drawn quite differently. In America there are two great women's organizations which, while agreeing on most points in the equality program, disagree emphatically, even violently, on the question of whether women should have special restrictions put upon their industrial activities. And I should say that there are women of all shades of political opinion in both groups. In England, on the other hand, all three feminist groups (Women's Freedom League, National Union, and Six Point Group) are as one man in their opposition to "protective" laws applying only to women, while the women who find their public expression through the Labour Party seem to speak with corresponding unanimity in favor of such laws. And of course the feminist opposition to these laws is disposed of by such labor women as Marion Phillips and Margaret Bondfield as a "bourgeois" attitude due to the feminist's complete ignorance of industrial conditions. Indeed, Dr. Phillips, who is chief woman officer of the Labour Party, has assured me more than once with complete statistical finality that I would not be able to find one single Labour or Socialist woman in all England, or any woman who has had an opportunity to study industrial conditions, who was opposed to the law prohibiting night-work for women.

Well, I have found one. Her name is Mary J. Bell-Richards. She lives in Liecester, and is head of the Women's Section of the National

Equal Rights, 3 October 1925.

Union of Boot and Shoe Operatives. She was a delegate to the Conference of Labour and Socialist Women at Marseilles, and one of the most extraordinary women I met there.

It would be difficult to find a labor leader with a more genuinely proletarian background than Mrs. Mary Bell-Richards. Her "opportunity" to study industrial conditions commenced when she was ten years old and first went to work in a shoe factory in Liecester. It continued for twenty-five years during which she became an expert in skill and speed and familiar with every step in the process of making a pair of shoes. When she was twenty her mother died and she was left with an invalid father and five younger brothers and sisters to look after. This meant a "double" life—cooking, sewing, washing for a family after her day's work at the factory was done. For years she had no recreation except to go to chapel and sing one evening a week. But she was gifted with extraordinary health and ability. She was always the "smartest" girl at the factory and could make the highest wages. Her strength and courage for life held through all those years; and she managed to launch the five children on their own working lives. Meanwhile she herself had become a leader in the union, and at thirty-five was elected head of the Women's Section of the National Union of Boot and Shoe Operatives, a position which she has held for fourteen years.

Here she is at fifty—vigorous, well-dressed, thirty-five in appearance and carriage, without a gray hair in her head—a responsible trade-union executive, no longer working in the factory but representing all the women in this great trade, individually and collectively, in their relations with their employers. What does she say about these laws which "protect" and at the same time "restrict" women in their working lives?

We had been discussing feminism in various phases as we dined together at the close of the conference, and finally, because she seemed so very decidedly my kind of a feminist, I decided to broach the question of special protection. I more than half expected to be put in my place as a bourgeois meddler.

"Mrs. Richards," I said, "you've been in industry all your life. Do you think women workers want special protective legislation?"

"No, we don't want it!" she exclaimed. "You can't protect

women without handicapping them in competition with men. If you demand equality you must accept equality. Women can't have it both ways."

"Then you don't believe in the no-night-work law for women?"

"No. Why should I? If men work at night there is no reason why women should not work at night. Let's have better laws for both. I know men who are stronger than women and I know women who are stronger than men. Of course we must protect children and I think we must protect women when children are born. But we ought to have no laws for women in general unless they also apply to men in general. That's what I say."

"If you demand equality you must accept equality." It will be on the basis of some such hard practical logic as that that this question of protective-restrictive laws will eventually be settled, I think, and I think it will be settled by women like Mary Bell-Richards.

London Letter—
The Married Teacher

Today I heard judgment delivered in the third of the married women teacher cases, and I never felt more sure that women in all Anglo-Saxon countries need a *bill of rights*. This was the case known as *Fennell vs. Borough of East Ham*. But since the judgment was but a reflection of the judgment of a higher court in the more celebrated Poole Case, and since the facts in all three cases are essentially the same, let me give a brief account of the Poole case.

On May 6, 1924, the Borough of Poole adopted a report to the effect that the retention of married women teachers was inadvisable, that they had therefore decided to dismiss them unless good reason to

Equal Rights, 30 January 1926.

the contrary were shown. ("Good reason to the contrary," it appears, had to do altogether with the husband's ability to support the married woman about to be dismissed, not in any sense with her record as a teacher, no matter how extraordinary.) The reasons given for this decision were (1) that a married woman should attend to her domestic duties, and that it was impossible for her to do both this and her school work efficiently; and (2) that to retain married women teachers who had husbands who could support them was unfair to young unmarried women.

Consequent upon this decision, a certain Ethel Short, who had been a certificated teacher since 1905, received notice, in common with certain other married women teachers employed by the Borough, to terminate her engagement in one month.

Mrs. Short brought an action against the Borough and won her case in the lower court. Mr. Justice Romer held that the local education authority was not justified in dismissing Mrs. Short solely on the ground that she was married, that their reasons were not educational, that their motives were alien and irrelevant, and the dismissal was therefore invalid and inoperative.

From this decision the Borough of Poole appealed and secured a reversal. The Court of Appeal handed down its "considered judgment" on November 20, 1925. In this judgment it is made clear that there was no question but that Mrs. Short had performed her duties satisfactorily and was an efficient teacher. On the other hand there was no question but that the Borough had acted in good faith. There was no suspicion of bribery or corruption. The sole question was whether the Borough had gone outside its province as an education authority, and whether therefore their action in giving notice of dismissal was *ultra vires*. The court concluded that the Borough of Poole was well within its powers in making the rule in regard to married women teachers and acting upon it. "To decide to employ only women whose whole lives should be devoted to teaching was not irrelevant." "The local educational authority was entitled to consider that the performance of domestic duties would tend to diminish educational efficiency, and that the supply of young teachers would be adversely affected by the employment of married women."

This decision is to all practical purpose final. The only appeal now is to the House of Lords and that is not likely to be undertaken; it would be costly and the chance of a Feminist victory almost negligible.

I don't know what legal stage this question has reached in the United States, but I feel sure that this decision in the Poole case is worthy of study over there. American judges have not ceased to quote British precedents. And certainly no precedent has been set up in modern times more firmly establishing the "subjection of women." We are accustomed to think of the Married Woman's Property Act as something achieved long before our time. We look back with some pity and condescension on the married woman of mid-Victorian days who could not hold property in her own name, whose earnings did not belong to her any more than if she were a minor. But here is a decision handed down in the year of our Lord 1925, 25 years after Queen Victoria was buried, which takes from the married woman, not to be sure, the property she has accumulated, but *her right to acquire more*, her right to continue to earn her living by the profession in which she is trained and experienced. By such decisions as this in the Poole case married women in tens of thousands can be (*and are being*) cut off in mid-career, women of the highest skill and proved ability in their chosen trades and professions forced back into the ranks of unskilled labor, their rich experience lost to the State, their years of faithful achievement to count for nothing in winning comfort, happiness, opportunity for themselves and their children.

The powers of these local educational authorities in England are on paper almost unlimited. They may "appoint necessary officers, including teachers, to hold office during their pleasure, and may assign to them such salaries as they see fit, and may remove any of those officers." But in actual legal practice their power is extremely limited. They must not dismiss teachers for a corrupt or collateral or an irrelevant reason. For example, in one of the cases quoted by Mrs. Short's counsel, *Sadler vs. Sheffield Corporation,* an Education Committee had been forced to reduce expenses and had decided to do it by dismissing some of the teachers over sixty years of age. The dismissal notices were held to be invalid and inoperative because they were based on financial and not educational reasons. And the elderly teachers were reinstated.

It is notoriously hard to get rid of an inefficient teacher as all school boards know. His or her tenure of office is almost a life grant. Yet by the Poole decision a way has been found to remove by wholesale superior teachers in the prime of life, teachers whose work is above criticism.

I can think of many amusing parallels. For example, "the Borough of . . . announces: Miss Jones, the splendid principal of our grammar school, has been offered the position of cook and housekeeper by the family next door, and so we feel obliged to dismiss her and make room for one of the young girls just graduated from training college. Miss Jones may not care to be a cook but since she has that privilege we don't think it right for her to continue to teach, valuable as her services are to the community." Or, "the Educational Committee of . . . Borough has adopted a rule to employ no more men teachers who have vegetable gardens, and to notify those men now in its employ who possess vegetable gardens or are contemplating acquiring one that they will be dismissed. We are actuated by the following reasons: (1) The place of a man with a vegetable garden is at home working in his garden. (2) We feel, as a general rule, that a man with a vegetable garden will, to some extent, suffer in his efficiency as a teacher. We have no evidence of this; in fact the vegetable gardeners whom we are about to dismiss are among our best teachers, but nevertheless, we feel that as a general policy our rule is sound from an educational standpoint. (3) A man with a garden will not starve. Therefore, it is unfair to continue paying him a salary as a teacher while men who have no vegetable gardens are waiting for posts."

It must be remembered that this decision in the Poole case undermines the professional security, not only of women teachers, but of thousands of women nurses, doctors, clerks, stenographers, staticians, experts of all kinds, heads of institutions, etc., in fact, I presume of all women employed by local public authorities throughout the British Isles.

British Feminists are not taking the decision lying down. A question has already been asked in the House. Capt. Walter Shaw (Conservative member), shortly after the Poole decision, asked the President of the Board of Education (Lord Eustace Percy) if he would not "initiate legislation or promulgate a departmental Order for the purpose of preventing local education authorities from dismissing teachers who have served them faithfully and well through a long period of years simply and solely because they have married." Lord Eustace Percy replied that he did not see his way to intervene in the matter, whereupon Lady Astor called his attention to the Sex Disqualification (Removal) Act and suggested that that should cover the case. Lord Eustace Percy did not agree.

This act, as most EQUAL RIGHTS readers will remember, was passed in 1919, shortly after the suffrage victory in England. By reason of it women were admitted to the practise of law, a thousand women magistrates have been appointed, certain university restrictions have been withdrawn, women have been admitted to jury service, etc. There is a clause in the act which reads: "A person shall not be disqualified by sex or marriage from the exercise of any public function or from being appointed to or holding any civil or judicial office or post." In the first of these teachers' cases it was hoped that the act would prove sufficient to prevent the arbitrary dismissal of married women. But as a check on the action of local authorities it has proved valueless. I don't quite know why. Apparently it is too general. On the basis of this experience the National Union of Societies for Equal Citizenship is drawing up a new and very specific bill. In its present form it reads:

"From and after the passing of this act it shall not be lawful for any government department or any local government or other public authority to make any rule or regulation whereby a person shall be disqualified by reason of marriage from being or continuing to be employed by such body, and any such provision in force at the passing of this act shall from such date be null and void; and in any contract of employment made by such department or authority whether made before or after the passing of this act, any stipulation providing for the resignation of an employee on marriage or for the termination of a contract on the marriage of an employee shall be null and void, and such contract shall be construed as if such stipulations were omitted therefrom."

The failure of the Sex Disqualification Act to cover these cases which it was obviously intended by its supporters to cover, demon-

strates the need for eternal vigilance to guard every advance we make
in this hundred-year war for equality. It should also make us glad
that we have a constitution in America, that a woman's bill of rights
can be written into that constitution which will forever prevent such
intolerable invasion of the rights of the free-born.

CRYSTAL EASTMAN.

P.S.—Will some one of our brave band get the opinions of half
a dozen infallible constitutional lawyers as to whether our amendment
will establish, once for all, the right of a public employee to marry
without being thrown on the street?

British Women Fire the First Gun in Their Second Suffrage Battle

---

It seemed an anachronism to be going to a suffrage meeting, but there
it was on the announcement, "A Public Meeting at the Caxton Hall,
Westminster, January 19, to demand Votes for Women on the Same
Terms as Men." And when I got inside it looked just like a suffrage
meeting too, not like one of the great roaring, laughing, passionate
meetings of the last years of our campaign, but like a suffrage meeting
of the late Nineties, perhaps. There were the two or three hundred
earnest believers scattered about trying to look like a crowded hall,
and there was the one pale, thinnish man caught in the ample row of
women speakers on the platform. And the opening speech, which, as
it happened, was made by the one man, sustained my illusion. This
gentleman's soothing and chivalrous effort to show that women are as
good and intelligent and brave, etc., as men that they really should

Equal Rights, 27 February 1926.

have the vote, was so exactly like the speeches I had heard men make at suffrage meetings which I attended with my mother 30 years ago, that I concluded none of it was real. I slipped down comfortably in my chair hoping to sleep as well as dream.

Just as I was "losing myself" I heard a quick nervous step and looked up to see a very small woman come rapidly down the centre aisle, step up on to the platform and sit down. "There is something vaguely military about her," I thought, "but she's not like a soldier, she's like a general." Perhaps it was her straight black coat with its stand-up collar. Perhaps it was her stiff black velvet hat with its distinctly Napoleonic suggestion. Perhaps it was her walk—that fast heel-walk so common to small people who have an extra ordinary amount of vigor and power to command. And again, perhaps it was an air she had, emphatically assured and yet emphatically alert; it is an air one often sees in a military man of high rank and small stature.

The big Napoleon hat was pulled over her copper-colored hair and almost over those round appealing mother-eyes of hers, but I could not mistake the big nose and determined little chin and the pale creamy skin—of course it was Ellen Wilkinson, M. P. And when, after a moment or two, she got up to speak, the whole meeting seemed to leap forward into the twentieth century, indeed, to the beginning of the second quarter of the twentieth century.

"I have just left a committee," said Ellen. "As I left I told them I was going to a suffrage meeting. You should have seen the astonishment on the face of every member of that committee! 'A suffrage meeting in 1926!' they said. 'Why, the only people that haven't the vote are girls. Surely you cannot think that is important with all the other things you are trying to do?" And that is the usual attitude.

"I need not tell you how short-sighted that attitude is. It is not only that our election law disfranchises certain women, or women of a certain age. That would be bad enough. But this law practically disfranchises a class—in effect it takes the vote from the great majority of single women wage-earners. No woman under thirty can vote and most of our women industrial workers are under thirty. But this is not all. The so-called residence qualification which looks to me very much like a property qualification disfranchises a vast number of single women of the wage-earning and poorer paid professional classes who are over thirty."

She went on to show how she had seen again and again since she entered Parliament that the government's mind is influenced by the fact that all these women are voteless. For example, "The widow's pension act discriminates all through against single women. Those who pay in more than they get out are largely women who have no votes."

"But it is not only in legislation that the vote counts. There is great exploitation of the young women workers in this country, no one can deny it. I am more and more convinced these low wages are determined not by the value of the work done, but partly by custom, partly by organization, and partly by *status*. It may seem far-fetched, but I am sure that *the inferior political status of these young women workers is reflected in their pay*. The fact that they do not vote is the fundamental reason why they don't get equal pay."

The rounds of applause that followed Ellen Wilkinson's last words rolled into the long applause that greeted Mrs. Pethick-Lawrence, who made one of the best speeches I have ever heard. I had listened to Mrs. Lawrence on peace, but never before on a Feminist issue. I find she has not only emotional power, but a shrewd wit, great cogency, and a gift of ridicule which, with her smile and her essentially generous personality, is as disarming as praise. "Why is the government afraid of women?" was the keynote of her speech. She began by describing a cartoon she had seen: a small man under a bed with a large woman standing over him, brandishing a rolling-pin or some such emblem and demanding that he come out. The man, cowering well under the bed out of her reach, is shouting; "I won't come out! I won't come out! I *will* be master in my own house!" This she suggested is the way the government is acting about the Equal Franchise measure. Mr. Baldwin, it seems, gave a sort of a pledge during the last pre-election campaign declaring his party to be in favor of equal political rights, but proposing that the question of extending the franchise be referred to a "conference" representing all parties.

"But, the Conservative Party's real attitude," said Mrs. Lawrence, "was shown at the debate a year ago. A perfectly good Equal

Franchise measure was introduced in a private member's bill. No one spoke against it. No member, now that all members are dependent on women's votes, would have dared to speak against it. If the government had allowed it to go to a second reading it would have carried. But Mr. Baldwin appealed to his party to vote against a second reading and in favor of his conference scheme. We must put no trust in any government whatever. We must take the matter in our own hands as we did before. There is not a moment to lose if women are to vote at the next general election."

And later, "the present franchise for women is an absurdity. It was as though the Government said, 'The women have worked hard in the war, we must do something for them. We'll give them the vote at thirty.' So this fantastic franchise was devised. Women are supposed to dread reaching the age of thirty. 'Well, now,' said the Government, 'you confess to being thirty, we'll give you the vote.' A sort of consolation prize.

"Why are they afraid? What is the matter with British women? Women of the United States, women of Canada, women of Australia, even women of many States of India have the vote on equal terms with men. What is the matter with the British women? It is said that if all women were given the vote they would be in the majority, a majority of perhaps two million. But aren't these women British? Are they an alien section? What is there to be afraid of?"

The rest of Mrs. Lawrence's speech was devoted to rousing the meeting to enthusiasm to take up this fight in the old spirit, to rededicate themselves, as Miss Wilkinson had said, and "get this irritating restriction out of the way." At the close she came back again to the earlier note with a telling word on Britain's favorite boast. "We like to sing, 'Britons never, never shall be slaves.' But Britain will never be really free until every British child is born of a free woman, and until every *British man drives out of his heart this fear of women.*"

There is a strong conservative trend in England now toward raising the voting age to 25. The Premier himself has spoken in approval of it. And it seems likely that Mr. Baldwin's desire to get the Equal Franchise matter referred to a "conference" is two-fold; to delay the full enfranchisement of women by involving it with a general discussion of the reform of the franchise, and to gain a hearing under apparently progressive auspices for this alarming Tory proposal to advance the voting age. Both Miss Wilkinson and Mrs. Lawrence made clear their opposition to "votes at 25." What British Feminists are demanding is the vote for women on the same terms that men vote *now*—no raising of the voting age. "This is a real danger," said Miss Wilkinson. "It is an effort to disfranchise youth. This country is too old anyhow. We are governed by old men."

The last speaker, Miss Emily Phipps, is a woman whose name is not yet known to American readers, I think. She is the editor of the *Woman Teacher,* and one of the most valued leaders in the women teacher's fight for equality. She is also a barrister, and was one of the pioneer women candidates for Parliament in 1918. Miss Phipps kept up the spirited standard of this really remarkable meeting. Her speech was full of laughter and full of important facts and figures.

"There are five million women disfranchised under our present laws," Miss Phipps explained, "and only three million men. And three million of the five million women are over thirty. This is of course explained by the 'residence' qualification which is quite different for men and women. A man has to prove merely that he lives somewhere. A woman has to prove either that she occupies premises of the annual rental value of £5, or that she is the wife of a man who occupies such premises. If she does not 'occupy premises' in the legal sense but is a lodger she must prove that she owns her own furniture. This disfranchises at one blow nearly all domestic workers. And it disfranchises a vast proportion of single women wage earners, clerical workers, and even teachers who are notoriously low-paid, and who are forced to live from hand to mouth in 'furnished rooms.' There it is then, our fancy franchise—because I haven't a chest of drawers I cannot vote.

"And what reason do its defenders give for this legal absurdity? 'We must disfranchise some women. If we gave the vote to them all they would be in a majority.' But what is a two-million majority in a democracy? This so-called reason is just the rationalization of a fear. And the fear is based on a fallacy, *i.e.,* that women will all vote alike. But we know there is no issue on which all women think alike, hardly one on which all Feminist women think alike."

Miss Phipps, too, called for fighting on the old lines with banners flying and women marching with a fiery determination in their hearts.

This meeting which I have been tempted to review in such detail is the beginning of a campaign on which all British Feminist groups have united this year. One good hard push and the thing will be done.

British Women Condemn
Sex Restrictions in Industry

This has been a great week for suffrage in London. At the invitation of the St. Joan's Social and Political Alliance, Mme. Malaterre-Sellier, secretary of the *Union Française pour le Suffrage des Femmes,* crossed the channel in order to issue personally an invitation to British women to attend the Tenth Annual Woman Suffrage Congress to be held at the Sorbonne in Paris, May 30 to June 6 next. Mme Malaterre spoke at crowded meetings on Thursday and Friday evenings. She is a woman distinguished in many fields. During the war she received the Croix de Guerre and the Legion D'Honneur for war service. In 1918 she was awarded the Prix Audiffred de l'Academie Francais for a most remarkable act of heroism. She also undertook valuable social work during the war, founding antituberculosis and milk depots in the liberated districts. Since the war she has become an active leader in the peace and Feminist movements, acting not only as Secretary of the Union Française but as president of its Paris group, as a member of the executive board of the I.W.S.A., as president of the peace section of the French National Council of Women, and as vice-president of the Women's League of Nations Union.

Equal Rights, 27 March 1926.

Despite her many achievements and distinctions Mme. Malaterre is young and handsome, and she has that rare, mysterious gift of
eloquence. (Sometimes I think it is merely the power of feeling
intensely, feeling to the full the meaning and purpose of the words
spoken, and feeling at the same time the beauty of the words
themselves.) She asked us to come to the Sorbonne in May as though
the privilege of asking us were a great dramatic opportunity in her
life, and as though she were calling us to start a revolution.

The Congress has been fixed for the end of May with an eye on
the French Senate which meets in June. The suffrage measure which
passed the Deputies last year was defeated in the Senate by 21 votes.
And it is hoped that this great gathering of women from all over the
world in Paris just as the French Senate opens will have its effect on
those twenty-one votes.

On Friday of last week also, occurred the second mass-meeting
in the Equal Citizenship Campaign, upon which all the Feminist
groups and scores upon scores of other organizations have united this
spring. Its object is to complete the enfranchisement of British
women. The present measure, by which women over thirty may vote,
has no basis in reason or justice and, moreover has the distinct effect
of disfranchising more than half of the women industrial workers. A
unique feature of this meeting was the reading of greetings and
messages of encouragement from Mrs. Pankhurst who happens to be
in London now, and from Lord Oxford (formerly Mr. Herbert
Asquith).

Of far greater interest to me than these public meetings,
however, were the sessions of the annual council meeting of the
National Union of Societies for Equal Citizenship. It was this society,
(as perhaps some faithful reader will remember)—the largest, oldest,
and most conservative of British Feminist groups—which last year
re-affirmed its conviction "that legislation for the protection of the
workers should be based not upon sex but upon the nature of the
occupation," and regretted "that certain of the Washington conventions are not in accordance with these principles."

Resolutions may not amount to much in the history of progress,
but they indicate its direction. At last week's meeting the
N.U.S.E.C. passed six resolutions dealing with protective laws,

which for vigor and emphasis, and for vigilant attention to specific violations of the principle of equality, leave nothing to be desired. From the debate which raged around these resolutions one may fairly assume that the question of sex restrictions in industry has become a major Feminist issue in Great Britain.

There was, to begin with, a decided attempt made to modify the attitude of the Union by substituting for last year's pronouncement (quoted above) the following:

"This Council recognizes the danger that protective legislation for women workers may result in the arbitrary restriction of their wage-earning opportunities, and calls upon the N.U.S.E.C. executive to take cognizance of the course of such legislation with a view to detecting and combating its abuse."

This substitute resolution was proposed by Mrs. Stocks, who is chairman of the executive; it was supported by such women as Madeleine Simons, a well-known Fabian and co-worker of Beatrice and Sidney Webb; it was known to be favored by the president and most distinguished member of the Society, Mrs. Eleanor Rathbone. Nevertheless, it had no chance. And I was interested to find that one of the younger women who opposed the substitute and believed it a dangerous attempt to weaken the stand of the National Union on industrial equality is a labour woman, Miss Monica Whately, active member and speaker in the Labour Party and a prospective Labour candidate for Parliament. It is good to find an occasional Feminist in the Labour Party.

Indeed the intention of the delegates was by no means to weaken their opposition to restrictive laws, but rather to emphasize and define it.

Thus, in re-drafting their immediate program, Point No. 4, which reads "Equal pay for equal work and equality in industry and the professions," was specifically defined to include:

"(a) The abolition of the customary division of labour into men's and women's work.

"(b) The application of the principle that protective legislation shall be based on the nature of the work and not upon the sex of the workers."

Next came three resolutions dealing with proposed labour legislation in Great Britain, which I quote in full:

1. "The N.U.S.E.C. calls upon the Government in its promised consolidating and amending Factories Bill so to frame its provisions for the safeguarding of the worker, including those dealing with hours of labour, periods of employment, sanitation and ventilation, rest, medical attention and examination, and general supervision of health, that they shall apply to men and women equally.

". . . And protests against the inclusion in any such bill of provisions which give the Secretary of State unlimited powers to exclude female young persons on the ground of sex from any process or to limit the conditions of their employment.

2. "That in view of the attempt made during the debate on the Expiring Laws Bill to restrict still further the already limited freedom of women in industry, by prohibiting their employment on the two-shift system, and in view of the fact that this system has in those cases in which it has been permitted had beneficial effects, this Council calls upon the Government to promote legislation permitting the employment of women on the shift system.

3. "That if a bill on the line of the Lead Paint (Protection Against Poisoning) Bill, 1925, be introduced during this session, this Council demands that it shall not include Clause 2 of that bill, which would have the effect of closing the painting trade to women and of limiting apprenticeship to male persons only."

Finally a long resolution was adopted demanding international action. It began by calling attention to the efforts of the International Labour Office "to standardize internationally a system of differential restrictive legislation against women workers," and urging "international action to combat the underlying fallacies of this so-called protection of women." The resolution then went on to ordain two courses of action: the National Union should (1) "co-operate with individuals and organizations in other countries who oppose restrictive legislation"; and (2) *"seek to have the following resolution placed upon the Agenda of the International Woman Suffrage Alliance Congress in May:*

" 'This Congress holds that all regulations and restrictions which aim at the true protection of the worker must be based not upon sex but on the nature of the occupation; and that any international system of differential legislation based on sex, in spite of any temporary advantage, must develop into an intolerable tyranny and result in the segregation of women workers and impose fresh handicaps on their capacity as wage-earners.' "

What does the adoption of this resolution mean? It means that the entire British delegation will go to Paris in May committed to asking the I.W.S.A. to call the highly benevolent designs of the International Labour Office for woman's protection an "intolerable tyranny," as indeed they are.

Woman's Party Accepts Paris Congress Repulse As Spur to a World-Wide Feminist Movement

Leaders Felt Triumphant in Defeat, Viewing Rejection by Suffrage Alliance as Challenging Idea of Equality With Men

With the sure instinct of self-preservation, the old bottle has rejected the new wine—by a vote of 123 to 43 the International Suffrage Alliance has refused the application of the Woman's Party for affiliation.

What was the formula of rejection? How did they do it and yet preserve the outward forms of democracy and a fair hearing? And, finally, what will this rejection mean in the history of feminism?

We will take the official reasons first. These were read to the congress on the morning of the vote in English, French and German. They cover two closely typed pages, so I can merely summarize and comment on them here.

First come three paragraphs to explain that the constitution of the Woman's Party is in perfect accord with the alliance. "It is not because of its advocacy of industrial equality that the Woman's Party is to be excluded. The alliance allows complete freedom on the

The World, 27 June 1926.

particular question of protective legislation. Many of the delegations are divided. Even on the board there is difference of opinion."

This explanation was emphatically necessary, for everybody knew there was a very strong minority in the alliance opposed to protective legislation at the Rome Congress in 1923. No one was quite sure that it had not become a majority. In fact, three days before the congress opened one of the five special "commissions" of the alliance, the Commission on Like Conditions of Work, had held a large preliminary meeting and by a vote of 71 to 38 adopted a set of resolutions condemning special protective legislation, and denouncing the benevolent efforts of the International Labor Office to restrict the freedom of women in industry in terms as emphatic and thorough-going as though they had been chosen by Alice Paul herself!

Woman's Party Eager for Action

I think the board was sincere in thinking that the exclusion had nothing to do with the protective legislation issue. But as a matter of fact it had everything to do with it. The Woman's Party not only believes in industrial equality, it believes in fighting for it and getting it. If they had been admitted into the alliance they would have joined forces with the industrial equality group already there (a large and able body of delegates, if not one-half) and their demand would have become a demand for action. That would have split the alliance.

It is all right for the lion and the lamb to lie down together if they are both asleep, but if one of them begins to get active it is dangerous. The believers in equality and the believers in special protection can live together in the same International Alliance, so long as their beliefs are merely academic. But suppose the equality group should organize an international lobby and begin to dog the footsteps of the I.L.O.—as they would be sure to do within six months with the help and inspiration of the Woman's Party. Would the alliance survive that?

Now let us come to the reasons for the rejection of the National Woman's Party as officially set forth.

Reason number one states that the League of Women Voters is

opposed and makes a reference to its "loyal and generous support of the alliance." Here at least is a practical reason—i.e., the alliance cannot live without the legaue's financial support, which will be withdrawn if the Woman's Party is admitted.

"They sold us out for $3,000!" remarked one of our flippant younger members when she was told later in the week that the treasurer of the alliance, after forty-five minutes of pleading, had raised $3,150 to carry on until the next convention, of which $3,000 had been pledged by America, to be paid at the rate of $1,000 a year. "Three thousand dollars from the women of all the world! And at a luncheon in Paris two days after we were thrown out of the alliance we raised $6,000 in ten minutes from a handful of American women in Paris."

Mrs. Catt's Opposition Given as a Reason

Reason number two stated the opposition of Mrs. Carrie Chapman Catt, "founder of the alliance and President for twenty years." Here is sentimentality for you! All honor to Mrs. Catt. I heard her preside at a Suffrage Congress at Budapest in 1913, in the days when this alliance was in its first strength and glory, and she was magnificent. But they do her no honor who would drag forth and emphasize the little-mindedness of her declining years.

Where are we now? A policy of caution—penny wise, pound foolish. And a sentimental loyalty to a past leader. Are these sound foundations for an international policy of strength and growth? Surely there must be a better reason for rejecting a new source of power.

Reason No. 4—"The press campaign of the Woman's Party." We don't like it. "It has shown that the body in question would not be a source of strength to the alliance, but quite the contrary."

Somehow this has a familiar ring. It reminds me of the conservative Suffragists of early days who would not consent to have a procession "because it would destroy the effect of all the good, quiet work we are doing." Let me quote to you what Lady Rhondda said about our press campaign in Paris. She was speaking at a little luncheon which was arranged in Paris to celebrate our defeat and at which she and Mrs. Belmont were guests of honor. She said:

"Ladies, you will remember that the head and front of your offense was concerned with the press. You were accused, you will remember, of seeing to it that the National Woman's Party got mentioned in the press. Well, I was so determined to find out just what the trouble was that I read right through all the press cuttings relating to the Congress. Certainly a good seven-eighths of those cuttings seemed to me to bear traces of having originated with your very able Press Secretary. But so far from the Woman's Party being unduly pushed it was the Congress that received first place every time.

"The Woman's Party was wonderfully little pushed, considering that it was responsible for the cuttings. It seemed to me to show—for a political organization—a most unusual modesty. But what did seem clear to me when I had finished was that if the Woman's Party had never come to Paris not one word about the Congress would ever have appeared in the press. In fact, ladies, the difference between you is pretty obviously this: You believe in having a good press while those responsible for the organization of the Congress believe in having a bad press. Possibly they do not think it is very ladylike to have a good press."

Early Arrivals Are Gaining Ground

I have now summed up the official reasons why the National Woman's Party was excluded from the International Alliance. Obviously those reasons by themselves would not have been enough to satisfy the delegates.

Something had to be done to make sure of an unfavorable vote by the Congress. The Committee on Admissions had done its best in the early spring by a flat "refusal to recommend the affiliation" of the National Woman's Party without any reasons given. To this the Woman's Party had replied by sending to Paris not only the two fraternal delegates who were to state its case before the Congress but a party of twenty-five or thirty supporting members as a demonstration of good will. These women, through their excellent publicity and through the splendid personal impression they made on the early arriving national Presidents and delegates, were rapidly making friends for the Woman's Party, and the idea of receiving it into the International despite the advice of the Admissions Committee was gaining ground.

Something had to be done. A joint meeting of the board and the national Presidents was called three days before the convention opened, and two representatives each of the Woman's Party and of the League of Women Voters were asked to appear.

Miss Doris Stevens and Mrs. Clarence Smith appeared for the party, Miss Belle Sherwin and Mrs. A. Gordon Norrie, for the league.

I have heard at least seven accounts of that hearing, and all accounts agreed that the Woman's Party won its case. Miss Sherwin had nothing much to say except that the Woman's Party was impossible to work with. Mrs. Norrie, in attempting to corroborate this from her experience of legislative work on equality bills in New York State, revealed considerable lack of information concerning the actual situation which, after a few words of explanation from Mrs. Smith, she graciously acknowledged.

Miss Stevens, in a brief statement, made clear that the Woman's Party approached the International with a genuine desire to help. She followed with a modest record of the history and achievements of the party, which was enough to convince the national Presidents that its help in the international movement would be exceedingly valuable. And Mrs. Smith, from her background of five years' legislative work for the Woman's Party in New York State, was able to show that it was the party which had done active work for the equality bills in the State and it was the league which had refused to co-operate.

Both Woman's Party representatives made an excellent impression. After hearing them most of the Presidents had reached the same conclusion—these are splendid, intelligent, honest, able women. Their only crime is that they believe in a program of full equality and that they are determined to achieve that equality and not merely pass resolutions about it. They are just what we need in the I.W.S.A.

If the national Presidents had voted immediately after that hearing they would have voted to recommend the affiliation of the National Woman's Party. There seems to be little doubt of that.

Secret Came Out Behind Closed Doors

But this "hearing" was only part of the board's plan, and the least important part. After the four representatives left the room there followed a secret session in which all proceedings were in strict confidence.

In effect the Presidents were told: "Disregard the results of this hearing and the excellent impression these two women have made upon you. We will now tell you the real reason why we cannot admit them into the alliance." Then a letter was read from Mrs. Catt (in strict confidence) condemning the party and all its works. Other accusations were made, specific and general. What was not said was implied. One or two of the Presidents protested, but no discussion was allowed. It was arranged that the Presidents should meet again the next morning at 10 and vote whether or not to recommend the admission of the Woman's Party.

Of this confidential session and of the accusations made we of the Woman's Party were of course in complete ignorance. We thought our hearing was a genuine one and that we had won on the basis of the facts. When the Presidents voted next morning (again without discussion and in spite of several protests), and we learned from the press that the vote had gone heavily against us, we could not understand it.

I have described this clever bit of organization trickery not because I feel particularly indignant about it but because it was so very smooth. The open hearing, with every chance for question and answer, everything fair and square and above board, followed by the secret session, with "confidential" accusations, no chance of a hearing, no question or answer, no discussion. What could be simpler?

"Whispered" Hints Of Grave Charges

So much for the method. The International Board felt that it was fighting for its life; it must make sure that the delegates would turn us down on Monday morning. It had accomplished its object. It had started a "whispering" campaign against us.

Innocent delegates, asking why we were not to be admitted,

were told in an ominous whisper, "Personal reasons!" And the Presidents, meeting privately with their delegates on the day before the congress, talked of "grave charges," "absolute secrecy," "must stand by the board," &c.

Not all the Presidents were lost to us by the "secret accusations." Quite a number were roused to indignation in our behalf. One, Viscountess Rhondda of the Six Point Group in England, publicly withdrew the application of her society for affiliation (already accepted by the board) in protest against the methods used to secure our exclusion.

And before the vote of the congress was finally taken on Monday morning a half dozen leading women among the delegates spoke vehemently in our behalf. Others were ready to speak if time had been allowed. Throughout this storm of protest, however, the board sat calmly on the platform, undisturbed; its work had been done— the vote was safe.

After our fate had been decided, after we knew that our application had been finally rejected by a large majority of the delegates themselves, we felt, of course, the usual relief. But we felt also very decidedly elated. This was to be expected at first because of the fine fight that had been put up for us by our new friends among the delegates. But, mysteriously, this quiet little feeling of triumph stayed with us all that day. And on the next day, when we went in a body to greet Mrs. Belmont on her arrival from America and tell her that we had failed, we were still feeling pleased with ourselves in some unaccountable way.

Felt Triumphant Even in Defeat

The following day, Wednesday, was the day of the luncheon to which I have already referred. When I arrived at the restaurant I noticed the same look of triumph in people's faces. And later, when the talking began, there was the little note of victory in every speech. Why was it, when we had come so far to get into the International and had failed, that we felt so glad about it?

Suddenly, in the midst of that luncheon, I knew why. Two new convictions were born of the tempest in Paris roused by the Woman's

Party's application for membership in the International Alliance and its inglorious rejection—convictions which are destined to mean infinitely more to the progress of feminism than our acceptance in the International could ever have meant. At the luncheon on Wednesday those convictions became articulate, they were recognized and acclaimed for the first time. It was for this, I thought, that we came to Paris.

"What is the real reason that you have been turned down?" asked Lady Rhondda on that occasion.

"Would you like to know? Putting aside all the reasons given, the real reason is that you are feminists. Just that. It may seem to you at first sight an odd reason for which an international alliance of Woman Suffragists should turn you down. But I do not need to tell you, you who work in the woman's movement, that all Suffragists are not feminists. In fact, one may divide the women in the woman's movement into two groups; the feminists, and the reformers who are not in the least feminists, who do not care two pence for equality for itself, who, in so far as they are interested in it at all, are merely interested in it as a means to an end."

"For instance, nearly all women reformers wanted votes for women because they believed that the woman's vote would further the reforms that they had at heart—infant welfare, prison reform, temperance and a dozen other things. Now every woman's organization recognizes that reformers are far more common than feminists, that the passion to look after your fellow man, and especially woman, to do good to her in your way is far more common than the desire to put into every one's hand the power to look after themselves—always all these organizations therefore have so arranged their programs as to attract if possible both feminist and reformer.

"Some of them so arranged it as not to bother about the feminist, to concentrate upon the reformer. The result is that the reformers are in the majority to-day in the woman's movement and are in a very big majority over the feminists in the I.W.S.A. There are, in fact, very few pure feminists in that body. But your organization is one of the very few in the world to-day which is purely feminist, and the very sight of it and of you makes the reformer shiver. She has a feeling that instead of being allowed to potter away at welfare work, at protective work for women, she will be forced to move swiftly toward that complete equality of opportunity between men and women for which in her heart she is not yet ready.

"And so the reformers, when they saw you advancing toward the I.W.S.A., were terrified and they rose in their big majority and barred the way. They were frightened of the glare of the dawn breaking in on their comfortable twilight.

"I believe that this action of the I.W.S.A. has taught us a lesson, has taught us that however closely we may co-operate with the reformers in working for individual reforms, we must, if we are to keep our faith whole, actually work together with those of a like faith. We must separate the sheep from the goats.

"They have shown us who are feminists, feminists first and last, where we are drifting to and where our spiritual home really lies. They have made us feel that we are one body, the feminists of the world."

Another speaker at the luncheon said: "There are many very valuable bodies that exist mainly or solely for purposes of deliberation, for the exchange of ideas and the recording of progress. And most international bodies are by their very nature of this kind.

"But in the feminist international movement this sort of thing will no longer suffice. A new danger has arisen. A new enemy has appeared. It is no longer enough to meet once in three years and report on our separate contests each with his own national tyranny. We have an international tyranny growing fast upon us. I refer to the International Labor Office of the League of Nations. Seven years ago it was no bigger than a man's hand, to-day it is a cloud that darkens the sky.

"It is a tyranny all the more dangerous because its designs are so benevolent, all the more to be feared because it is a super-Government, organized and financed to do good to the entire world. When this I. L. O., this sacrosanct body of super-reformers, presumes to issue to the world as the word of final wisdom its decree that women must not work at night, then I say the enemy is at our gates. It is time to give the deliberators and keepers of records a room to themselves and call in the experts on action."

I hesitate to put these two new convictions into words of my own. They are expressed in the quotations I have given.

The feminists of the world must find each other and unite on a policy of action. It is thus that the new international will be born.

The Great Rejection: Part I

I am almost ashamed of my good luck as a member of the Woman's Party. Without having done anything to deserve it I seem so often to turn up at moments of triumph like this. For, make no doubt of it, the rejection of our application for membership in the International Woman Suffrage Alliance last Monday by a vote of 123 to 49, like so many famous defeats, has turned over night into a victory.

Let me tell the story. With regard to the events preceding the opening of the convention, about which you must have read so many conflicting stories in the press, I shall try to write as though I were drafting an affidavit because I think it is so important for our members to have a clear and accurate record of those events.

Early in May, Abby Scott Baker, National Political Chairman of the Woman's Party, and Anita Pollitzer, National Secretary, our advance heralds, arrived in Paris, and began to explain, both through social contacts and through the press, why they had come. Miss Pollitzer tells me that she found the press on the whole interested, friendly, and co-operative. Her press campaign was genuine, it was brilliant, it was successful. Mrs. Baker, who gave herself especially to meeting the International officers, the National presidents and the early arriving delegates, explained that our group was coming to

Paris to help strengthen the International Feminist movement, and especially to support those who were working within the Alliance for a program of complete industrial equality; she said that we were asking for admission to the International, but whether in or out, our purpose would be the same. Her efforts were equally successful, as all who know her must realize that they would be.

On Monday, May 24, Doris Stevens, National Vice-President of the Woman's Party, arrived in Paris with twenty-five other members of the Woman's Party. On May 25 Headquarters were opened at the Hotel Lutetia, (where the International officers and a large number of delegates were stopping), and the work went forward with the same spirit and purpose, but on a larger scale.

On Thursday, May 27, the Woman's Party representatives were asked to send two of their number to appear at a joint meeting of the International Board and the National presidents, which was meeting to determine whether to recommend to the delegates favorable or unfavorable action on our application for affiliation. Miss Stevens, as head of the delegation, and Mrs. Clarence Smith, New York State Chairman of the Woman's Party, were chosen. Permission was secured for Burnita Shelton Matthews to accompany them, as the member best informed on the legal aspects of our work.

Two representatives of the League of Women Voters, Belle Sherwin and Mrs. A. Gordon Norrie, appeared at the same time to set forth their reasons for protesting against our affiliation.

This was of course a private hearing; my account of what took place is based on reports from Miss Stevens, Mrs. Smith, and Mrs. Matthews.

Miss Stevens spoke first, making her statement both in English and in French. Her opening remarks I quote in full:

"The National Woman's Party, desiring to do everything possible to help further international co-operation among women, has applied for affiliation with the International Woman Suffrage Alliance.

"We would like to join with you to hasten the day when men and women throughout the universe shall enjoy, if they choose to exercise them, equal political, social, civil, and industrial rights.

"We offer our strength, our devotion, whatever practical and spiritual forces we have at our command, to the International Woman Movement.

"Since the subjection of women is world-wide, we feel that this subjection can be removed finally and permanently only through international co-operation.

"Then too, there is this human reason. The hostility to those who are working to lift the position of women, which all of us as nationals, bear in our own countries, needs to be washed away from time to time and replaced by the refreshment and regeneration which come from association with our colleagues in the same undertaking. This heartening regeneration we would get from association with you.

"Since we have been told that the aims and purpose of our organization meet with your requirements of affiliation, the National Woman's Party therefore lays before you for consideration its application for membership in the Alliance."

Miss Stevens then asked the board and Presidents if they would like to have some information about the National Woman's Party, and, receiving an eager assent, proceeded to give a brief resume of our history, our achievements, and our principal activities.

Miss Sherwin, president of the League of Women Voters, was then called upon in opposition to the Woman's Party.

Mrs. Norrie made an attempt to corroberate Miss Sherwin's statement from her experience.

Questions were asked by a few of the presidents, friendly comments were made, it was obvious that the statements of Miss Stevens and Mrs. Smith had cleared up doubts and difficulties and that the tide had begun to turn in our favor. The feeling of the presidents had been manifestly relieved and was exceedingly friendly. Our representatives came away feeling that there was a very reasonable chance that the presidents might decide in our favor.

Meanwhile no official notification had reached us from the board concerning our rejection.

On Saturday afternoon, at the request of Mrs. Corbett Ashby, Miss Stevens again appeared before the board, this time without the presidents. She asked Mrs. Smith and Mrs. Baker and Mabel Vernon, executive secretary of the Woman's Party, to accompany her. After a long informal discussion, which seemed to lead nowhere, our representatives retired, feeling that the International Board would like to find some way of getting rid of our application without bearing the onus of rejecting it.

Two hours later Frau Schreiber, German member of the board brought us the following joint statement which it was officially proposed we should sign:

"Publicity concerning the admission of the National Woman's Party to the I.W.S.A. might convey a false impression to the public.

"Therefore the facts must be stated as follows: Before any decision has been put to the congress a meeting between the board of the I.W.S.A. and representatives of the N.W.P. has taken place where the controversial points concerning the admission of the N.W.P. have been discussed and cleared. It was stated that they did not touch questions of principles but methods of work. It was felt that this difference of method might make co-operation in one organization difficult and impede the full development of work. It was therefore agreed that it would prove more useful if the N.W.P., maintaining its liberty, continued to act independently without affiliation. Both organizations are willing to work side by side, each according to its traditions and convictions, fully aware of the great aims that unite them.

"Representatives of the N.W.P. will be cordially welcomed as fraternal delegates of the I.W.S.A."

This statement the Woman's Party representatives refused to sign, feeling in the first place that we had no authority to do so, that the statement was entirely contrary to our purpose and instructions, and in the second place that the statement did not in any way express our own views or wishes.

This was on Saturday afternoon. It was not until Sunday evening at seven that official notification reached us that our application for affiliation had been unfavorably acted upon by the board and national presidents.

On Monday morning at 9.30 at the commencement of the first business session of the Congress, we were to be given 10 minutes in which to present our case to the delegates. Before I proceed to set forth what happened in that Monday morning session—one of the most dramatic sessions surely in the history of the Alliance—I must go back to relate two important incidents.

Among the special commissions set up by the Alliance for the study of certain questions is the "Like Conditions of Work Council." On Friday afternoon this commission held a preliminary conference, presented its report, and won a decided victory for the principle of industrial equality. A resolution adopted at the Rome Congress declaring that "no special regulations of women's work different from regulations for men should be imposed *contrary to wishes of the women concerned*" was enormously strengthened by omitting the phrase in italics. This carried by a vote of 71 to 38.

Thus on the very day when the presidents had voted to exclude the Woman's Party from the International, a very large number of the delegates (nearly one-half) voted to endorse the principle to which the Woman's Party is most signally devoted, and for which it has fought more consistently and more vigorously than any other Feminist organization throughout the world.

Another thing that encouraged us mightily was the fact that on Saturday afternoon the Six Point Group, of which Viscountess Rhondda is president, withdrew its application for affiliation in protest against the methods used in connection with the application of the Woman's Party.

The Great Rejection: Part II

Proceedings began on Monday morning with the admission of a dozen new societies on the recommendation of the board, some of them from countries never represented in the Alliance before, some of them additional societies from countries already represented in the

Equal Rights, 26 June 1926.

Alliance. In the latter group was the Women's Freedom League of Great Britain and La Ligue pour les Droits des Femmes de France.

Next in order came the reading of Lady Rhondda's letter of withdrawal to which I have already referred. The letter follows:

Hotel Lutetia, Paris,
May 30, 1926.

To the President, Congress of the International Woman Suffrage Alliance,
The Sorbonne.

DEAR MRS. CORBETT ASHBY:

It is with the most profound regret and with a deep sense of the gravity of the step which I am taking that I write to withdraw the application of the Six Point Group for affiliation to the International Woman Suffrage Alliance.

The methods used in respect to the request for affiliation of the National Woman's Party and with a view to preventing that affiliation have been such that it would not be possible for the Six Point Group to associate itself with them. There is therefore no other step open to me but to withdraw our application for membership.

You will know with what reluctance I have been brought to this conclusion; I am sending you this letter as I feel that I must make my position clear to the Congress.

Yours sincerely,
RHONDDA, *President,*
The Six Point Group.

Following close upon this letter of withdrawal from the Six Point Group which had already received the sanction of the board came the rejection of the National Union of Women Teachers and the League of the Church Militant, two societies which had applied for affiliation and been disapproved by the board. A leading representative of each of these societies was given a few minutes in which to protest against the decision of the board, but in each case the board was sustained almost unanimously. The decision was a perfectly understandable one, based upon the nature and objects of each organization, not in any degree upon personal considerations.

At this point in the proceedings there was a general stir, a tightening of nerves, a straining forward for better sight and hearing—the case of the National Woman's Party was about to be taken up.

Miss Frances M. Sterling, of Great Britain, treasurer of the International, who seemed to be in charge of these admission proceedings began by reading slowly and distinctly the statement which follows:

"The board and presidents regret to be unable to recommend the admission of the National Woman's Party. It is perfectly clear that the constitution of the National Woman's Party is perfectly in accord with the constitution and aims of the Alliance. The resolutions voted in Rome show the position of the Alliance toward women in industrial legislation:

"That the right to work of all women be recognized and no obstacles placed in the way of married women who desire to work. That no special regulations for women's work different from regulations for men should be imposed contrary to the wishes of the women concerned. That laws relative to women as mothers should be so framed as not to handicap them in their economic position, and that all future labor regulations should tend towards equality for men and women.

"By our By-Law No. 1 we allow complete freedom to each auxiliary on the particular question of protective legislation. Many of the national delegations are divided and even among the board members there is a great difference of opinion.

"The reasons for the decision taken are as follows:

"1. The board and presidents felt that great weight must be given to one of their foundation members, representing an immense organization in the country, and which for the first nine years of the Alliance's existence was the only suffrage society in that country; and which further has, by its generous and loyal support built up the Alliance in its older days and supported it through the terrible years of the War.

"2. The board and presidents also laid great weight on the advice given by the Founder and president for twenty years, Mrs. Chapman Catt, whose wideness of outlook and superiority to personal considerations is known to us.

"3. This request has also raised the difficulty of admitting second societies which instead of complementing each other, are definitely and constantly opposing each other.

"Further, and more serious even, than any difficulties likely to be created in one country, the board and presidents considered that the methods of work of the National Woman's Party would make co-operation with our organization difficult if not impossible—as an example:

"4. The press campaign of the National Woman's Party during the last three weeks, both abroad and in France, has been conducted on lines dictated solely by the interests of their own organization and to the detriment of the interests of the Alliance and has showed that the body in question would not be a source of strength to the Alliance but quite the contrary. After carefully reasoned appeals from three members of the board to them to discontinue this campaign on the sole grounds of the interests of the Alliance, they themselves offered to give a promise to discontinue that action and to allow the French press to receive its Congress news solely from the official press bureau and Committee. Nevertheless numerous articles have continued to appear, showing that no effective action had been taken to prevent their recurrence. It seems evident that if the National Woman's Party failed in efforts to stop publication of material already given out, they should have informed the Alliance in order that joint and effective measures should be taken. This example, corresponding to all the information already received, produced the conviction that the ad-mission of the National Woman's Party at the present time would seriously damage the harmony and power of working of the Alliance."

In the hush that followed the reading of this document Mrs. Corbett Ashby asked if Miss Doris Stevens was in the room. Miss Stevens explained that Miss Vernon was to represent the Woman's Party on this occasion. And Mable Vernon made her way quietly to the platform and began.

Let me pause at this point to say that the Grand Amphitheatre of le Sorbonne has the most inhuman acoustics known to history. It had been impossible to hear anybody except Miss Sterling up to this point. And she had managed to make her words reach us only by speaking very, very slowly and with great strain and stentorian effort.

As Mrs. Corbett Ashby explained at the beginning, the place was good enough for speaking if full, but practically hopeless when nearly empty, as it was during the business sessions of the Congress. There were some two hundred delegates on the floor, a scattering hundred of visitors and press on the first rising tier of seats, and then two deep, vast hooded balconies absolutely empty. Five thousand more people could have been seated. The words of nearly every speaker were lost in echoing space almost as they left her lips.

Now a remarkable thing happened when Mabel Vernon spoke. By some mysterious instinct which goes with the orator's genius, she knew how to conquer those baffling spaces. Her words fell on our ears as clearly, as softly, as graciously as though we sat in a little Quaker meeting house.

"We came to offer all that we have of strength, ability and devotion to the world-wide woman's movement," she began. "I can do no better than to quote for you Miss Alice Paul's reply when she was asked by the President of the Alliance to send a letter setting forth 'the points on which our application for membership were based.' 'We do not know,' Miss Paul wrote, 'we do not know that we have any point to put before the Convention except the desire to offer our aid to those who are working in the International woman movement.' . . ."

"Some of the objections now advanced to the acceptance of this offer," Miss Vernon went on, "are amusing to us. For instance, your board and presidents give as a serious reason for rejecting our application to your body, a difference of opinion as to how a press campaign should be conducted. We have no apology to offer for our press campaign. We consider such an objection too trivial for consideration. . . .

"In order that the objection of your foundation member in the United States may be rightly understood it must be stated at once that there is a sharp difference between the League of Women Voters and the National Woman's Party. The League stands for regulation of women in industry. The Woman's Party stands for complete equality of men and women in industry and in every other department of life. By its own confession the League of Women Voters seeks the measure of equality in which it believes by 'slow and cautious methods.' The National Woman's Party works with rapidity, determined to gain for the women of this generation full control over their own lives and equal control over the world in which they live. . . ."

Passing soon from consideration of objections, Miss Vernon briefly stated the principles and hope of the Woman's Party and closed with a reference to the international field: "And while we are working for these aims in our own country we are joining hands with the women of every other country that we may help end the universal subjection of women. So long as this subjection is world wide the work to end it must be world wide. Therefore, regardless of your action here today, we of the National Woman's Party are in the International Woman's Movement; we are bound to contribute to it our strength and devotion."

I have given a sketch of what Miss Vernon said. It was a most moving plea for honesty and large-mindedness. Before Miss Vernon had come to her last word, almost half a dozen delegates were up asking for the floor. But before the Chairman recognized any of them she read to the Congress a letter she had received from Miss Pollitzer in final explanation of the French press incident. Miss Vernon in considering the fourth paragraph of our indictment had asked why this letter had not been read to the Congress in connection with the statements made about the Woman's Party publicity campaign. And Mrs. Corbett Ashby took the first opportunity to read it. The letter follows:

Paris, May 30, 1926.

DEAR MRS. CORBETT ASHBY:

I have, of course, heard of the discussion of the Board meetings concerning the Woman's Party publicity in the French Press, and want to write to you to say, what it has hardly seemed to me necessary to say, that after I promised you on my own initiative that I would not see the French press, I did not.

The material which they subsequently used they got from the first interviews I had before our conversation. When I saw the editors on my arrival I gave them material for immediate use. I gave them no stories with advance release dates. After my talk with you and a talk with Madame Malaterre, I took to the *Journal* and *l'Intrasigeant* letters correcting their mistatements as to the names of officials of the Alliance.

The promise I made to you has been kept in its entirety, and it is hard for me to believe that it has become necessary for me to assure you of this. I am sorry to go into all of this now when I think our whole minds should be on Equal Rights and the advancement of the position of women—the purpose for which we came.

Very sincerely,
ANITA POLLITZER,
National Secretary.

The delegates who wanted to speak remained standing during the reading of this letter. The room was tense with excitement.

Miss Chrystal Macmillan of Great Britain was in the first to be granted the floor. Unfortunately a two-minute rule was adopted for the discussion. If they had made it five minutes instead of two I believe the occasion would have been even more memorable than it was. Miss Macmillan has been a leading figure in the Alliance for many years and was for some time on the Executive Board. Of recent years she has headed the Commission on the Nationality of Married Women. She is a splendid big Scotch woman with a fine head of short gray hair.

"I shall try to make two points in my two minutes," said Miss Macmillan. "First: America is a great industrial country where it is most important that industrial restrictions against women should be watched and fought. The fact that the American society now affiliated with us does not deal with industrial restrictions is the greatest possible reason for bringing in to the Alliance the Woman's Party, which does. And second: We should not put forth foolish reasons like these about publicity methods. There was clearly some degree of misunderstanding, we all know how these misunderstandings arise, even on a small committee. And we are a great political organization; we should not stand on methods."

Next came Lady Rhondda, explaining that she had never hated to come to a conclusion so much as she had with regard to withdrawing the Six Point Group's application for membership in the Alliance, but that she had felt in honor bound to do it. "I have read all the press cuttings and I found nothing objectionable. It is a matter of opinion—some like a big press and some like a little press. And one thing more I wish to say. If you vote to keep the Woman's Party out you will be voting for the past. If you vote to take them in it will be a vote for the future."

Miss Eleanor Rathbone, president of the largest and most conservative society in England, then rose to plead with the delegates to uphold the board. "You have elected a board, you have elected your presidents. They have consulted together and come to a conclusion. You are bound to uphold them, to trust in the wisdom of their decision." (When this typical "organization" plea is made I always wonder, "Why have delegates met at all, then?") Apparently Miss Rathbone is more conservative than her organization, for nine out of the twelve British delegates voted for us.

Next our good friend Mrs. Pethick-Lawrence gained the floor to say with great earnestness, "I hope you will think very carefully before you break the unity of the woman's movement by excluding this strong and vital element in it. Out of love and devotion to the whole movement I ask you not to split it by excluding the Woman's Party." Mrs. Lawrence has recently been elected president of the Women's Freedom League of Great Britain which was finally taken into the Alliance at this Congress. She was followed by Miss Anna Munro, the former president, who merely said, "I belong to a society that has waited eighteen years for admission, and I wish to say that I hope you will admit the Woman's Party today."

The delegate from Palestine, Dr. Rosa Straus, an exceedingly able woman, declared that there would be grave danger in not admitting a society which in spirit and purpose was so closely akin to the great majority in the Alliance. In support of this fact she instanced the very heavy majority against special restrictions in the Like Conditions of Work Commission which had met on Friday.

Finally Miss Belle Sherwin spoke on behalf of the League of Women Voters. "We do not like to protest against the admission of another society," she said. "We would not do so if we did not think it necessary. It is not so much a question of principle between us, nor of legislative differences. That is not the starting point of our opposition. It is because we are convinced of the impracticability of a working alliance between the National Woman's Party and this body."

On this closing note the vote was taken—49 for our admission, 123 against.

The Great Rejection: Part III

"If you vote for the Woman's Party, it is a vote for the future! If you vote against them it is a vote for the past!"

With these words Lady Rhondda had ended her two-minute challenge to the International Woman Suffrage Alliance during the brief debate allowed before the delegates were called upon to vote on the question of the admission of the National Woman's Party. And it was with these words ringing in our ears that we listened to the taking of the vote, and heard the final verdict, 123 to 49 against us.

When we left the Congress Hall and drifted out into the streets of Paris (sunny for the moment), it was with a sense of elation rather than of defeat. *"The future is with us,"* that was the burden of our thought and conversation.

On the next day which was Tuesday, June 1, the sense of elation, mysteriously, had grown rather than diminished. When, that afternoon, we went to greet Mrs. Belmont at the Gare St. Lazare, on her arrival from America, we were feeling so cheerful that she could hardly believe the story of our defeat.

On Wednesday, June 2, the Woman's Party group had arranged a small luncheon in honor of Mrs. Belmont and Lady Rhondda at the Restaurant Laurent. It was a "last moment affair," organized in less than forty-eight hours, perhaps with the idea that we would like to console and consult with each other, and with some of our new-found friends among the delegates after our rejection by the International.

Now, strange to say, this affair refused to observe the decencies of the occasion and express a little solemnity and regret. There was an irrepressible note of triumph about it from start to finish. There were some 125 women present, of whom about twenty-five were of our own party, perhaps a dozen were Americans visiting in Paris, and the rest were delegates from the congress. At least six of the national presidents came, possibly more. And there was Mme. Maria Verone, president of La Ligue des Droits des Femmes, which is not affiliated with the International. In all fourteen different nations were represented.

Mme. Verone, who spoke first because she had to hurry off to an important case, is a French "avocat" known for her eloquence. She had read of our rejection by the International but declared it nothing to be discouraged about. "They call you extremists," she said, "but I am head of an organization which has taken the same position your society takes for thirty years. I am with you altogether in your demand for full equality in the industrial sphere as in every other."

Mrs. Belmont's words of greeting to those who had gathered in her honor, contained no hint of regret, no suggestion of indignation, indeed, no reference whatever to the action of the International Alliance in refusing membership to the Woman's Party. She was a general reviewing her troops, greeting new allies, admonishing all to go forward, strong in the faith and confident of the end. I quote what Mrs. Belmont said in full:

"As president of the National Woman's Party, I am most happy to welcome our Feminist colleagues and friends from many countries. One of the purposes of our coming to Paris at this time was to make closer and more intimate ties, as well as to make more effective contacts, with those who feel as we do about the great importance of this woman movement. This our organization has done. Working friendships which will endure even after we have returned to our respective countries.

"It is a heartening sign indeed to see stirring among women throughout the world a wholesome impatience against our subjection. And we ought to be more impatient than we are. There is no

Crystal Eastman in Croton.
Annis Young collection

Crystal's mother, Annis Ford Eastman, at Glenora on Seneca Lake.
Annis Young collection

Crystal Eastman with her father in Croton.
Annis Young collection

Roger Baldwin, Crystal Eastman, a conscientious objector and Ruth Pickering in front of Crystal's studio at Croton, June 1917.
Fuller collection

Ruth Pickering, Alexander Trachtenberg, Alston Dana, Winthrop D. Lane and Crystal Eastman holding her son Jeffrey Fuller, Croton, 1917.
Fuller collection

Crystal Eastman on the beach at Martha's Vineyard, 1920.
Fuller collection

Ruth Pickering, Margaret Lane(?) and Crystal Eastman on the beach at Martha's Vineyard.
Fuller collection

Crystal Eastman and Jeffrey in Croton, 1920.
Fuller collection

Crystal Eastman and Jeffrey in Croton, 1921.
Fuller collection

*Crystal Eastman,
Annis, and
Leonard Woolf,
London, c. 1923.*
Annis Young
collection

*Crystal Eastman
with Jeffrey,
London, c. 1924.*
Fuller collection

Crystal Eastman with Jeffrey, London, 1926.
Annis Young collection

Walter Fuller in London, c. 1927.
Annis Young collection

Crystal Eastman with Annis in Walter's studio, London, 1927.

Annis Young collection

virtue in sitting quietly by and accepting the slow processes of the evolution of an idea. If we choose we can greatly accelerate these processes. We of the National Woman's Party work to hasten the day when women throughout the world shall stand as equal partners with men in the great adventure of life.

"We look to the day when the present hostility to women's fullest creative development shall be wiped away, to the day when women's contributions will be accepted in friendly encouragement.

"It is of paramount importance that in this century when the nations of the world are endeavoring to achieve closer understanding and co-operation, the voice of women in all international councils shall speak with authority.

"Have confidence in your own judgment; trust yourselves; do not listen to the voice of fear; speak out your minds, speak out your opinions. Even though those opinions differ from those of your neighbors, silence in face of injustice is unworthy. Let us all together bear witness, everytime we are called upon to do so, that we will not cease for a single day until all women are completely emancipated."

The next speaker was our other guest of honor, Viscountess Rhondda, whose address appeared in EQUAL RIGHTS June 19. I must say a few words about this remarkable woman who played such a large part in our Paris adventure. (To begin with I am sorry she is a viscountess; my ancient American revolutionary forbears and my modern proletarian revolutionary sympathies are agreed in protesting against hereditary titles. As they have never agreed about anything else, I can't help mentioning it.)

Margaret Thomas, now Lady Rhondda, was the only child of David Alfred Thomas, owner of large coal properties in the Rhondda Valley, South Wales. Thomas was a distinguished Welsh Liberal, a rare personality, and an exceedingly gifted administrator. He was given a peerage in recognition of his great service to the country as food controller during the war, but consented to accept the title only on condition that it should be inherited in the female line. When Viscount Rhondda died shortly after the war he left to his daughter not only his title but full possession, direction and control of his extensive properties, exactly as though she had been a son.

Lady Rhondda was passionately devoted to her father. For some

months after his death she gave herself up to writing and compiling
the story of his life, and created a beautiful book, worthy of him and
worthy of her. Then she turned wholeheartedly to Feminism. All her
gifts, all her dreams, all her ambitions have since then been concerned
with the cause of making women free.

She founded the Six Point Group and through it has played a live
part in getting the various post-war Feminist measures through
Parliament. She made her fight to get into the House of Lords. She
founded *Time and Tide,* the brilliant Feminist weekly of which she is
co-editor with Helen Archdale. In all this work she has shown herself
to be an effective, political writer, a humorous and original speaker,
and as an administrator, shrewd, swift and decisive.

I have given this brief account of Lady Rhondda because it
should be known in America how significant was her withdrawal of
the Six Point Group application for membership in the International
at this time. It should be realized from what a background of power
and achievement and distinction she speaks.

The Woman's Party never had a tribute more generous, more
deeply understanding than that paid by Lady Rhondda at the
Restaurant Laurent on June 2. A good deal of our sense of joy and
success on that occasion came from her mood. She is young, not much
more than forty—a lovable person, shy and rather beautiful. And she
looks as fresh and strong and confident and happy as though she had
just begun her working life.

Lady Rhondda learned her Feminism at the militants' school
and has never lost their fire. She loves to laugh. She loves to fight.
When she calls upon the real Feminists of the world to find each other
it is the call of a comrade. Perhaps it is the call of a leader, too.

There were many other speakers at our luncheon that day, and
all of the same opinion, i.e., that something had come out of the
application of the Woman's Party and its rejection that would mean
more to the future of Feminism than our admission to the International Alliance would have meant. We listened to words of encouragement from Greece, Spain, and Egypt as well as from France and
England. A number of our own group responded, Abby Scott Baker
(who was in the chair), Anne Martin, Anita Pollitzer, Florence Bayard
Hilles—all in very good form.

But perhaps the most memorable words spoken were those of Elsie Hill, who brought us word of an actual battle over protective legislation during these very days while the congress was debating the issue.

France has adopted the highly benevolent night work convention established by the International Labour Office of the League of Nations. As one result all women telephone operators have been taken off and men put in their places. What does this mean for the women? It means that they work during the seven busiest hours at a nerve-racking occupation without relief, while the men, coming on at nine o'clock in the evening take the seven easiest hours during which they have two hours off for rest and are paid 3,000 francs more per year than the women. On the night before our luncheon the women telephone operators, who are organizing against this outrage, held a meeting which was broken up by the men's union.

This news, straight from the industrial field gave point and purpose to all our talk. It made sharp and clear the need for a Feminist party of action in the international field. Those Paris telephone girls are fighting an *international* tyranny. There is no international body of women to speak for them, much less to fight for them.

Lady Rhondda was quite right when she said that the majority of the delegates to the I.W.S.A. were social reformers and that they rejected us because we were Feminists. But I think that was not the only reason. The British delegates, the Scandinavians, are in intellectual conviction, as "extreme" Feminists as the members of the Woman's Party. In the language of their resolutions they are as uncompromising enemies of "protection" as we. Yet they live in amity with the League of Women Voters and the other reformist groups in the Alliance. The trouble with the Woman's Party is that in addition to the purity of its Feminism it has a capacity and reputation for *action.* They were more afraid of what we would do than of what we would think.

The expedition of the Woman's Party to Paris has demonstrated that there is at present no Feminist international with a purpose and plan of action. . . . The future is ours!

Recent Developments in England

Women in England are beginning to wonder whether the House of Lords, so long an enemy to woman suffrage, is going to prove an ally to feminism, in its later and more advanced phases. Six months ago the Lords startled the radical world by passing a resolution in favor of birth control, to be specific, a resolution requesting the Ministry of Health to withdraw its prohibition against the giving of birth control information to married women in public welfare clinics. Ten days ago, the Lords took a hand in the industrial equality dispute, and while the Feminists did not win their point they received some valuable and highly intelligent support.

The debate arose on the Lead Paint (protection against poisoning) Bill, which has already passed its third reading in the House of Commons and came before the House of Lords on November 18. The bill provides certain new safeguards against lead poisoning for all those engaged in the painting trade, and then proceeds to prohibit altogether the employment "of women and young persons in painting any part of a building with lead paint." It will have the effect of completely closing certain well-paid sections of the painting trade to women.

Owing to the efforts of a new and very energetic group of Feminists, called the Open Door Council, a number of the Lords were prepared for this amendment and well-schooled in the "equality" argument against it.

The exclusion of women from the painting trade in England as in America, rests on a medical theory that they are more susceptible than men to lead poisoning, and that lead poisoning in the mother frequently causes miscarriage. Yet advocates of exclusion admit that there is no absolute proof of women's greater susceptibility. And, as for the racial argument, there does exist proof that the evil effects of

Equal Rights, 22 January 1927.

lead poisoning are transmitted through the poisoned father no less than the poisoned mother.

This was made clear by Lord Balfour of Burleigh, who moved to amend the prohibiting clause so as to make it apply to "young persons" but not to women. To exclude women from a trade on a medical theory about which there is so much doubt and so little evidence, he concluded, is to play into the hands of "one of the most powerful vested interests which exists—the trade unions. The protective regulations are always put forward by trade unions on humanitarian grounds, but while no doubt many people in trade unions honestly want them on that account, I am bound to say that there is another motive at work, and that is that they want to keep women out of the job."

More important, because of his very high standing in the medical world, was the long and carefully-reasoned speech of Lord Dawson of Penn. I quote two paragraphs:

"If you take the figures at present available, there is very striking evidence that lead attacks women more often and with greater severity than men. But those figures are mainly taken from the old days in the Potteries when women undertook the less skilled, the more dangerous forms of work. They were economically in a less fortunate position, and they were less protected; and there is certainly ground for the view that a large part of that proclivity of women was the result of their economic position rather than of their sex characteristics. Unless a further inquiry is undertaken in the light of modern knowledge I should doubt very much whether there is a case for excluding women from the painting trade."

Coming to the question of pregnancy, Lord Dawson said, "It is quite true that lead is a dangerous poison in that it produces abortion and miscarriages. But—the lead poisoning, in bringing about miscarriages, very often goes through the male as well as the female. The figures are most interesting as well as tragic. For example there is one set of figures affecting workers in lead mines, where the wives have never worked in the lead mines and the men do work in the lead mines, and 40 per cent of a given block of pregnancies miscarried. There you have the poison carried by means of the man. And there are other figures bearing that out. Therefore if you exclude the women and leave the men, and your regulations are bad, you will still have your miscarriages. If your regulations are good, I think you will find that women and men will be protected alike."

Viscount Haldane and Lord Phillimore followed Lord Dawson to the same effect, and only one member, Lord Desberough for the Government, defended the exclusion of women from the painting trade.

What most surprised and amused the Feminists was the support they received from Lord Banbury of Southam, one of the most irreconcilable opponents of woman suffrage.

"I think it is the first time I have ever spoken in this house, or in the other house, in favor of women," said Lord Banbury, "but being an individualist, and the Government having approved of giving the vote to women, I venture to say that if a woman is fit to vote for a member of Parliament she is also fit to decide whether or not she should paint a house."

"Or take poison?" A "Noble Lord" interrupted.

"Yes, or take poison. I do not believe in all these paternal regulations, and I cannot conceive how anyone can contend that a woman who is 21 years of age and is capable of voting, is not capable of deciding whether or not she should occupy herself in painting."

Despite the able putting of their case the women lost. The clause excluding them from the painting trade carried by a vote of 35 to 17. However the members of the Open Door Council feel well satisfied with their first effort.

The establishment of this new group is significant. Although there are four active Feminist societies in England which include among their objects the breaking down of all barriers to industrial and professional equality, nevertheless it has been thought necessary to form another with that as its exclusive purpose. Its object reads:

"To secure that women shall be free to work and protected as workers on the same terms as men, and that legislation and regulations dealing with conditions and hours, entry and training, shall be based upon the nature of the work and not upon the sex of the worker.

"And to secure for women, irrespective of marriage or childbirth, the right at all times to decide whether or not they shall engage in paid work, and to ensure that no legislation or regulations shall deprive them of this right."

What Is Real Protection?

American women in London are watching with interest the preparations that are being made for a Feminist attack on the Factories Bill which will soon come up for its second reading in the House of Commons. The bill, which is a 100-page effort to amend and consolidate the factory legislation of the last half century, contains, of course, many clauses "protecting" or, as the Feminists regard it, "restricting" women workers. For example, seats must be provided for female employes, "women and young persons" are prohibited from cleaning machinery in motion, lifting loads beyond a certain weight, working in certain zinc and lead processes, working more than 48 hours a week, working at night, etc.—it is the so-called "welfare legislation" for women workers with which we are familiar in most of the States.

From a Feminist standpoint, here in England as in America, it is considered an added aggravation that for purposes of factory legislation women are classed with "young persons." "In factories as elsewhere," say the British Feminist organizations, "women must be treated as adult citizens; protective laws must be based on the nature of the work and not on the sex of the worker."

Some weeks ago an all-day conference was called by the N.U.S.E.C. (National Union of Societies for Equal Citizenship) to consider "What is the real protection of the woman worker?" Thirty-three women's organizations sent representatives.

"I could make out a good case for specially protecting men,"

Equal Rights, 19 February 1927.

said Dr. Jane Walker, a leading woman physician of London, who
opened the conference. "It is time some attention was paid to vital
statistics. More boys are born than girls, yet more girls survive.
There are always more widows than widowers, there are two million
more women than men. In other words, woman's survival rate is
greater than man's, and women are getting stronger all the time. If
either sex needs protection, it would seem to be the men."

"The provisions of this Factory Bill are excellent," Dr. Walker
went on, "if applied to *men and women,* but they are devilish if applied
to women only, because they interfere with her earning capacity.
Most of these provisions are relics of the last century, of early
Victorian times, anyhow. Take the one about cleaning machinery,
and read the arguments that were made for it in those by-gone days—
"The *long hair, long skirts* and *many petticoats* worn by women make
them more liable to danger!" And think of how women dress today!
What could be better than the short hair, short sleeves and sheath
skirts up to her knees of the factory girl today? She is far better
equipped, actually, for handling machinery than is a man with his
floppy coat and baggy trousers.

"I remember when bicycles came in,—and I believe bicycles
were the beginning of woman's emancipation,—there was a great
outcry from the doctors. It was not good for women to ride bicycles,
they declared, and we had to have a committee of investigation to
prove that it did women good. It was the same way with aviation.
When a woman wanted the pilot's certificate in aviation, she was
refused. And the Medical Woman's Federation appointed a commission of experts to inquire into the physical fitness of women to be
aviator pilots!"

Dr. Walker was supported by another physician, Dr. Christine
Murrell, who declared that the motive of this legislation was either a
sentimental one or a self-interested one. It was very often to get rid of
a competitor. She had attended the famous Washington Conference
when the "No night work" convention was passed. "You don't
believe women ought to work at night?" she asked one of the
enthusiastic advocates of this measure, "Then we will have no night
nurses?" "Oh, yes," replied the reformer. "Of course, we must have

night nurses." "It seems," went on Dr. Murrell, "that women are excluded from night work only when it is especially well paid work and when their services are not needed by the community."

It was Mrs. Elizabeth Abbott, chairman of a new Feminist group called the Open Door Council, who took up the limitation of the working day for women.

"The eight-hour day which men have secured through their unions is not the same thing as the eight-hour day imposed by law on women. The union makes its own regulations, its own provisions for exceptions, over-time and holidays. For women these important matters are fixed by law; they are not allowed to make over-time. This alone is enough to exclude them from many trades. What we ask for women is not only the same laws but the same regulations and regulating machinery."

"They say that it is impossible to organize women. But look at the war years. In 1914 there were 472 women organized in agriculture, in 1917 there were 3,392. In potteries the number of organized women increased from 1,900 to 25,000, in tailoring from 14,000 to 111,000; in the paper and printing trades from 6,000 to 60,000. You can organize women if you give them equal pay and treat them as comrades."

Mrs. Abbott quoted Emma Patterson, a great leader of working women in the '80's and '90's, who founded the Women's Trade Union movement in England. She, it seems, had opposed special protective laws for women and had warned the working women of England against them. Mrs. Abbott's point was that all these laws, even when they do not actually close the door on the woman worker, surround the employment of women with so many time-taking, costly and troublesome special provisions that an employer will naturally avoid employing women if he can, and hence women are seriously handicapped in competition.

Several women's trades unions were represented at the conference, and most of their delegates spoke and voted against the Feminist resolutions. They felt that the Feminists could have spent their time better in trying to increase the safeguards in the Factory Bill. However, Miss McGuire, secretary of the Association of Women

Clerks and Secretaries, spoke with some sympathy of the Feminist effort, and was only concerned that in amending the Factories Bill, there should be no loss of standards, that it should be so amended as to "secure for men adult workers the shorter hours and such other benefits as are now provided for adult women workers."

Here is a question the Feminists must agree on, before they go far in their campaign for industrial equality. Are they going to level up or level down? Are they going to insist that men workers be brought under the safety and health regulations that now apply only to women? Or are they going to insist that women be taken out from under those regulations?

Judging from this first conference, it seems that the British Feminists will favor the "levelling up" form of amendment. The chief resolution passed at the conference calls upon the Government "to amend the Factories Bill by incorporating in it the hours proposal of the Washington Hours Convention," (i.e. of the International Labour Office of the League of Nations), "thereby securing for all adult workers the same conditions of employment as regards hours of labor, including nightwork, overtime and holidays; and to apply all provisions for health, safety and welfare to all workers irrespective of sex."

At the close of the conference Miss Cicely Hamilton, novelist and playwright, caused some laughter by suggesting that this campaign against special protective laws adopt as its slogan, "The human female is not a disease." She also said she would like to appoint a commission of women doctors to investigate men in order to determine if possible why they have such a "feeble hold on life."

"It is not only that so many more girls survive than boys though more boys are born," said Miss Hamilton, "but that they survive when so little care is taken of them. Until recently very little was thought of girl babies in England, nobody bothered much about them. But boys were precious, every care was taken of them. And it is well known that the women of England have had less to eat. And they have been maltreated by their husbands, many of them. And yet they cling to life. Men are strong muscularly, no doubt, but in general endurance women are far ahead. Observe carefully a girl and a boy starting off for a long cold ride on a motor cycle. Note how differently the two are dressed. It is not difficult to tell which of those two is the hardiest human animals."

Although there are four active Feminist societies in England which include among their objects the breaking down of all barriers to industrial and professional equality, nevertheless it has been thought necessary to start a new one with this as its exclusive purpose. Last May, just before the International Feminist Congress in Paris, the Open Door Council was organized, made up of prominent representatives of all four British Societies, including the presidents of three.

Miss Chrystal Macmillan, the Viscountess Rhondda, Miss Helen Fraser and Mrs. Pethick-Lawrence, women who vigorously supported the National Woman's Party in its application for admission to the International in Paris last June, are active in the Open Door Council. Its object reads:

"To secure that women shall be free to work and protected as workers on the same terms as men, and that legislation and regulations dealing with conditions and hours, entry and training, shall be based upon the nature of the work and not upon the sex of the worker;

"And to secure for women, irrespective of marriage or childbirth, the right at all times to decide whether or not they shall engage in paid work, and to ensure that no legislation or regulations shall deprive them of this right."

It was this group that brought about the remarkable debate on the Lead Paint Bill in the House of Lords in November, in the course of which Lord Dawson of Penn, Lord Balfour of Burleigh, and Viscount Haldane, very ably presented the Feminist case against excluding women from the painting trade. The council is now engaged upon the preparation of an amendment to the Factory Bill designed to do away entirely with the differentiation between men and women workers.

There is no doubt that the advanced standpoint of the British Feminists on the matter of industrial restrictions will have an influence on the American woman living in London. It will make her regard with more understanding and tolerance than do many of her sisters at home, the fight which the National Woman's Party is making for equality on the industrial field.

Women, Rights and Privileges

Feminism has entered upon a new phase; no longer content with asking for their rights, women have begun to question their privileges. They have begun to examine, with some shrewdness, the whole body of more or less benevolent legislation which has been gradually built up during the last half century for the "protection" of women in industry. For a good many years the British feminist societies have been declaring in annual resolution that "legislation for the protection of the worker should be based not upon sex but upon the nature of the work." This year, for the first time, I believe, an effort is being made actually to amend existing and proposed labour legislation in accordance with that principle. The 102-page Factories Bill, which will soon come up for its second reading in the House, they think, affords a good place to begin.

Recently an all-day Conference was called by the National Union of Societies for Equal Citizenship to discuss the question: "What is the real protection of the woman worker?" Thirty-three women's societies were represented and the following resolution was carried, not unanimously but by a good majority.

> This Conference calls upon the Government to amend the Factories Bill by incorporating in it the hours proposals of the Washington Hours Convention, thereby securing for all adult workers, male and female, the same conditions of employment as regards hours of labour, including night work, overtime, and holidays, noting that the night work provisions therein contained may not be of practical effect in the case of women till after 1930*; and to apply those provisions of the Bill concerning general safety (including protection from machinery and the institution of fire drill), lead

---

* This refers to the International Labour Office Convention prohibiting night work for women in "Industrial undertakings," which was adopted by Great Britain in 1920 under an international agreement that it should remain in force for ten years.

The Outlook (London), 5 February 1927.

processes carried on in places other than factories, and special provisions and regulations for health, safety, and welfare to all workers
irrespective of sex.

In America a violent controversy over this question of special
protective laws (or "restrictive" laws, as the feminists regard them)
has been going on for some years owing to the activities of the
National Woman's Party. Shortly after the woman suffrage amendment passed, this organisation, which holds the same views as the
National Union of Societies for Equal Citizenship, Freedom League,
Six Point Group, and other British feminist societies, secured the
introduction of another amendment to the national constitution,
which reads: "Men and women shall have equal rights throughout
the United States and every place subject to its jurisdiction." This
amendment, if enacted would make unconstitutional and inoperative
all so-called protective laws for women. Reformers and welfare
workers, who saw the results of their life-work threatened were up in
arms against the Woman's Party and its amendment. And nearly all
women leaders of the reformist and humanitarian type, including the
officials of the Women's Trade Union League, joined the opposition.

Despite the outcry the American feminists have stood their
ground. Not only have they continued to press their equality amendment, but they have appeared before one state legislature after
another, when it was proposed further to restrict the hours of working
women, insisting that the proposed restriction be applied to men and
women alike. And gradually they have gained strength, their demand
has come to seem less preposterous to the general public. Most
important of all, despite the official opposition of the Women's Trade
Union League, they have found support among women industrial
workers, especially among the higher skilled, many of whom have
found in protective legislation more tyranny than benevolence.
Women, for example, who have been shut out of a number of the
higher paid trades by the law prohibiting them from working at
night, support, for the soundest economic reasons, the feminist
demand for like conditions of work for men and women.

In the Scandinavian countries special protective legislation has
been a live feminist issue for many years. To-day, in Denmark, it is
proposed to enact into law the International Labour Office Convention

prohibiting night work for women; feminists and women trade unionists are making a united stand against it, and, according to all accounts, will succeed in preventing the adoption of the law. Owing to the effort of the feminists Holland abandoned differential legislation in 1919, and made its laws regulating night work and hours of labour generally apply to men and women alike.

In every highly developed industrial country, once women have secured the suffrage, this question of protective legislation is bound to come up. The modern woman is seriously demanding equal opportunities in every field. With some reason she questions whether factory laws which class her with children and young persons and hedge her employment round with special restrictions which do not apply to men are not a handicap in competition. She is beginning to demand not that protective legislation should be abolished, but that it should be made to apply to men and women alike. At the Rome Congress of the International Woman's Suffrage Alliance in 1923 protective legislation had already become an absorbing topic of discussion and debate; at the Paris congress of the same body last June it was the dominating issue. And while the feminists failed to bring the Congress to an expression of unqualified opposition to protective legislation on a sex basis, they came very near it.

It is not unlikely that a new woman's international will be formed in the near future for the special purpose of dealing with the International Labour Office of the League of Nations, a body which seems determined to protect women at any cost. One of its earliest Conventions which has been adopted by a great many governments, decrees that "Women without distinction of age shall not be employed during the night in any industrial undertaking." In 1921 an attempt was made to extend this prohibition to agriculture by a *Recommendation* that:—

> Each member of the International Labour Office take steps to regulate the employment of women wage-earners in agricultural undertakings during the night in such a way as to ensure to them a period of rest compatible with their physical necessities and consisting of not less than nine hours, which shall, when possible, be consecutive.

This sudden concern for the health of women when they set out to earn their living in competition with men seems a little suspicious to the feminist.

"What working-class mother of small children ever had nine hours' consecutive rest?" she asks. "What trades union husband ever felt that it was his concern to see that she should have? How often does the eight-hour-day man get up to prepare his own breakfast with the benevolent intention of reducing his wife's working day from fifteen hours to fourteen?"

Whatever one may think of protective legislation in general, the night-work prohibition seems to be a gift horse women [would] do well to look in the mouth. Nobody, man or woman, really prefers to work at night. He takes a night-work job because no other job is available, because he can make more money that way, or perhaps because he has some responsibilities which make a day-time job impracticable for him. It is, to say the least, an arbitrary and fantastic sort of philanthropy to close this opportunity to adult women.

Letter to the Editor of *Time and Tide*

SIR,—No one can doubt that the resignation of eleven hard-working members of the N.U.S.E.C. Executive on March 5th was the result of a genuine and very important difference both of opinion and temperament, and that it will therefore promote clear thinking in the feminist movement. But I believe the "equalitarians" would have done more toward setting the National Union's house in order if they had gone to the root of the trouble, if, instead of attempting to define the relative "equality content" of different features of the program, they had directly attacked the unnatural compromise revealed in the avowed "Object of the society:—

> "To obtain all such reforms as are necessary to secure a real equality of liberties, status and opportunities between men and woman *and also such reforms as are necessary to make it possible for women adequately to discharge their functions as citizens.*"

Time and Tide, 18 March 1927.

On the single obvious demand for the franchise nearly all public spirited women were united; they were all feminists together without question of kind or degree. But after the suffrage victory they inevitably "reverted to type," as one might say. The humanitarian type said to itself, "Thank God, that's over. Now we can stop demanding our rights (which never came natural to us anyhow) and turn once more to the various reforms which we believe will benefit the human race. And, as we go, we can clear up those minor inequalities which still exist between men and women."

The "pure feminist" type said, "Thank God, that's over. Now we can go on with the programme of feminism. We can begin to attack the subjection of women in its other forms, many of them as deep-rooted and menacing to freedom as was our disfranchisement."

In some countries, as in America, this "reversion to type" led to a complete re-alignment of forces. In England, at least in the case of the N.U.S.E.C., it led to compromise, an unholy and unworkable compromise. The first half of the "Object" quoted above is a clear and complete statement of the feminist objective. The second half, which I have put in italics, is pure social reform. It is worse than that; there is a humble pious tang about it, as though women were still in a state of tutelage, needing special training to fit them for the great privilege of citizenship.

What does it mean—"Such reforms as are necessary to make it possible for women adequately to discharge their functions as citizens"?

I am told that it is under this clause that the N.U.S.E.C. supports the League of Nations:—"women cannot adequately discharge their functions as citizens until we have peace." Well, neither can men. On the same ground, I presume, the N.U.S.E.C. would explain its attempt to settle the general strike;—"Women cannot adequately discharge their functions as citizens with industry at a standstill." True. Neither can men. And the argument for including "smoke abatement" in the N.U.S.E.C. programme was, no doubt: —"Women cannot find their way to the polls through the fog." But again what about men? Is their eye-sight better?

There is hardly a reform advocated, from breast-feeding to free university education for which it cannot be claimed that it will make better citizens. But what has all this to do with feminism? Are not all these reforms as important for the male citizen as for the female citizen?

The "equalitarians" have declared that they do not intend to leave the National Union, but to "work within it for its return to right lines." May I suggest that the first thing to do is to get rid of that meaningless blanket-reform clause which confuses and befogs the declared "Object" of the society? There need, then, be no longer a juggling with "Equality A" and "Equality B." There would be but one clear test. And it would be possible to discuss without confusion whether such measures as birth control and motherhood endowment belong in the feminist programme or not.

Such border-line issues, which cannot perhaps be stated literally in terms of equality because the functions of male and female parents are so different, nevertheless in the minds of many clear-thinking feminists, bear as directly and as vitally upon the problem of equalising the status of men and women, as any other feminist issues.

To confound feminists of this persuasion with those who would make peace, pure milk and piety part of the feminist programme, does nothing for our logic nor for our fighting strength.—Yours, etc.,

CRYSTAL EASTMAN.

6, Upper Park Road, London, N.W.3.

Equalitarian vs. Reformer

By a curious chain of circumstances it came about that I took part in the stormiest battle that has stirred the ranks of British women since pre-suffrage days, when militants and constitutionalists so passionately opposed each others' methods—a battle which ended in the dramatic resignation of eleven leading members of the executive, and

Equal Rights, 4 June 1927.

which has left a deep cleavage in the ranks of the oldest suffrage society in Great Britain.

Protection versus equality for women in industry, birth control and family endowment versus "straight" feminism—in general the same issues that concern and divide the leading women's organizations in America, were the issues round which the storm raged in London. But the "line-up" is surprisingly different here.

In their demand for the franchise nearly all public-spirited women, both in England and America, were united; they were all Feminists together without question of kind or degree. After the suffrage victory they "reverted to type." The humanitarian or social reform type said to itself:

"Thank God, that's over. Now we can stop demanding our rights (which never came natural to us anyhow), and turn once more to doing good, to the various reforms which we believe will benefit the human race. And as we go we can clear up those minor inequalities which exist between men and women."

The equalitarian or pure Feminist type said:

"Thank God, that's over. We have taken the first step. We have established for women the elementary right of citizenship. Now we can go on with the Feminist battle until we have established a real equality of status and opportunity for women in every field."

In America this "reversion to type" led to a complete realignment of forces, to the development of two national organizations, often violently opposed to each other, not merely on matters of tactics as in presuffrage days, but on matters of principle. Witness protective legislation.

In England it led to compromise. There was a special reason for compromise in England; the suffrage victory had been but a partial one. Five million women were still voteless. And leaders of all types felt that they must keep their forces intact until the franchise had been granted to women on the same terms as men. In 1920, shortly after Parliament had granted the suffrage to women over thirty, the National Union of Societies for Equal Citizenship, hoping to hold together both Feminist and reformist types among its members, adopted a new "Object," as follows:

"To obtain all such reforms as are necessary to secure a real equality of liberties, status and opportunities between men and women, and *also such reforms as are necessary to make it possible for women adequately to discharge their functions as citizens."*

This blanket-reform clause which I have put in italics was designed to include and did eventually include everything from birth control to the League of Nations. It was an unnatural, unworkable compromise and now at last, after seven years of dissension, it has gone to pieces.

Strange to say, the inevitable split came just on the eve of an important deputation to the Prime Minister to demand the extension of the franchise to women under thirty. The eleven "equalitarians," as they call themselves, the Feminist half of the executive, resigned in a body publicly the last day of the Conference. The following Tuesday was the day set by Mr. Baldwin to receive the united deputation of suffrage societies, the first deputation of its kind since 1918.

"At least they might have waited till after Tuesday!" said the shocked and startled delegates to each other.

"I consider this most discourteous," said Mrs. Corbett Ashby, International President, who happened to be in the chair that morning. "There is no excuse for members of the executive to make such an announcement publicly to the Conference without giving notice to the board."

"This is a terrible blow!" said Miss Eleanor Rathbone, president and leader of the humanitarian group in the National Union. "I beg these members to reconsider. I call upon the Conference to ask them with all possible urgency to withdraw their resignations for the moment, at least until after the deputation to the Prime Minister. And I appeal to the press to disregard the announcement of the resignations."

But it was too late. Feeling was too tense. The press already had the story, and none of the resigning members would reconsider.

The wonder is not that the split has come, but that the lions and lambs have been lying down together so long in this British society. If you can imagine Mrs. Florence Kelley acting as president of an organization in which slightly less than half of the members and her strongest co-workers on the Executive Committee were stern follow-

ers of the strict Feminism of Alice Paul—if you can imagine a
program which on the one hand denounced protective laws for
women and on the other advocated birth control and the League of
Nations, you will get some picture of the National Union of Societies
for Equal Citizenship.

I never before realized how strong is the instinct for compromise
among the English.

Much is known in America about the English militants, about
the adventurous exploits of the Women's Social and Political Union,
founded by the Pankhursts. But of this older, more "regular" suffrage
society with an even longer name, almost nothing is known. Yet its
history is in many ways as unique if not as romantic. For one thing
the National Union of Societies for Equal Citizenship—commonly
called the N.U.S.E.C.—throughout its long life has been dominated
by just two leaders.

When far back in 1866 a group of women in London drew up
the first suffrage petition which John Stuart Mill presented to the
House of Commons, Millicent Garrett, then a girl of nineteen, was a
member of the group. By the following year, 1867, when the first
woman suffrage society was formed, she had become an active leader
and she continued to be an active leader in the movement until the
vote was won in 1918.

It was Millicent Garrett, now for many years Mrs. Fawcett, who
in 1897 gathered together the suffrage societies which had sprung up
all over the country and founded the National Union, of which she
became president and remained president until 1919.

Along in the late nineties, another very strong personality
became prominent in the organization, Eleanor Rathbone of Liverpool, a woman some thirty years younger than Mrs. Fawcett,
daughter of a famous line of Liverpool shipbuilders. Her father and
her grandfather were Liberals of great wealth and more than local
distinction. Both had devoted their lives and their fortunes to fine
generous schemes of constructive philanthropy.

Eleanor Rathbone was a born social reformer, it was in her
blood, in her early training and environment. Millicent Fawcett, on
the other hand, was a Feminist of the old school. Throughout the last
twenty years of the suffrage campaign these two powerful leaders

worked side by side in the National Union, and when Mrs. Fawcett decided, after the victory, that the time had come for her to retire from the presidency, she chose Miss Rathbone as her successor with the unanimous consent of the members.

But Miss Rathbone had not held the leadership for three years before she inaugurated a change of policy so emphatic that Mrs. Fawcett felt obliged to resign. To resign from her own society, which she had created, nursed through its infancy and ruled for half a century!

You see, Eleanor Rathbone, though she was a passionate suffragist, is not primarily a Feminist but a social reformer. After the vote was won she "reverted to type."

During the war Eleanor Rathbone had had charge of the distribution of separation allowances to the wives and children of soldiers from the Liverpool district. As a result of this experience she had become a convinced believer in what is known as "family endowment." This is a system, already quite generally adopted in the poorer industrial districts of France and Germany, by which through direct taxation, a small allowance is paid to a mother for the maintenance of each child. The idea is to relieve poverty by adjusting wages to need, by equalizing to some extent the economic position of the father of a family with that of the single man.

Miss Rathbone has written a book about family endowment, and is becoming known throughout the world as one of its most distinguished advocates. Through her influence as president, the N.U.S.E.C. was persuaded first to study the scheme and finally to advocate family allowances as part of its program. It was at this point that Dame Millicent Fawcett left the society. She does not believe in family allowances; she thinks they would destroy family responsibility, and she feels that the scheme has no place in the Feminist program.

In the same way, with the approval and support of Miss Rathbone, though it was not a pet reform of hers, birth control became part of the N.U.S.E.C. program. A good deal can be said for both these reforms from a Feminist standpoint. They seem to me to bear with considerable directness on securing equality of status for the married woman. But your pure Feminist is apt to be a bit of a doctrinaire. She likes to advocate something that can be stated literally in terms of equality. The equalitarian contingent in the Union was not pleased with this enlargement of its program, but they bowed to the will of the majority.

Meanwhile another big issue had arisen—protective laws, or restrictive laws as the Feminist prefers to call them, for women in industry. On this issue the equalitarians had their way. Year after year they succeeded in passing, against the pronounced opposition of Miss Rathbone who as a reformer believed in protective laws, a resolution declaring that protective legislation should be based on the nature of the work and not on the sex of the worker, and another making it clear that when the Union said equality, it meant equality in industry, too.

This accounts for the fact that at the International in Paris last June, as many American Feminists will remember, nine out of the twelve British delegates voted for the admission of the National Woman's Party, while their president, Eleanor Rathbone voted against its admission.

Now we come to the annual conference of 1927, which I attended. The large active executive of twenty-four members, almost equally divided between humanitarians and equalitarians, had by its own confession spent the year in dissension and wrangling. They had begun to feel that the situation was impossible. Each group decided to try to strengthen its own position by a vote of the conference.

Miss Rathbone, for her group, proposed an amendment intended to weaken and modify the Union's declared opposition to protective legislation. Her amendment was finally carried, after hours of heated discussion, by a vote of 81 to 80.

The Feminist group, on their side, introduced a general resolution to the effect that equal franchise, equal moral standard, equal pay and opportunity in industry and the professions, be given precedence in the program; that family allowances and birth control involve the principle of equality *to a lesser degree* and should be dealt with secondarily. After a discussion even longer and more heated, this resolution was lost.

Thus, the equalitarians lost on both counts, and their answer, as we have seen, was to resign. Technically, it is a victory for the humanitarians, but, as Lady Rhondda points out in her lively Feminist weekly, *Time and Tide,* it is "victory at a heavy cost. Miss Rathbone has lost from the executive all the old powerful personalities who were with the Union in the old days before the vote was won. She has lost too the most enterprising of the younger women. One is reminded of the saying of Pyrrhus: 'Another such victory and we are undone.' "

"If you set yourselves to work for pure equality between the sexes and nothing else," said Miss Rathbone, in the course of the final debate, "you are following an arid, barren and obsessing idea." And yet this "arid idea" seems to attract the freshest, youngest and warmest personalities in the movement. Lady Balfour of Burleigh, who acted as spokesman for the eleven who resigned, belongs to the new order of Feminist. She is, I should say, barely a voter, hardly over thirty, slim, tall and charming, and the mother of three or four small children. Like Lady Astor, she has a devoted Feminist husband in the House of Lords, who works in close co-operation with her. She is extremely modern. She believes in birth control and works for it. She believes in family endowment and is a member of the Family Endowment Council. But she wants to take her Feminism straight. "Equality first" is her motto.

Lady Balfour in her turn is some thirty years younger than Miss Rathbone. It is not inconceivable that she has been chosen by destiny as the third leader in a century of British Feminism.

Two

CRYSTAL EASTMAN
ON REVOLUTION

AGAINST IMPERIAL WARFARE: THE WOMAN'S PEACE PARTY AND THE AMERICAN UNION AGAINST MILITARISM

To Make War Unthinkable

SIR: If it is not too late I should like to comment on your editorial of July third, entitled "The Deeper Preparedness."

You say: "Both pacifists and militarists—to use inaccurate but convenient words—proclaim their interest in peace. It remains for the public to require both of them to explain the foreign policy they have in mind before they proceed to adopt means of carrying it out."

Speaking as a pacifist, I reply that with every surface appearance of common sense you are "putting the cart before the horse." Beyond advocating what is an inherent and inevitable part of the pacifist platform, i.e., a non-aggressive national policy, it is not necessary for the peace movement to concern itself in the first instance with questions of international policy. National disputes will arise—they are unavoidable—so long as separate nations exist. Our concern is with the method of settling those disputes. Our function is to

Letter to the editor, *The New Republic*, 24 July 1915.

establish new values, to create an overpowering sense of the sacredness of life, so that war will be unthinkable; so that when international disputes arise, even of the most grave character—when lives have been lost, when our rights have been clearly invaded—we shall not turn to wholesale, deliberate destruction of life as the means of settling those disputes, of avenging those deaths, of asserting those rights.

Our function, again, is to devise the substitute, or substitutes for war—to start the political genius of the world thinking, inventing, along this line. We did not wait for the last word on individual rights before establishing courts to adjudicate them. Quarreling persists among men, but duelling has been abolished. Pacifist agitation is directed primarily, and rightly, I think, against the prevailing archaic and barbarous *method* of determining international disputes. No amount of wisdom and forbearance and generosity will prevent disputes arising. The flag will be insulted here and there, boundary questions will come up, trade disputes will arise, American lives will be lost, the national honor will be offended, no doubt to the end of time, or for centuries to come; let us be "prepared" for those contingencies by all means, but prepared to meet them in a civilized, grown-up way, not by the flourish of the big stick, and the slaughter of thousands. That is the pacifist's concern.

Finally, the peace movement is essentially international in character. No world court or international federation can be established unless there is a strong desire for it in many nations. Therefore the pacifist agitation cannot concern itself too closely with questions of purely national policy. Beyond insisting that each nation should be non-aggressive, beyond insisting that national integrity be preserved, and such trade freedom and possibility for expansion be allowed each nation as are necessary to its successful national existence, and asserting his willingness to have these matters left to an international body in which each nation has just representation, the pacifist, it seems to me, need not concern himself with national policies.

Especially is it important that in the present controversy he should not lose himself in the necessarily involved discussions of national policy. The immediate function of the pacifist in America to-day is to fight the agitation for increased armament as a step in the wrong direction, as a long backward step away from the achievement of his ideals. We are not in any immediate danger of invasion, probably not for ten years. During that time we have the opportunity to inaugurate some sort of world understanding which shall remove once and for all the danger of such invasion and the necessity of providing against it. If now we take the fatal step of large increase in armament, inevitably we shall arouse suspicion and unfriendliness, no nation will believe us when we talk of a democratic world federation or a league of peace; we shall have lost the opportunity of centuries. That is the pacifist's "ideal" reason for opposing the advocates of "preparedness," so-called. His "practical" reason is that a big increase in armament on the part of an important neutral nation at a critical time like this, is most obviously playing with fire—it is inviting war upon us.

CRYSTAL EASTMAN BENEDICT.

New York City.

"Now I Dare to Do It"

An Interview with Dr. Aletta Jacobs, Who Called the Woman's Peace Congress at The Hague

---

Aletta Jacobs, first woman physician of Holland, founder and head of the Dutch suffrage movement, who spent some weeks in America on a mission which brought her to the White House, was telling me how she found courage to call the Woman's Peace Congress at The Hague last spring.

The Survey, 9 October 1915.

Much has been written of that remarkable gathering but the vigorous-minded woman who conceived it and with characteristic directness "put it through" is comparatively unknown to us in America. She is, however, one of a group of "international" women who are challenging public opinion with the idea of world union for peace.

"You see," she began, "at Buda Pesth in 1913, it was agreed that we should hold the next biennial meeting of the Woman Suffrage Alliance in Berlin in 1915. The German women wanted us. But then the war came, and early last winter a letter reached me, as one of the national suffrage presidents, saying that of course the war would make it impossible to hold the meeting in Berlin, and strongly recommending that the convention be given up.

"But I thought at once, just because there is this terrible war the women *must* come together somewhere, some way, just to show that women of all countries can work together even in the face of the greatest war in the world. Women must show that when all Europe seems full of hatred they can remain united. I felt that the alliance had to do that and we should invite the alliance to meet in Amsterdam. But several of the allied countries voted against holding an international meeting during the war and therefore the invitation was not accepted.

"I received, however, many letters of sympathy with the plan from individual women in belligerent and neutral countries, and from Miss Macmillan of England a plan for a meeting of individuals. The other members of my board of the suffrage society did not agree on this plan of a congress of individuals, but I thought it a good plan and decided to do what I could personally.

"I therefore invited as many women as I could reach in different countries to discuss together what the congress should be and to make up the preliminary program. When the answers came, so many were in favor that I thought,—'now I dare to do it.' "

This meeting was held in Amsterdam on February 12 and 13, 1915. Five women came from Great Britain, four from Germany, three from Belgium, and several from Holland. Agreeing that there should be no discussion of the causes or conduct of the war, but that all minds should be concentrated on methods of bringing about peace, these pioneers made Dr. Jacobs chairman of the organizing committee and the call went out to the women of all nations in her name.

The next question put to Dr. Jacobs was this: "Was the Hague gathering more than a splendid expression of the growing solidarity of womankind the world over? Do you think it will lead to something constructive?"

"Of course, it will." Dr. Jacobs replied. "It already has. As the convention voted it, I went with Miss Addams to carry our resolutions to the governments of Great Britain, Germany, Austria-Hungary, Switzerland, Italy, France and Belgium. But when I got back to Amsterdam the first thing I did was to open headquarters for the International Committee of Women for Permanent Peace, the permanent organization formed at the congress, and to engage two secretaries to commence the work.

"The work we have planned is an enormous undertaking. First we must keep up the bond between pacifist women in all countries. We must act as a clearing house through which they can communicate. We have already begun issuing bulletins. Here is one, for instance, telling what the Swedish women have done since the congress—how on June 27 they held peace meetings in 343 places at one time—crowded, enthusiastic meetings, and secured the signatures of 88,784 women to our Hague resolutions. News like that sent out to the women of other countries will inspire them to act, you see, and thus the organization will grow.

"Next we must help to organize the pacifist women in countries not yet roused, like Switzerland, for instance. Then, of course, we must have an international organ soon to make a stronger bond.

"But the immediate project for which we must be ready any minute, is the calling of a second congress. This was agreed on by the women at The Hague. As soon as negotiations for peace begin, we are to send out invitations for a second congress to be held in the city where peace is made. There will be five women from each country to sit in continuous session and consider terms of peace and send in their suggestions from time to time to the negotiators. At the end of this session there will be a big congress of women going on, with twenty voting members from each country."

There was no need to ask Dr. Jacobs whether to her mind such a congress of women would have an influence on the deliberations of the negotiators. She goes further and believes the coming—and staying—of world peace will depend largely on women. When I asked her if she thought we might see the end of war in a generation or two or if it would take centuries of education to bring it about, she said: "Oh, no. Women will soon have political power. Woman suffrage and permanent peace will go together. When the women of a country are eagerly asking for the vote, and a country is in the state of mind to grant the vote to its women, it is a sign that that country is ripe for permanent peace.

"Yes, the women will do it. They don't feel as men do about war. They are the mothers of the race. Men think of the economic results; women think of the grief and pain, and the damage to the race. If we can bring women to feel that internationalism is higher than nationalism, then they won't stand by governments, they'll stay by humanity."

There is a resolution in the Hague platform calling for a conference of neutrals to propose terms of peace. I was interested to get Dr. Jacobs' impressions with regard to the European neutrals— Holland, Switzerland, Spain and the Scandinavian countries—and their attitude toward this proposal.

"I can only speak for Holland," she said. "But the other European neutrals must be in the same situation. The Dutch are strong pacifists. Of course there are people in my country who believe in war, but what they preach is not popular. I have heard some of them speak, and they were hissed by the audience—sometimes hissed right off the platform. But in spite of the temper of the people these have been critical times in Holland.

"It is hard for you to realize how close the war is to us. It is at our very doors. We can hear the cannon and the bursting shells. The results are always coming over our borders. That, of course, makes us feel the horror of it more than you do here, but it means too that we are more closely involved."

"So the neutral governments had hardly thought of using their good offices to stop the war, until the women came together and proposed it?"

"Yes, that's it. The women thought of it."

"Well," I asked, "suppose there is a neutral conference of some kind, don't you think there should be a woman on it?"

Here Dr. Jacobs smiled—the knowing tolerant smile of a mother for her boys. It made her seem less of a feminist. "Men, you know, like to do things for themselves. They have more confidence in a proposal if it is made by men than if it is made by women. So, we don't care so very much about having women in the Conference of Neutrals, *if only the right men can be found.*"

That is after all the amazing thing about these women "internationlists." They do not seem to be driven by personal ambition, and yet they tackle big, unheard-of undertakings like the Hague meeting and succeed with them. Simplicity, directness, the glorious courage of children to whom everything is possible because it is untried,—these are the qualities women are bringing into the new world councils. They are priceless qualities, and the spirit of these women will be felt whether any of them receive official recognition or not.

A Platform
of Real Preparedness

That these are critical times for America in her relation to the rest of the world, no one denies. The question is: What are the real dangers that face us, and how can we best meet them. At one extreme we have the various defense leagues that are urging upon the country in great haste and excitement a large increase in armament as the only "safeguard." At the other extreme are a few serene non-resistants who would have us meet every conceivable national emergency by laying

The Survey, 13 November 1915.

down our arms. Standing between these two groups is a steadily growing body of thoughtful citizens by no means to be dubbed advocates of "peace at any price," whose counsel to America throughout these critical months has been "Trust Wilson and keep your powder wet," and who see with regret that the administration has at last been stampeded into a big defense program.

So far we have been playing a role of negation, or at best have set remote plans for world federation against immediate demands for preparedness. Congress convenes December 6. It is high time we had a program.

This country now spends about $300,000,000 a year on national defense, approximately 30 percent of our entire federal expenditure. Our navy ranks third in the world. In 1912 we spent about $2.65 per person for defense, France $6.65, Germany $4.81, and England $7.80 per person. Considering our geographical position and comparative freedom from international complications, our expenditure for national defense seems reasonable. If, then, our defenses are in such desperate condition as the experts say they are, is not our first move to find out how all this money is being spent? To root out the graft and inefficiency and establish good organization and modern methods? To say to Congress: "Gentlemen, before you take $500,000,000 more from our pockets for national defense show us how the last $250,000,000 was spent. Show us why we don't get better defense for our money." Surely this is common sense. By all means on the first day of congress let us have a bill ready, calling for a public and expert investigation of the state of our defenses, with a report in three months. Let that be the first plank in our platform.

Second, national manufacture of armaments,—this we can surely demand with one voice. And the hottest advocates of preparedness must join us. For who should be more anxious than they to clear the air of suspicion, to establish beyond reasonable doubt that the anxiety for adequate defense is in all cases a disinterested anxiety?

But, the alarmist cries, this is no time for investigation and long-drawn-out debates over Socialistic legislation. This is a time of danger! Let us vote the increase first and investigate afterwards. Is it really then a time for desperate, eleventh-hour legislation to save the nation? It is claimed that we need increased armament, not for aggression but for defense. Danger means, then, danger of attack, of invasion. What are those dangers that threaten us?

The German invasion war-scare we need not consider. Those who in their sober moments can see in the present world situation an immediate danger of a German fleet bombarding our ports and a German army invading our country will not be reading this article.

First, then, the Philippines—there is a strong conviction that Japan is jealous of our rule in those far-off islands. Granting that these imperial "possessions" of ours do constitute a danger, it is hardly one to warrant emergency legislation. With Japan still burdened by the debt of her last war, busily engaged in securing a firm foothold in Manchuria and Mongolia, and deeply involved in the present European conflict, that danger is not immediate. We have time to reconsider our Philippine policy. And to many of us, who are out of patience with America's recent imperialistic ventures, it would seem the part of wisdom to hasten the independence of the Philippines, instead of getting ready to fight out this question with Japan. Surely there is no benefit conceivably to be gained for us, for the Filipinos, or for humanity at large, by our continued rule over those islands, which would warrant us in entering upon an international conflict to maintain that rule. By all means let America be free from incongruous possessions as well as from entangling alliances, and let Philippine independence in 1916 be the third plank in our program.

The next source of danger commonly mentioned as a reason for a vast increase in army and navy is California's oriental exclusion policy on the Pacific coast. That is a real difficulty. Here we must not merely abandon a policy inconsistent with the healthy growth of a republic as in the case of the Philippines, we must change our feeling about an alien race, and solve a knotty industrial problem. This will take time, and fortunately again we have time.

As a first step toward preventing war over this matter, let us on the first day of congress appropriate $5,000,000 for an "oriental-occidental-understanding foundation" to be established in California, where the young men and young women of the West and the East can study each other's national characteristics and their respective countries' problems of labor and expansion under the wisest sociologists and economists. Let us establish 500 interchanging scholarships

K. Patterson
5/5/93

between Japanese and American universities; let us appoint a federal commission to study oriental immigration—its real effect on both countries—to make the facts known here and in Japan and to devise wise immigration laws.

Yes, $5,000,000 or even $1,000,000 appropriated for some such plan as that, which would show in its very wording a friendly spirit toward the oriental peoples, would do more to avert war with Japan than $500,000,000 worth of battleships to show her we're "ready for her."

And now we come to the Monroe Doctrine, chief bulwark of the "preparedness" campaign. Are we not bound, they say, to protect those South American republics and doesn't that mean we must be ready to fight? Surely the Monroe Doctrine as it stands contains the germs of future trouble, but again, I insist it does not constitute an immediate danger. Only a strong nation will challenge it and the strong nations will all have their hands full for some time to come. We must keep cool-headed enough to see that there is a certain security for us in the fact that most of the world is fighting. The European War is, to be sure, a warning, but at the same time it is a guarantee against immediate danger. It gives us time to think. And while we are thinking, why not seriously propose a democratic union of American republics as a substitute for the Monroe Doctrine and all its dangers?

Such a federation, already forshadowed in President Wilson's A.B.C. gatherings, would be established first in the interests of mutual understanding and good will. And this is extremely important, for it is well recognized by international students that the Monroe Doctrine in its modern interpretations may get us into trouble with South America as well as with Europe. But our pan-American federation could stand for something more. It could stand for the maintenance of republican ideals. Thus, we should abandon an uncomfortable and possibly indefensible doctrine, at the same time preserving in modern and acceptable form its valuable feature. We should rid ourselves of the temptation to establish profitable protectorates in the South American countries and disarm the growing and perhaps warranted South American suspicion.

To make this proposal concrete, the fifth plank in the new

platform might call for a small commission to confer with the other American republics concerning the advisability of forming a permanent union for our mutual benefit.

Now, many people would follow us on such a program and yet try to reserve the right to shout for preparedness at the same time, reasoning that even if we do bring our foreign policies into line with the new spirit of internationalism, there is no harm in increasing our fighting strength, we might as well be ready for trouble. Such loose thinking, such "bad psychology" makes it imperative for the pacifists to emphasize continually as a corollary to this constructive program, the great urgent reasons for holding America back from any unusual defense measures at this time.

With most of the world at war, our rights are bound to be trampled on here and there. It is a dangerous time for us—every morning we seem to face a new crisis. A fire as big as that with only the ocean between is bound to scorch us. It is only by keeping cool, by playing the hose on our roofs all the time, by stowing all inflammables and combustibles out of sight, that we can keep from catching fire. To start in just now on a great program of military and naval expansion, to spend millions on submarines and battleships, to increase the standing army, to start military training camps, to talk, think, and act "preparation for war," is psychologically speaking, like pouring kerosene on the roofs instead of water. Sparks are bound to fall—if they fall on cool wet roofs there is a chance of their going out. If they fall on dry roofs prepared with kerosene, what chance is there?

For those who think this country can best serve humanity by staying out of the war, a program of immediate military expansion is foolhardy. Suppose, however, we do adopt such a program, and, suppose owing to fortunate circumstances, to the early ending of the war, to the growing determination of sensible men not to go to war, to cool leadership at Washington, or to all of these causes, suppose we escape becoming involved in the war, in spite of our state of aggressive preparedness, is there any harm done? Yes, there is.

To one with a feeling for the deep currents of history it is clear that a destiny awaits this country, the opportunity of centuries. At the close of this greatest of wars America can, *if her people stay in the right frame of mind,* initiate some new kind of world understanding which shall make war between civilized nations unnecessary, impossible.

This is no idle dream. World peace is desired by all the real, organic groups of every nation—capital, labor, science, religion, finance, etc. Interests are agreed on this that are opposed on almost every other issue. Only a method is lacking. Here, we can say without national egotism since our opportunity is due not to superior intelligence, but to fortunate circumstances, here America's opportunity lies. All our national energy and genius should be directed toward putting this idea of a world federation into workable form, acceptable to all nations. We must be ready in mind and spirit for our destiny.

Now, two opposing fervors cannot possess a mob at the same time. America cannot be thrilled with its destiny as the inaugurator of world peace, and be caught up at the same time in a kind of fear-engendered, jingo-patriotic, pugnacious emotionalism that will vote $500,000,000 for new battleships on the chance of German or Japanese invasion. The national genius cannot be directed to war preparation and *genuine* peace preparation at the time time. If we are to fill the public mind with the kind of enthusiasm which will be necessary to make us a power for world union, we cannot at the same time rouse it with pictures of Germans bombarding New York and of Japanese possessing California.

The amount of the people's money that would be spent on the new battleships is by no means negligible; but the amount of national spirit, pride and patriotism, that would be spent on such a program would beggar us for years to come so far as national action toward world peace goes.

So much for the effect of increased armament on our own national psychology. How about Europe? Will those nations watch our preparations for war without suspicion? If they do it will be contrary to all history. It is only in its own eyes that a nation arms for defense. If at the peace when it comes, we face exhausted Europe, armed as we never have been before, with our editors boasting from San Francisco to Boston, that now at last America is ready to meet the world, in what spirit would our world federation proposals be received? (If indeed, it is conceivable that we could have intelligent proposals of that nature to make after devoting ourselves for months to preparations for war.)

This, then, is the truth about the preparedness advocates. They are urging upon us a large increase of armament: at best an emergency measure, the evil consequences of which all Europe cries to high heaven today. And *there is no excuse for it*—no emergency, no danger of immediate invasion. More, they are urging this step upon us at a time of great national excitement when it might be just enough to tip the scales for war. And finally, they urge it upon us although it means abandoning the brightest hope a nation ever had.

Suggestions for 1916–1917

A Review

We should face the new year, not so much in the mood of defeated reformers doggedly pressing on, as in the mood of fighters who have held their ground and even made a little headway against tremendous odds. It is true that the army was increased (on paper) from 100,000 to 180,000 and that the National Guard has been put on a Federal subsidy, but the demand for a standing army of 250,000 was decisively beaten and the Administration's plan for a Continental Army was dropped overboard early in the fight. It is true that conscription was artfully included in that bill, but Congress was unaware, the people didn't dream of it, and we can probably have it repealed at the short session. It was accomplished through an oversight, not by a real winning of public opinion.

It is true that New York State passed extreme militarist measures, providing compulsory military training and conscription, and

American Union Against Militarism pamphlet, October 1916.

that similar legislation threatens in other states. But the New York
laws were hastily, quietly, passed. The opposition is now thoroughly
awake, and the chance to repeal them is excellent.

It is true that Congress passed the largest naval appropriation
bill in the history of the United States—yes, in the peace history of
any country,—but it was forced to concede the Hensley paragraphs
providing for the abandonment of the program if an adequate
international agreement develops after the war. And far more important than anything else in the general progress of our fight, are these
so-called Hensley paragraphs, which are safely incorporated in the
huge Navy Bill. They read as follows:

> "It is hereby declared to be the policy of the United States to
> adjust and settle its international disputes through mediation or
> arbitration, to the end that war may be honorably avoided. It looks
> with apprehension and disfavor upon a general increase of armament
> throughout the world, but it realizes that no single nation can disarm,
> and that without a common agreement upon the subject every
> considerable power must maintain a relative standing in military
> strength.
>
> "In view of the premises, the President is *authorized and requested
> to invite, at an appropriate time, not later than the close of the war in Europe,
> all the great Governments of the world* to send representatives to a *conference*
> which shall be charged with the duty of formulating *a plan for a court
> of arbitration* or other tribunal, to which disputed questions between
> nations shall be referred for adjudication and peaceful settlement, and
> *to consider the question of disarmament* and submit their recommendation
> to their respective Governments for approval. The President is hereby
> *authorized to appoint nine citizens* of the United States, who, in his
> judgment, shall be qualified for the mission by eminence in the law
> and by devotion to the cause of peace, to be representatives of the
> United States in such a conference. The President shall fix the
> compensation of said representatives, and such secretaries and other
> employees as may be needed. *Two hundred thousand dollars,* or so much
> thereof as may be necessary, is hereby *appropriated* and set aside and
> placed at the disposal of the President to carry into effect the provisions
> of this paragraph.
>
> "If at any time *before the construction* authorized by this Act *shall
> have been contracted* for there shall have been established, with the
> cooperation of the United States of America, *an international tribunal*or

tribunals competent to secure peaceful determinations of all international disputes, and *which shall render unnecessary the maintenance of competitive armaments,* then and in that case *such naval expenditures* as may be inconsistent with the engagements made in the establishment of such tribunal or tribunals *may be suspended,* when so ordered by the President of the United States."

Here, if we can get a strong enough public opinion back of it, is our congressional authority for ditching part, at least, of that preposterous naval program, for sinking the dreadnaughts before they are built. Here indeed is a new precedent in naval bills,—"We authorize you to build these ships, but we authorize you also to try to get the other nations to stop building theirs: if you succeed, then *don't build ours."* If the next to the last page of the Navy Bill works, many previous pages of it may become so much waste paper.

The Year Ahead

We propose then the following plan for the next year's work of the American Union Against Militarism.

(1) By bringing popular pressure to bear on Congress, by deputations, public hearings, and the widest possible publicity, we must compel the repeal of the *Hayden "joker" in the Army Law, which provides for conscription in case of war.* And we must increase rather than relax our vigilance in forestalling all other attempts at militarist legislation in Congress, such as the Chamberlain bill for universal military training, and the War College bill which would give military authorities power of censorship over the press in time of war.

(2) We must cooperate with local peace organizations in their efforts to *keep military training out of the public schools* and in their fight against *conscription* and compulsory training in the state laws, by providing effective literature and promoting publicity.

Simultaneously with the opposition campaigns outlined above, we propose to commence these two affirmative programs:

(3) *Create nation-wide publicity about the Hensley paragraphs* in the Navy Bill, and encourage delay on the ship-building program until the international agreement plans can be tried. Let every despairing pacifist in the country, every exhausted anti-militarist, every lover of

democracy, every radical, every man who objects to having the taxes wasted, every trade-unionist, every ordinary citizen who dislikes to feed the war trust,—let them all know that there is an "if" in the Naval Program, that a good share of the $315,000,000 can be saved to the people, if we can hold up the new building contracts until an international understanding is under way. Under the law, contracts for certain of the ships must be let before March 1, 1917. But that gives us time enough to tell the whole world about the Hensley paragraphs, and the practical hope they hold out for world-wide, organized peace. Once center public attention on those paragraphs and the enthusiasm for expensive battleships will die down; we can then rely on the inevitable slowness of a government department when it is not being watched, or we might even secure an amendment to allow further delay.

Then we can begin to suggest nine citizens for the international conference—we should secure an audience with the President to propose our candidates, and cable that story to the world. We should ask him what he can do at once to convince the people of all nations that he takes those paragraphs as seriously as any other legislation in 1916. He's bound to make an earnest statement. This story alone and the story of the big "if" in the contracts will do something to take the challenge and threat out of our new Navy Law.

There's no limit to the enthusiasm we can arouse over such a prospect. We'll have all the munition makers openly against us. It will be a glorious fight.

(4) Finally, *we must make the most of our Mexican experience.* We must make it known to everybody that the *people* acting directly—not through their governments or diplomats or armies—stopped that war, and can stop all wars if enough of them will act together and act quickly. We must celebrate this fact in some great and dignified way. The militarists will be quick to take the credit for peace. Let us too take time to claim our victories. We can contrast vividly the Civil Joint Commission at Atlantic City with a modern battlefield, and make it our rallying call for new support, new members, and new glory.

Then let us seriously and patiently construct the machinery for instant mobilization of the people for the prevention of any future war that might threaten this country. A war of simple wanton aggression against the United States is unthinkable. There would always be misunderstanding, false national pride, secret diplomacy, financial interests, something crooked at the bottom of it. And our plan for getting the people of the two countries into instant actual contact with and understanding of each other would always prevent it.

This would seem to be the way to begin: first, build up our own organization so that it is a real power in the land and known among liberals *all over the world.* Then educate our membership in what is expected of them if war threatens—so that we can have almost instant mobilization for service. Then get in touch with organizations like ours in other countries—especially those countries expected to be our enemies. Get them to select likely "Joint Commissioners" who would start to meet ours on an hour's notice. (Our Mexican-American Commissioners have all pledged to start for the border on an hour's notice if war threatens again and their services are needed.) *Have the names and addresses ready.* (We wasted twenty-four hours in the Mexican crisis because we didn't know the name of a single Mexican who would act with us. There's provincialism for you. Let our plan be the beginning of a *practical* internationalism.) Also get these leaders in foreign countries to send us their membership lists. We could then distribute the names among our active members and pledge them to cable at least one "enemy" a message of good-will to stave off war, if we send out the word. Imagine it! a thousand cables from "enemy" to "enemy" stating the firm friendliness of the people and their determination not to fight—all in 48 hours; and meanwhile the heads and subheads of organizations busy cabling stories to foreign papers, and a joint conference on its way to meet and *hold the peace.* There never could be a war if our peace forces could mobilize like that in 48 hours.

And there is no step of that program more quixotic or impossible than the El Paso Conference seemed at first.

The Machinery

For such a program (1-2-3-4) we need a big membership,— 10,000 before the year is out. We have on hand, 1,000 contributing members, 5,000 non-contributing members, and 60,000 likely names. We can build such an organization if we have the money to reach these people.

We must have a free hand for all the literature we need, and a genius to design it.

Our publicity department,—clever and competent as it is— must be ever bigger and better equipped, and we must begin to make it *international*. (Right out of a clear sky with no experience we tackled a problem of international publicity in the Mexican crisis. And perhaps the $300 we spent on telegrams and cables during that critical 48 hours in June was more important than we know in preventing war. Perhaps our feeling of good-will really reached the Mexican public in that way and made them endure the irritating presence of American troops a little longer in patience. Perhaps it kept Carranza from despairing and yielding to his angry soldiers. Perhaps it strengthened President Wilson in his determination to treat Mexico as the United States would like to be treated.)

We must not drop back. We must go ahead. Nothing must be too new and daring for us. What succeeded with Mexico will succeed with Japan, but we must be ready. We must be able to mobilize— hands and hearts and minds across the sea,—in forty-eight hours.

CRYSTAL EASTMAN,
Executive Secretary.

October 1916.

War and Peace

The radical peace movement, barely two years old, which is America's best answer to the war in Europe, has three main emphases: to stop

The Survey, 30 December 1916.

the war in Europe; to organize the world for peace at the close of the war; and to guard democracy (or such beginnings of democracy as we have in America) against the subtle dangers of militarism.

With regard to the first aim, the moment of achievement seems to be at hand. Surely the President's note makes the possibility of neutral action for peace almost immediate. If now we can gather together and express an overwhelming public opinion in support of that note our task will be done. The liberal and pacifist groups in the belligerent countries will do the rest.

As for international federation at the end of the war, this is the supreme moment for action. We have the hope of the world in those Hensley clauses of the navy law which request the President to summon the nations into conference at the close of the war to "consider disarmament" and organize for peace. The establishment of an international tribunal to settle disputes between nations has become a political possibility. We, the United States of America, through the action of our Congress, have taken the first step.

To make the Hensley clauses live in the mind of every American, to make them dominate the thoughts of the President, to make them ring through Europe as a promise of relief, to make them known throughout South America as a guarantee of our good faith, to accomplish this *now* before the war is over—and then at its close to create such a demand for action on them that President Wilson will not sleep until he has written and dispatched to the heads of all the governments a classic summons to the World Congress which shall end war! There is a New Year's resolution for every pacifist in America.

But what shall we do, meanwhile, about the growing demand for compulsory military training and service in this country?—a demand stimulated by the self-interest of capitalists, imperialists and war traders, but supported by the sincere emotions of thousands who call themselves democrats? To defeat this combination we need the constant, uncompromising opposition of all those lovers of liberty who can *think*. We must make this great American democracy know, as we know, that military training is bad for the bodies and minds and souls of boys; that free minds, and souls undrilled to obedience are vital to the life of democracy. We must make them see the difference between equality and freedom; if forced military service is "democratic," in the same sense prison life is democratic.

To repeal conscription where it has crept into our laws, to keep Congress from passing the Chamberlain Bill for universal training, to keep the other states from following New York—to hold the fort for liberty over here, until the nations are actually gathering to establish organized lasting peace—until, in short, every fool can see the folly of war preparations—that is the pacifists' third task for 1917. It is a task worthy of the grimmest and the gayest fighters among us.

Crystal Eastman
to Emily G. Balch
14 June 1917

Confidential

I have received within a week two letters, one from Miss Wald and one from Mr. Kellogg, explaining that the recent action of the Committee in voting to continue the Bureau of Conscientious Objectors as a department of the American Union Against Militarism marks such a division in interest and such a departure in policy that they are persuaded of the wisdom of resigning. Both reached this conclusion with regret and both letters express the friendliest hopes for the success of the program undertaken by the majority of the committee.

Of course resignations are bound to come; committees always split up eventually. I would only hope that when the American

AUAM Papers, Swarthmore College Peace Collection, Swarthmore, Pa.

Union Against Militarism Committee breaks up, it will break up over some really fundamental difference in belief, or some essential division over policy. Neither, it seems to me, is present in the immediate difficulty. It is a difference of emphasis, and of temporary emphasis at that.

Indeed, I feel so strongly that the time for parting is not yet, that there is still strength and not weakness in our Union, that I have asked Miss Wald and Mr. Kellogg to give us a week to consider the whole field of our activities and our possible future before formally submitting their resignations.

As a basis for such consideration, may I submit the following analysis of the positions taken by Miss Wald and Mr. Kellogg, with my own reaction to the points made by them?

Miss Wald feels that the program proposed for the development of a Conscientious Objectors' Bureau, "if consistently developed, must inevitably lead to a radical change in the policy of the Union. We cannot plan continuance of our program which entails friendly governmental relations (at least opportunities to get before the powers that be and possibly obtain governmental cooperation for our program) and at the same time drift into being a *party of opposition* to the government."

Two things might be said concerning this point: First—opposition to the extreme "preparedness" program, promoted by the Administration in the winter of 1915–16 was, more than any other one thing, the reason for our existence in the beginning. This was what made us unique among peace societies. Our opposition to so-called "preparedness" was consistently and boldly maintained, yet we were able always to secure an interview with the President or with any Department we thought it necessary to approach. And our views, in the matter of the Continental Army, of universal service, in the various Mexican crises, in the suggestion of "armed neutrality," etc., were, to say the very least, taken seriously. We were never denied a hearing, nor limited to so brief a hearing that it could be called a mere empty courtesy. In spite, then, of our radical opposition to the Administration in the matter of "preparedness," we have been counted on, I believe, to keep the President and others in touch with the widespread liberal (as opposed to "extreme radical") anti-militarist sentiment and opinion in the country throughout these troublous times.

Now in our defence of the Conscientious Objector—in our effort to secure a lenient administration of the Conscription Act—in our determination to maintain "liberty of conscience" in this country so far as we can—war or no war—we are not by any means as directly an "opposition party" as we were in the "preparedness campaign."

The President himself has said:—"This is by no means a conscription of the unwilling." He has put into the War Department, not avowed militarists, but men like Baker, Keppell, Walter Lippmann. It is as though he said to his old friends, the liberals:— "I know you are disappointed in me—you don't understand my conversion to the draft—my demand for censorship. I have reasons, plans, intentions, that I can't tell you. But as guarantee of good faith I give you Baker and Keppell and Lippmann and Creel, to carry out these laws. No matter how they look on paper—they cannot be Prussian in effect with such men to administer them."

So long as this policy continues, so long as the President is so obviously bidding for liberal support, it is our chance as an organization, no matter what doubts we may maintain as individuals, to take the opening, to assume that the President in his own way is still keeping faith with the liberals, to *believe*, officially at least, that he does not intend a conscription of the unwilling, and endeavor at every point (through advising the War Department at Washington, by the closest watch of local tribunals, by becoming a clearing house for complaints of injustice, by furnishing such information, advice and aid as will give the individual Conscientious Objector a chance to make his case with dignity and effectiveness) to aid the President in so administering the law that it may become in effect merely an efficient organizing of the fighting forces of the nation, not a means of forcing men into the army against their conscience. Thus we might really help, and not hinder, the Administration.

If, as the war goes on, it becomes more and more the deliberate and obvious intention of the government to militarize this nation, thoroughly and completely, for the sake of creating and maintaining a completely efficient war machine, the American Union Against Militarism must become, deliberately and obviously, the focus for the opposition. At that time our Committee might have to break up. But why cross the bridge till we come to it? At present, taking the President at his word and counting his War Department appointments as in some degree significant, our plan for maintaining free speech, free press, and free assembly, should logically command the support of those liberal democrats whose avowed leader the President until recently has been.

Mr. Kellogg shares Miss Wald's view, and, as I see it, goes farther. Mr. Kellogg is more interested in the international aspect of our work, in hastening a liberal peace and proceeding to organize the world for democracy, than in the struggle to hold the fort for democracy against militarism at home. And he feels that the American Union Against Militarism, having espoused the cause of the Conscientious Objector, is no longer in a position of influence and power in the "drive for peace."

He says:—"I am not blocking the prosecution of war, now that the decision has gone against me. Rather, I am still for the drive for peace, to outflank the war. And I feel that the institution of the Conscientious Objectors' Bureau, as an integral part of the American Union, will so throw the organization out of balance both in our own absorption in it and in the public estimation, as to put us in a position of attempting to paralyze the government and incapacitate us for constructive action."

Mr. Kellogg describes the opportunity that exists for gathering up the vast body of liberal opinion behind a drive for "liberal statement of peace terms and a negotiated liberal peace." Surely we are all with him in this hope, in this effort. But Mr. Kellogg believes that the American Union Against Militarism, having established a Conscientious Objectors' Bureau, is no longer fit for that task. We cannot combine, he says, "an aggressive policy against prosecution of the war with an aggressive policy for settling it through negotiations and organizing the world for democracy."

It seems to me that Mr. Kellogg has made a fundamental mistake. As I see it, our attempt to have the Conscription Act administered with due regard to liberty of conscience, is no more an aggressive policy against the prosecution of the war than is our attempt to save free speech, free press and assembly from the wholesale autocratic sweep which war efficiency dictates.

If we proposed an anti-recruiting campaign Mr. Kellogg's point would be well taken. If we set out, as the Republicans are doing, to criticise and find fault with every act of the Administration, in its conduct of the war, again his point would be well taken. But ours is not a policy of obstruction. Ours is a "democracy first" movement. And our Conscientious Objectors' Bureau is only part of that movement.

However, if undue emphasis is put on the Conscientious Objectors' Bureau, if it commences extensive activities without a statement of where it comes in in our general scheme, what Mr. Kellogg fears might come true—we might well become so hopelessly identified in the public mind with "anti-war" agitation as to make it impossible for us to lead the liberal sentiment for peace. To avoid this danger, I would suggest an immediate statement to the Press, and a reorganization of our work, making one legal bureau for the maintenance of fundamental rights in war time—free press, free speech, freedom of assembly and liberty of conscience.

To quote again, Mr. Kellogg says:—"I believe there are great reaches of public opinion in this country, in England and France and Russia that could be banked up behind such a program (i.e. liberal statement of peace terms, and a liberal negotiated peace, which shall lay the framework for internationalism). In this country these people are not for the war. Neither would they respond to anti-war agitation. They do not need to be converted against war. They do want to be shown a way out of a bad business. I think I can help."

Well, I, too, think I can help. So, I believe, does every member of our Committee. His hope is our hope—"to enlist the rank and file of the people, who make for progressivism the country over, in a movement for a civil solution of this world-wide conflict and fire them with a vision of the beginning of the U.S. of the World."

But shall we not be stronger, individually and collectively, to work toward that end by continuing to stand together in the American Union Against Militarism? We have a start; we have a name; a membership; a certain standing and influence, both at Washington and in many liberal circles throughout the country. We have an unusual combination of influential people in our Committee. These are assets.

Perhaps to all this, Mr. Kellogg would say:—"All that is true, but when we voted to take up the Conscientious Objector, the die was cast. We can no longer make that wide appeal." But is Mr. Kellogg right?

Will there be a hundred liberals whom we can count on our side in working for a liberal negotiated peace, whom we can not *also* count on our side in working to save this country from the disgrace of forcing young men to kill and be killed in a cause which their reason and conscience do not support?

Read this from the last issue of *The New Republic:*

"If at any time during the discussion it had been asserted that conscription was to be used as a measure, not only of sending American soldiers to Europe, but of coercing unwilling minorities into the firing line, it would have been overwhelmingly defeated. No one can deny there are minorities of Americans who, for various reasons, do not support this war. *The New Republic* has insisted from the beginning that the government in adopting conscription should show every consideration to conscientious objectors. This now appears all the more essential. We ought to have little difficulty, with less disturbance to industry than under the voluntary system, in selecting 500,000 or 1,000,000 young men who are willing, if necessary, to give their lives for present American purposes. Let this be done; let us not arouse the bitter internal dissension and petty local tyranny which would surely result from an attempt to coerce the men who, for reasons of conscience, claim exemption. Having adopted conscription for democratic purposes let us not turn it into an instrument of tyranny."

This article is significant. Here is the administration's own organ, as we might say, which fought for and secured conscription, now standing with us in maintaining that it must be administered with the widest tolerance for the "unwilling minorities."

If *The New Republic* believes that we should "show every consideration for the Conscientious Objector," surely we shall not weaken, but, rather, strengthen our appeal to the rank and file of liberal opinion in the country by taking up his cause.

One last word: Mr. Kellogg and Miss Wald both feel so cheerfully sure that the American Union Against Militarism can go on better in its present mood without them, and that their more constructive international peace plans can go on better without the American Union Against Militarism and its consistent stand against militarism.

This seems to me an unwarrantedly optimistic conclusion. We need them; we need their wisdom; their balance; their influence. They form a necessary sympathetic bond between what might be called the revolutionary and the non-resistant motives that make up our combination. On the other hand, I feel that they may need us in the new effort. I believe that any thorough-going movement for a democratic peace, for world organization, for universal democracy must rest on a clear understanding of each nation's problem in guarding its own democracy against militarism, and an unequivocal avowal of intention to fight the manifest encroachments of militarism at home. Otherwise, the movement will lack reality, valiant people will lose faith in it, and it will go the way of all peace movements.

The two go hand in hand. Some of us reason this way:—"War is intolerable; we must get rid of war. Moreover, militarism, which is a fruit of war, endangers democracy. We must fight militarism in all its phases, keep it from spreading and growing, even while we are working to abolish war itself, the source of militarism."

Others of us reason this way:—"The greatest danger to democracy today is militarism. I will fight militarism at every point. But there would be no militarism without war. Therefore, without relaxing my vigilance in combating all the manifestations of militarism (lest the ugly thing grow while I'm looking away) I will also join hands with all those who are working to abolish war itself."

Neither effort can be real or intelligent or altogether sincere without the other. The American Union Against Militarism has been a synthesis of the two. By all means let it continue.

AUAM Press Release
August 9, 1917

Protesting against the wide spread report that conscientious objectors to military service will be shot as deserters, The American Union Against Militarism, thru its executive secretary, Crystal Eastman, last night appealed to President Wilson to allay the growing fear that an era of Prussian frightfulness is to be instituted in America by this Government.

The letter states that members of the Union cannot believe that the words of General Crowder have been correctly interpreted, and that they are convinced that President Wilson will promptly correct the unpleasant impression made by the press interpretation of General Crowder's statement, and will state his own attitude with regard to the conscientious objector. The letter follows:—

May we call your attention to the fact that Brigadier General Crowder's statement of August 4, allows the inference that conscientious objectors may be court martialed and shot? We refer to the following paragraph with regard to the treatment of those citizens who fail to appear before the Exemption boards in answer to summons under the Draft Act:

"When the time allowed for making these claims has elapsed, these persons will be enrolled as in the military service. They will then be ordered to appear as soldiers. From this point on they will be under the swift and summary procedure of court martial. Failure to report for military duty when ordered to do so constitutes desertion. Desertion in time of war is a capital offense."

The press has widely interpreted this as a threat of the death penalty for all who, for any reason, refuse to take part in this war. On the heels of this startling announcement comes the news that a

Swarthmore College Peace Collection, Swarthmore, Pa.

Federal District Attorney is demanding death for those citizens of Oklahoma who recently armed themselves to resist the draft.

Mr. President, we realize, of course, that from a purely military point of view, resistance to authority—refusal to obey commands—is the final crime, demanding the extreme punishment. In Prussia it would be idle to question it. But this is America. We have here a great free civilian population, unused to military dictation. You know, as we do, that there are a great many thousands among our hundred million who, rightly or wrongly, disapprove of this war and are unwilling to fight in it. Some few will have the courage of their convictions, and will refuse to fight. That these must suffer imprisonment is a foregone conclusion. But that they should be executed, or that a responsible officer should be allowed to threaten them with the death penalty is something which we believe you, as the elected head of this great democracy and as Commander in Chief of the army, will not tolerate.

May we therefore urge you to take such steps as will correct the unfortunate impression made, and at the same time make clear to the country your own attitude toward the conscientious objector?

Respectfully yours,
CRYSTAL EASTMAN,
Executive Secretary.

For the American Union Against Militarism.

Woman's Peace Party
of New York City
70 Fifth Avenue

for peace by negotiation without annexations or indemnities, — the people's program for a settlement of the war.	*for free peoples, free markets, free seas, world union for disarmament, —the only guarantees of a democratic and enduring peace.*

Honorary Chairman
    MRS. HENRY VILLARD

Honorary Vice-Chairmen
    MARICE RUTLEDGE HALE
    MARIE JENNEY HOWE
    ELLEN N. LA MOTTE
    ROSE SCHNEIDERMAN
    MARY SHAW
    LILLIAN D. WALD
    ANNA STRUNSKY WALLING

Vice-Chairmen
    MADELEINE Z. DOTY
    FLORENCE GUERTIN TUTTLE
    MRS. JAMES P. WARBASSE

Secretary
    A. EVELYN NEWMAN

Executive Secretary
    MARGARET LANE

Chairman
    CRYSTAL EASTMAN

Treasurer
    MRS. HENRY G. LEACH

Executive Board
    THE OFFICERS
    EMILY GREENE BALCH
    MRS. VICTOR D. BRENNER
    MARION TILDEN BURRITT
    MRS. ALLSTON DANA
    FLORENCE C. ENO GRAVES
    MRS. HAROLD A. HATCH
    ANNE HERENDEEN
    JESSIE WALLACE HUGHAN
    EDITH KELLY
    FREDA KIRCHWEY
    FOLA LA FOLLETTE
    M. AGNES WILSON

Cover page for "Our War Record: A Plea for Tolerance," Woman's Peace Party of New York City, pamphlet, 1 January 1918, Swarthmore College Peace Collection, Swarthmore, Pa.

Our War Record:
A Plea for Tolerance

It is true that we opposed the entrance of this country into the war and used every honorable means at our command to prevent it. We believed that cooperation with other neutrals would have furnished a method of maintaining our joint rights without recourse to war, and at the same time a means with which to hasten peace negotiations in Europe. We especially urged that if a democracy is to go to war it should go by direct mandate of the people through a referendum. After war had become a fact, we further urged that conscription was no fit weapon for a democracy to fight its wars with, that forcing men to kill and to be killed against their will does violence to the vital spirit and essence of democracy.

However, once the war and conscription became the law of this land, our agitation against them ceased. Common sense as well as loyalty and the habit of obedience to law counseled this course. We have never in the slightest degree urged or suggested resistance to the selective service law nor followed any other policy of obstruction.

What then has been our position, what have we asked of our government during these critical months? Briefly this:

To begin with, we have insisted not merely upon the right, but upon the need for a full, free and continuous discussion in the press and on the platform of America's war aims and peace terms. We have urged this that the militarists and imperialists might be exposed, that ignorance might be destroyed, that we might be faithful to the declared ideals for which our armed forces are fighting, and that the whole world might know us as the enemies of German aggression but no less the friends of a German democracy.

We have at no time demanded an immediate peace or a separate peace. But, when revolutionary Russia first pronounced its simple, generous, practical peace formula—no forcible annexations, no punitive indemnities, free development for all nations,—we urged that our government should respond, stating its willingness to make peace on this formula. When the German Reichstag passed a resolution substantially endorsing this formula, we asked our government to welcome the resolution officially, and thus strengthen the hands of the German liberals who were struggling to make it the avowed policy of their government. When the President replied to the Pope, we rejoiced to find him clearly standing for the Russian formula and we advocated a further step, i.e., that our government should support the long unheeded request of Russia for a restatement of the Allied aims,—a policy now supported by the Marquis of Lansdowne.

Today we are still urging this step. But we also look ahead to the inevitable cessation of hostilities, to the peace conference which must come. We are urging that the ultimate agreement to be reached by the nations at that conference shall include Free Markets and Free Seas, Universal Disarmament, and A League of Nations, the obvious essentials of an enduring peace. And since we are wise enough to know that these ends cannot be achieved at a gathering of military personages and appointed diplomats, we are demanding direct democratic representation of the people of all countries at the peace conference.

This is our complete war record. We hold that there is nothing treasonable or unpatriotic or even emotional about it. On the basis of that record we ask protection from the government for our propaganda no matter how unpopular it may become. We ask tolerance from those who think our ideas are wrong. And from those who think our ideas are fundamentally right, whether they agreed with us about the question of entering the war or not, we ask friendship and loyalty and support.

CRYSTAL EASTMAN.

January 1, 1918.

A Program for Voting Women

Why a *Woman's* Peace Party?, I am often asked. Is peace any more a concern of women than of men? Is it not of universal human concern? For a feminist—one who believes in breaking down sex barriers so that women and men can work and play and build the world together—it is not an easy question to answer. Yet the answer, when I finally worked it out in my own mind, convinced me that we should be proud and glad, even as feminists, to work for the Woman's Peace Party.

To begin with, there is a great and unique tradition behind our movement which would be lost if we merged our Woman's Peace Party in the general revolutionary international movement of the time. Do not forget that it was women who gathered at The Hague, a thousand strong, in the early months of the war, women from all the great belligerent and neutral countries, who conferred there together in friendship and sorrow and sanity while the mad war raged around them. Their great conference, despite its soundness and constructive statesmanship, failed of its purpose, failed of its hope. But from the beginning of the war down to the Russo-German armistice there was no world step of such daring and directness, nor of such honest, unfaltering international spirit and purpose, as the organization of the International Committee of Women for Permanent Peace at The Hague in April, 1915. This Committee has branches in twenty-two countries. The Woman's Peace Party is the American section of the Committee, and our party, organized February 1 and 2, is the New York State Branch.

When the great peace conference comes, a Congress of Women made up of groups from these twenty-two countries will meet in the same city to demand that the deliberate intelligent organization of the world for lasting peace shall be the outcome of that conference.

Woman's Peace Party of New York City pamphlet, March 1918. Swarthmore College Peace Collection, Swarthmore, Pa.

These established international connections make it important to keep this a woman's movement.

But there is an added reason. We women of New York State, politically speaking, have just been born. We have been born into a world at war, and this fact cannot fail to color greatly the whole field of our political thinking and to determine largely the emphasis of our political action. What we hope, then, to accomplish by keeping our movement distinct is to bring thousands upon thousands of women — women of the international mind — to dedicate their new political power, not to local reforms or personal ambitions, not to discovering the difference between the Democratic and Republican parties, but to *ridding the world of war.*

For this great purpose we have an immediate, practical program. We shall organize by congressional districts and throw all our spirit and enthusiasm and the political strength of our organization to the support of those candidates who stand for our international program. If the candidate is a Socialist, all right. If the candidate here and there is a woman, so much the better.

To be concrete, we shall go before each candidate in each district of this state with the following definite propositions:

As a candidate for the Congress, which will be in session while the problems incident to the settlement of the war are before the world, *we ask you to indorse the following proposals:*

A democratic league of all nations, based upon: Free seas, — Free markets, — Universal disarmament, — The right of peoples to determine their own destiny.

The development of an international parliament and tribunal as the governing bodies of such a league.

Daylight diplomacy, with democratic control of foreign policy.

Legislation whereby American delegates to the end-of-the-war conference shall be elected directly by the people.

Furthermore, that America's championship of the principle of reduced armaments may appeal to the rest of the world as disinterested and sincere, *we ask you to oppose* legislation committing this country to the adoption of universal compulsory military training.

As the candidate stands or falls by this test, so he will win or lose our support; and we believe that by next fall our support will be something to be reckoned with. There are thousands of radical women in this state, whose energies, whose passion for humanity, have been released by the suffrage victory of last November. Among them are experienced workers, speakers, organizers, writers. Every day more of these women leaders come forward and reveal themselves as eager, thinking internationalists. They are caught and held by the intellectual content of our program and its great world purpose. They will work with us, and I may say seriously that we expect to measure the effects of our campaign in the character of New York State's representatives in the next United States Congress.

Thus we shall play a part in building the new world that is to come—a great part; for, unless the peoples rise up and rid themselves of this old intolerable burden of war, they cannot progress far toward liberty.

CRYSTAL EASTMAN, Chairman,
Woman's Peace Party of New York State,
March, 1918.   70 Fifth Avenue.

FROM REFORM TO SOCIALIST REVOLUTION

Work-Accidents and Employers' Liability

In these days, there is almost a craze for investigation into social and industrial conditions. This sort of study, which involves going into people's homes and asking questions about personal affairs, is justified, it seems to me, only when there is a pretty strong conviction of the existence of a wrong big enough to warrant the interference of society, and of such a nature that society can right it. Investigation just for the sake of investigation does not appeal to me. Social investigators should know what they are driving at. They should have not only evidence that there is an evil but a rough plan for remedying it in mind before they commence an investigation.

Before we began the Pittsburgh Survey, in which my part was a study of work-accidents, there had been for some years a growing conviction that our laws do not furnish just and proper compensation

The Survey, 3 September 1910.

to workmen injured at their work, or to the widows and children of workmen killed. This conviction was based on a vast number of unconnected incidents, individual experience, newspaper stories, magazine articles, and the like.

Such was our evidence that a wrong existed. Had we any reason to believe that it was a wrong which legislation could remedy? We knew well enough that no law could really comfort the mother for the death of her son, nor compensate the stricken widow and children of a workman killed, nor make up to a man for the loss of his strong right arm. But we did believe that some law could be devised which would take from the injured wage earner and his family part of the economic burden of his accident, some law by which society should make up to them at least a share of their income loss, and thus keep them from destitution. We were the more sure of this because such laws had already been adopted in nearly every European country. It was to get a reliable collection of facts to substantiate our conviction, and give weight to our demand for legislation, that the study of industrial accidents in Pittsburgh was undertaken.

We soon found that there is no complete public record of industrial accidents, and at that time there was none in any state. At the coroner's office, however, there was a record of every fatal accident in the county. We got permission to use these, and made a record of every industrial fatality reported to the coroner during the twelve months from July, 1906, to July, 1907, taking down on a separate card for each case, the name and address of the man killed, his age, occupation and conjugal condition, the name of his employer, the circumstances of the accident, the names of important witnesses and the verdict.

The plan was to learn from the evidence in the coroner's record, how each accident happened, and to learn from visiting the family what happened after the accident, *i.e.,* how great a financial loss was suffered by the family of the workman killed, how much of this was made up by compensation received from the employer, and how the family was affected in its economic life by the accident. When we had done this with the fatalities, we followed the same course with the records of three months' industrial injuries which we secured from the hospitals.

We found that in one year 526 men were killed by accidents of employment in Allegheny county: 195 steel workers, 125 railroaders, 71 miners, and 135 miscellaneous workers, including house-smiths, carpenters, electric linemen, elevator men, teamsters and quarrymen. Of these, nearly half were American born, 70 per cent were workmen of skill and training and 80 percent were under forty years of age.

An analysis of these fatal accidents according to personal responsibility, based largely on evidence given at the inquest, showed roughly this result: for 30 per cent of the accidents no one was responsible; for 30 per cent the workman killed or his fellow workmen were responsible; for 30 per cent the employer, or someone representing him in a position of authority, was responsible, and for 10 per cent both employer and workman were responsible.

If there were time for a further analysis of these groups of accidents, it would show that while sometimes the workmen's carelessness is exasperating heedlessness, oftener it is ignorance, or inattention due to long hours and intensity of work, or recklessness inevitably developed by a trade which requires daring; that while sometimes the employer's carelessness is deliberate disregard for safety in the construction of his plant, oftener it is the human frailty of his agents, the hasty mistaken orders of foremen, or the putting off of necessary repairs from day to day so as not to delay the game—an ordinary outcome of competition. In short, one must conclude that these accidents seldom can be laid to the direct personal fault of anyone. They happen more or less inevitably in the course of industry. If it were carried on slowly and carefully with safety as the first concern of all, there would be few accidents, but carried on as it is today in America, there are many accidents.

With this conclusion in mind, let us turn to what happens after the accident. The first thing to notice is that the person injured or killed is always a worker, an income producer. No helpless children, no feeble old men, no idle women perish in these disasters. So nearly every work-accident leaves a problem of poverty behind. We found that of the 526 men killed in the year's accidents, 258, or almost one-half, were married men regularly supporting their families (more than 470 children under sixteen were left fatherless by the fatalities of the year); of the single men and boys killed, only 38 percent were quite without dependents.

Speaking in terms of economics, then, the most serious feature of the usual work-fatality is the permanent income loss which it means to the family affected. Perhaps it is only the dollar or two over and above his board which a minor son contributes every pay day; perhaps it is the father's regular twelve or fifteen dollars a week upon which the typical young family is wholly dependent. According to our figures, 63 per cent of work-fatalities means the sudden cutting off of the sole or chief support of a family. Permanent injury to a worker may mean a bigger economic loss to the family than his death, and the lesser injuries, while they mean but a temporary loss, may have serious economic consequences in the life of a family.

No investigation was necessary to prove that work-accidents mean, in the first instance, income loss to the workers' families. Under American laws and customs, is any considerable share of this loss shifted to the industry in the course of which the worker suffered his injury? That was the central question of the Pittsburgh accident study. Here is the answer. Among the families of married men killed, one-half suffered the entire loss, *i.e.,* they got from the employer either no compensation whatever, or merely funeral expenses. Only one-fourth of these families got more than $500. Among the families of single men with dependents, 65 per cent stood the whole loss and only 17 per cent got more than $500.

In injury cases we found roughly the same proportions—56 per cent of married men, 66 per cent of single men with dependents and 69 per cent of single men without dependents—stood the whole income loss resulting from their injuries.

The share of the burden borne by employers as a whole can be better understood from these figures: For the 139 cases of married men killed, where we learned both the yearly wages and the compensation, the total compensation was $74,305; the total yearly wages $109,262. Thus the total compensation paid to the dependent widows and children amounted to less than three-fourths of their first year's income loss.

It seems hardly necessary to prove by statistics that these innumerable income losses resulting from work-accidents, borne as we have seen wholly or almost wholly by the workers and their families, result in hardship and privation. Yet to determine this by actual investigation was part of our task. The following figures give some idea of what a work fatality means in the home: Among 132 families where a husband and father had been killed, 53 of the widows went to work, 22 children were taken out of school and put to work, and 19 families moved to poorer quarters—all this within a year after the accident.

These three items upon which we have definite figures merely suggest the problem of poverty which those families had to face. One-half of the work accident victims were earning less than fifteen dollars a week—obviously not enough to carry adequate life insurance at the high rates necessitated by their occupations. The economic struggles of a family suddenly deprived of that small income can be left to the imagination.

Have we any reason to think this situation is peculiar to the Pittsburgh district or to Pennsylvania? Can we of other states comfort ourselves with the thought that our laws are fairer, that our employers are more above self-interest, that more injured workmen are compensated in other states? I think not.

During the past year, the New York State Employers' Liability Commission carried on an investigation similar to the Pittsburgh study. Here are a few of the figures resulting: In 236 fatal cases, to more than half of the dependent families no compensation above funeral expenses was paid. In 1,040 temporary disability cases, 44 per cent did not receive even medical expenses from the employer.

The Wisconsin Industrial Insurance Commission found that out of 306 injury cases, less than a third received anything more than medical expenses, while in 51 death cases only one-third of the families were paid more than $500.

As to actual results in the families, the New York commission found as follows: Among 186 families of married men killed, 93 widows went to work, 9 children under sixteen went to work, 37 families reduced rent, 33 families had received aid, 10 families were destitute.

It seems to me there is little need for further investigation. The facts of the situation are fairly well established for every state which has the same general laws in regard to an employer's liability for injury to his employes. We are forced to conclude, with the New York commission in its first report:

that only a small proportion of the workmen injured by accidents of employment and the dependents of those killed get substantial damages; that comparatively few of the workmen in occupations which involve special hazard are earning enough to enable them to provide adequate insurance against it; that, therefore, through accidents of employment thousands of workingmen's families are brought to extreme poverty and privation, the state suffers through the lowered standard of living of a vast number of its citizens and the public is directly burdened with the maintenance of many who become destitute.

The law which governs this whole situation and which in its main features is the same in almost all the states, is the law of employers' liability. It is a law based on fault. The injured workman can recover only when he can prove that the accident resulted from negligence in his employer, and by no means always even then. For the law holds that the workman assumes all the ordinary risks of the trade, all the risks due to the negligence of fellow servants, all the risks due to the negligence of his employer—such as defective machinery, absence of guards, etc.—if he knew about them and kept on working just the same. Moreover, if the workman's own negligence contributed in any degree to the accident, he cannot recover no matter how gross the employer's negligence was. Now it is clear that under this law the workman's chances of recovery are very slim. Practically his chances are still further reduced by the fact that his case loses and the employer's case gains by the inevitable delay in the courts; that the witnesses are almost always in the employ of the defendant, and that the defendant is usually a big corporation which can fight forever, and the plaintiff an injured workman or a widow and children in immediate need of funds.

The outcome of this law, as we have seen, is that the bulk of the accident loss rests on the workman injured and his dependents, bringing hardship, sometimes extreme poverty and even destitution, upon them.

This is the most serious indictment of the law, but many other things can be said against it. Most people have a vague notion of the evils connected with "employers' liability." "Ambulance chasers" pursuing the injured workman to his home to stir up litigation, or extracting enormous contingent fees from the distracted widow; claim-agents in league with hospital authorities, securing valid releases from men too sick to know their legal rights, or bribing witnesses to disappear; liability insurance for which the employer pays thousands of dollars every year and from which his injured employes reap almost no benefit; lawsuits bitterly fought, lasting often several years, to determine fine points of legal negligence, while the children of the workman killed are starving or dependent on charity—these are some of the mental images suggested to us by the phrase "employers' liability." And there is too much truth in them for comfort. To quote again from the New York report:

> Because of the uncertain and arbitrary chances of recovery under our system (of employers' liability), the state is put to the cost of much fruitless litigation and employers pay out enormous sums to protect themselves against liability on account of industrial accidents, from all of which the victims of those accidents reap little benefit; the system is slow in operation, is an encouragement to corrupt practices on both sides, and is a great source of antagonism between employers and employes.

Is there a remedy? Accidents of employment, as I have suggested, are not for the most part due to the direct personal fault of any person. They occur in the course of industry. Danger is inherent in modern methods of production, construction, transportation—accidents are to a certain extent inevitable, men are bound to be killed and injured.

Our law, nevertheless, disregards all this; it is based on fault just as it was in the days when one man's carelessly hitting another with his hoe was the typical work-accident. Moreover, it has been very narrowly interpreted against the interests of the workman. The way to cure such a situation is to fit the law to the actual conditions of modern industry—to abandon the law based on fault and put in its place a law based on the principle that every industrial enterprise should regularly share the loss resulting to the workmen injured in its accidents.

Such is the law in almost every civilized country except the United States. In England, for instance, since 1897, employers have been required to compensate all their employes injured, and the families of those killed, according to certain limited uniform rates. By adopting some such law, I believe we might hope to accomplish three things:

> Save almost all of the tremendous waste of money and honesty and good will involved in the present system, by doing away with litigation over questions of negligence in such cases.
>
> Provide an important incentive for the prevention of accidents by making each serious accident a direct, sure and considerable expense to employers.
>
> Shift a share of the economic loss of each accident from the family affected, by way of the employer, to the whole body of consumers, by making accidents a regular cost of industry.

How to get such a law in America is another story.

There have been at least nine state commissions appointed within the last few years to inquire into this subject and devise a remedy. The Connecticut, Massachusetts and Illinois commissions have reported, but without results in legislation. In the two latter states new commissions have recently been appointed. The commissions of Wisconsin and Minnesota are expected to report soon. Those of Ohio and New Jersey are just commencing their labors.

The New York commission, appointed in June, 1909, submitted its first report to the Legislature March 19, 1910, recommending two measures. One of these provides several important amendments to the employers' liability act. It greatly modifies the assumption of risk rule, places upon the employer the burden of proving contributory negligence and makes employers liable for negligence of employes "entrusted with any superintendence," or "entrusted with authority to direct, control, or command any employe in the performance of the duty of such employe." After having thus increased the liability of the employer, the bill introduces an elective compensation plan by declaring that "when and if any employer in this state and any of his employes shall consent to the compensation plan" therein described, by filing such consent with the county clerk, then, in case injury thereafter results to such employe, compensation shall be paid regardless of negligence according to a uniform schedule, four years' wages for death and half wages for disability up to eight years. This bill has become law. But the employers' liability amendments included in it find precedent in the laws of other states, and the compensation scheme presented, since it is purely voluntary, cannot be said to be a radical step toward the substitution of a compensation for a liability system.

The other bill, known as the "compulsory compensation act for dangerous employments," which has also become a law, is the first of its kind in this country and warrants the attention of all who are interested in this reform. It applies only to the following specified employments in which of necessity the trade hazard is great:

1. The erection or demolition of any bridge or building in which there is, or in which the plans and specifications require, iron or steel framework.

2. The operation of elevators, elevating machines, or derricks, or hoisting apparatus used within or on the outside of any such bridge or building for the hoisting of materials for such erection or demolition.

3. Work on scaffolds of any kind elevated twenty feet or more above the ground, water, or floor beneath in the erection, construction, painting, alteration or repair of buildings, bridges or structures.

4. The construction of tunnels or subways.

5. All work carried on under compressed air.

6. Construction, operation, alteration or repair of wires, cables, switchboards or apparatus charged with electric currents.

7. All work necessitating dangerous proximity to gunpowder, blasting powder, dynamite or any other explosives, where the same are used as instrumentalities of the industry.

8. The operation on steam railroads of locomotives, engines, trains, motors, or cars propelled by gravity or steam, electricity or other mechanical power, or the construction or repair of steam railroad tracks and roadbeds over which such locomotives, engines, trains, motors or cars are operated.

The bill provides for the compensation by employers of all workmen injured in these employments by any accident due in whole or in part to the fault of employer, or any of his officers, agents or employes, and also by any accident due in whole or in part to "a necessary risk or danger of the employment or one inherent in the nature thereof."

The schedule of compensation provided is, in case of death four years' wages, not to exceed three thousand dollars; and in case of total or partial disability, fifty per cent of the earnings of the injured person payable weekly, but not more than ten dollars a week, during the continuance of the disability, not to exceed a period of eight years.

This bill does not take away any of the rights of action now existing either at common law or under any statute, but provides that the person suing must elect at the time of bringing his action whether he will pursue his rights under the compensation act or under the existing liability laws, and such election is final.

Both laws became operative September 1.

This second measure has received much adverse criticism, particularly at the hands of those who are eager to see workmen's compensation established in America. The members of the commission have been challenged to explain, first, why we limited the operation of the compensation principle to a few dangerous trades, and, second, why we provided for compensation only in case of accidents due to negligence or to a risk of the trade instead of for all accidents in the course of employment. I am glad of an opportunity to answer those questions.

In the first place, a very little experience in law-making is enough to teach one that doing a thing is a very different matter from telling how to do it. Especially is this true in regard to labor legislation in the United States. There are two chief reasons why in this country we cannot as a rule go ahead and pass a labor law when we see that it is good. In the first place, there is our interstate competition; we have legislative lines between the states, but no commercial barriers. This gives the manufacturer a substantial reason back of his protest against laws which will increase his cost of production; he can in fairness argue that if laws are passed in his state requiring compensation for all injured employes, while his competitors in neighboring states go on as before, he cannot "stay in the game." Whether we sympathize with his plight or not, we must recognize the effectiveness of his argument before our state legislatures.

In the second place, we have written constitutions, state and national. Certain provisions in these documents, originally intended no doubt to safeguard the rights of the people, serve often, so it seems to some of us today, to deny the rights of the people. But here again it seems wise to understand thoroughly and reckon with this difficulty rather than to pretend it is not there.

In drawing up a workmen's compensation bill, the New York commission had to face both of these difficulties, and the bill we recommended was our way of getting around them. It may have been good or bad judgment but it was an honest and painstaking effort.

To begin with, we purposely left out the manufacturers so far as possible, in the belief that we could get the new principle—limited compensation for industrial injuries based not on negligence but on trade risk—established more easily in connection with industries not directly involved in interstate competition such as railroading and building, then in connection with manufacture where the additional cost to employers would be an almost insurmountable argument against it; and when once enacted into law and "tried out," as it were, we believed that the principle of workmen's compensation would soon become generally accepted as just and reasonable; that the new system would be found to entail advantages to the employer which would offset its additional cost, and that therefore it could rapidly be extended to cover all employment in which accidents commonly occur.

Second, as to the constitutionality of the proposed measure: without going into the "reasons why" which are hard to explain, let me say that all but two of the lawyers whom we consulted told us that a general compensation act covering every accident in the course of employment would violate both the state and national constitutions. Instead of going ahead and pretending we could not see this obstacle, we tried to find a way around it. Further study and consultation resulted in the conclusion that a compensation law limited to obviously dangerous employment and based upon the risk inherent in the employment, would be upheld, the theory being that since the state can, if it likes, prohibit a dangerous enterprise, it can, *a fortiori,* exact certain conditions from those undertaking it—for instance, that they shall insure their employes against the risk involved. The "risk involved," however, cannot be made to cover every accident possible in the course of that employment but only those resulting from its inherent dangers. Upon this theory our bill was drawn. I believe it will be found to cover practically all serious accidents in the employments to which it applies. It is difficult to think of a bad injury or a fatality in railroading or construction work, for instance, which would not be due "in whole or in part" either to a failure of the employer, or some of his "officers, agents or employes," or "to a necessary risk or danger of the employment or one inherent in the nature thereof."

To sum up this defence: we drew the bill so that it should apply largely to employers not directly competing with employers in other states, because we believed that by thus taking away the one solid economic argument of the opposition we could get the bill passed, and because we believed that to get in the entering wedge containing the new principle was the important thing for us to do—the rest would take care of itself; and, again, we limited the compensation principle to obviously dangerous trades, and to accidents due to the inherent risks of those trades, in order to have a sound argument for the constitutionality of the measure.

As might be expected, I am an enthusiastic advocate of this compensation law enacted on the recommendation of the New York commission. The more I think about it the surer I am that it is right. For, as I see it, the fundamentally important step in this reform is to establish the principle that the risks of trade, borne through all these years by the workmen alone, should in all wisdom and justice be shared by the employer; and our bill, limited as it is, if enacted and upheld by the courts, must go a long way toward fixing that principle in American law.

The Three Essentials for
Accident Prevention

When I read in the newspaper the day after that terrible fire in Washington Place two weeks ago, that a relief fund had been started,

American Academy of Political and Social Science Annals, July–December 1911.

that so and so and so and so had contributed so and so much, and the Red Cross had opened an office in the Metropolitan Building to "administer the fund," it turned my soul sick. When I read in the Bulletin of the New York Department of Labor, among particulars of fatal accidents in 1908 such records as this: *"Helper—flooring factory— age 18—clothing caught by set-screws in shafting; both arms and legs torn off; death ensued in five hours,"* my spirit revolts against all this benevolent talk about workingmen's insurance and compensation.

When great unforeseen disasters like the San Francisco earthquake come upon humanity by act of God, we can be thrilled and uplifted by the wave of generous giving which sweeps over the country—we can be comforted by contributing a little ourselves to aid the survivors. And when we are thinking of the deadly list of unpreventable work accidents—the blast furnace explosions, the electric shocks, the falls—it appeases our sense of right a little to realize that we are working away as hard as we can for a law which will assure a livelihood to the children of the victims. But when the strong young body of a free man is caught up by a little projecting set-screw, whirled around a shaft and battered to death, when we know that a set-screw can be countersunk at a trivial cost, when we know that the law of the state has prohibited projecting set-screws for many years, then who wants to talk about "three years' wages to the widow," and "shall it be paid in instalments, or in lump sum?" and "shall the workman contribute?" What we want is to put somebody in jail. And when the dead bodies of girls are found piled up against locked doors leading to the exits after a factory fire, when we know that locking such doors is a prevailing custom in such factories, and one that has continued in New York City since those 146 lives were lost in the Triangle Waist Company fire, who wants to hear about a great relief fund? What we want is to start a revolution.

That is why I am glad that for once I have a chance to talk about preventing accidents instead of about paying money to the victims.

If we undertake to stop this unnecessary killing and injuring of workers in the course of industry, we must pause and consider what are the essential weapons of our campaign.

The first thing we need is information, complete and accurate information about the accidents that are happening. It seems a tame thing to drop so suddenly from talk of revolutions to talk of statistics.

But I believe in statistics just as firmly as I believe in revolutions. And what is more, I believe statistics are good stuff to start a revolution with. We must know how many men are killed and injured at their work every year in every state, not only in mines, railroads, and factories, but in all the building trades, in tunnelling, in engineering work of all kinds, in the loading and unloading of vessels, in water transportation, in teaming, and all the risky occupations of the city streets, in washing office windows, in agriculture, in the business of distributing gas and electricity, in the installation of telegraph and telephone lines. We must know not only how many are killed, but how many are killed in proportion to the number employed—the relative danger of the occupation. And about each of these accidents we must find out all we can, not only how it happened, and what machinery was involved, but what time of the day it happened; how long the injured man had been working; what were his regular working hours, etc. We must try to get every fact that will enable us to analyze accidents with a view to prevention.

How can we get such information? It is comparatively simple: require each employer engaged in any industrial pursuit to report every accident to his employees in the course of work. Minnesota has had such a law for a year, and under it has been able to record all but about 5 per cent of its industrial accidents. Many employers are not used to reporting, of course; but the Minnesota Labor Department secures a first notice of almost every accident through its newspaper clipping service, and, if in the course of a few days no notice comes in from the employer, they send him the clipping with a polite notice of the law's requirement and a blank form for him to fill out. In this way, I am told, the backward employer is soon induced to fall in line and do his own reporting. As a result of its new accident reporting law, the Minnesota Labor Department has issued the first complete study of a year's industrial accidents I have ever seen. They found out for instance, that although mining, railroading and lumbering are the most dangerous industries of the state, contracting work follows close with 37 killed and 717 injured. In agriculture, 12 were killed and 51 injured; in the operations of public utilities corporations, 19 were killed and 207 injured; in teaming, 7 were killed and 17 injured; and so on. In New York since September, 1910, accidents in the building trades have been reported, and Illinois has a law requiring all accidents of employment causing death, or disability of more than 30 days, to be reported. But with these exceptions: I believe no state goes farther than to require accident reports for factories, mines and railroads. Minnesota's new law increased their accident reports from 1,590 in 1908 to 8,671 in 1910. If in Minnesota in one year 7,000 additional industrial accidents came to light under a complete reporting system, imagine what the number would be in Pennsylvania and New York, with their population six or seven times as great.

The New York State Employers' Liability Commission found that out of 554 fatal work accidents in the coroner's files, 325 had not been reported. And out of 451 injury cases taken to hospitals, only 56 had been reported to the Labor Department. These unreported accidents were not for the most part factory or railroad accidents which should have been reported, but accidents in other employments of which the state does not pretend to keep record.

Of course, in maintaining that complete accident reports are a first essential for accident prevention, I assume an intelligent use of them. We must have a grouping of accidents around the danger points in different industries and a very painstaking impartial intelligent study of their causes by the statistician with conclusions which will be of practical use to the inspector in his next rounds—not a mere cut and dried analysis of the accidents according to whether the employers reported them "due to negligence" or "inevitable." For this work we must have a statistician who looks upon his compilations not as an end in themselves, but always as a means to prevention. A chief statistician with a great deal of common sense and a positive zeal for preventing accidents—that is what we must have in every labor department. And we must give him money enough to do his work.

I have always had an idea, too, that the law should provide for a certain publicity for these statistics. For instance, if every newspaper were required to print once a year the particulars of all fatal work accidents in the twelve months preceding, officially issued by the statistical bureau of the labor department, would it not help to keep us interested? And, if in addition certain simple and obvious statistical conclusions were printed; such as these for instance: In 1908, out of 257 industrial fatalities reported to this department, 26 were caused by men getting caught in belting, shafting, gearing, or other machinery, which could have been guarded so as to make the accident impossible; 21 were caused by men falling down elevator shafts or getting caught and crushed between the floor or walls and the elevator, accidents which would have been impossible on properly guarded elevators. Would not such statistics, published in the daily papers over the official signature of the Commissioner of Labor, help to keep the revolutionary spirit alive in us?

I have not looked into this matter yet, but I believe newspapers are required to publish certain matters of public concern, such as tax sales. Surely, these accident statistics are of equal public concern.

The second essential is a department for enforcing the accident prevention laws, commensurate in equipment and in power with the importance of its duty. The question whether accident prevention should be the exclusive duty of a special department or entrusted to the factory inspection bureau of the labor department, along with the enforcement of child labor laws, and the inspection of sanitary conditions, is one it seems to me which should be profoundly considered, but it is not a part of my plan to discuss it here. Clearly, whatever department is expected to enforce the laws for safeguarding life and limb, should be given money enough and power enough to do it.

In New York we have a fairly comprehensive law in respect to the guarding of machinery and other measures for safety in factories. The business of seeing that this law is complied with in the factories of the state, is entrusted to the chief factory inspector, who is paid $3,000 a year, and his fifty-two deputies, who are paid from $1,000 to $1,200 a year. But accident prevention is not the only business of this force. They must also enforce the laws in regard to child labor and hours of work, and sanitation and ventilation and lighting of factories.

So much for equipment. Now as to power. The violation of a safety provision in the labor law is a misdemeanor for which the employer may be fined from $20 to $50 for the first offense. The prosecution is conducted by the labor department in the lower courts.

How does this work out? In 1909, there were seven prosecutions for violation of the safety laws, with this result: three suits were unsuccessful; in two, sentence was suspended; in two, employers were fined. The total fines amounted to $35.

This small number of prosecutions might, of course, be coexistent with complete enforcement of the law. But it is not. The number of employers prosecuted seems to bear no relation to the number of employers who violate the laws with regard to accident prevention. For instance, in the same year during which there were seven prosecutions, there were among the 2,947 accidents reported to the department, 779 accidents classified as follows:

Accidents due to gearing	320
Accidents due to set-screws	337
Accidents due to shafting	73
Accidents due to belts and pulleys	49
	779

We may fairly assume that most of these accidents resulted from violations of the statute which requires all "gearing, shafting, set-screws, belts and pulleys to be properly guarded."

In fact, the prosecutions are used only as a last resort to compel obstinate employers, who have been given three or four distinct warnings, to comply with the order of the department. And then, after the prosecution is commenced, and even after the employer has been convicted, if he can show that he has at last complied with the law, the judge suspends sentence.

Such is the equipment and authority of the executive department to which the state entrusts the enforcement of its accident prevention laws. The same description would serve, I believe, for almost any other state. In short, factory inspection for safety has hardly been seriously commenced. Reasonable safety provisions in the labor law continue to be violated with impunity all over the state, while the records of utterly needless injury and death go on piling up in the labor department.

Well, what can we do about it? First, it seems to me we must get into the minds of the legislators an altogether different conception of what a labor department should be. They must recognize that the administration of labor law is rapidly coming to be the most important function of government. We must give our labor department more dignity, better equipment, more power.

Compare the salaries of the chief officers of the labor department in New York State with some other departments. Our Commissioner of Labor gets $5,000. Our forest, fish and game commissioner gets $6,000. Our superintendent of banks, our superintendent of insurance, and our commissioner of excise, each gets $7,000. Compare also these items: the labor commissioner, himself on a salary of $5,000, has $2,400 to pay his counsel and $3,000 to pay his chief statistician, while the Public Service Commission of the Second District, composed of five men on $15,000 salaries, has $10,000 to pay its counsel, $6,000 to pay its secretary, and $5,000 to pay its statistician.

So much for the heads of departments. Judging from the salaries paid, it is clear that the state does not yet recognize the relative importance of its labor department. But further than this and more important, the appropriation for the department does not allow for a sufficient number of intelligent well-trained men to do the actual work of inspection. There are in New York, fifty-two factory inspectors whose salaries range from $1,000 to $1,500, the majority at $1,200. By covering seven establishments a day they usually manage to visit each factory once a year.

It is not remarkable that there is no real enforcement of the safety laws in factories. A yearly visit from an untrained $1,200 man whose duty of inspection covers child labor, hours of work for women and minors, sanitation, ventilation and lighting, as well as the guarding of machinery, is not going to be very alarming to an employer who does not want to spend the time and money to make his workshop safe. Even if a violation is noted and an order for compliance issued by the labor department, his chance of getting into serious trouble by continuing to violate the law is pretty small, with only two employers fined in 1908, and three in 1909.

To put the labor department in a position to carry out the law's intent and really prevent unnecessary accidents by requiring safeguards wherever practicable, I think we must pay higher salaries at the top, high enough, for instance, to get a first-class counsel and a skilled engineer to devote their whole time to advising the commissioner in their respective fields. Then we must have a somewhat larger force of inspectors, more highly qualified for their task and much better paid, with salaries graded so as to tempt capable men to make factory inspection their life work. Thus, we could create a department with the wisdom and ability to do its work. But how can we give it power?

I should say, first, we must cease to make light of violations of the safety provisions in the labor law by classing them with petty offenses for which a $20 fine is imposed. If the deliberate refusal to comply with a reasonable order of the labor commissioner, requiring the guarding of a dangerous machine is any kind of a crime, it is one that calls for a heavy penalty. It is difficult to see why a railroad should be fined $5,000 for refusing to comply with an order of the Public Service Commission, while a factory owner is fined $20 for refusal to comply with an order of the labor commissioner. The suggestion was made to me the other day that an increase in penalties, far from resulting in fewer convictions, would result in more convictions, and might largely do away with the practice of suspending sentence, for this reason: from the express provision for a petty fine for violations of the safety laws, the judicial mind infers that the lawmakers did not consider the violation a serious one, and therefore inclines to indifference and leniency, whereas the duty of imposing a heavy penalty would tend to make the judge give real thought to the case. There seems to me to be wisdom in that suggestion. Indeed, it is worth considering whether we should not provide a penalty heavy enough to take these cases out of the lower courts entirely.

But nothing we can do to the system of fines and penalties will give the labor department power enough to put the safety laws into immediate effectual operation. I should like to see some state try this: First, give the commissioner power to make rules for safety in different trades, rules which shall have the force of statutes. And then give him expressly by statute summary power, in case his orders are not complied with, to call on the police and close up a factory, prohibit all operation of it, until his orders in regard to safety are carried out, this summary power to be exercised, of course, only after due notice.

This sounds alarming, autocratic, too much like Germany. But would that power in a labor commissioner really be anything to fear? Would he be likely to make unwise use of it? Every employer against whom it was exercised would have his appeal to the courts as to whether the order of the commissioner was a reasonable one. By praying for a temporary injunction to restrain the commissioner from shutting up his shop, the employer could protect himself against grave loss and secure a speedy hearing. There is little doubt but that the court would give him every chance. And with this review in sight, there is not much reason to fear that the commissioner would make arbitrary use of his power.

It is this sort of a summary power we deem it necessary for a health department to have. A health officer can prohibit the occupation of a tenement when its unsanitary condition menaces the health of its tenants. Why cannot the labor commissioner prohibit the operation of a factory when its unsafe condition menaces the lives and limbs of its employees? It seems to me that laws in regard to safety, even more than laws in regard to health, demand this method of enforcement. A summary method is one which stops the danger at once and leaves the employer to commence an action in the courts to vindicate his right, instead of requiring the commissioner of labor to commence an action in the courts to vindicate his authority *while the danger continues.* Clearly the old way safeguards property at the risk of human life. The new way would safeguard life at a very little risk to property.

So far, I have imagined a complete system of accident reports, handled with transcendent intelligence by a superhuman statistician, and published for the enlightenment of a body of eager-minded public-spirited citizens. To this picture I have added that of a high-salaried, well-trained, fully-equipped labor department with power to make safety rules having the force of statutes; I have provided heavy penalties for violation of these rules to be imposed with discretion by judges aroused to the importance of their duty; and I have given the commissioner of labor summary powers to enforce compliance with his orders.

Now we come to the third essential—a new system of liability known as *workmen's compensation,* which makes every serious accident a considerable cost to an employer and thus insures his invaluable co-operation with the labor department in promoting safety. After all the prevention of accidents in modern industry is too difficult a problem to be solved by statistics and statutes and summary powers; little can be done without the active co-operation of employers. In order to secure that co-operation, let us then quite frankly make the most of the economic incentive, establish a system of liability by which an employer can reduce his accident costs, not by hiring a more unscrupulous attorney and a more hard-hearted claim agent, but only by reducing his accidents.

Let the employer once realize that the accident, insure as he may against it, has its inevitable and definite effect upon the cost of production, and his zeal for preventing accidents will be constant. His superintendents and foremen will be made to see the effect of every accident upon their department cost sheets, and, knowing that their hope of retention or advancement in the service depends upon their efficiency in keeping as low as possible the ratio of cost to production, they will become the most aggressive fighters for accident prevention.

And the workman, while he has now, in the instinct of self-preservation, the strongest possible reason to protect himself against accident, will give far greater attention to the safety of the men about him when he finds out that carelessness brings down upon him the wrath of his foreman. To-day a man is fined or laid off or dismissed for the careless operation of valuable machinery; under workmen's compensation, he would be fined or laid off or dismissed for indifference to the safety of his fellow-workmen.

Thus, when all has been said that can be said for the importance of a wise and efficient and powerful factory inspection department, it must be admitted that the all-important thing in accident prevention is to let the economic necessity of reducing accidents enter effectively into the calculations of the "powers that be"—those who determine how often chains are to be inspected; how soon defective cars are to be retired; what signaling system is to be installed for those working in defenceless positions, whether cranes are to be stopped when repairs are made on the runway; what part of the work is to be done by ignorant foreigners; at what speed work is to be carried on; all those details of operation so intricately connected with the management of each enterprise that they cannot be reached by law, but must depend upon the will of him who directs the enterprise. And it is to be hoped that our state legislatures will not overlook this: that in granting larger appropriations and new powers to the labor departments, they will not fail to secure the co-operation of employers in accident prevention, by the enactment of workmen's compensation laws.

Editorials, Introductory Issue of *The Liberator*

Never was the moment more auspicious to issue a great magazine of liberty. With the Russian people in the lead, the world is entering upon the experiment of industrial and real democracy. Inspired by Russia, the German people are muttering a revolt that will go farther than its dearest advocates among the Allies dream. The working people of France, of Italy, of England, too, are determined that the end of autocracy in Germany shall be the end of wage-slavery at home. America has extended her hand to the Russians. She will follow in their path. The world is in the rapids. The possibilities of change in this day are beyond all imagination. We must unite our hands and voices to make the end of this war the beginning of an age of freedom and happiness for mankind undreamed by those whose minds comprehend only political and military events. With this ideal THE LIBERATOR comes into being on Lincoln's Birthday, February 12, 1918.

THE LIBERATOR will be owned and published by its editors, who will be free in its pages to say what they truly think.

It will fight in the struggle of labor. It will fight for the ownership and control of industry by the workers, and will present vivid and accurate news of the labor and socialist movements in all parts of the world.

It will advocate the opening of the land to the people, and urge the immediate taking over by the people of railroads, mines, telegraph and telephone systems, and all public utilities.

It will stand for the complete independence of women—political, social and economic—and an enrichment of the existence of mankind.

It will stand for a revolution in the whole spirit and method of dealing with crime.

It will join all wise men in trying to substitute for our rigid scholastic kind of educational system one which has a vivid relation to life.

It will assert the social and political equality of the black and white races, oppose every kind of racial discrimination, and conduct a remorseless publicity campaign against lynch law.

It will oppose laws preventing the spread of scientific knowledge about birth control.

THE LIBERATOR will endorse the war aims outlined by the Russian people and expounded by President Wilson—a peace without forcible annexations, without punitive indemnities, with free development and self-determination for all peoples. Especially it will support the President in his demand for an international union, based upon free seas, free commerce and general disarmament, as the central principle upon which hang all hopes for permanent peace and friendship among nations.

THE LIBERATOR will be distinguished by complete freedom in art and poetry and fiction and criticism. It will be candid. It will be experimental. It will be hospitable to new thoughts and feelings. It will direct its attacks against dogma and rigidity of mind upon whichever side they are found.

Thus far the working-class government of Russia has appropriated the banks and the banking system of the country and repudiated the national debt; it has taken possession of the entire mining district; it has declared the munitions factories state property without compensation; it has supported the control of other factories, and their

profits, by workingmen's committees; it has decreed the land of
Russia to the peoples who work upon it, and the land is now actually
held in common by those people. And on this day, January 20th, the
Marxian premier, Lenine, has suspended and dismissed the democratic parliament as "a relic of Bourgeois society," and declared
Russia to be a Socialist republic in which the Congress of delegates
from the Workers', Soldiers', and Peasants' Unions is the sovereign
power. Thus comes into actual existence that "industrial parliament"—the crowning and extreme hope of the Socialist dream-
theory.

To our American bourgeois newspaper correspondents this all
appears rampant disorder and blind mixture of events, defying and
denying human intelligence. But to everyone who has read the
Communist Manifesto, it is so sublimely ordered and intellectual a
performance as to dispel all pessimism of propaganda forever, and
raise intelligence and the dissemination of ideas to the highest place
in their confidence. Without doubt it is the most momentous event
in the history of peoples. And if such an event can be shown to be no
accident or mystery, but the orderly maturing and accurate enactment of ideas full-born in a great mind sixty years ago, and cherished
and disseminated in the meantime by all those who had strength to
believe, then indeed there is hope that intelligence may play its part
in every event. Never in all history before could one so joyfully and
confidently enter upon the enterprise of publishing and propagating
ideas. Dedicating our admiration to the fearless faith in scientific
intelligence of Karl Marx, and our energy to hopes that are even
beyond his, we issue **THE LIBERATOR** into a world whose possibilities of freedom and life for all, are now certainly immeasurable.

Their Utmost Hope

In his address to Congress on January 8th, President Wilson
said: "It is our heartfelt desire and hope that some way may be opened
whereby we may be privileged to assist the people of Russia to attain
their utmost hope of liberty. . . ."

He professed to be speaking for the American people, and we
hope that he was. He was speaking for us. And we would only wish
to add two things to his words before the world. First, that the people

of Russia, a vast majority of them comprised in the Left Wing of the Socialist Revolutionaries and the Bolsheviki, have set before themselves a hope of liberty that involves the ownership and control of all land, plants, and machinery by those who work them, and the abolition of profits and wage-dependence altogether. We should like to add in parenthesis after the words, *utmost hope of liberty,* the words, *See the Communist Manifesto.*

And then, second, we should like to add for ourselves, that it is *our* heartfelt desire and hope that some way may be opened to awaken in the people of the United States that same "utmost hope of liberty," and that we may be privileged to assist them to attain it.

The Socialist Vote

There is a pretty widespread impression that except in Wisconsin the Socialist vote on November 5 was discouraging. We do not find that impression borne out by the figures in New York City. It is true that London, Hillquit, Nearing and Lee were defeated for Congress, but in each of their districts it was a two-party fight; we cannot hope to defeat fusion in the first contest.

The important question is, how much did the Socialist vote increase? This question is complicated in New York, of course, by the new women voters. It is estimated that they added 40 per cent to the vote. Compare the highest vote given in Greater New York to any Socialist candidate on the state ticket in 1916—42,000—with the highest vote for any Socialist candidate on the state ticket in 1918—106,000. Allowing for the 40 per cent general increase, we still have a Socialist increase of nearly 50 per cent.

This increase is by no means limited to the five "hopeful" districts in which the campaign work was concentrated. It is a steady general growth, most striking in some of the most obscure districts. In the Seventh, for instance, the vote jumped from 452 to 5,500.

The Liberator, December 1918.

Apparently there is no smallest district in which the vote has not increased. In 1916 the lowest vote in any Assembly district was 26, and there were six districts under 100 votes. In 1918 the lowest was 247, and there were only nine districts under 500.

The steady growth of the Socialist vote is always remarkable. This year it is amazing. A party which has consistently opposed what proved to be a popular war—in an election held at the very moment of victory—adds 50 per cent to its vote! Politically speaking, this is impossible. That it happened demonstrates once more that the Socialist party is only incidentally a political institution; it is something politicians cannot understand, a deep-rooted faith and a thoroughly understood intellectual conception which must grow because it satisfies the vital desires of real human beings. It also demonstrates the folly of those social patriots who went all over Europe saying that the Socialist party in America had destroyed itself.

Aeroplanes and Jails

The Fourteenth Congressional District, where Scott Nearing is running for Congress, contains in addition to a great East Side section, that mysterious part of the world known as Greenwich Village. Most of Greenwich Village, if it remembers to vote at all, will vote the Socialist ticket. A year ago the vote for Mayor in this district stood, Hylan, 6,206; Hillquit, 5,689; Mitchell, 5,553. Consequently, if there had been again three candidates in the field, a Socialist would have gone to Congress this fall without doubt. But, not without some grumbling, the Democrats finally consented to allow La Guardia, the Republican, who now represents the district, to stand as their candidate. So the contest is between Nearing and La Guardia.

The interesting thing about La Guardia is that though duly elected in 1916 to represent the wishes of 300,000 citizens in the national congress of the United States, he has spent the last sixteen months in Italy flying. Of course this clearly violates a Constitutional provision. The men voters of the district have not seemed to care whether their representative went to Washington to help make the laws or went soldiering to Europe. When the new women voters of this district endeavored to have his seat declared vacant in accordance with the law they were met with respect and assurances that they were in the right, but no action.* When they cabled their protest, asking him either to resign or to come back and tend to business, La Guardia gaily cabled back that he wasn't worried about his district— he knew he was serving his country better "sitting in an aeroplane in Italy than sitting on the plush seats of the House of Representatives."

No doubt he was right.

We wonder if it is generally known that the Socialist party, which may elect seven men to Congress, has an Executive Committee of fifteen members, five of whom are in prison and three others under indictment? If a Republican congressman can serve his constituents from an Italian aeroplane, perhaps a Socialist Committeeman can serve his party even better from an American jail.

* The Woman's Peace Party of New York petitioned the Speaker of the House to remove La Guardia [B.W.C.].

The Liberator

A Journal of Revolutionary Progress

EDITORS, MAX EASTMAN, CRYSTAL EASTMAN
ASSOCIATE EDITOR, FLOYD DELL
BUSINESS MANAGER, MARGARET LANE

CONTRIBUTING EDITORS:

Cornelia Barns, Howard Brubaker, K. R. Chamberlain, Eugene V. Debs, Hugo Gellert, Arturo Giovannitti, Charles T. Hallinan, Helen Keller, Robert Minor, Boardman Robinson, Maurice Sterne, Alexander Trachtenberg, Louis Untermeyer, Clive Weed, Art Young

Editorials, *The Liberator*, February 1919

A League of Which Nations?

Some good friends of the LIBERATOR are disturbed at our want of enthusiasm for the League of Nations. We believe in a League of Nations as the one thing that will ever remove the menace of nationalistic war from the earth. We believe that it must be a definite, concrete, continuous and working federation of the peoples. We believe that such a thing may come to pass in the near future, and we will work for it. But we do not discover in the victorious governments that are meeting in Paris, nor in any of the delegates of these governments, the least disposition to establish such a federation of the peoples. We are not free to say all that we might of these governments, but we can say that the hands they clasp over the council table will be red with the fresh blood of the freest people on earth.

We have read with diligence the manifesto of the "League of Free Nations Association" to which are signed the names of many radical-minded people, and one at least who used to call herself a revolutionist, and we subscribe to much of the abstract wisdom therein contained, but we find the manifesto altogether timid and reticent upon the one question that will determine whether the League is to be a League for peace, or a League for counter-revolutionary war—the question of the admission of Russia. Having been thoroughly drilled by one of the chief sponsors of this association, Professor John Dewey, in the knowledge that every question that arises in the complex of events is a specific question, we do not ask ourselves, "Do you support a League of Nations?" we ask ourselves, "Do you support this League of Nations? Do you think the international proletariat ought to support this league of nations?"

The Liberator, February 1919.

And our answer is, *they ought to support it when the Soviet Republic is invited to enter it upon equal terms with the rest.* Until then they ought to concentrate their mind and energy upon their own league, their own nations. They ought to see to it that the great power and determinor of the world's future shall not be the League of Business Politicians at Versailles, but the New International, the League of the Working Classes of the World.

And the sharpness of this alternative—let it be understood—is the work of the Business Politicians, not of the revolutionary proletariat. The Soviet Republic has demanded admission to the armistice, has applied for representation at the peace conference, has appointed its delegate. Its envoy at Stockholm has offered terms and concessions to the Allied governments that shock the heart, they show so sacrificing a devotion to the ideal of peace. And the reply has been silence, or criminal slander and renewed invasions of Russian territory. Upon this foundation there can be no league of the peoples of the earth, there can be no peace.

Those radical-minded idealists of the League of Free Nations Association might see this, I should think, and even though they cannot take their stand with the proletariat, they might concentrate their zeal for the League of Nations, upon a bold demand for the recognition of the Soviets—without which the League will be a compact of tyranny, and with which it may conceivably become a means to make the world more peaceful, more reasonably resigned to the agony of its transformation.

The only revealing thing Wilson has said in Europe is that he "would go crazy if he didn't believe in Providence." Most of the people in Europe apparently would go crazy if they didn't believe in Wilson. Let us hope that Providence has some sense of personal responsibility.

Political Prisoners

The Department of Justice reports that there have been 1,281 cases under the Espionage Act. Of the defendants, 252 pleaded guilty and were sent to prison, 237 were convicted after trial, and 792 cases are pending. The Department does not report any acquittals. In addition to this there are no doubt thousands of cases under the draft act. There are hundreds of conscientious objectors—some of them technically classed as deserters.

A complete catalogue of all these cases is being prepared by the Civil Liberties Bureau. The Department of Justice has declined to furnish them with any statistics beyond the figures above, and they are compelled to gather their information from the press and from personal sources. Readers of THE LIBERATOR who know of cases which they believe deserve to be included in a general amnesty, are requested to communicate with the Civil Liberties Bureau, 41 Union Square, New York. Send them the name of the defendant and your address, so that they can write for more information if they require it.

The Allied Intervention in Russia and Hungary

If there had been no disinterested idealism introduced into the war by Woodrow Wilson, and the Allies had simply proceeded to "lick" Germany in a straightforward fashion, the terms imposed upon her would no doubt have been extremely severe. The victors would have taken away all of her non-European territory, and probably about a quarter of her European territory, reducing her empire from 1,236,600 square miles to about 160,000 square miles. They would have robbed Germany of her navy, demolished her army, deprived her of the right to build a new navy or organize a new army, razed her principal fortifications to the ground, and prevented the rebuilding of them, emasculated her national stronghold, the Kiel Canal, taken a bloody vengeance upon some of her military and poltical leaders, stolen her marine cables, stolen her merchant marine, deprived her of

Unsigned editorial, *The Liberator*, June 1919.

the freedom of the seas, placed her under heavy economic disabilities, exacted money payments to the extreme limit of her productive ability over several generations, and united in a League or Alliance to perpetuate their ascendency and the subordination of the rest of the world. In other words, they would have reduced Germany from a first-class to a second-class power for all time. And the bulk of the advantage, both in territory and in world-control, would have gone to England. There is no doubt that some such cynical and irresponsible butchery of one empire in behalf of another would have been perpetrated, if it had not been for Woodrow Wilson's disinterested idealism.

But that is just a summary of what has happened with Wilson presiding over the job. So what did his disinterested idealism amount to? It amounted to a heroic determination to surround himself and the general public with a blinding vapor of self-righteous emotion all the time that the job was being done. That determination he carried out. That is his contribution to history.

The International Class Struggle

In this ultimate exposure of the piratical purpose at the heart of the war for democracy, how happy are all the revolutionists who oppose it—and how humbly penitent, if they ever failed or faltered for a moment in loyalty to the great truth that it was entrusted to them to know! Let there be no more failure and no more faltering. These imperialistic pirates who have ripped open and mutilated the wounded body of the German nation after surrender, are at the same time engaged in the cold-blooded murder by starvation of hundreds of thousands of men and women and little children in the towns and cities of European Russia. They are starving them because that is the only way they can prevent the truth that has been demonstrated in Russia from becoming known to the whole world. And while they are starving them, they are supplying arms and ammunition and soldiers to the few remaining minions of the Czar and of Big Business to shoot them down. And they are raiding and slaughtering the people of Hungary in the same deliberate manner and for the same desperate purpose. Remember with what horror we read only a year ago that the Germans were "closing in on Petrograd" and "plunging toward Moscow" in violation of an armistice and of the rights of a defenseless nation? Remember how these Germans were played up in the papers as dishonorable robbers and butchers of men, until even some of us socialists who ought to have known better, were almost ready to enlist against them under the colors of the Allies? And now in the same columns of the same papers we read that the Allies are "closing in on Hungary," the Allies are "plunging toward Budapest," in violation of an armistice and of the rights of a defenseless nation. Do we have to be instructed that the Allied Governments, too, are dishonorable robbers and butchers of men? It is all very plain now even to the mind of a child. The war for democracy, the war that we who love the people of the world and care about their peace and freedom and happiness, have to wage, is the war between the Communist International and the League of Imperialist Nations. The line is so clearly and fearfully drawn that there can be no doubt and no confusion in the heart of any socialist any longer.

We cannot treat with these, the murderers of our comrades. We cannot send delegates to them to plead and persuade, to beg for amnesties for our prisoners, to pray for the incorporation of social reform measures in the constitution of their League of Nations, as the Berne conference did. It is time for all pleading and appealing and associating ourselves with these governments to cease. It is time for us, in every act of our organization and in every word from our press and our platforms, to wage the class war against them.

That is the reason why the entire Socialist Party of Italy, through its executive committee, has withdrawn from the old international which organized the Berne conference of Social Patroits, and affiliated itself with the third international summoned by the Soviet Government in Moscow.

That is the reason why the Socialist party of Switzerland, although the Berne conference was held in their own capital, refused to send delegates to that conference.

That is why the Socialist parties of Serbia, Rumania, Denmark and Norway refused to send delegates to that conference.

That is why Loriot, the spokesman of the Left Wing of the French movement, denounced the Conference, saying:

"You have come together not for the purpose of finding a Socialist solution for the tragic problems that have followed in the wake of this greatest of all capitalist crimes, but for the purpose of finding some sort of justification for the governmental, nationalistic, chauvinistic neo-war-Socialism that flourished upon the ruins of the Socialist movement after the outbreak of the war.

"You are here, not in order to give expression to your determination to fulfill your Socialist ideals, but in order to document the agreement of the International with the policies of Wilson, the representative of American multi-millionaires.

"You have met, finally, and above all, to condemn the tremendous struggle for freedom that is spreading out from Russia all over Western Europe. . . ."

That is why the socialists of the Left Wing in almost every other country have their own organization and their own spokesmen and their own press, through which they have repudiated the Berne Congress and the old international which organized it.

And that is why at last, even in the United States, we have a Left Wing, with its own organization, and its own spokesmen, and its own press. We know that the international class struggle is being fought to a finish in Europe, with all the weapons and forces of propaganda that are available on either side. There is no middle ground left. Every thinking man and woman there is either for the revolution or against it. And every one here too. And we are for it, and we can not tolerate the silence of the official party in this the most critical hour in all the history of the revolutionary hopes of mankind.

The Last Excuse

There have been three pale ghosts of reasons advanced for Allied intervention in Russia:

First, it was necessary to "reconstitute the eastern front" against Germany. Germany is vanquished, the eastern front is west of Poland, and this pale ghost is fled.

Second, it was necessary to "extricate the Tchecho-Slovaks from Siberia." The Tchecho-Slovaks have been offered free transportation home to their own country by the Soviet Government, and two thousand of them are in jail for refusing to fight the battles of the Allies. This ghost is making but rare appearances.

Third, it was necessary to re-establish "democracy," which had been overthrown in Russia when the Soviet government dissolved the Constituent Assembly. Now comes the news, in a letter from Maxim Litvinoff, that *"the committee of the Constituent Assembly has proposed to the Soviet Government an alliance for joint action against Koltchak."*

Thus vanishes the last pale ghost of a reason for invading Russia. But Lloyd George and Woodrow Wilson and Clemenceau and the Mikado—champions of democracy, champions of the Tchecho-Slovaks, champions of an "eastern front" four thousand miles from the enemy, champions of any bundle of the old clothes of a dead pretense that will cover their naked imperialistic designs, continue to ship arms and ammunition and soldiers to Koltchak to do murder in support of the corrupt and bloody regime of the Czar.

The Mooney Congress

"Shall we call for a general strike May 1st or July 4?

"Shall we abandon all political efforts, all attempts to influence governors, presidents and legislatures and resort direct to the economic weapon, or shall we give them one more chance by sending a committee to Washington and another to the California Legislature, and in case these efforts fail, resort to the strike on a date to be fixed here and now?

"Shall we strike for the release of all political and class-war prisoners, or shall we, as a matter of tactics, strike for the freedom of Mooney alone,—with the thought that once feeling the power we can use it for anything we want afterwards?"

The Liberator, March 1919.

These were the main questions fought out at the Mooney Congress in Chicago January 14–17. No one dared to doubt the wisdom of calling a general strike,—it was the *date* over which the "reds" and the "machine" wrangled. It was not the ultimate use of the economic weapon that the "conservatives" questioned but the abandoning of all the old methods in the meantime.

From this it is clear that the most cautious conservative at the Mooney Congress was a radical,—would have been a "red" at any A.F. of L. Convention. And if you have heard that the conservative forces after a lively struggle captured the convention, remember that these words "radical" and "conservative" have no fixed meaning, they are comparative terms.

On Wednesday, the second day of the convention, two members of the Italian labor commission now in this country, Carlo Bozzi and Amilcare De Ambris—who had been invited by the officers of the Mooney Congress to attend, sent an extremely polite note, saying that they would wait in their hotel until "the right time for them to come." Immediately after the usual formal motion was made to "endorse their communication and invite them to attend as fraternal delegates," a dozen men were on their feet. The first to make himself heard was Turko, a blacksmith from Seattle. "I am an Italian," he cried, "I know! These men don't represent Italian labor. They represent the most imperialistic government in the world!" . . . Here his voice, all fired up for passionate speech, was drowned in the confusion of fifty or a hundred men asking for the floor. First to make any impression on the noise was Batt of Detroit, waving the January LIBERATOR over his head and shouting that he had some important information for the Convention. In five minutes of near-silence he read Trachtenberg's* description of the Italian Mission.

"I guess," he concluded, "that mission represents the Italian labor movement about the way the Gompers-Spargo-Russell Mission to Europe represented us!" Then more confusion, and out of it suddenly R. F. Dunn, electrical worker, editor of the Butte *Daily Bulletin,* whose speech that morning had won him virtual leadership

* Dr. Alexander Trachtenberg, editor of the *American Labor Yearbook,* lectured on the international labor movement at the Rand School and had a regular column on working-class movements around the world in *The Liberator* [B.W.C.].

of the "radicals," moved an amendment to the motion, that "the officers immediately wire Eugene V. Debs asking him to address the convention." This was received with a roar of surprise and joy and relief, and was carried with only a scattering half dozen "noes." And then the original motion to admit the Italian Mission was firmly and unanimously voted down.

Just before the vote was taken I heard a despairing growl from the Irishman who had moved to welcome the mission—appealing to the Chair—"Ain't you goin' to give me a chance to answer them Guineas?"—meaning Turko, I suppose. But he was lost and forgotten, even by the Chair, in the glowing demonstration of intelligent class-consciousness which claimed Debs, the indicted Socialist, and rejected the emissaries of a great capitalist government, however disguised.

This was the great moment of the Convention. I tell it now because I want to make clear at the start that there were no conservatives at the Mooney Congress.

There were a few flowery words about Wilson from the Irish Chairman, Ed Nolan, and a sentence or two in defense of July 4th, as the day we "threw off the yoke of England," and therefore a fitting day to strike,—this by John Fitzpatrick, candidate for mayor on the new Chicago Labor Party ticket,—also an Irishman. Otherwise not a bit of flag-waving that I can recall, at a convention held not three months after "our victorious armies forced Germany to her knees," in the greatest war of the world.

As for Gompers,—he might never have been born. I don't think his name was mentioned except in two resolutions calling for his resignation, which of course were suppressed in committee. Yet this was a convention of delegates from A.F. of L. unions. Credentials from I.W.W. unions and Socialist party locals were not accepted. The Railroad Brotherhoods and the Amalgamated Clothing Workers of America were the only unions outside the A.F. of L. that were allowed representation.

How, then, could it be intelligent and class-conscious? Or if it was, why isn't every A.F. of L. convention intelligent and class-conscious?

The answer to that question goes to the heart of the trouble in the American labor movement. It is a matter of the basis and machinery of representation.

In school we used to study about "pure" democracy and "representative" democracy, but they never told us about representative democracy "once removed." An A.F. of L. Convention is a delegate body—*made up of representatives from other delegate bodies.* It represents the union rank and file in much the same way that the United States Senate represented the people of the United States before we had direct election of senators. You remember, by special provision of the wise fathers in 1796, who feared the Bolshevist tendencies of a lower house elected directly by the people, this popular body was to be checked by an upper house,—a senate, elected by the state legislatures, two from each state. After a century and a quarter, we found that this indirect method of representation gave us almost a fixed upper house, practically a "House of Lords," corporation lawyers who held office year after year, sometimes 20 or 25 years. And so at last, in 1913, we changed the Constitution to provide for "direct election of Senators."

Almost any system of representation can get into the control of a machine. The difference between an indirect and a direct system is that with the former the machine can never be dislodged, with the latter you can once in a while, by superhuman efforts at a time of great public indignation, loosen the clutch of the machine.

Local 97 of the United Garment Workers, for instance, elects a delegate every year to the annual convention of the Garment Workers' International. At that convention five delegates are elected to the Annual Convention of the A.F. of L.,—representative democracy once-removed, just like the old Senate.[1] But it is worse than that, for the constitutions of most of the Internationals provide that two of the five delegates must be the President and Secretary! There is machine control made absolutely permanent—fitted in and nailed down.

So it is easy to see why the Mooney Congress—delegates elected

---

1. A few local unions, without national or international affiliations, send representatives direct to the A.F. of L. Also some of the Internationals provide for a formal referendum on delegates to an A.F. of L. convention, but nominations are made at the International convention so that the character of the delegation is determined there.

directly by local unions[2]—differed in temper and intelligence from an A.F. of L. Convention.

One further question bothered me: Why was it also so much more radical than the conventions of the various Internationals, where delegates are elected directly by local unions? These conventions, while far less reactionary than the A.F. of L., are still as a rule fairly conservative and "regular" bodies. The answer is that the organization heads (the "machine"), in the various trade organizations didn't consider the Mooney Congress important; the local union membership sent the delegate it wanted to send. Elections were not controlled and directed in the well-known ways. It was not, in the opinion of the trade-union leaders, a Congress which threatened or affected their position, in any way. So they left it alone. And the Congress was something like a spontaneous expression of the organized workers of this country, the first gathering of its kind. Therein lies its significance.

If we want to determine the temper of the workers in America at this moment of hasty demobilization, increasing unemployment and continuing judicial oppression, and make a shrewd guess as to what will happen in the next five years, the recent Mooney Congress is our laboratory—not the formal proceedings of the A.F. of L.

The Mooney case was such an old story.[3] It was not easy to be excited about it any more. I felt, I think everybody felt, that when the Governor of California, under threat of a general strike last December, saved Mooney from hanging and condemned him to life imprisonment, he had taken the dramatic force out of the Mooney agitation and it would be impossible to revive it. But we reckoned without Edward D. Nolan, Secretary-Treasurer of the International Workers' Defense League. Nolan is the slender fighting Irishman with uplifted boyish face, who presided over the Chicago Convention. As a determined labor leader, friend and co-worker of Mooney's,

2. Only 148 out of 1182 delegates were sent by Central Labor Bodies and State Federations; the rest directly represented local unions.

3. An "old story," only if you do not know the details. Send for "Justice and Labor in the Mooney Case" compiled by E. B. Morton, if you want to read a story of criminal prosecution more ingenious and fascinating than the Dreyfus case. Price, 15 cents. Order from the International Workers Defense League, 307 Russ Building, San Francisco, Cal.

Nolan was arrested in the Preparedness Day affair—"indicted at my request without a single word of evidence," as District Attorney Fickert boasted in the hearing of Detective Matheson,—but never brought to trial. Nolan spent nine months in jail. He came out to find the San Francisco labor leaders, powerful but treacherous, silent on the Mooney case; the A.F. of L. formally protesting about it but doing nothing. I guess he cursed them in his Irish heart and vowed he'd get his friends out, if he had to reorganize the American labor movement to do it. Nolan had not been out of jail an hour before he became the driving spirit and directing genius of the International Workers' Defense League. This organization which has the backing of 54 local unions and Central Bodies of the San Francisco Bay District, has had full charge of the defense. Its organizers have gone up and down the land from coast to coast, addressing local unions, Central Bodies, Mass meetings, and every sort of working-class gathering, raising money and rousing public opinion for the Mooney case, and finally calling into existence this stormy congress of 1,200 delegates which voted to organize a general strike on July 4, 1919, if Mooney is not granted freedom or a new trial before that date.

It was a great achievement. You couldn't blame them—Nolan and Johannsen and Patterson and the other organizers—for their pride in it, for their belief that the Convention was *theirs,* for their determination that it should not get out of their hands, that when its work was done (the work which they had created it for—the freeing of Mooney) it should adjourn and go home, and under no circumstances take action on the burning questions of the day, lest its express object should be endangered and the power and prestige of the I.W.D.L. be lessened. You can understand that. It is a rare organizing genius who can see the child of his dreams, perfected by his thought and labor for a certain task, seized by destiny for another— even if a greater—purpose, and see it with equanimity.

It was that inevitable organization point-of-view around which the conflict raged at Chicago. When Dunn, the revolutionary editor of the Butte *Daily Bulletin,* said in his first speech, "There seems to be some danger of this defense of Mooney ceasing to be a principle and becoming an industry," I don't think that he meant any ugly insinuation. He meant to criticize that inevitable anxious care with which people guard the existence of the things they have created, or with which they are identified, or upon which their livelihood and positions depend. Many delegates came here with a great shining hope that this Mooney congress might be the beginning of the Revolution in America; others wanted the strike called to demand the freeing of all political and class-war prisoners; others, the ablest group, wanted to make it the beginning of labor organization on industrial lines. Opposed to these half-articulate demands of the delegates was the hot determination of the "machine" that nothing should be mentioned—let alone acted upon—at the convention except the Mooney case. This conflict of purpose was evident during every moment of the convention. Watchfulness, fear, suspicion on both sides.

"We got you here—by God! you've got to do what we want, or organize a convention of your own! This Convention will adjourn the minute the Mooney case is disposed of"—from the organizers.

"We're here—1,200 strong—the first really representative gathering of American labor. It's a great and terrible moment in the history of the world. We've got the right to take any action we want to. And anyhow, nothing on God's earth will make us adjourn without demanding 'hands off Russia,' and 'freedom of all political prisoners' "—from the delegates.

Which side won? Well, I think it was fifty-fifty. Briefly, this is what happened. In the first battle, over the admission of I. W. W. and Socialist Party delegates, the organization won, but it meant the exclusion of only 8 or 10 men, and no change in the temper of the Convention. I heard that 38 out of the 40 Seattle delegates carried both cards; when excluded as representing I.W.W. unions they offered their A.F. of L. cards, and were admitted. But they kept the red cards in their pockets and the I.W.W. spirit in their hearts. As for Socialist party delegates, they were excluded—but I heard of none going home. Apparently all who came on were also trades union delegates, and as such were admitted. So the first contest which the so-called "conservatives" won was over a principle, not a reality. All the thoughtful "reds" were glad of this technical exclusion of "red" delegates, because it left clear in the public mind the fact that a gathering of "regular" trade union delegates had taken extremely radical action.

The next great battle—over the Italian mission, with the

sudden test vote on Debs, already described—was a shouting victory for the revolutionary delegates present. That was on Wednesday, the second day. Thursday was a day of general speech-making, waiting for the Resolutions Committee, marking time. Friday morning's session began with the reading of the Mooney resolution from the platform by Anton Johannsen, and that precipitated the third contest. The Committee resolution was briefly this:

1st. That an effort be made to secure legislation in California which will result in the granting of new trials to Thomas Mooney and Warren K. Billings, such legislation now pending before the California Legislature.

2nd. That a committee be appointed to proceed to Washington in a final effort to secure Federal Intervention in the Mooney case, as had been recommended in two separate reports filed by officials of the United States Government, thereby removing the Mooney case from the jurisdiction of the California Courts, and placing it under control of the Federal Courts.

3rd. That the entire labor movement of the United States be requested to proceed with the taking of a vote on the question of a general strike to commence July 4th, 1919, should Mooney's release not be received by that date, and to remain in full force and effect until new trials are granted or liberty is restored to Thomas Mooney and Warren K. Billings.

A four-hour debate followed. Concerning the first point nobody seemed to care, although little faith was expressed as to success with the California legislature. On the calling of a General Strike all were agreed,—that's what they had come for, to a man. The date—July 4th—was a disappointment to the Western delegates. Many came from unions which had already taken a strike vote for December 9th and were holding it in abeyance. To them July 4th seemed too many months away. In the West they seem sure of the success of the strike. As Hunter of New Mexico expressed it, "When Mr. Capitalist crosses the Mississippi after this strike is called, he'll have to grease his own hand-car!"

On the other hand, the Committee argued for time to inform the rank and file in the East, time to organize, and they were supported by some of the wisest from both groups, and from East and West. For instance, Jim Lansbury, representing 18,000 boiler makers of Seattle, said "I've had the pleasure of sticking two $1,000 bills through the bars of Tom Mooney's cell from the Boiler Makers of Seattle. We voted 8 to 1 to go out on December 9th, and that vote holds. I tell you, the Pacific Coast would go out tomorrow. But the East is different. We've got to organize and it takes time to do it. I'm for July 4th."

The strongest argument for May 1st as opposed to July 4th was made by Kate Greenhaughl of Seattle, an able Socialist spell-binder, one of the "wild" ones.

"What is holding us back when the case of Mooney has gone round the world?" she asked. . . . "If we were ready for a general strike on December 9th to keep Mooney from hanging, why wait till July 4th to call a strike for his freedom? . . . July 4th is too late. . . . Demobilization will have taken place—the country will be full of unemployed—the employers will have months and months to prepare. . . . And July 4th is the Masters' day—it is the day when your Masters set you free to celebrate. . . . Why start a strike on a day like that? Why stop work on the one day in the year when you're allowed to stop work? . . . May 1st is the Independence Day of Labor—July 4th is a national day—May 1st is an International Day. . . . Why should we wait? . . . This is the only civilized country in the world where the prison doors are still swinging in for political prisoners now that the war is ended!"

There was reason as well as poetry in the choice of May 1st; it might have carried if Kate Greenhaughl had made her points and sat down, and if she had not been followed by other spell-binders who got up to make a point, but became intoxicated by the chance to make a speech, until the delegates were weary and in a mood to do what the Committee suggested.

The clash over dates brought out the fireworks, but the fundamental division of practical policy that morning was on the second clause of the Resolution,—sending a Committee to Washington to try for Federal intervention as a preliminary to calling the strike.

The practical, and it seemed to me superficial, argument for leaving this measure in, was strongly put by Johannsen, speaking for the Resolutions Committee. "The idea of the Committee," he said, "is that we should go to Washington with the threat of the General Strike to give us power. It's true that there is only one law for the working-man—economic power. But we must use the agency of the government when we can. After all, Densmore, a government agent, was responsible for the most valuable document in the entire Defense Campaign, and who knows whether Woodrow Wilson has played his last card in the Mooney case? Who knows whether William B. Wilson has played his last card? We don't want to strike for fun! We don't want to strike if we don't have to."

The practical and at the same time profound argument for resorting to the economic weapon directly, without any further parleying with Presidents and Congresses and legislatures, was made by Dunn, who moved to strike out the clause about sending a Committee to Washington. Dunn, who spoke seldom and always spoke quietly and briefly,—getting the attention of the delegates at any time as soon as they could see he wanted to speak,—was unusually quiet and brief in this argument: "We've been at this two years. We've exhausted every legal means. No further consideration is going to be given the case through legal channels, we *know* it. We must use our money not for lobbying but for organization. I understand the A.F. of L. maintains a lobby at Washington—let them take up the legal end. Not one cent of our money should be spent in appealing to the legislative bodies of this country. We need all our time and all our money to organize a general strike."

The finest speeches at the convention were made in support of this non-compromise position. I remember especially Charles Nicholson, General Executive Board member of the Machinists' International, who said he spoke for his whole official family and for a union of 300,000 members. He not only spoke for direct resort to the strike, recalling the threatened railroad strike three years ago and its immediate result in legislation, but strongly suggested continuing the strike for the sake of the 8-hour day. "You talk about prisons," he said, "but do you know that conditions in prison are often better than outside? When you go behind prison bars, by God, you get the 8-hour day! But outside how many of you do? Strike, call a general strike by all means, and when you strike *don't go back at least until you've got the 8-hour day.*"

And there was R. T. Sims, the colored brother from the Municipal Janitors Union of Chicago. He spoke that morning against the waste and compromise of sending a commission to Washington.

They made him stand on a chair, and there was a special friendly warmth in the applause with which they welcomed him. Sims was one of the older delegates. He looked like a tired janitor, especially his feet. And despite the warmth of his welcome, I felt a little sorry for him at first, as he stood rather unsteadily on the chair facing the great crowd of his white brothers. But when he began to speak I could see that he was a master. First he told the story of the two farmers and the mad dog. The mad dog rushed for one farmer, but the farmer grabbed a pitchfork and met the dog with that and killed him. Then the other farmer who owned the dog came running up, and saw that his dog was dead, and wrung his hands and cried, "Oh dear! oh dear, dear! Why didn't you knock him on the head with the butt end of your pitchfork? Why didn't you go for him with the other end of your fork?" "Well," said the first farmer, "Why in the name of hell didn't the son of a gun go for *me* with the other end?"

"No," Sims went on, "it's not commissions—it's not lobbies—but the strong arm of labor, and labor alone, that will win this fight. It is not publicity we want; it is action. I have no faith in their Washington. I have no faith in their Constitutions, but I have faith in labor." Sims was the only one who spoke of the unorganized; he said he believed when the time came "thousands that never carried a card will strike too. . . . I come from a small union, but I feel that I represent my race, and I want to say that 12,000,000 negroes will be lined up on the right side." His own simple earnestness and sincerity made you for a moment believe his prophecy. And then he dedicated himself, his own life, in a few honest words,—"I have been behind prison bars, I'm ready to go again. I'm ready to die in this fight if necessary,"—and sat down.

So the strongest and sanest, it seemed to me, both of those who spoke in the debate that morning, and of those whom I talked with afterwards, were opposed to the Washington lobby.

And they were right. Nothing could be devised which would deflect money and energy and enthusiasm away from the business of organizing a general strike better than maintaining five leaders in Washington to try for federal intervention. It sounds practical but it is profoundly impractical. It is true that the threat of a strike may force federal intervention. But the threat of a strike will be taken much more seriously—and lead much more surely and directly to federal intervention—if those in charge of making that threat come true, turn their backs on Washington and quietly get down to business. The presence of a lobby won't make Washington aware of the reality of the threatened strike. The total *absence* of a lobby—the complete cessation of all appeals and requests and arguments and resolutions and delegations—may.

On this point, however, as well as the date, the "organization" had its way. The Mooney resolution went through as presented. However, it was a close vote, and many agreed that a vote early in the debate would have gone the other way, that many who were worn out by speech-making, and hungry, voted for the Committee's Resolution as the line of least resistance.

On the matter of Russia and political prisoners, the Committee was wise enough by the fourth day to see that they must concede something. Mild resolutions involving no action, asking for the withdrawal of American troops from Russia, and the freeing of political and industrial prisoners and conscientious objectors were presented by the Resolutions Committee on Friday afternoon, following the Mooney Resolution, and carried almost without debate. This was in a sense a victory for the "reds"—but nothing to boast of.

Following this, after two or three perfunctory Committee reports, the reading of the names of the Federal intervention committee, and a word of thanks to the Chicago Federation of Labor, the Congress was suddenly adjourned. This was the real "coup" of the organizers, the only thing one cannot forgive them. To call 1,182 delegates to a Congress and adjourn them before they wanted to adjourn, before they had made any provision for a second Congress, for perpetuating and developing their new representative machinery,—that was ruthless, unnecessary, shortsighted. The International Workers Defense League, a local California organization, calls into existence a national Congress, first of its kind in American labor history. It might be expected that the I.W.D.L. would then sink itself and merge into a new nationally representative organization, growing out of the Congress. But no! Back into the bottle goes the genie. Back home go the delegates, leaving the whole future in the hands of the I.W.D.L., as before.

And yet perhaps it doesn't matter. Labor in America has held a great Congress without so much as a by-your-leave from Samuel

Gompers. It has voted a general strike in complete defiance of the A.F. of L. and all the sacred labor-contracts which it has sworn to uphold. That is a blow at craft unionism stronger than any other that could be struck.

The most intelligent, perhaps the most important, resolution of the whole convention—calling for the appointment of a Committee to carry on the educational propaganda necessary "to reorganize the rank and file of the American labor movement on an industrial basis as a reflection of the industrial character of production," was ruled out by the Committee as "foreign to the call of this convention." If opened up for discussion, this practical plan of action would have carried the convention. But after all, a general strike is a *general strike*. If Ed Nolan and his organizers leave the Washington lobby to its own devices, and set out now to prepare the rank and file for that strike vote—if they can put it over on July 4th, all will be forgiven. A successful general strike will be the beginning of the breakup of craft unionism.

Perhaps, as Dunn said to me, "we'll skip over the stage of industrial-unionism here, in America." We were talking over the Convention and its abrupt ending on Friday. I had asked him what he thought of some of the leaders.

"Oh, they're all anarchists, that's the trouble,—metaphysicians. And they can justify everything they do, because they don't hold with group action anyhow."

"You call them anarchists. What are you?" I asked.

"I don't know what I am. I don't call myself anything. But I'll tell you what I think is going to happen, and then you can call me anything you like. Craft-unionism is out of date, it's too late for industrial-unionism,—mass action is the only thing—mass action."

"What do you mean? How will it come?"

"Well, unemployment will increase, there'll be starvation, and some day the banks will fail, and the people will come pouring out into the streets, and the revolution will start."

"Do you think it's going to come with violence and bloodshed?"

"That depends on how much the privileged class resists," he said quietly.

And this man looks as little like an agitator as—well, as Lenin does. He is strong and thick-set, with a powerful closecropped head and a big neck, and stern bulging eyes. He's an electrical worker by trade—now editor of the Butte *Daily Bulletin,* a paper owned by the Metal Trades Council of Butte. He's a member of the Montana State Legislature. And he was the one man to whom that turbulent thousand-voiced Congress of labor would stop and listen—quietly, as though they were learning—whenever he decided to speak.

During the last day's session at Chicago a telegram came announcing the decision of the Seattle Ship Workers to go out on January 21st. On the way home news reached us of the New York Waist Makers' vote to strike. A few days later came the victory of the Amalgamated—an outlaw union, cast off to die by the A.F. of L. five years ago, quietly winning the 44-hour week for 250,000 clothing workers! And now the textile-workers of Lawrence, the silk-weavers of Paterson, the miners of Butte, come forward to make industrial history again. These strikes are symptoms, just as the Mooney Congress was, of a new spirit in American labor. Where does it come from?

Everybody knows. It is no secret. Vandenbergh, a young painter and paper-hanger from Minneapolis, expressed it when he said good-by to us in Chicago:

"It's the Russian comrades who are doing it—it's the Bolsheviki. Their spirit is creeping all over the earth . . . like a prairie fire . . . when it's all burned out the new grass will grow—I'm going back to tell my kids the Bolsheviki won!"

In Communist Hungary

Before the war, they told me, Bela Kun was an obscure Socialist secretary in a small city of Hungary, employed by a Workingmen's Insurance Association. During the war he was one of those fortunate

The Liberator, August 1919.

military prisoners in Russia who saw the Revolution. He organized thousands of Hungarian soldiers for the Russian Red Army, was prominent in the Revolution, served close to Lenin, and became an intimate and trusted lieutenant. Lenin had planned to send him to Germany, but at the last moment changed his mind and sent him to Hungary. He arrived last November, and at once began a revolutionary agitation. At the time, there was no Communist movement in Hungary. The present Commissars were for the most part inactive members of the Socialist party. Bela Kun had hardly arrived, however, before the strong men came out of their obscurity in the discontented ranks of the party, and joined him. By February they were all in jail—the whole Communist executive. Another executive was formed at once and the agitation went on, but this time completely underground. The proletariat was turning more and more toward the Communists.

During all this period Karolyi, the pacifist liberal who had dismissed the Hungarian army, was premier. There was no force to defend the bourgeoisie; the Communists felt that a single demonstration of power would deliver the city into their hands. They planned a coup. Two cannon were secretly placed on the mountain across the river, from which the city could be bombarded, and a great street demonstration was arranged for Sunday, March 23d. At the climax of the demonstration it was planned to demand the immediate release of Kun and the other leaders; and if they were not free within two hours, to bombard the city. But the demonstration never occurred. Hungary did not even come this near to a violent revolution. By Friday, March 21st, the Big Four's ultimatum had been received, making such inroads on Hungarian territory that even Karolyi was unwilling to accept it. He prepared to evade responsibility by handing the government over to the Social Democrats. But the Social Democrats were wise; they did not venture to accept it alone. They realized that they could not succeed without the co-operation of a certain group of strong men in the city jail. So they went to the jail, then and there accepted the Communist platform, and formed a government with Bela Kun, each group being equally recognized in the division of offices.

On that same night, Friday, March 21st, Bela Kun walked out

of jail, ruler of a completely blockaded nation of nine millions, pledged to abolish private capital and establish a Communist society, and at the same time to lead his country in a desperate war of defense on four fronts—Rumanian, Serbian, Czecho-Slovak and Italian.

Bela Kun is a young man (they are all young)—probably 29 or 30. He is stocky and powerful in physical build, not very tall, with a big bulging bullet-head shaved close. His wide face with small eyes, heavy jaws and thick lips is startling when you first see it close—I am told it is a well-known Magyar type—but his smile is sunny and winning, and he looks resolute and powerful. He has a superhuman capacity for hard work. His title is Commissar of Foreign Affairs, but there is not the slightest doubt in anyone's mind that he is in every sense the head of the government. He is described by his comrades as a "great agitator," a man of real revolutionary talent, a "genuine Socialist statesman," the "first statesman Hungary has had in seventy years." Their eyes glow with pride in him. "The rest of us are nothing," said Lukacs, Commissar of Education. "We do our part, but there are hundreds like us in every country." It is nothing to the European movement whether we are hanged to-morrow or not. If Kun were killed it would be a serious loss to the revolution."

Bela Kun gave me a written message to the workers of America, which I cabled for publication in the July number of *The Liberator.* He also gave me written answers to some of the questions that were in our minds in America. He said that they had learned much from the experience of Russia—both what to do and what to avoid. Perhaps it was a reflection of his own personal growth in Russia that made him say, "We certainly learned, from the Russian example, self-sacrifice."

He also said, "We learned the proper form of dictatorship there."

I asked him whether the Hungarian dictatorship was more or less strict than the Russian, and he said it was more strict. "The Russians made many experiments," he said, "before they found the proper form of dictatorship. We have been saved those experiments."

I asked him whether he found necessary a complete suppression of free speech and press, and this is his reply:

"We do not practice general suppression of free speech and free

press at all. Workmen's papers are published without the intervention of any censorship. Among workingmen there is perfect freedom
of speech and of holding meetings; this freedom is enjoyed not only
by the workmen who share our views but also by those whose views
are different. The anarchists, for instance, publish a paper and other
printed matter. There are also citizens' papers, for instance, the *XX
Szazad* (*Twentieth Century*), a periodical published by the society for
sociology, without any control or restriction being exercised upon it.
We only suppress bourgeois papers having decided counter-revolutionary intentions.

"We are doing this not because we are afraid of them, but
because we want in this way to obviate the necessity of suppressing
counter-revolution by force of arms."

He did not say how long he thought the dictatorship of the
proletariat would last, but he was very emphatic in describing it as a
condition which belongs only to the period of transition from
capitalism to communism. I quote his words again: "We consider
the dictatorship as a transitional form of government only, justified
by the state of revolution and war alone. As soon as the danger of
counter-revolution is over and peace returns it will be possible to
establish in all respects real and complete freedom of speech and
press, which up to now has never existed. For up to now the so-called
freedom of press was really a privilege of capitalist interests only."

In answer to my question about bloodshed—whether it will be
possible for the Hungarian government to establish communism
without violence except against invading armies, he said: "Not
completely. It has happened several times that persons have attacked
us with the force of arms and killed some of our political delegates. In
such cases we have, of course, to make reprisals against the murderers.
*We are doing, however, everything in our power to persuade our former
oppressors, by the demonstration of our strength, to refrain from every attempt
to impose their yoke on us again.* Our effort has been so far successful;
only very slight bloodshed has occurred. What some foreign papers
have published to the contrary is absolute falsehood."

In regard to the attitude which communists should adopt
toward the centrists, the pacifists—men like Longuet in France and
Robert Smillie in England—he said: "We do not consider them
adversaries and we profit by every occasion to distinguish them clearly

from people like Renaudel and Scheidemann. We hope that within a short time they will come to see their place on our side."

Of course, we would all like to ask Bela Kun a thousand questions, seeing that we cannot reach Lenin, but these are the principal ones to which I secured his answer in his own words for quotation.

Another interesting figure is Lukacs, the Commissar of Education. He is thirty-four—"One of the oldest," as he quaintly says—a slender, fair-haired, studious Jew with blue eyes, and spectacles. His father was a very rich banker—the head of the biggest bank in Hungary. Lukacs was wholly a student. He asked nothing of life but leisure and a chance to study philosophy. He was a Socialist, but inactive because he was disgusted with the compromise parliamentary policy of the party. A month after Bela Kun's return he had become an active leader of the Communists. Now he is the Commissar of Education over Sundays, but acts as "political commissar" for one of the Red Guard companies at the front on week-days. He goes about in a leather uniform, an earnest little professor, very learned and intelligent, very kindly and humorous, and awfully amused at his sudden transformation—pleased, too, I think, especially at the army end of it.

Each company has a soldier in command, and a "political commissar," who acts as his colleague, to keep up the "revolutionary morale" of the Red Guard. I suppose he is the revolutionary counterpart of the chaplain and the Y. M. C. A. But he fights, he goes into battle with the soldiers.

Lukacs is interested in his educational reforms. Teachers' salaries under him have been raised to the highest rank—650 kronen a week. It is just what the commissars get.[1] But Lukacs is more interested now in the army. He is as proud of the fighting spirit of his company of Red Guards as Napoleon ever was of his chosen troops.

"When the Rumanians first attacked, our Red Guards quite simply ran away!" he says, "but now they are strong and eager. The army is five times as strong as it was on May 1st. It numbers between 80,000 and 100,000 men."

I found Lukacs and the others supremely confident of military

---

1. 650 kronen to-day is about $35.

success. They smile at the suggestion that the small governments now surrounding them might defeat the Red Army. The power of the Entente to crush them they acknowledge, but they have a sure and smiling faith that the workers of the Entente countries will prevent this. All these young leaders live in confident hope of new revolutions. The only question debatable is *where* the next one will break out. Capitalism they speak of always in the past tense: "Capitalism was. . . ."

Confidence, amazing confidence, not only in their power to establish Communism, but in the complete success of Communism when established, the power of this idea to save the world and make everybody happy, is the irresistible quality in these men. For instance, Julius Hevesi, Commissar for Social Production, who explained the whole process of socializing production to me, insisted that it had all been very easy. And when I asked about distribution— were there no difficult problems in distributing the product under Communism?—he could think of no problems. Distribution will be easy enough, once Hungary has possession of her coal mines and the other sources of raw materials upon which her productive industries have always depended.

Hevesi is an engineer, a university graduate, who was for years an ardent Communist—as it seems most of the Hungarian engineers were. He is a slight, dark man, very well dressed—a delicate oval face, black eyes and mustache. He might be a neat little French or Italian officer.

I will describe, if I can, the exact process by which private capital was abolished, as Hevesi explained it to me.

The morning after Bela Kun came out of prison placards throughout the city announced the establishment of the Communist Republic, and commanded all commercial and industrial establishments to close for three days, during which time they must make an accurate and exhaustive inventory and deliver it to the government, *under penalty of death.* The threat was believed, and all business men, both great and small, hastened to obey. After this was done, factories employing under thirty people were allowed to continue on condition of accepting the new scale of wages. All factories employing more than thirty people were as rapidly as possible "socialized"—that is, *the government took the place of the shareholders.* All who really did any work were left at their places. The owner was offered the post of manager at 2,000 kronen a month; if he declined, things went on without him. According to Hevesi, their plan differs very much from syndicalism. "Under syndicalism," he said, "industries could be continued that we do not consider important." Every factory is the common property of the whole people, and is under centralized control. The workmen elect a controlling council, which has general direction, but the final power rests with a special commissar appointed by the Central Government. I suggested that this sounded a little like State Socialism, but Hevesi reminded me that they had abolished private capital!

Wages everywhere were raised, wages of the unskilled the most, on the whole. Sometimes they were raised as much as 100 per cent. Three classes of workmen were established:

Skilled to receive 5–8½ kronen per hour (25–42 cents).
Semi-skilled to receive 4–5½ kronen per hour (20–33 cents).
Unskilled to receive 3–5 kronen per hour (15–25 cents).

The workmen's controlling council in each factory determines which workmen belong in each class. Otherwise it has no control over wages.

The syndicalist tendency, however, is to express itself in an industrial parliament, or congress of production, to be made up of the commissars and delegates from the trades unions. But, according to Hevesi and Lukacs, the Communist State is not to be established on a basis of industrial representation as we have understood the Soviet State in Russia to be, but on a basis of geographical representation. All the workers in a certain district will elect a representative. It is on this basis that the present Buda-Pesth Soviet is constituted. And the first All-Hungarian Congress of Soviets—to be held on June 16th—is to be elected in the same way. The industrial parliament is to be a sort of co-ordinate advisory body. In the progressive adjustment of these two bodies, of course, lies a vital development for the future.

Unemployed relief is paid, if necessary, but nearly all the unemployed are absorbed by the Red Army.

Communist distribution is hardly as yet to be described, because, owing to the blockade, the lack of materials, the alarming
shortage of coal, very little is being produced. Distribution of
necessities is managed through the co-operatives with the aid of some
small commercial shops, which are being incorporated as branches of
the central distributing system. The plan is to have a distributing
center for every five hundred families. Goods are also being distributed through a central bureau on requests by the unions. The
distribution of luxuries in a starving country under blockade is not,
of course, a pressing problem.

The stores are still closed. Gray iron shutters throughout the
shopping districts deny you even that idle pastime of looking in the
store windows at what you can't afford to buy. You know what a city
is like on Sunday. Well, in Buda-Pesth, Monday, and Tuesday, and
Wednesday, and Thursday, and Friday, and Saturday are just like
Sunday—and Sunday in a bone-dry town. Complete prohibition was
almost the first decree of the Communists.

Houses

I shall never go into a big, comfortable house again, whether it
is the house of a Socialist professor or a railroad president, without
quietly figuring up the number of rooms and the number of people,
to determine whether the family will be allowed to continue in
possession of the whole house when communism comes. So real was
my experience in Hungary. Vago, Commissar of Housing, who looks
like a college hero—big, brown, handsome, and built like an
athlete—smilingly assured me that the new Communist rule of one
room per person, until all are housed, is actually in force in Buda-
Pesth. Of course, each family is allowed a kitchen, and people who
work at home—writers, artists, professors, etc.—may each have a
workroom in addition. Many of the rich people have moved out of
their big houses into hotels, or have left the country. Some, however,
are living in the three or four rooms allowed them in their own
houses. The housing room thus gained is being used as rapidly as
possible to relieve the over-crowding of the poor. Of course, it is not
simple. Kitchens have to be put in. But it is being done.

The summer villas on the mountain are turned into homes for convalescent children. I saw one, a great white palace of twenty-eight rooms, which had been occupied by one man with his son during only two or three months in summer. It is transformed into a gay and spacious getting-well place for thirty children, light tuberculosis cases, with doctor and nurses employed by the State. I did not see many people that looked happy in Buda-Pesth, but those children did. They were lying out on a big stone balcony in sea-chairs, wrapped each one in a red blanket, talking and laughing together. They thought one of our party was Bela Kun, and roared a joyful greeting to him.

There are five hundred children on this mountain. There would be five thousand, I was told, if they could get beds. I thought for the thousandth time how bitterly tragic it is that these great experiments in government must commence at a time when material conditions are so desperate. But, as Lukacs said to me, "It is not an accident that revolution and starvation come hand in hand."

There is one commodity of which there is no shortage—water. Buda-Pesth is famous for its baths—big, well-equipped baths for the middle class and luxurious baths for the rich. For two days a week now all these baths are given over to the children of the city; 70,000 boys and girls from the public schools, between nine and fourteen, "go through" the baths every week. I saw five hundred boys in the midst of it. First they come along in line, naked to the waist, carrying their little coats and blouses, for a five-second medical examination, long enough for the doctor to discover heart weakness or skin trouble. Their heads are looked at, too, and shaved if not perfectly clean. Then they take off the rest of their clothes in little dressing rooms and run along down to the big steaming dark baths, first for a cursory scrub from one of the bathers, then into the hot tank, and at last, with a whoop of joy, into the big swimming tank, hundreds of them together.

The baths are dark, just as the hotels are dark, because there is such a shortage of coal that only absolutely essential bulbs can be lighted. When I was in Buda-Pesth the Hungarians had just one coal mine left in uninvaded territory. I could understand how, earlier in June, when in a victory over the Czechs they won back two coal mines, a great public rejoicing was held, with dancing in the streets. Lack of light would kill the revolutionary spirit in me almost sooner than lack of food. I shall never forget the dim and dreary gloom of the Hotel Hungaria, where I stayed and where the young Commissars lived. Yet their eager spirits seemed untouched by it.

Banks

How about banks? How about farms? How about money? Food? I can hear your questions, but my time was very short.

The Soviet State has taken possession of banks exactly as it has taken factories. The Soviet steps into the place of the shareholders, and hires the employees. Sometimes the rich banker becomes the manager, employed by the State at 2,000 kr. a month. That is what Lukacs' father is doing. I asked Lukacs how his father liked it, whether he was reconciled to the new order. He said: "Well, not quite. He doesn't say anything to me, of course, but I think he has some secret plans. I think perhaps he is plotting to overthrow us. And the funny thing about it is that the day he gets back his fortune is the day I get hanged!"

Bank deposits have not been disturbed, but each depositor can draw only 2,000 kr. a month, and that only if he proves that he has no other source of income. Jewels and other valuable private possessions in excess of a certain generous allowance were taken from the bourgeoisie at the beginning. The immediate purpose of these measures was to prevent anyone in Buda-Pesth from getting more than his share of food. In Vienna—another blockaded city—the poor are absolutely starving, and the former middle class, still living in comfortable houses and big apartments, look pinched and are obviously undernourished, while the rich are living well. In Buda-Pesth, as a result of these measures, everybody is hungry. There is that satisfaction. As Lenin is reported to have said about Russian Communism, "We have demonstrated that we can distribute *nothing*. It remains for us to prove whether we can distribute *something!*"

Hungary, it seems, was the one well-fed country of Central Europe during the war, and twenty miles from Buda-Pesth there are eggs and milk and good things to be had for real money to-day. But the small farmers, whose private ownership has not been disturbed, distrust the new government, will not take Soviet money, and, it is said, are hiding their food.

"All right, if they're hiding their food we'll go out with machine guns and get it," said Bolgar, the Soviet Ambassador at Vienna to me. (He, by the way, is an old American I.W.W., for ten years editor of a Hungarian paper in Boston.) But I have more faith in the distribution to the towns of surplus produce from the big estates, which are being communized and operated by soviets formed of the former landlords' employees. With the blockade cutting off raw materials, and the foreign invasion preventing access to all but one of Hungary's own coal mines, it will be, of course, next to impossible for the city workers to make anything to exchange for the farm produce which they need. It is a pretty tight situation. The leaders know it, despite all their bold courage. There is almost a desperate note in the Hungarian appeal to the workers of the Entente countries:

"Comrades, the Russian and Hungarian workers *alone* cannot achieve victory for the revolution, not even if the German working class ranges itself beside them. To-day there is only *one* power which can save the Russian and Hungarian revolutions and lead the international revolution to victory. And that one power is *you,* workers of the Entente countries. *On your shoulders, comrades, rests to-day the tremendous responsibility for the future of the working class revolution, which is the future of humanity.*"

There is no use having any illusions about the revolution. It was born in starvation, and its first business is war. There is no freedom, no plenty, no joy, except the joys of struggle and faith. Cherished dreams of scientists, educators, artists, engineers, who were waiting for a free society, must be set aside, while the whole proletariat organizes in desperate haste to check the invading hosts of the enemy. And war means recruiting propaganda, conscription, military discipline, the death penalty, the whole damnable business of organized dying and killing. Max Eastman said in Madison Square Garden two years ago, "When our own war comes you'll know it, because it won't be necessary to conscript the workers to fight in it." I thought he spoke a profound truth. I do not think so now. When we heard about those democratic regiments formed in Russia after the first revolution, I thought, "This is a real workers' army." Now I know there can be no such thing as a democratic army. People don't want to die, and except for a few glorious fanatics they are not going to vote themselves into the front line trenches.

"We are in the war," said Lukacs, when I cried out against the shooting of six men from that first regiment which "quite simply ran away at the first fire." "In war, fugitives and traitors must be shot. If not, all right, then, let the Czechs in and the revolution will be lost."

I hope there is some pacifist revolutionary with an answer to that. I have none.

The Red Army was recruited at first by spontaneous volunteering on the part of thousands. It was encouraged later by unemployment. The closing of the cafes in Buda-Pesth, for instance, must have driven hundreds of workers into the Red Guard. It was stimulated by a brilliant and overwhelming propaganda. Finally, they resorted to conscription—not as we know it, but through the trades unions. Decrees were posted calling upon each trades union to draft a certain number of its members for the Red Army by a certain date.[2]

Recruiting

The Red Army recruiting propaganda interested me perhaps more than anything else I saw in Hungary. I remember when I first caught sight of big photographs of Lenin decorating a newsstand. It was the same friendly, quizzical, half-smiling picture we had on our January cover, and it suddenly peered out at me through the murky dimness of a country railroad station, where our train stopped for an hour on the all-night trip from Buchs to Buda-Pesth. I must have been a little lonesome, because I felt like crying when I saw Lenin's face, and I said to myself, "Lenin is my father, and I am coming home!"

Next morning in Buda-Pesth I found the newsstands, the pillars, the walls, every blank space, shouting with revolutionary

---

2. It must be understood that those decrees are inescapable. Nobody takes any chances with the dictatorship.

posters. It seemed to me that Por and the other Commissars of Propaganda, in the two short months of their work, had put the National Security League, the American Defense Society and all the other patriotic poster designers of America wholly in the shade. The revolutionary placards are all red, almost wholly one color. They are everywhere, on every wall of every street—enormous sheets many of them, some good drawings, some bad; very daring and simple; all emphatically modern. One is a great bold red figure running with a flag—"To Arms!" There is a soldier charging with a bayonet—"He who is not with us is against us!" "Save the Proletariat," "Defend the Revolution," "Join the Red Guard!"—these are the phrases repeated again and again—but never a word about Hungary, never a note of nationalist appeal.

At the moving pictures it is the same.[3] All these recruiting posters are thrown on the screen. Then come Red Army scenes— soldiers marching to the front, warships on the Danube, battle scenes, wounded Red Guards. Everywhere the desperate appeal to arms, but never a suggestion of nationalism. This seems to me immensely significant. It is a tribute to the sincerity and purity of purpose, the intellectual integrity of these revolutionary leaders, that never, even in the darkest hour of despair, did they appeal to the people to defend Hungary against invasion from its ancient enemies, Italy, Bohemia, Roumania. It would have been so easy, but it would have been false. It would have made impossible the tributes and pledges of faith and friendship which I heard given to the Buda-Pesth Soviet by Roumanian, Italian, Czech and Serbian workers' represen- tatives. They brought greetings from workers of these nations to the Soviet government of Hungary and proclaimed their devotion to that government almost within sound of the guns of their invading armies, marching to destroy it.

In all the theaters of Buda-Pesth now the International is played. In the movies the words are put upon the screen and the people sing it. You "have to stand up"—the same sort of social compulsion, perhaps, that our patriots exercised upon us in New York during the

---

3. Theatres, of course, are already communized, actors, singers and managers employed by the State, and tickets sold through the Unions.

war. One day I met an American newspaper correspondent, who was cursing life under the Soviet regime. He could see no hope short of the day when "all these Jews will be hung up there along the castle wall where they belong."

"Why," he said, "I used to love the Hungarian opera. Now I can't even go to that, because they play the International and you have to stand up. I wouldn't mind standing up for the Hungarian national hymn, but I'll be damned if I'll stand up for the International!"

It is a small incident, but I think it shows how rapidly all our passionate national hysterias—amazingly vital as they often are—will pale and disappear beside the deeper realities of this new struggle.

The great war is over. The Revolution has begun. And we've got to choose new sides. The other day in the British Parliament Winston Churchill, Secretary for War, in the course of his reply to Colonel Wedgewood's able arraignment of British intervention in Russia, turned suddenly to Wedgewood—a Liberal who recently joined the Independent Labor Party—and asked ironically:

"If my honorable and gallant friend is so enthusiastic about these Bolsheviki, why doesn't he go and join them?"

Without a moment's hesitation Wedgewood replied seriously: "If this is going to be a class war, that's my side."

And so it goes.

British Labor Is Moving

It was my good fortune to see the great British Labor Party, at its official convention on Friday, June 27th, vote overwhelmingly in favor of industrial action to stop the Allied butchery and torture of

The Liberator, September 1919.

Soviet Russia. It was a 2 to 1 vote on a motion to instruct its National Executive "to consult the Parliamentary Committee of the Trades Union Congress with the view to effective action being taken . . . by the unreserved use of their Political *and Industrial Power,*" to stop Allied intervention in Russia, "whether by force of arms, by supply of munitions, by financial subsidies, or by commercial blockade."

This action was not taken blindly or with temporary emotion. The use of "direct" or industrial action for political ends has been quite widely and on the whole respectfully discussed in the British press for the past two months. Liberal editors have gone out of their way to praise the strike as an excellent weapon for achieving industrial ends—wages, hours, conditions of labor—but to warn against it as dangerous, undemocratic, and unconstitutional when employed for political ends. The old line labor leaders, like Clynes, Ben Tillett, and Havelock Wilson, have made it clear that they are in violent agreement with the capitalist editors on this point. Arthur Henderson, also, of course, is firmly and sadly opposed. Henderson is still executive secretary of the Labor Party, but nevertheless, with his black coat and his general air of being a shrewd and solid banker superintending a Sunday School, he belongs irrevocably to the past, and he seems to me to realize it. The Labor Party Executive did their best to keep the issue from coming up at the conference. They urged, in their report to the conference, that "if the British labor movement is to institute a new precedent in our industrial history by initiating a general strike for the purpose of achieving not industrial but political objects," the trade unions themselves, and not the Labor Party, should determine the plan.

The chairman in his opening remarks declared: "Either we are constitutionalists or we're not constitutionalists. If we believe in the efficacy of the political weapon—and we do, or we wouldn't have a labor party—then it is both unwise and undemocratic, because we were defeated at the polls, to turn round and resort to the industrial weapon."

But the new leaders, Smillie, with his 600,000 miners behind him; Frank Hodges, the keen young miners' secretary who has won distinction on the coal commission; Bob Williams, General Secretary of the Transport Workers who carries the majority of their votes;

Cramp, President of the Railwaymen's Union; the Glasgow men, David Kirkwood and Neill McLean, M.P.; the Manchester group, all these declared themselves in favor of a general strike in defense of Russia. They did this clearly and intelligently and without illusions as to its possible consequences.

"They call this measure unconstitutional," said Bob Williams, who is a big Welshman, fiery, eloquent and humorous, "but I tell you the constitution of the Trades Union movement is what circumstances make it. Is the war against Russia a constitutional war? There is much talk about the Triple Alliance, but it isn't only there that the workers are ready. Churchill has thrown down a challenge on this Russian matter and I believe at least a million, the pick of the British workers, are ready to accept it. All we ask is an opportunity for trades union workers to determine the question. Unless the leaders act, the workers will act by themselves. . . . And what's more the soldiers and sailors and police cannot be relied on to defeat a general strike if and when one takes place. The soldiers to begin with aren't very reliable; the sailors are more unreliable than the soldiers; and the police are more unreliable than the sailors!" Shouts of laughter and applause followed this. Williams seems to be accepted as an orator chiefly, a man who perhaps goes farther in a speech than in action.

Smillie is just the opposite type—a man whose thoughts and plans, I am sure, go ahead of his public utterances. Smillie had fought this question out in the meetings of the Triple Alliance, and he must have known which way the strength of the Congress lay, for he just said enough to show where he stood, and sat down. These were his points: (1) It is a strange and sinister thing to find Mr. Henderson and the Executive Committee of the Labor Party taking the same position on this question that every exploiter of labor in the country is taking. (2) What is called direct action may be constitutional action. For every trade-unionist to stop work at once might be perfectly constitutional. It would be justified if the cause was sufficient. (3) It is impossible to draw the line between political and industrial questions. Nationalization of the mines is certainly a political question, yet no one will deny that the government was forced to action in this direction by the miners' strike, and the Executive Committee of the Labor Party will congratulate the miners on their action. (4) Direct action does not mean an end of political action. Labor failed in the elections because the workers are not sufficiently class-conscious, and because they were deceived by the government. Now it is our duty to let our 62 members in parliament know what we want—by industrial action.

Next came James Seddon, M.P., of the Dockers' Union. He was greeted with "Hello, Jimmie—another forlorn hope!" An oldish man with a caved-in face, he managed with the help of the Chairman's frequent appeals, "Give order, will you please! Shut up and give order, will you?"—to state the ancient case.

"What's the use of talking about industrial action? There are 4,000,000 trade-unionists, yet we got only 2½ million votes in the general election and a large part of these were from the middle class. (As if this weren't the very central argument for direct action!). . . . There is a more comfortable way of dealing with Churchill, when the next election comes around, yes even if it takes four years (cries of "How about Russia?" "What will happen to Russia?") it's better than risking civil war. A general strike will mean a revolution. You'll be letting mad dogs loose, you'll be encouraging an element rife today in the trades union movement, *an element you can't control,*" etc.,

He was perfectly right. It would be letting loose an element which he and his type—labor leaders, as one speaker put it, "who like to be called level-headed trade unionists in the Capitalist Press"—cannot control.

Then followed Bromley, an engineer who briefly supported Smillie, "We've been betrayed politically. We mustn't take it lying down. We must swing the industrial movement back of the political movement and unite them."

The opposition countered again with an M.P., but by this time the delegates, knowing how they were going to vote, were very impatient and unruly. The Chairman, a likeable Irishman named McGurk, made a last desperate appeal—"There were no interruptions when Williams spoke, or when Smillie spoke or when Bromley spoke. Well for God in heaven's sake, be tolerant now and give order!" This won Brace a chance to say that he "knew no more slippery slope" for labor to start on than this one of industrial action for political ends. "We've been declaring we should soon have a labor government—we must have faith, we must use the trades unions to build up the political party. We must have patience, we must educate the worker. . . ."

So it went. Every opponent of industrial action called attention to labor's defeat at the polls as a warning and thus gave his case away. For if labor in Great Britain, though strong industrially, is weak at the polls, there must be something the matter with the polls as a register of labor's will. Labor is weak politically because all the institutions which influence and control its political mind—schools, churches, movies, newspapers—are capitalist institutions; and labor is strong industrially because it can't be so easily fooled about questions immediately relating to the job, and because its industrial mind is influenced more and more by its own press and institutions. Moreover, the only kind of education labor needs just now is the realization that political questions are fundamentally industrial. One of the women delegates made an unconscious comment on political methods, that amused the conference. She was pleading for support for some parliamentary measure. "Just deluge the Government with resolutions," she said, "so that their waste baskets will be bulging with your letters!"

The debate which had started rather informally over the clause in the executive's report quoted above, was sidetracked for a day and a half, on the chairman's guarantee that it should be resumed on the introduction of the formal resolution. When the time came, the resolution was formally moved by "Councillor" Davies—a Welsh miner now in the Manchester Town Council. It was seconded by Neill McLean, a Glasgow engineer, one of the I.L.P. candidates returned to Parliament last December. He is a real labor member, who laid down his tools on "the Saturday," as they say, and took his seat in Parliament on "the Monday."

Ben Tillett began the attack. He is a short powerful man, an able and moving speaker, but he was helpless with this modern audience. He tried the time worn dodges to rouse labor against the Socialists.

"This conference is 99 per cent trades union and 1 per cent professional politician," he said. "The 1 per cent moves this resolution. Do we want to be led by the nose by professional politicians?

We've got the fighting to do. We know these eloquent speakers, we've seen how they act when it comes to a fight. The lions on the platform have very often proved to be rats when the soldiers turned on them. . . . For this conference to pass such a resolution is an insult to the workers. . . . I tell you the Trade Union movement will not allow you to boss them"—and so on, until they booed him down.

Then young Frank Hodges, earnest and fine, a miner educated at Ruskin College, now Secretary of the Miners' Federation, quietly repeated the earlier arguments, closing with these sentences, "I think the Parliamentary Party would welcome that industrial support which would make it a power in the House of Commons. In every great political question labor must be backed by what will always be the greatest power of the workers, their industrial power. This country can move through to the social revolution perhaps in a different way from any other. But if you deny it a chance to move through those channels provided in the Labor Party and the Trades Union Congress, it will move some other way, perhaps not for the best."

J. R. Clynes, M.P., dean of the labor politicians, was the last speaker. He is a neat little gray-haired man—always re-elected to the labor party executive despite his reactionary tendencies, because of his ability. He said nothing new except this: "If you try to terrorize this government by a general strike, you'll establish a dangerous precedent. Suppose a labor and socialist party gets in power—will you give another class the same right to terrorize a labor government?" The cries of "Yes-Yes!" "Let them try it!" "There won't be any classes!" which greeted this stroke seemed to grieve him, and he soon sat down. After this the direct actionists would listen to no more speeches. They demanded the vote and got it!

1,893,000 for the resolution.

935,000 against.*

Of course it is merely an instruction to their executives to consult the parliamentary committee of the trades union. It is not action. But in the light of all the events and discussions which led up

---

* They come as instructed delegates and vote by the card system, one card for every 1,000 votes. Miners, railway men and transport workers make up more than half of the vote in favor.

to this vote, its significance is very great. Six days before at a
conference in Manchester representing 70 trade union branches,
several trades-councils, and a number of Socialist branches, a Hands-
off-Russia Committee was formed to arrange a series of sectional labor
conferences culminating in a national unofficial labor conference to
determine the question of industrial action on behalf of Russia. And
four days before, the Triple Alliance executive, representing the
Miners' Federation of Great Britain, the National Union of Railwaymen and the Transport Workers Federation (over a million workers
in all), decided to convene a full delegate conference in London, July
23rd, to decide what action, if any, should be taken in order to
compel the Government to repeal conscription, cease intervention in
Russia, raise the blockade, and release conscientious objectors.

The Labor Party convention contained 975 delegates, representing millions of voters of whom 99 per cent are trade union members.
Its vote was a vote for action at a time when action was under
consideration by the most powerful unions. Such a vote passed by the
delegates of a political party cannot but indicate an even greater
readiness for action among the rank and file.

I saw the proof of this two days later at a meeting in Manchester.
It was an I.L.P. or Socialist meeting, but it was also distinctly a labor
meeting, a working-class audience and every speaker a trade unionist.
These are some of the statements which won the enthusiastic approval
of the crowd:

"The Trades Unionist movement can either become direct
actionist now or be left behind."

"Don't let us apologize about the Bolsheviki—if we are sincere
we know that we are Bolsheviki, everyone of us. They are our
comrades. . . . You tell me the press calls them murderers. Well, so
does the press call you murderers when you go on strike. . . . All
those Glasgow workers were murderers to the Provost Marshal, when
he sent the soldiers out to shoot them down. The Press tells you the
Bolsheviks believe in free love! Was there ever a Socialist or labor
leader that rose to a position of power that they didn't make the same
attack on him? The accusations they make against the Bolsheviks are
the accusations they will make against you when you show your
power."

"It's the duty of every working man and woman in Great Britain to see that Russia wins through. If Russia wins through Germany will win through. If Germany wins through France will win through. And then by God we'll win through!"

"You've got to have industrial action, you'll always have to have it. I'm not sure even if you get a labor majority, that you'll get a labor government."

"If ever we get a working-class tribunal of justice, I want to see Winston Churchill in the Dock—that hero of Sidney St., who has become the assassin of new republics!"

And finally the chairman, who is President of the Trades and Labor Council of Manchester (a city of a million) and a strong industrial unionist:

"If I ever vote for a labor member of Parliament it will be to close the House of Commons. If we get control of the industries, and establish our central committee representing all the industries, we can take care of everything. We won't need the House of Commons."

"We want soviets!" somebody called out. The chairman proposed "three cheers for the Revolution!" and they were given with a will.

Later By Cable

As was expected, the Parliamentary Committee of the Trades Union Congress, when requested by the Labor Party executive to convene a special meeting of the Congress to consider the proposal of direct action, refused. On July 23rd the Triple Alliance (Railroad Workers, Transport Workers, and Miners) in a full delegate conference at Caxton Hall, London, voted by an enormous majority—217 for, 11 against—to take a strike vote. The strike ballot, which is now being distributed, reads: "The government having refused to abolish (1) Conscription, (2) Military intervention in Russia, (3) Military intervention in trade union disputes,—

"Are you in favor of withdrawing your labor to enforce the abolition of the foregoing?"

Smillie is all hope. I will send an interview with him for the next number.

The Workers of the Clyde

"Well, Wullie Gallacher's cam oot. And they're sayin' the treaty is signed and they're going to have peace, but they're not. *Wullie Gallacher's not goin' to let 'em have peace!"*

Thus spoke John Maclean, on Thursday, July 3d, 1919, in the Paisley Town Hall, where three thousand Clyde workers had gathered to welcome the chief hero of the 40-hour strike after his three months in Edinburgh jail. "Our annual meeting to celebrate William Gallacher's release from prison," the Chairman called it. And there on the front row of the platform beside his beaming wife sat the hero— a trim, square-shouldered young lightweight with a red rose in his button-hole, healthy rosy-cheeked and smiling, like a boy home from school. Through six long speeches of tribute he sat with downcast eyes, quietly blushing, and never looked up. It may be an annual performance, but Gallacher isn't used to it yet. Surrounding him were the chief figures in the great strike, behind him a socialist chorus, girls all in white, below him rows of hard-headed Scotch machinists, munition makers and shipbuilders, all in their working clothes with caps on, typical Clyde workers, the sort of men that kept Glasgow, despite all governmental blandishments, an anti-war city throughout the five years.

This meeting was the final chapter of the story of the first general strike in Scotland.

The Clyde is a muddy, uninteresting river 100 miles long, which rises fifteen hundred feet up in the hills of Lanarkshire, and flows west across the narrow part of Scotland into the sea. Fourteen miles up from its mouth lies Glasgow. The history of Glasgow and the Clyde is the history of the industrial revolution. For along the valley of this river lie the largest coal fields and the richest iron-ore mines in all the British Isles. It happens that Fulton, Bell and Watt were all originally Clyde men. After the invention of machinery,

Glasgow which had been a thriving little seaport of 14,000, serving an agricultural and wool-producing hinterland, became in one short century a great dark smoky city of a million people, surrounded by a dozen ugly industrial suburbs. And half a century later, when men learned to make ships of steel, the Clyde became the greatest shipbuilding river in the world. The Pittsburg worker must bring his iron-ore from some place away up in the Great Lakes region, a thousand miles away, and he must send his finished steel to far-off harbors to be made into ships. But the Clyde worker finds iron-ore, coal, and a 200-acre harbor right at hand. No wonder that more ships were built on the banks of the Clyde before the war than in England, Germany and America put together.

But the Clyde workers do not all build ships. The kindred trades flourish there. They make boilers, locomotives, bridges, machinery, tools. And thousands of them are miners. Bob Smillie, a Lanarkshire miner, is a Clyde man. Keir Hardie, too, worked in the coal-fields area of the Clyde valley. But the Clyde worker about whom this story is written, works in the shops and is called an "engineer."

Well, during the war, of course Glasgow became one of the greatest munition-making centers in the Empire. Yes, the Clyde made munitions and sent thousands of kilted bare-kneed lads to the front, but the Clyde never gave its heart to the war. From the great Keir Hardie Memorial meeting in 1915 when Robert Smillie said, "Fellow workers, this war which has killed Keir Hardie is a capitalist war," to the day of the armistice, there wasn't an hour when it wasn't safer to hold a peace meeting than a war meeting in Glasgow. Night after night John Maclean and James MacDougal held their peace meetings right opposite the recruiting office. The crowd grew and they were unmolested. In 1917 Helen Crawfurd of the Women's International League conducted an out-and-out peace crusade, with processions, banners, street-meetings and all, after the fashion of suffrage days—and no one dared interfere with her. In fact there were 4,000 shop-stewards organized to protect peace meetings. A certain number of these, each one with 18 inches of lead pipe under his coat, would be detailed to attend whenever trouble was expected. Glasgow was ready for anything.

The rent strike was typical. In 1915 when munition workers

began to stream into the city, there was an attempt to raise rents. But the women, wives of soldiers and munition workers, wouldn't hear of it. They refused to pay more rent and when ordered out of their flats they refused to move. Suddenly, within six hours, there appeared in windows all over the city, placards announcing in big red letters their calm defiance of law and authority, "RENT STRIKE. WE ARE NOT REMOVING." They meant what they said. In each house one woman would be stationed as a picket to watch for trouble. On the approach of landlord, sheriff or rent collector, she would give the signal and twenty or thirty angry women would run out of their apartments and meet him on the stairs, sometimes armed with flour, sometimes with water, sometimes just with words. In any case he retired. It looked as though it would take machine guns to get any of these women out of their apartments. Finally, however, ten were arrested. When word was carried to the engineers in the shops that these women were on trial before the Sheriff for refusing to be evicted, they dropped their tools and came running in thousands to the Sheriff's office. They gathered on the square outside, a great threatening determined mob, with John Maclean standing up somewhere, exhorting them, "Now you're out, let the war go to hell!" The Sheriff telephoned in haste to London, and then adjourned the case. In two days the old rents were restored—and a Bill enacted preventing eviction except after a court trial. Then the engineers went back to work.

But the most characteristic demonstration of Glasgow temper was on the night when Lloyd George and Arthur Henderson came up to explain the government's plan for introducing unskilled labor into the munition shops for the duration of the War, contrary to union rules. The Clyde Workers' support for their scheme,—known as 'dilution of labor,' was so vital to the government that Lloyd George came up there himself. Thousands gathered in the largest hall of Glasgow to hear what he had to say. As a diplomatic stroke, David Kirkwood, one of the leading shop-stewards, was chosen to introduce the Prime Minister, and carefully instructed beforehand to speak of him as the "Right Honourable David Lloyd George." Kirkwood is a plain spoken man, and no respecter of persons. "Fellow-workers, this is Lloyd George," he began, and turning to the Prime Minister, went on, "and I may say to you, Sir, that we view every word that comes from your mouth with suspicion. We've had your 'ninepence for four-pence' bill,[1] and we've had your Munitions Act, and now you're bringing us your dilution of labor scheme, and we don't trust you. But, fellow-workers, I beg you to listen to the man and give him a fair hearing."

The meeting never got far beyond that introduction. The men sat in grim silence while the Premier staggered through a few sentences of patriotic eloquence, but when he came to "our boys in the trenches," one old fellow called out, "We're not here to talk about boys in the trenches. We've boys in the trenches ourselves. We're here to listen to your dilution of labor scheme." After that the interruptions were continuous, until a man in the back of the room began to speak so powerfully that the whole audience turned round to listen to him, and Lloyd George had to give up and sit down. Then pretty soon the meeting got up and went home.

This blessed British custom of heckling public speakers, even the high and mighty, certainly develops character and keeps the soul alive.

Kirkwood, Maclean, Gallacher and Arthur McManus—those are the names I heard oftenest in Glasgow. They are all engineers except Maclean, and all are Socialists, but each one represents a slightly different group. David Kirkwood, whom I met at the Labour Party Conference in Southport, is on the Executive of the Independent Labour Party. He stood for Parliament in the last election, and claims that he got more votes than any other I.L.P. candidate in Great Britain. His fame rests, however, on his industrial activities. During an earlier strike, in 1916, he and nine other engineers were "deported" from Glasgow and "interned" in Edinburgh for 14 months. For some time Kirkwood was kept under guard. One night his soldier guard turned on him and said: "God! I hope I'll have a chance to shoot you." When Kirkwood asked him why, the soldier said: "Why, we hate you worse than the Germans. You're the fellow that brought the men out on the Clyde, and let us down over there. We'd like

1. A reference to the Workman's Insurance Law.

nothing better than to kill you and your kind. You're enemies." They argued through the night, but the soldier held to his convictions. Last June, two and a half years later, a man came up to Kirkwood after one of his speeches, and said: "Do you remember me? I'm the soldier that wanted to shoot you in Edinburgh jail. Well, I just wanted to tell you I was wrong and you were right. I've found it out now."

That's a true story. I know the soldier's name and address. Kirkwood is one of these quiet-looking, apparently commonplace individuals who is continually having adventures. He sees his life as a series of dramatic events, and that is what it is. Kirkwood is no good in a strike, they say—excitable, sentimental, always "striking an attitude." But no one—surely no one speaking the English tongue—can tell the story of a strike with more warmth and color, with a more perfect narrative art, and with more fire and passion and purpose, than Kirkwood can. If he never has any more adventures, and just goes around to labor meetings telling the story of those he has had, he'll play a big part.

John Maclean's relation to the movement is, I think, not unlike Kirkwood's, although Maclean is an intellectual. They both have a lovable but unmanageable recklessness. "You never know what he's going to do," is said of both of them. But Kirkwood is a little inclined to melancholy, while Maclean is the cheeriest firebrand you ever saw. He is a mild-mannered, smiling conspirator, with a round-eyed, apple-cheecked face, and white hair. "Be cheerie, comrades," he says, "you never can win a revolution without being cheerie." Maclean believes in Revolution *now*. Since the defection of Hyndman and his pro-war followers, he is perhaps the most distinguished member of that small intellectual doctrinaire left wing group called the British Socialist Party. When I first met Neil Maclean, who is an I.L.P. man and member of Parliament, I thought, "There won't be much in common between this man and the revolutionary Bolshevik consul of the same name." But Neil smiled at such a notion. "You'll find all the Macleans have about the same reputation," he said, "and it's a very bad one."

Then at the Paisley meeting it was John Maclean who proposed sending greetings to Neil—the one member in the House who refused to rise for "God Save the King" on the occasion of Lloyd George's triumphal return from Paris with the peace treaty in his pocket.

"Neil and I have learned to call each other cousins," he said, "and I congratulate him on keeping his head and his seat. It doesn't matter whether a man is standing up for his class, or sitting down for his class, we're with him."

Apparently in Scotland the different socialist groups are not very far apart. It seems to be more or less an accident which one a man belongs to. They all work together when there is anything to be done.

Maclean's appointment as Russian Consul for Scotland was not a surprise. He had helped to send both guns and pamphlets to Russia from a Scottish port before the revolution of 1905, and he was one of those who welcomed the terrorist refugees who began to land in Scotland in 1907. Petroff, who arrived in 1908, became his close friend and co-worker. When Maclean started the "Vanguard" to beat Hyndman's pro-war "Justice," Petroff became the London agent for it. And later, at the time of Maclean's first arrest, Petroff came up to Glasgow and took over his classes. (Of course long before this Maclean had lost his position as a teacher of Economics in the city schools, and had started his own socialist classes—out of which evolved the Scottish Labour College of which he is now director.) When, soon after the first Russian Revolution, Maclean came out of prison, he started a campaign for the release of Petroff and his wife and Tchicherin, who were at that time held in England. But it was not until after the Bolshevik revolution in November when Trotsky demanded their release and threatened to imprison Sir George Buchanan, the British Ambassador, that the Russians were set free, and allowed to go home. They told Petrograd about Maclean, and his appointment followed. He learned it from the press. The official confirmation never reached him, and all the money he ever received was $250 from Litvinoff just before the latter sailed for Russia. He opened headquarters, nevertheless, and actually acted as Consul—listening to the troubles of the Russian workers of Glasgow and helping them where he could—until April 1918, when he was arrested a second time. This time he got five years, but working-class pressure forced his release soon after the armistice. As a candidate for parliament, nominated while in prison and released only nine days before the election, he polled 7,000 votes.

"What were you arrested for?" I asked him.

"Well—things I said in speeches. The first time it was under D.O.R.A.[2] I was speaking outdoors. Somebody called out, 'Why don't you enlist?' I said, *'I've been a member of the socialist army for five years; God damn all other armies!'* "

"And the second time?"

"Oh, the second time, I guess they didn't need D.O.R.A. to get me. I was urging the people to seize the municipal buildings and banks and electric power stations. I wanted them to start the revolution."

John Maclean and Arthur McManus certainly stand at the left of the Left of the British movement, yet both were Parliamentary candidates last December. Sylvia Pankhurst seems to be the only socialist leader who refuses to have anything to do with political action. Maclean says: "I don't scorn any method. I would use all methods." McManus, who is a leading figure in the shop-steward movement and also in the revolutionary Socialist Labour Party, got 4,000 votes last December on a straight Bolshevik platform—and sees no harm in that fact.

McManus is a "wee fellow," as they say in Glasgow, a rough overworked, undersized, undernourished little fighter, who went into the shops when he was thirteen. He is now perhaps twenty-seven, and recognized as one of the intellectual leaders of the left wing.

In Glasgow, second city in the Empire, both industrial and political expressions of the revolutionary movement find their strongest support. The Socialist Labour Party, which is really the Communist Party of Great Britain and definitely affiliated to the Third International, publishes its monthly journal, the "Socialist," from Glasgow. The "Worker," organ of the Shop Steward Movement (that name can't be Scotch; nobody but an Englishman would express a revolutionary intention in such terms!), is also published in Glasgow.

2. Defense of the Realm Act.

McManus is a frequent contributor to both. He is one of those night and day agitators, always running off to make a speech somewhere. And when he's lucky enough to have a job, *i.e.,* when the demand for labor is so great that some firm will risk employing a known revolutionary agitator, he's an engineer in the shops.

McManus is probably the most able intellectually of the group I met in Glasgow, but I think he is a little too bitter and scornful to make a great leader. He thinks Glasgow should have started the revolution in January. He condemns the leaders and scolds the workers for their failure, making the mistake which is not uncommon among left-wing leaders, of not always identifying himself with the movement. He is a little too given to saying "you" instead of "we" in his speeches. Gallacher, on the other hand, no less eager and ready, no less a scientific revolutionist in mind and spirit, is more generous and more just. He is no fool where a leader has proved false or weak, but he is less ready to condemn. He, too, had a secret hope that the 40-hour strike might "start something." But he identifies himself with the failure, if it was a failure, and is already looking ahead with a warm-hearted faith in his fellow-workers.

William Gallacher was born in Belfast but has lived all his working life on the Clyde. He has been chairman of the Clyde Workers' Committee since its formation in 1915. To understand what that means I must try to explain the Shop Steward Movement, or the "unofficial" movement as it is now commonly called in Glasgow. It seems to be a movement within a movement, a system of workshop committees within the existing trade unions. It is an attempt to capture the trade union movement for the workers, to take it out of politics and bring it back home. Its leaders attack the trades union system not only because it separates the workers into 1,100 different unions but also because its unit is *the branch, (i.e.,* all the members who live in a certain area irrespective of where they work) instead of *the workshop.* They would apply the Soviet idea now to trades-union organization, making a small number of workers (15 to 200) in a certain shop of one plant the unit, and one of their number, called a shop steward, elected and recalled at any time, the representative. The stewards in each shop form a shop-committee. There is a convener of shop stewards for the whole plant, and a plant committee on which each shop committee is represented. From these various plant committees a local workers' committee is chosen, such as the Clyde Workers' Committee, of which Gallacher is chairman. Sheffield and Coventry also have local workers' committees, and others are just about to be formed. But these committees, designed of course to represent all the industries of a district, actually represent so far only the engineering, shipbuilding and kindred trades. And the further development of the scheme by the formation of national industrial committees, and a single national workers' committee elected from these, is as yet only sketched in the literature of the movement.

The shop steward idea offers a radically new plan of representation for the labor movement; the unit of production is made the unit of representation, and it is kept small enough so that there can come no separation between the leaders and the rank and file. There is nothing revolutionary about this; in fact many employers strongly favor the formation of shop committees because they obviate the necessity of dealing with outside trade union officials. But the revolutionary purpose is clear in the minds of the founders of the movement; it aims at establishing industrial unionism ad workers' control just as definitely as the I.W.W. And the machinery of representation lends itself to revolutionary activity. Moreover it gives the workers a strong weapon for organized defiance of the trade union leaders when they prove false, and for forcing their hands if they go too slow. The Glasgow 40-hour strike is a complete illustration of that.

It was Gallacher who gave me a connected story of the strike. Fifty-four hours? Forty-seven hours? Forty-four hours? Forty hours? No; *thirty hours,* six hours a day for five days a week—that's what the miners were demanding, and that's what the Glasgow engineers really wanted. The shorter hours movement was of course primarily for self-preservation, to make place for the thousands of men and women that were emptied out of the streets after the armistice when the wheels began to stop, and for the demobilized soldiers that would come trooping back home looking for work. But it was also an expression of the weariness of these workers after the long war-strain, and a desire for more life, freedom, leisure, education, happiness.

The A.S.E. (Amalgamated Society of Engineers) had voted to demand a reduction of ten hours, making a 44-hour week; its leaders were pledged to this. But after a conference with the employers they distributed a ballot among the men calling for a vote on 54 hours and 47 hours—no mention of 44 hours. The men were confused, they voted of course for 47 hours, but they knew that they had been tricked, and the shorter hours agitation increased. The shop stewards, seeing the opportunity, kept up the agitation, until all the shops were discussing not 44 hours, the original demand, but 40 hours, and 30 hours, and a ways and means committee had been appointed to consider a general strike. On January 11, four days after the 47-hour week went into effect, 200 shop-stewards were in conference with Gallacher in the chair. They had unanimously condemned the 47 hours, and were considering what action to take to get a further reduction, when in came a delegation from the "official" movement, headed by Shinwell, chairman of the Trades Council, to say that they were heart and soul with the rank and file, and suggest "joining forces." A joint committee was formed that day representing the Glasgow Trades Council, Joint District Committees of the Shipbuilding and Engineering Trades, the Scottish Trades Union Congress, and the Shop Stewards. Shinwell was made chairman. It was agreed that the workers in each shop should vote whether to demand 40 hours or 30 hours, that another conference should be held in one week, to ascertain the result, and the joint committee should then call a strike to enforce the finding. On January 18, this conference was held—300 delegates representing not merely the Clyde Valley, but most of industrial Scotland. When reports from all shops were in, it was clear that a decided majority had voted for 30 hours, but by general consent it was decided, in order to carry the big minority with them, to make the 40-hour demand.

On Monday, January 27, the strike was called. Fifty thousand came out the first day; by Wednesday 100,000 were out. Shipbuilding yards and engineering shops were empty, and many other trades responded. There was a central strike committee, a daily strike bulletin reaching 20,000 in circulation, and daily mass meetings of 20,000 gathered inside and outside St. Andrew's Hall.

Mass picketing was the feature of this strike. Five to ten

thousand workers would gather at the gates of a plant at closing time, line up on each side of the road, and when the men came out they'd have to "run the gauntlet,"—not hurry past a hundred odd discouraged pickets, but make their way slowly, one by one, through a narrow lane grudgingly allowed them by the vast crowd of jeering fellow-workers outside. This method never failed. Shop after shop came out, and when they came out, they were the most eager to try the same game on the next shop. Mass pickets of women, the engineers' wives, were found even more effective. The big industrial suburbs were tackled in this way, 5,000 men marching from Glasgow to Paisley, for instance, to picket one shop.

In two respects the strike leaders miscalculated: the municipal employees, despite the presence of their organizer on the joint committee, did not come out; and the response expected from Sheffield, the London district, and the other big engineering districts, failed to come. Gallacher and the other "unofficial" leaders expected workers of all these districts to fall in line, follow Glasgow and make the 40-hour week a national demand. It didn't happen.

Every strike has its crisis. In Glasgow it was Bloody Friday. January 31st. Two days before, a deputation had gone to the Lord Provost (Mayor), and secured a promise that he would communicate with the Prime Minister and Sir Robert Horne (Minister of Labor), place the 40-hour demand before them, and have an answer ready for the strikers on Friday. When Friday came, owing to the efforts of the strike committee and the Bulletin, 40,000 people had gathered in George's Square in front of the municipal building, waiting for the word from London. Kirkwood, Shinwell and Neil Maclean were sent in to get it. They were kept waiting a long time. The crowd was getting impatient. The police armed with their batons were ranged in long rows fronting the Municipal Chambers. Suddenly, trouble started in a far corner of the crowd. Two men were injured by automobiles, and the strikers asked the police to turn all traffic up another street, keeping it out of the square. The answer of the police was a baton charge. Gallacher saw it from the base of a monument in the square, from which he was addressing the crowd.

"I saw the police start, the whole lot of them, driving the crowd, beating them with their batons. I never saw such a sight.

They pressed the crowd so hard that a flagpole in front of me was bent over. And the people were helpless. They were packed in a tight mass, so they could hardly move when the rush came; they were taken by surprise, and *they had nothing in their hands.* It was a paved square, there weren't any stones to pick up, there wasn't any fence or railing to break up. They had nothing but their bare hands. If the boys could have laid their hands on *anything,* it wouldn't have gone the way it did. Well, in a minute, it seemed, I was left alone on the plinth, men were lying all around me trampled and muddy where they had been battened down. I saw a woman lying face down, all in the mud, where she'd been left. I jumped down and lifted her up. Then I ran to an officer and said, 'For God's sake, get this stopped.' He only swore at me. Then I saw the chief, standing and looking on while the police drove that helpless crowd across the square. I didn't stop to think, but just ran up and hit him a terrific blow in the jaw. He's a big man, but I knocked him out. Then in a moment three or four of them were on me. I kept hitting up—hitting them in the jaw from underneath." Here Gallacher jumped up to illustrate, his eyes shining, and his smile as sweet as ever. "But pretty soon they had me down. I was dazed, not really hurt. They picked me up and carried me into the Municipal Chambers under arrest."

Meawhile, the deputation inside, still waiting for the Government's answer, heard the sounds of battle and came running out to the square. Kirkwood, with his usual sense of the dramatic, when he saw what was happening, raised his arms above his head in a gesture of amazement and horror. At that moment he was bludgeoned from behind by a policeman's club, and carried unconscious and bleeding into the Municipal Chambers. He had received the Government's answer. Gallacher, by this time quite recovered, saw them bring Kirkwood in, and helped to bring him back to consciousness, and bandage his broken head. Then together they saw the victims carried in, one striker after another beaten into unconsciousness.

"Suddenly," said Gallacher, "I saw a sight that was like the sun on a rainy day. I saw *policemen* being carried in. 'Thank God!' I said, 'thank God! The boys have found weapons at last.' "

Next day he learned that a lorry of beer bottles on its way to a nearby "pub" had been commandeered by the strikers and used with some effect on the charging police. By this time the strikers had learned that Gallacher and Kirkwood were arrested; this and the lorry of beer bottles turned them from driven sheep into angry and determined men. Almost anything might have happened. The authorities knew this; in their panic they came and begged the two leaders in order to save terrible bloodshed and loss of life, to go out and tell the crowd to go home. The more cautious strike leaders took the same line. But the men on the square were in a different mood. They sent in word. "Say the word, boys, and we'll stay here till kingdom come. Give us half-an-hour, Davie, and we'll annihilate every policeman in Glasgow."

Kirkwood and Gallacher were finally persuaded to go out on a balcony and tell the strikers to go home, after which they were led off to jail. That was the beginning of the end. Shinwell and twenty others were arrested that night. The next morning troops had arrived, several train-loads of them, with machine-guns, tanks, aeroplanes, etc. The sympathetic strikes all over the country, which the Clyde was hoping for, did not take place. Finally the A.S.E. executive, acting with the government and employers, *suspended the Glasgow District Committee.* On February 11, the strike was called off. Two months later Gallacher and Shinwell were sentenced respectively to three months and five months in prison.

I asked Gallacher if he was glad or sorry he had told the crowd to go home that Friday in the square.

"I couldn't do anything else," he said. "They put the decision on me. I was safe inside. I couldn't say, 'Go ahead and get killed.' If I had been outside I could have said, 'Come on—it's worth getting killed for,' but being inside myself, how could I?"

Gallacher is the sort of leader the Shop Steward Movement is designed to produce. He has never had a salary, never even had his expenses paid by the movement. He is a skilled brass-finisher, has always worked at his trade when he wasn't in jail, and wants to go right on doing it. He has no political ambition; I don't know that he is even definitely affiliated with any one of the three socialist parties. Nor does he want to be a labor organizer. He wants to *agitate on the job.* Perhaps the best thing about these labor leaders of the new order—next to their determination to keep on being workingmen—

is their love of poetry. It is so common that I wasn't surprised when I asked William Gallacher what message he would send from the Clyde to the workers of America, to hear him begin quoting Whitman—

"Come, my tan-faced children,
Follow well in order, have your weapons ready.
Have you your pistols? Have you your sharp-edged axes?
Pioneers! O Pioneers!"

The Socialist Party Convention

"We must make clear what kind of socialists we are. We must have a key-note in this campaign," said Holland, the clearest-headed leader of the Minority in the Socialist Convention. "Is the key-note to be— 'We are the only 100 per cent American party destined to uphold the Constitution of the United States,' or is it to be. . . ."

But he never made clear the alternative. Nor did any other member of the Minority make it clear. They were an earnest and honest Minority—about one-third of the delegates, and they could see that something was wrong with the Majority, but they had no firm ground of their own from which to attack it. They were soft and vague and unorganized and entirely spontaneous in their attacks. The effect of their presence, therefore, was merely to modify in a few points the glaringly conservative measures adopted by the Majority and lend the support of their numbers, and their sincere revolutionary intentions, to a movement absolutely controlled and guided by persons with contrary intentions.

The Liberator, July 1920.

It seems to me that the key-note of any socialist campaign at the present time must obviously concern our attitude toward the decaying institutions of political democracy. And there are just two possible attitudes. On the one hand we can say something like this:

"Despite the complete breakdown of the most essential democratic institutions during the past four years, commencing with the overthrow of the vital guarantees embodied in the first amendment to the Constitution, and reaching its climax when Congress twice refused to seat a man duly elected to represent his district in that body because he was a socialist, and when the Legislative Body of our largest state arbitrarily expelled five Socialist members, thus denying the very principle of majority representation on which the Republic is founded, nevertheless we reaffirm our faith in democracy, we assert our abiding belief in the sacredness of its institutions, we declare that progress can continue only by a return to those institutions: and whereas all other political parties have basely forsaken the Constitution we declare our everlasting allegiance to it, we feel ourselves called by destiny to restore political democracy and bring this erring nation back to the faith of its fathers."

On the other hand we can say something like this:

"The last four years in America have demonstrated as never before in the history of the world, that human liberty cannot be secured or maintained through the institutions of political democracy. Those vital safeguards of the First Amendment, never of much practical value in protecting the poorest workers, were completely abandoned by the government in the first week of war and have never been restored. Without freedom of speech, of assembly, of the press, the principle of majority representation is a mockery. The denial of these rights is a virtual disfranchisement of the workers. But not satisfied with this, the ruling class, by twice refusing to seat a duly elected Socialist Congressman and expelling five duly elected Socialist assemblymen from the New York State Legislature, has proved that any inconvenient provision of the constitution can be set aside, and has taken a long bold step toward openly disfranchising all who advocate fundamental changes in the form of government. These developments do not surprise us. They merely confirm our opinion and serve to emphasize a cardinal point in our socialist philosophy, that the state under capitalism, whether it be a democratic or an autocratic state, is bound to be, not a reconciler of, or arbitrator between classes, but an agent of

the exploiting class. They serve to recall to reason those socialists who have put democracy before socialism, who have vainly expected the capitalist state to maintain democratic institutions against its own interest, and to stand quietly by while socialists, exercising their constitutional rights, vote to destroy it. The experiences of the last four years, which after all have been but the logical development of democracy under capitalism,—have recalled us from those childlike dreams to the stern realities of the class-struggle.

"Therefore, while we unite with all honest liberals in demanding the 'restoration' of civil and political liberty in America, we know that the way to 'restore' liberty is to destroy the capitalist system. And while we shall continue to exercise our political rights, whenever and wherever a capitalist government allows us, we know that the great hope of realizing socialism lies in the leadership of the masses by the workers organized in the industrial field, and that the chief function of a political party of socialism is to define, interpret and explain the industrial struggle, and educate the workers to play their historic part."

The choice was made between these two possible "key-notes" long before the convention began. The Stars and Stripes were as thick to the square inch on the walls of Finnish Hall, May 10th to 17th, as they can possibly be in Chicago or San Francisco. "Back to Democracy and the Constitution" was the key-note.

"I don't want any dictatorship, I want democracy," shouted Berger. And what Berger says is usually what the other right-wingers think. Berger would rather go on fighting for his life and liberty and his right to sit in Congress in this capitalist democracy, than take a chance under a rough-and-tumble working-class government, and he says so. Ex-Assemblyman Waldman is also frank about his opinions. When he said up at Albany that he preferred the government of New York State to the Soviet government of Russia, it was not a false and cowardly admission. He knew he would feel more at home sitting on the steps of the Capital at Albany with the door shut in his face, then he would as a re-callable delegate to an industrial Soviet under communism, and he said so. Ex-Assemblyman Solomon's contribution at the Convention was equally frank: "I am proud of being 100 per cent American," he said, "I support the Constitution. It is Sweet and Lusk who have betrayed Americanism."

Indeed the Preamble of the platform itself, drafted it is understood by Hillquit, makes this key-note of the Socialist campaign quite clear.

"In the short space of three years," it says, "our self-styled liberal administration has succeeded in undermining the very foundation of political liberty and economic rights which this republic has built up in more than a century of struggle and progress. . . .

"America is now at the parting of the roads. If the outraging of political liberty and concentration of economic power is permitted to go on, it can have only one consequence, the reduction of the country to a state of absolute capitalist despotism.

"The Socialist Party sounds the warning. It calls upon the people to defeat both old parties at the polls, and to elect the candidates of the Socialist Party to the end of restoring political democracy and bringing about complete industrial freedom."

These leaders of the Socialist Party seem to have forgotten what it was like before the war. They talk about profiteering as though it were a new phenomenon, as though "charging what the traffic will bear" were not always the principle under which capitalist business is conducted. They talk about civil liberty as though it were a blessing enjoyed by all prior to April 3, 1917. Have they forgotten Ludlow and Lawrence? Have they never read the findings of Frank Walsh's Industrial Commission? Don't they know that there has been no free speech in Homestead since 1892, nor in any other unorganized steel town? Don't they realize that the shooting of five detectives in West Virginia last month was the final flaming revolt against conditions of feudal tyranny which have prevailed in non-union mining towns for thirty years? Consider an ignorant foreign miner living in a company camp in West Virginia, with no right to go or come except on a company pass, with no right to attend a meeting, with company detectives watching to see that he doesn't get together with four or five fellow workers and talk things over, with company guards ready to shoot down any union organizer who attempts to get in and teach him his rights. He has been in that situation ever since he came to this country. What is the sense in telling him that he was free up to April 3rd, 1917, and now we are going to restore that freedom?

Surely a socialist ought to know that the First Amendment is as good to-day as it ever was. And it was never any good in a crisis. It has never been proof against a strain. The war was a very big strain, that's all. The contest of industrial forces set going by the war is a bigger strain still, and the breakdown of democratic institutions is correspondingly more complete. Our revolutionary understanding ought also to be more complete.

But the war, which brought socialists and liberals together in the fight to maintain civil liberty, was as bad for the socialists as it was good for the liberals. The fight for free speech demanded constant reference to the Constitution and the Declaration of Independence. To demand that these documents be lived up to, was the most revolutionary thing a socialist leader could do, except go to jail. And from demanding that they should be lived up to, some of these leaders have apparently gotten into the habit of believing they will be lived up to, and that when they are, that will be the Social Revolution.

Hillquit spoke playfully perhaps when he said that the Socialist Party is "the only conservative party in the United States," but he stated the literal truth. The two old parties have progressed rapidly during this military and economic crisis. They have thrown over the old-fashioned political ways of thought, along with the old documents, and are bending almost all their energies to perfecting the economic dictatorship of the capitalists. The Socialist Party leaders have taken the opposite course. They have abandoned their former economic view-point, ceased to criticize the political forms of democracy, and taken refuge in pre-Marxian documents like the Constitution and the Declaration of Independence. They are the party of old-fashioned Americanism.

Their preamble could be taken over verbatim by Hiram Johnson if he should bolt the Republican convention next week. And their whole program would make an excellent getting-together ground for the Committee of Forty Eight, the Labor Party and the Non-Partisan League when they meet in Chicago next July. There is something in it for everybody; cancellation of war debts, democratically elected international parliament, free trade, disarmament, and self-determination for the liberal pacifists; election and recall of federal judges, direct election and recall of President, an easier method of amending the constitution, for the civic reformers; an anti-injunction clause, child labor, minimum wage, and shorter workday provisions for "labor." It goes without saying that "trade with Russia," "Recognition of the Irish Republic," Amnesty, and Repeal of the Espionage Act are included. The Social Worker will be glad to find government insurance covering sickness, accident, old age and unemployment. The Single Taxer is well provided for. And of course there is a comprehensive government ownership plank, with a sort of Plumb Plan provision for administering publicly owned industries "jointly by the government and representatives of the workers," for those who are socialistically inclined.

As for the Declaration of Principles—it seems to have been written with the double purpose of fooling the party rank and file by half a dozen paragraphs of good socialist theory, and fooling the Department of Justice and the New York Assembly by a naïve insistence on the party's innocence of the intentions implied in that theory. A characteristic sentence is this:

"The Socialist Party seeks to attain its end by orderly and constitutional methods, *so long as* the ballot box, the right of representation and civil liberties are maintained."

The italics under "so long as" are mine.

Several thousand political and industrial prisoners already serving long sentences in jail and no end to the prosecutions; excessive bail a common place; search, seizure and arrest without warrant a notorious practice; martial law in every big strike district; the socialist and labor press struggling against complete post-office tyranny; free speech so dead that hundreds of bourgeois liberals,—clergymen, editors, lawyers, even a senator and congressman or two,—are out crusading to revive it; Berger twice thrown out of Congress; the five Socialist Assemblymen just picking themselves up from the steps of the State House at Albany;—What more do they want?

What wonder that capitalist editors in New York believed these Socialist leaders to be insincere, and merely adopting a fake platform as camouflage for a secret revolutionary plot? The press thought they were insincere because it could not believe that they were so simple.

But I can testify that there were no revolutionary plots, secret or otherwise, in the air at that convention.

There was just one moment in the whole week when the spirit of revolution breathed over it. That was on Thursday afternoon, the fifth day, when Debs was nominated for president. Debs' friend, Henry of Indiana, in an awkward little nominating speech, told of his recent visit to Atlanta—of how as he walked along the prison corridor with the guard he caught sight of that beloved figure, the great, gaunt man in prison clothes. He told of Debs' sudden childlike joy and surprise on seeing him,—the beaming smile, the long arms stretched out, the simple human cry, "Oh, comrade, I am so glad to see you!" . . .

Why is the thought of Debs in jail so heart-breaking? It isn't because he is sixty years old. It is because he has the heart of a child,—warm, trusting, merry heart,—and who can think of a shut-in child without crying?

Tears and cheers dissolve for the moment most differences, but nothing will make Engdahl and Kruse and Glassberg and Holland and Tucker and Dreyfus, and the rest of that large Minority, *who actually represented Debs' opinions at this convention,* forget what happened the next day. The Illinois delegation had come instructed to censure the lawyers who defended the New York State Assemblymen at Albany. Friday was their last chance to do it, for not a word about the Albany affair had been allowed to creep into the proceedings of the convention, and they had to make their own opportunity. After warning everybody that they were going to do it, and that they were doing it in no unfriendly spirit but rather for the sake of harmony and unity, they drafted and introduced a resolution of "regret." Tucker read it. It specifically mentioned three statements taken verbatim from the record at Albany.

(a) That in case of attack upon this government by the Soviet government of Russia, American socialists would fight for the U.S. government and against the Soviet government.—*Hillquit.*

(b) That the government of New York State is preferable to the Soviet government of Russia.—*Waldman.*

(c) That the provision which requires an elected socialist official to place his tentative resignation in the hands of his constituents on taking office, so that he can be recalled if he ceases to do their will, is a dead letter.—*Gerber*.

After quoting these statements, the resolution continued on its gentle way: "We regret that these statements were made and we declare that they do not truly express the position of the National Socialist Party."

But all that gentleness was wasted. They might just as well have said, "We heartily condemn and excoriate these base betrayers of our cause." For the moment Tucker stopped reading, Hillquit, no longer suave and satirical, but ugly with anger, arose to his feet, demanding *a vote of censure* on those who had introduced this resolution! His motion was lost in a general storm of indignation against the Illinois delegation, but before a single word had been allowed in defense of the resolution, Meyer London moved that it be expunged from the record. And while a half dozen minority members were still demanding the floor, and protesting their desire to "explain," and while Hillquit, London and the other Majority leaders were shouting "No! No! Sit down! We don't want to hear you!" London's motion was put and carried in a toss.

That was the real spirit of the ruling groups of the Socialist Convention. And it convinces me that Debs would not have been their chosen candidate if he hadn't been safe in prison, where he will lend them the glory of his name without the embarrassment of his clear-thinking revolutionary leadership.

But why not go back further? I like to think that if Debs had been "out" last summer, if his wisdom and experience and generous spirit had been at the service of the growing numbers of the left-wing,—as, granting his freedom, I think it would have been, we should have had a different sort of split. Instead of the more actively discontented left-wingers being forced out to form a new party, the more hopelessly conservative right-wingers would have been forced out to form a new party, or to affiliate in some way with the growing Labor Party as many of the honest reformists among them desire to do. That would have left the American Socialist Party in the control of its genuine majority, unmistakably communist in thought and purpose, and definitely affiliated with the Third International.

The British
Labour Party Conference

It is very unlikely that all the delegates to the recent British Labour Party Conference agreed with Mr. Sidney Webb when he declared in his presidential address that "Robert Owen and not Karl Marx was the founder of British Socialism." The true believers might well have replied, "There is no British Socialism. There is only Socialism and it is international." But there was no spoken protest and Mr. Webb's able address, with its insistence on political democracy and a gradual progress, with its emphasis on "brotherhood" and consequent disavowal of the class war, was allowed to stand as the keynote utterance of the conference. Sudden increase in power and responsibility have had their usual effect; these Labour Party leaders seem to walk a bit soberly to-day, as though they feared they might wake up some morning and find the destinies of the Empire actually in their hands. The conference was considerably enlivened by the expulsion of four Scottish members from Parliament, and it was enormously cheered and heartened by the opportunity to welcome Robert Smillie as a Labour M.P. It is the general opinion that Mr. Smillie will help to give unity and coherence to His Majesty's Opposition. There is such confidence in his honesty and intelligence on all sides, that he may even be able to reconcile the emotional Scotch extremists and the parliamentarians. It is felt that if Mr. Smillie believed certain "economies" meant the death of little children he would be quite capable of calling a man who urged them a murderer but that he would know how to do it in parliamentary language.

Time and Tide, 6 July 1923.

APPENDIX

Portia Appointed by
the Governor

Miss Crystal Eastman,
the One Woman of the Fourteen Members
of the Employers' Liability Commission,
of Which She Is Secretary,
Investigates Industrial Accidents—
Scope and Intent of the Work

A few years ago there was a popular belief at the University of Pennsylvania that for a standard of feminine loveliness—well, unloveliness—all you had to do was to glance over the Law School co-

New York Herald, 24 April 1910, Magazine Section.

eds. The co-eds were treated with according chivalry. When one managed to survive the first year she was looked upon with a kind of awe; otherwise she wasn't looked upon at all.

The woman lawyer usually is pictured as sacrificing beauty to brains. Her bulging brow swallows up the rest of her face, and she's rather glad of it. Portia in floating garments, with curls peeping from under a fetching bonnet, parades only through the pages of Shakespeare or behind the footlights. And even then, to be taken seriously, she has to obviously masquerade as a man. The beauty of to-day who walks the devious ways of legal knowledge is apt to be a militant suffragette, regarding law merely as a side issue to the great cause.

That is why a gasp of pleasurable astonishment is the result of your first meeting with Crystal Eastman. For Miss Eastman, in spite of a fine brow, has brown eyes that laugh and dimples which she finds rather difficult to suppress. Likewise, she has youth, a charming, girlish manner—and seems to delight in making you overlook the fact that her name trails an A.B., for which Vassar is responsible; an M.A., bestowed by Columbia, and an LL.B., the result of a law course at New York University. These titles are as a court train— mere adjuncts to the attractive woman.

You look at Miss Eastman, talk to her, and come rapidly to the conclusion that the State was wise in appointing her the one woman among thirteen men of the Employers' Liability Commission. The commission, of which Miss Eastman is secretary, has been formed to investigate industrial accidents and prepare a report on the same for this session of the Legislature.

When the Governor of New York selects a young woman of— well, I'm not quite sure, but decidedly young, anyway, to fill a post of great responsibility, she must possess a personality of vital interest to the outside world.

In a suite set high up in the Metropolitan Building there's a large outer room whose occupants at desk and typewriters look up in quick welcome when an athletic blue serge figure and a face already smiles swing in from the corridor like the embodiment of fresh air, fun and big vitality. Each morning between nine and ten Miss Eastman hurries through the larger room and into her private office, a diminutive place, half window, the rest cased in shining metal like a vault for valuables. The telephone jangles—there's not a second of feminine uncertainty in the conversation that follows, not an instant's hesitation in directions given.

An incident in the life of Crystal Eastman's mother offers, I think, a key to the daughter's character. The wife of the Rev. S. E. Eastman, though intensely and, what is more, intelligently interested in her husband's work, was first of all the home woman, devoted to her three children and entirely apart from the class known as "professional." When the two brothers of Miss Eastman were still small boys, and she herself was scarcely eight years of age, the father fell ill, without expectation of recovery. The necessity of supporting the family devolved upon the mother, and, with that quiet resource which occasionally astonishes one in the gentlewoman, she took her husband's place in the pulpit, proving herself so thoroughly efficient that when he finally recovered they continued to work together. They have now Park Church, Elmira, N.Y.

"Not that my mother is any more the professional woman now than she was years ago," Miss Eastman added, in telling the story. "She's brilliant and capable, but in temperament she tends all the other way."

And in the mother you have the secret of Crystal Eastman's success—Pluck!

Just before her graduation from New York University, in 1907, she faced the allurements of beginning the practice of law on about $5 a week.

From Two Standpoints

"You see, I hadn't any money to begin with," she explained, leaning forward earnestly in her wide desk chair. "Then I learned that the Pittsburg Survey was sending investigators to study conditions in the great steel district of Pennsylvania and an opportunity to investigate industrial accidents for them was open to me. That's how I came to take up this work. I'd been interested in the Employers' Liability law for a long time."

"From a humanitarian or legal standpoint?" the writer interrupted.

"Both. I considered it bad law, and unjust, unfair to the

employe. But principally, it interested me from a legal viewpoint." The lawyer triumphed over the woman. "I went to Pittsburg expecting to be there about two months and stayed more than a year. Eight months after my return to New York, I began work with the commission."

Just a word of this Liability law and its relation to the numbers swallowed up each year in the great maelstrom of industry, or better still, some stories from accident cases investigated under Miss Eastman's direction. In hearing her discuss the work, you feel the force and sincerity of the woman, but none of that fanaticism usually credited to the feminine enthusiast. When she thinks her assistant may have more intimate knowledge of any particular case, she refers unhesitatingly to him. The following are a few of the stories related to the writer:—

John Simpson, engineer, had for thirty-eight years been employed in iron works in Twelfth street. One day he was given a "green" helper. Simpson objected, but on being assured that the man was competent began during the noon hour to make repairs on an engine. The helper, through a mistake, started the engine. Simpson was mangled, crushed like a fly on a cartwheel.

His widow went to the company that had for so many years employed him. They sent her to the liability insurance company with which they were insured. There the claim adjuster rather scoffed at the possibility of her having any claim, since the law provides that a master is not held liable for the negligence of his employes if the person injured is a fellow-worker—not a stranger, that is. Finally he agreed to settle for $200. Again she went to her husband's firm. They deplored the fact that under their agreement with the insurance company, by which all such cases were immediately turned over, they could do nothing. Her husband had worked for them so long that they would have liked to assist her, but they were helpless in the matter.

An act to provide compensation—but limited to a certain proportion of wages earned—without considering the question of negligence, is now being urged. This would do away with the necessity for a medium to settle damages, as well as the eternal question of interminable litigation.

It is remarkable the ingenuity displayed by the type of lawyer known as "ambulance chaser." A woman living in Second avenue was called to the nearest telephone, which happened to be located in a corner drug store. There she was informed by the police that her son, employed by the Interborough Rapid Transit, had been hit by a derrick mast while going under a bridge, and instantly killed. The woman, too stunned to realize her loss, hurried home. When she reached her flat in the tenement house she found a lawyer already waiting to take her case.

During the days that followed she was fairly besieged, a steady stream of strangers offering to make a fortune for her. One even exhibited as a testimonial the photograph of an eighteen thousand dollar check he insisted had been recovered by him in a similar accident case. In the face of such evidence it is scarcely astonishing to find the poor hastening to place themselves in the hands of the magician.

The woman in this case, however, finally settled for substantial compensation, one of the few instances, according to Miss Eastman's investigation, in which a fair sum has been paid without lawsuit.

Another Story

A contrasting story is that of an Italian killed in March, 1908, while at work on a building in Lexington avenue. He had started work only that day. The scaffolding where he stood had been broken and carefully nailed over. But it broke just the same and the man was killed. A troop of lawyers instantly descended upon his flat in East 108th street and his widow was forced to barricade herself against them. She locked her door, for several days allowing no one in the place, even barring neighbors who might have helped her. Then she appealed to the company that had employed her husband. They would look into the matter, they said, but at present could do nothing. That was two years ago. Friends at the time gathered together $30 for her. The oldest child, a boy not yet eighteen, is now out of work; the youngest is a baby, born after the father's death. There are five others, who manage to struggle along in the miraculous way hungry children often have.

In the following case a coroner's jury censured a landlord for the death of a man employed as janitor, yet nothing was done in the way of compensation. The husband of Mrs. Rapp, a Russian of the better class, was the janitor of a Thirteenth street house owned by a woman living abroad. Rapp informed the agent that the dumbwaiter rope was in bad condition. The agent looked at it, declared it to be safe and nothing was done in the way of repair. The next day the rope broke. The dumbwaiter fell and struck Rapp, causing his death.

Immediately the agent tried to get rid of the widow, children and baby grandchild of the victim. He wanted to put them out before the week of customary prayers and mourning had passed, but tenants of the house raised such an outcry, threatening to leave in a body, that the woman was permitted to remain two weeks longer.

Speaking English with difficulty, Mrs. Rapp later allowed herself to be taken to a lawyer, who has given her principally promises. Had her husband not been insured in a fraternal order of which he was a member the woman and her family would have become charges of charity. Now she helps things along by washing, scrubbing and cleaning houses.

The Public Service Commission receives a report of all railroad and street railway accidents to the individual workman. Those in factories are reported to the State Labor Commissioner. But in the case of building trade accidents no statistics are to be had save the few that labor unions can supply.

Francis Bashton acted as night watchman where a stoop was being taken down and Fifth avenue widened. He had often told his wife it was a dangerous place and poorly protected. One morning he was found in the basement, dead. There is no knowledge of when the accident occurred, the man having fallen, probably, through uncertain planking. Whatever the cause, immediately after his death proper protection was placed about the opening.

The man's wife was treated in accordance with the lack of definite knowledge. She was offered $200 by the same claim adjuster that had disposed of the case previously mentioned. Finally she decided to accept the sum, but was put off a month, while the incident was forgotten and the witnesses scattered. Then came a letter informing her that the insurance company could give her nothing. The woman, who is ill, cannot attend to the matter herself and her two daughters, telephone girls earning $5 a week each, are too busy to give the time to it.

These, as I have said, are but a small fraction of the instances the investigations of Miss Eastman have brought to light.

Her sympathies are like the Tower of Pisa, strong enough to lean definitely in one direction—that of organized labor—without fear of sinking or falling to the level of prejudice. A paragraph from a paper read by her recently at a meeting in Rochester of the New York State Bar Association will explain her attitude toward cases of the kind above mentioned.

"Would it be any more just," she says, in speaking of the injuries and deaths which occur in the course of work, "to shift all this great economic loss from the largely inevitable accidents of industry over on to the employer merely because he owns and controls the enterprise? Perhaps not. I suggest merely that the loss be shared between the injured workman and his employer. For all these years we have implied in the contract of hire an assumption of risk on the part of the workman on the ground that his compensation was adjusted to cover that risk. Now let us turn around and imply in the contract of hire an assumption on the part of an employer to insure his workmen against risk—to a limited amount, say one-half of the loss involved."

It's quite possible that some of those who listened to such words of wisdom emanating from lips red and well formed though firm may have found their thoughts wandering during the progress of the address. Eloquence will emphasize a woman's attraction! For the further edification of these, no doubt, as well as the numbers who were not present, the paper has been printed and five thousand copies ordered for distribution

The Woman

It is one of the freaks of fate that the only daughter of a family should have chosen to follow the most difficult, most tortuous road to success. Of Miss Eastman's brothers one is a doctor, the other head of the Men's League for Woman's Suffrage. Comparatively easy callings, both of them. For the doctor of to-day in these United States need only make a specialty of soothing overwrought feminine nerves and he finds the flag of "Excelsior" floating at no great distance ahead; while the suffragist of masculine gender is a hero of the hour. But to be a woman and lawyer at one and the same time means to make good in both capacities before you'll be trusted in either.

The tone of Miss Eastman's present work is not all drab. In going over the following story her brown eyes snapped merrily. It was the straw held until the last to tickle one into laughter.

There's nothing extraordinary, to be sure, in the Lothario who leaves his wife, save perhaps the fact that the one in question, an engineer, took with him their two children when he disappeared from the home in Floyd street, Brooklyn. Later we find him "married" once more and living in East Seventy-fifth street, New York.

That was his place of residence when Nemesis descended in the form of an ashlift that crushed him to death. Wife number one, learning of the accident, immediately looked up her successor, to offer condolence, it may be. The other had received $75, half of the compensation obtained by her lawyer. She gave her visitor a glimpse of the latter's two children, displaying at the same time a baby of her own. Amenities were exchanged, an amicable agreement made, and now the women with their three children are living together comfortably in Floyd street, Brooklyn.

Talk about accepting the goods the gods provide!

Just as the Englishman enjoys nothing so much as settling his affairs across a satisfying dinner, so anything not immediately connected with her own office work is disposed of by Miss Eastman at luncheon. Over the table the writer discovered that she is an ardent champion of the shirtwaist strikers. A chance remark that vanity, a love of pretty things beyond the limit of their pursestrings, was responsible for their dissatisfaction called forth a vehement defence of them. Were it not out of place that discussion might here be set down. When Miss Eastman argues the woman promptly gives place to the lawyer, clear headed, clear eyed, decisive, the adversary in every word and gesture. No, there's nothing particularly friendly in her method of argument. Needless to say, on this occasion the lawyer won out—perhaps that is why the writer modestly refrains from elaborating.

It seems almost superfluous to add that Miss Eastman is a suffragette. She is—and working with all the strength of her broad shoulders to push the cause.

Yet in spite of her many irons in the fire of activity she does not scorn the feminine arts and graces. The mention of music promptly arouses her enthusiasm and she naively suggests that she has rather a good voice herself. She enjoys the theatre as much as any girl and laughs at the idea of banishing the frivolities of life because one happens to be engaged in serious work. Neither, by the way, does she snap her fingers at the idea of matrimony.

And that is the crowning beauty of Crystal Eastman. She's as clear as her name, well balanced, natural and normal.

Before she leaves the temporary quarters of the commission, in the Metropolitan Building, her book, "Work Accidents and the Law," based on her studies in and about Pittsburg, will be published by the Russell Sage Foundation.

It is easy to picture her, when that work on which she is now engaged has been completed, flinging herself into the practice of law with the same energy and ability. But, on the side, there comes a vision of staid Judge and belligerent opponent when they face this modern Portia of dancing eyes and real—not to say bewildering—dimples.

Miss Eastman was asked to glance over parts of the foregoing. To the astonishment of the writer she made a significant cross at the last word of the last line.

"Can't you cut this?" she asked modestly. "I hate to have—them mentioned."

The writer gazed at "them." "How could we?" she puzzled. "They're there, aren't they?"

"But I can't help that!" The woman triumphed over the lawyer, and laughed.

The writer, being also a woman, smiled "I dare say you wouldn't if you could," she replied.

Crystal Eastman in Hungary

It will be good news to the readers of *The Liberator* that one of its editors, was the first American Socialist to carry greetings in person to the new Soviet Republic of Hungary. The following account of Crystal Eastman's address to the Central Council in Budapest, was translated from a Soviet paper by the correspondent of the New York Globe.

"Miss Crystal Eastman of New York brought greetings from the American workmen, and said it was the most beautiful moment of her life when she could address the central council of the Hungarian Soviet republic.

"Describing the American labor movement, Miss Eastman said that the capitalists had placed in prison thousands of the workers and their leaders. Thus the old leader, Debs, was given ten years because he talked against war. (Cries of 'That was a shame!') Four very young Russian children, including a young girl, were condemned to twenty-five years in prison because they said in a pamphlet that President Wilson was a hypocrite. They said that he was talking of freedom and at the same time was trying to destroy the new freedom of the Russian proletariat.

"Miss Eastman ended her speech with the statement that the American movement, just as every other movement of the world, can only aid in the world revolution. The victory of the Russian proletariat which has come over to Hungary will spread to all the other countries of the word and likewise will lead to the liberation of the American proletariat. The speech was greeted with great applause. It was translated by one of the people's commissars. President Agostin begged the foreign guests (there were others besides Miss Eastman) in the name of the Soviet, to accept the thanks of the Hungarian Soviet and convey its greetings to the foreign workmen."

The Liberator, August 1919.

Feminist for Equality,
Not "Women as Women"

Crystal Eastman Explains
She Favors Election of Congressional Candidates
on Account of their Principles,
Not of Their Sex

By Elisabeth Smith

There was once a time when the face cards of a deck bore the likenesses of Caesar, Charlemagne, Alexander and David. Woman was not permitted a place in the pack.

Women have come a long ways since those days.

So far, in fact, that the names of five women candidates for Congress appear on the ticket for the coming election in the State of Pennsylvania. They are Mrs. Elizabeth R. Culbertston, Mrs. Jennie Dornblum, Mrs. Jessie Collet, Miss Anna Van Skite, and Mrs. Daisy Detterline.

These women all belong to the National Woman's Party and are backed by the party.

Which fact may cost them the vote of some women. Unkind Victorian ladies here and there have been known to hold a secret belief that some of the members of the National Woman's Party might sign themselves with the name of Celia C. Cuckoo.

It has remained for Crystal Eastman to extend, in our opinion, the olive branch to the enemies of the National Woman's Party and to advance the only sane reasons for the support of the party that we

New York Telegram and Evening Mail, 31 October 1924. Crystal Eastman was in 1924 the secretary of the Women for Congress Campaign Committee of the National Woman's Party. Sarah Pell, Charlotte Boissevain, Rosalind Fuller, Ruth Hale, Fannie Hurst, Ruth Pickering, Blair Niles, Doris Stevens and other of Crystal's longtime associates were members of the committee. [B.W.C.]

have heard. Possibly Miss Eastman's own vivid personality and forceful manner of presenting her arguments do quite as much to convince the listener as the argument which she presents.

"Women as Women? Never!"

The National Woman's Party is frequently quoted as holding that women should hold office merely because they are women. Miss Eastman has still another argument to offer.

"Women as women bore me to death," Miss Eastman began, and it sounded like a bombshell, in view of her feminist affiliations.

"To me it is comparatively unimportant whether or not these five women candidates are elected to office, although I have every hope that they will be," Miss Eastman went on to tell us.

"What is extremely important to me is that the Equal Rights Amendment is passed.

"I do not care whether this amendment is passed by men or women. I am for these women candidates not because they are women, but because they belong to our party, which is backing the equal rights amendment. It is difficult to get pledged backers of the amendment among men, and for that reason I am backing these women who will support it.

"I would not have a woman go to Congress merely because she is a woman. I would rather vote for a man that I know will be a strong backer of the equal rights amendment than for a woman that I know will be only a luke-warm backer of the amendment.

"I do believe these five women candidates would do well in Congress because they have shown that they have courage and determination in the fight for election that they have made. If they have courage and determination in this fight, they will have them in questions in general which may arise when they are in office.

"Interested in Equality"

"I am not interested in women just because they are women. I am interested, however, in seeing that they are no longer classed with children and minors. As long as they continue to be, their own

psychology suffers. The equal rights amendment will have a wonderful effect not only on the attitude of men toward women, but of
women toward women.

"Within ten years the battle of the protective laws versus
equality will be won. The question will be a dead issue. There will no
longer be any possible dispute as to whether or not women are on an
equal footing with men. It will be an accepted fact that they are.

"Many women who did not fight for suffrage will fight against
the protective laws. Women were fighting against these years before
suffrage was granted, and they will continue to fight years afterward
and until the battle is won.

"I can pay no greater tribute to the Woman's Party and to Alice
Paul than when I say that in a year and a half they can influence public
opinion, whereas methods different from theirs would take at least
twenty years to influence it.

"The leaders of the Woman's Party have that rare combination
of zeal, fanaticism, shrewdness, political judgment and executive
ability that makes for success.

"Women have a higher station in the United States than they
have abroad, but this country has far fewer women in public offices
than foreign countries. In foreign parliaments, women are well
represented. . . .

"Should Not Quarrel"

"I feel it is unfortunate there should be high words between
women in America today on the subject of equal rights. The women
who oppose the amendment are sincere. Many of them are good
friends of mine. I know they have their own point of view and their
reason for it.

"Both sides, however, should maintain a dignity of position.
Both sides should recognize that the other side has its arguments and
should respect them."

Crystal Eastman has long been known as a flaming feminist. As
she explained herself to us, she was "born to it." Her mother was a
woman preacher and from childhood Miss Eastman held advanced
views about women's rights.

Yet Miss Eastman, flaming feminist that she is, had admitted that women as women "bore her to death"; that she would not vote for a woman for Congress "just because she was a woman"; that the Woman's Party has "fanaticism."

It is these frank admissions of Miss Eastman's which make for much of her force and charm. She is no blind follower of any crowd or cult. She sees facts and blinks nothing.

She has only recently returned from abroad. Her husband is Walter G. Fuller, who is with the *Westminster Weekly*. Miss Eastman says that eventually she and her husband and their two children will divide their time between England and America.

Crystal Eastman

---

by Freda Kirchwey

Crystal Eastman is dead. And all over the world there are women and men who will feel touched with loss, who will look on a world that seems more sober, more subdued. In her short life Crystal Eastman brushed against many other lives, and wherever she moved she carried with her the breath of courage and a contagious belief in the coming triumph of freedom and decent human relations. These were her religion. She preached it in many places and in many forms. In the struggle for woman's suffrage and for equality between men and women; in her work for peace and the rule of reason among peoples; in the fight for social justice and human liberty—as feminist, pacifist, socialist—she fought for her faith. Her strength, her beauty, her vitality and enthusiasm, her rich and compelling personality—

Obituary, *The Nation*, 8 August 1928.

these she threw with reckless vigor into every cause that promised a finer life to the world. She spent herself wholly, and died—too young.

Crystal Eastman was a great leader. Those who knew her, know these words are not too strong. When she spoke to people—whether it was to a small committee or a swarming crowd—hearts beat faster and nerves tightened as she talked. She was simple, direct, dramatic. Force poured from her strong body and her rich voice, and people followed where she led. Her vitality overflowed into thousands of other feebler spirits and made them, for the moment at least, into the likeness of herself. In her personal as in her public life her enthusiasm and strength were spent without thought; she had no pride or sense of her own power. Her capacity for warm and generous friendships seemed unlimited.

Early in her life Crystal Eastman studied law and was admitted to the bar; but she gave up legal work to turn to social studies. She wished to come closer to human beings in their social and industrial lives and to bring a trained understanding to the devious causes of their troubles. She helped make the famous Pittsburgh survey for the Russell Sage Foundation; later she was appointed a member—the only woman member—of the New York State Employers' Liability Commission. She became its secretary and in 1911 published a masterly report on "Work Accidents and the Law." But Crystal Eastman came honestly by her zeal and her capacity for leadership, and social work could not hold her. Her father and mother, both Congregational ministers, were the center of intellectual vigor and freedom in their up-State town, and her mother particularly was an active advocate of "women's rights" in the days when such a stand took courage and humor and a readiness to endure ridicule and dislike. Crystal Eastman flung her ardent energies into the suffrage fight. She became State leader of the suffrage forces in Wisconsin in 1911 and 1912. From then on until the vote was won, she campaigned and spoke for suffrage. She was always associated with the more militant wing of the movement; and later she joined the Woman's Party and supported it in its fight for the "blanket amendment," although she was opposed to any narrow legal interpretation of women's rights.

As a feminist Crystal Eastman was more than an ardent, militant advocate of votes for her sex. She was to thousands of young women and young men a symbol of what the free woman might be. Unlike some of her contemporaries, embittered by the long and unreasoning struggle, she never lost her sense of balance or her friendly sympathy with men. She fought not for a sterile victory for her sex but for her religion—the triumph of freedom and decent human relations. Since they could be won only through the winning of equality and the vote—those must come first. But she was fair and steady and consistent. Equality worked both ways. It was not a gesture but a simple article of her belief that she should refuse alimony when she was divorced from her first husband. She is quoted as saying:

> No self-respecting feminist would accept alimony. It would be her own confession that she could not take care of herself. Alimony has nothing to do with the support of children, which, of course, must always be the mother's and father's joint responsibility whether they live together or not.

This acceptance of the responsibilities of freedom along with its privileges was a solid principle. She believed in absolute equality. She would have abolished, along with the legal discriminations against women, all the laws which favored them. This included every form of protection whether in the form of property, or alimony, or support by a husband, or industrial safeguards. One may question the social wisdom of her position, but no one could doubt its courage or sincerity. She saw in the light of her faith a world in which men and women worked and played and loved as equals; nothing less than this would satisfy her.

Once in New York, before the war broke over the head of a hopeful world, a series of meetings was held to discuss the perennial subject of women's advancement—their right to self-support; their right to every sort of job; their right, even when married, to keep their own names. Crystal Eastman tackled a bold subject. She discussed women's right to physical equality with men. With humor and vivid imagination she pictured a cheerful Utopia of young athletes of both sexes, the girls unhampered by preconceived ideas of what was fit or proper or possible for their sex to achieve. She drew her examples from circus tents and battlefields and the fields of

European peasants. She asserted that when women were expected to be agile, they became agile; when they were expected to be brave, they developed courage; when they had to endure, their endurance broke all records. As she stood there, herself an embodiment of tall, easy strength and valor, her words took on amazing life. Whether science would sustain her theories or reject them made little difference. The fact was that not one woman left that hall but felt a little taller, straighter, stronger, more self-confident; and not one man left without a stir of a new sort of respect for women somewhere beneath his ribs. Crystal Eastman created the thing she preached.

As a pacifist Crystal Eastman was also a militant. She was the vigorous leader of the Woman's Peace Party in New York State during the early years of the Great War, piloting that organization through stormy days when it was denounced as pro-German and when some of its members dropped off to support the war or to roll bandages. She turned the energies of this women's society into dramatic, vigorous protest and caught the attention of a country already sliding into the fatal whirlpool. With equal vigor she shared the labors of the editor of *The Nation* and other pacifists who founded the American Union Against Militarism, a body which stood firm even when the war itself trampled their protest under iron feet.

But pacifism had failed to save the world. In 1917 Crystal Eastman joined her brother Max on the staff of *The Liberator,* successor to *The Masses.* For two years they fought against war and in behalf of social change. They hailed the Soviet Revolution in Russia as the embodiment of their dreams. They watched with high hope the tide of revolutionary sentiment rise in Central Europe, as famine and the devastation of war and the truckling of the peace makers made the workers more and more desperate and conscious of their plight.

The tide of revolution subsided; and in the years which followed Crystal Eastman, living for the most part in England with her two children and her husband, Walter Fuller, devoted herself to a more quiet life of writing and speaking on subjects concerning women. But quiet was not her natural medium. She longed to get to work— and work meant America. It was almost exactly a year ago that she came to New York, determined to find herself again in the world of active affairs. The months which followed bruised her body and spirit; but only her death ended her hopes. She had been in this country less than a month when word came that her husband had died. His loss was an irreparable blow. She was herself ill, but she fought off despair and physical suffering. With a courage that now appears almost incredible she organized and carried through to a brilliant finish *The Nation's* Tenth Anniversary celebration.

Into that campaign she put all her old-time fire and imagination. She concealed even from herself the deadly force of the disease that had assailed her. Only when she had finished her work and gone home to rest did her illness finally overwhelm her. She faced this last fight with the same defiant courage that had carried many a battle in her earlier days. But the flesh was less strong than the spirit, and the deadly effect of nephritis could not be stood off by any courage.

Mingled with our sorrow and deep sense of loss, we shall always feel pride and gratitude that it was to *The Nation* that Crystal Eastman turned when she came back to America. Her spirit and her steady faith in peace and freedom and justice lent strength to our own purpose, and they will remain with us.

INDEX